I0125875

CANE ROVERS
STORIES OF THE CHINESE-
GUYANESE DIASPORA

by

Trev Sue-A-Quan, Ph.D.

Vancouver, British Columbia

甘

Cane
Press

© Trev Sue-A-Quan, 2012

All rights reserved, including the right to reproduce this book or portions thereof in any form whatsoever, unless given prior written permission by the publisher.

Published by:

Cane Press
240 Woodstock Avenue E.
Vancouver, B.C. V5W 1N1
Canada
Canereapers@ Lycos.com

Library and Archives Canada Cataloguing in Publication

Cane rovers : stories of the Chinese-Guyanese diaspora / [compiled by] Trev Sue-A-Quan.

ISBN 978-0-9733557-2-7

1. Chinese--Guyana--History.   2. Chinese--Foreign countries--Biography.   3. Guyanese--Foreign countries--Biography.   4. Chinese--Foreign countries--History. 5. Guyanese--Foreign countries--History. 6. Guyana--Emigration and immigration--History.   7. Oral biography.
   I. Sue-A-Quan, Trev, 1943-

DS732.C35 2012   305.895'100922   C2012-900876-1

Photo credits are shown in italics with the photos.

Front Cover: Background - Migrating snow geese over Vancouver. Collage - Cayman Islands, Beijing, New York, Harare, Singapore, Zurich, Paris, Shanghai, Baghdad, Fortaleza, Kinshasa, London, Sydney ,Vancouver, Tel Aviv, New Delhi.

Back Cover: Trev Sue-A-Quan (L) presenting his books *Cane Reapers* and *Cane Ripples* to Professor Wu Baiyi (R), Deputy Director of the Institute of Latin American Studies, Chinese Academy of Social Sciences, as arranged by Anyin Choo (Center), Guyana's Charge d'Affaires in China (June 2010).

CONTENTS

§ Autobiography edited by Trev Sue-A-Quan

* With Trev Sue-A-Quan

FOREWORD

Anyone following Trev Sue-a-Quan's research into the history of his Chinese ancestors and compatriots as they migrated from China to Guyana and later to other lands will be profoundly astounded by the voluminous facts he has accumulated and woven together to produce the most invaluable accounts that have enriched our knowledge and culture. At the same time, they have instilled in us a spirit of determination that anyone can succeed in any enterprise or challenge that may arise in life.

These qualities in Trev Sue-a-Quan's accounts – also vividly illustrated in his two previous books, *Cane Reapers* and *Cane Ripples* – are clearly evident as well in this publication, aptly titled *Cane Rovers*. In putting together this current work, he presents the history of individual Sino-Guyanese in a very interesting and rather unique manner by allowing these individuals to tell their own stories of their growing-up years, their own struggles to succeed in Guyana, their decisive actions to migrate to other lands and societies, and the various ways they conquered their problems, privations and pains of adjusting to new environments and making successes of their lives.

This book is specifically about the travails of migration and the struggles of existence in the wider Guyanese Diaspora. The general theme, though, of *Cane Rovers* is woven around the efforts of the Sino-Guyanese in adjusting to migration and its associated difficulties and displaying how through grit, determination, a little luck and assistance from family members and friends, they were able to achieve varying levels of success for themselves and their children.

As is well known, historians interpret and analyse history, but history itself is made by people, individually or as a group. *Cane Rovers* gathers together an array of men and women who roved from Guyana to North America, the Caribbean, England, Western Europe, equatorial Africa, South East Asia, Australia and even back to China, and they separately relate their individual histories which illuminate old distant memories of days of long ago.

The reader, being aware of Guyana's history, economy, geography and culture is reminded, for example, of the workings of the timber industry in the country's heavily forested interior during the late 1950s and early 1960s, the "good living" in the managerial quarters at Mackenzie during the heydays of the bauxite industry, the struggles of everyday life in the poorer sections of Georgetown and rural areas of Guyana, the political troubles in the 1960s and the establishment of the autocratic regime after 1968, and the angst of pulling up entrenched residential roots in Guyana and migrating to new lands and relatively unknown environments.

But at the same time, the accounts reveal the resolve of these persons to educate themselves despite the various adversities they faced and eventually making successes with their lives – both in Guyana and in the new lands that they adopted as their own.

The style of life of ordinary people in the non-Guyanese environment jumps up from these accounts and the social interaction is vivid in description. We learn of the dental eccentricities of one historical Chinese figure, we flinch and shudder over the privations and sufferings of the residents of Singapore during the Second World War, we grimace and "suck teeth" over the bureaucratic hurdles facing a migrant in Zaire (now the Democratic Republic of the Congo), and we experience the fears first-hand of the devastating hurricane in the Cayman Islands.

Permeating the life stories of the book's contributors is a high sense of morality and religious zeal. In the reports of Chinese migration to Guyana in the nineteenth century, not very much is mentioned of the religious affiliations of those early migrants. However, as they adapted to the new conditions they gravitated towards Christianity, the semi-official religion of colonial Guyana. Obviously, many of the early Chinese immigrants were already exposed to Christian teaching in China and some of them became zealous Christians in their new land. Actually, the vast majority of Chinese in colonial Guyana were Christians, and this had an effect on the naming of children and even in the modification of many Chinese surnames. This Christian zeal is evidenced in a few of the stories in this book, and this commitment in spreading the religious teaching in officially atheistic Communist China is indeed indicative of the firm commitment and outright bravery of those Guyanese Chinese who returned to their ancestral home to spread the gospel.

Trev Sue-a-Quan, the author and compiler, is featured prominently and his own experiences as a student in England and later as a young scientist in the USA and Canada demonstrate qualities of determination to succeed in whatever is aspired – whether as a scientist or an amateur/ professional musician. But what is even more remarkable is his courage to move to China to help develop scientific knowledge in a society where he was a complete stranger, with little knowledge of the culture and at the same time being absolutely ignorant of the language.

Actually, the exciting and interest-grabbing first person accounts in this book take the readers into the real areas of history that are rarely expressed in textbooks. Through the experiences of Trev and his wife, for instance, the travails of Chairman Mao's "Cultural Revolution" are clearly understood. I recall reading numerous books and newspaper articles of this period of Chinese history but rarely did I find expressions by ordinary people – and especially by a Guyanese – who actually lived through and experienced first-hand those trying times. The details of that period in Trev's book present a realistic down-to-earth character of Chinese society in that period of that country's history.

All those who have migrated from Guyana – no matter what may be their ethnic backgrounds – can easily identify with those whose experiences are expressed in this book. Most of those Guyanese who have migrated from the 1950s did so for various reasons – economic, familial, educational, and even political – and they established new homes in England, Canada, the United States of America and the English-speaking Caribbean. But some have ventured to other areas of the world where they had to assimilate in completely new cultures and learn new languages. Undoubtedly, they faced – and continue to face – all sorts of adversities, including ethnic profiling and discrimination. Yet the trend to study, work and save has remained constant and this has helped them to overcome obstacles in their way.

Here I must interject my own experience. I grew up in rural West Berbice and built up work experience in teaching and for a while – when I was pursuing university studies in the early 1970s – as a junior information officer in the Ministry of Foreign Affairs. I have lived outside of Guyana since November 1985. Along with my family, I resided for eight years in Freeport, Bahamas, where I practised my teaching profession. I never wanted to leave Guyana where I was a senior teacher, but, no doubt, due to political reasons, I was by-passed for promotion and I made a conscious decision to leave after the Bahamian job offer arose. Fortunately, assimilation was easy since the education system was similar to that of Guyana and the life-style was not much different. My two children adjusted very quickly to their new schools, and my wife was employed relatively quickly as a teacher as well. Further, the Bahamians were very accommodating, especially since Guyanese teachers were held in great respect.

After the political change in Guyana in October 1992, I was called back to Guyana by President Cheddi Jagan and appointed as ambassador of Guyana in the United States and also to the Organisation of American States. As the years moved on, I was subsequently posted to Venezuela and more recently to Kuwait.

In all of these places my family had to adapt to new situations and cultures, including languages, but due to our experiences over the years we have managed to fit in relatively easily into the new societies. Surely, being part of the diplomatic circuit has helped, since official assistance from the host countries have aided in the settling process.

During my travels I met numerous Guyanese of all ethnic background in many parts of the United States and Canada (especially in New York and Toronto which have huge concentrations) where they have generally fitted in very well as professionals, scholars, diligent workers and in some cases as local legislators. They have also formed support groups to assist health and education facilities in Guyana, even though some of the members of those groups have not returned to their old homeland for a very long while. In 1995, I met an elderly Guyanese gentleman in Chicago where he had resided since 1945. He knew of no relatives back in Guyana, but he was very nostalgic over his boyhood days in Georgetown, and although he had never returned to Guyana he was still donating funds to a Guyanese support group in that city.

I have had the pleasure of meeting Guyanese nationals in Western and Eastern Europe, in the Middle East, Nicaragua, Mexico, Guatemala, Brazil, Chile, and other areas of South America. And of course, I have visited Guyanese nationals in the huge Guyanese enclave in San Felix-Puerto Ordaz in eastern Venezuela where the Guyanese culture, traditions and language continue to proudly strive.

And in Guatemala, there is a small Indo-Guyanese community where all are relatives. Apparently, a few of them went there in the 1960s as agricultural workers in the sugar industry, and subsequently they sent for other relatives who soon assimilated into the Guatemalan way of life. The younger generation (children and grandchildren) are now all Guatemalans, but they all still maintain their Hindu names, religious traditions and continue to nourish themselves on Guyanese cuisine.

It is interesting that one of the contributors to this book lived in the diplomatic community for a number of years and she vividly spelled out her own tribulations after that period of her life came to an end. No doubt, her experience presents a lesson my wife and I have to consider when the time comes for us to settle back in everyday life away from the diplomatic hustle and bustle.

I have to mention something about the fears encountered by the Guyanese migrants living in the new land now regarded as their permanent home. These fears may be similar to those who continue to reside in Guyana. They include the dangers presented by growing crime, the economic crisis and the threat of losing employment, and the dread of their children becoming victims of violence.

That fear of losing a child is poignantly presented by one contributor, Mrs. Barbara Sohan, who relives the pains of not knowing for many months what happened to her daughter, Astrid, who worked at the World Trade Center on September 11, 2001.

Everyone remembers that fateful and horrible day when terror tore away the lives of those who died and those who remained to mourn – especially those who received the remains of their loved ones. Mrs. Sohan and the other relatives of those whose lives were shattered on that fateful day will always endure that pain. But they will always cherish the happy times that their loved ones shared with them. Surely, despite their crushing loss, they have all moved forward with their lives and have continued to make positive contributions to their communities and to the homeland of their younger days.

Like all others who have made their decisive journeys from Guyana to re-build their lives on foreign soil, they have had their days of disappointment, but they have climbed up from their knees to reach out to a positive future. It is an existence all will endure, for as another contributor to this wonderful book puts it, "There are clouds and there are rainbows."

ODEEN ISHMAEL
Ambassador of Guyana to the State of Kuwait
(*and formerly Ambassador to the USA, the OAS and Venezuela.*)

Kuwait City, December 2011

PREFACE

Cane Rovers is the third in a series of books that I have written describing the experiences of the Chinese who have lived in Guyana. As described in the first book, *Cane Reapers*, 13,541 Chinese arrived in the colony of British Guiana in the mid-19th century to serve as indentured labourers on the sugar plantations. After completing their five years of indenture, they were free to stay in the colony or return to China. The situation in China offered dim prospects for a better life and some instead chose to leave for other countries, particularly in the Caribbean area, where it was perceived that there was greater potential for personal and economic advancement. Many more remained in Guyana, settling there and becoming integrated into a multi-ethnic society. In the process of creolization, the Chinese descendants lost many of their connections with China, including language, dress, customs, and traditional values. The main distinctive characteristics retained were close family ties and the love of Chinese cuisine. Descriptions of the experiences of the Chinese as residents in Guyana were presented in my second book *Cane Ripples*.

Although comprising less than two percent of Guyana's population the Chinese community had become recognized as a significant contributor to the country's well-being particularly for the role in the middle economy – as traders, merchants and entrepreneurs. As a result the Chinese were named as one of the six peoples that make up the nation of Guyana. In the mid-20th century the local situation changed and a large proportion of the Chinese in Guyana migrated to other countries. The reasons for the exodus were varied – some were seeking further educational training, others were looking for professional opportunities or improved economic status. A significant number also left when the country changed from a British colony into an independent nation because they felt that conditions were no longer conducive to achieving their personal goals or expectations. At the same time, several developed countries in North America and Europe had opened their doors to new immigrants. Together, these "push" and "pull" aspects of migration resulted in a significant reduction in the numbers of people of Chinese ancestry remaining in Guyana.

The Chinese Guyanese traveled primarily to the developed countries and established themselves in all manner of occupations. For some, the transition was a relatively smooth one, while others faced significant challenges in being accepted into the society because of academic, professional, and social obstacles. Indeed, several left a "good life" in Guyana and had to start over from scratch, coping with fewer of the privileges to which they had become accustomed in Guyana. Those who ventured into non-English-speaking countries faced the additional challenge of dealing with and in a foreign language. Even those who settled in countries where English prevailed may have found that their spoken English, carrying a distinctive Guyanese lilt, caused them to be regarded differently . . . as aliens. These new immigrants had to learn to cope with the local brogue, whether that was the Cockney, Scottish, Jamaican, New York or Australian version of the English language.

As new immigrants, the Chinese Guyanese rovers would have brought with them aspects of both their Chinese and Guyanese upbringing and habits. They had to adapt to and accept the prevailing culture and customs, and just how much of their Chinese and/or Guyanese background was retained and how they influenced the transition was very much dependent on each individual and the environment. The ways that these interactions played out are described in this collection of short stories.

In the process of preparing this book I have been asked how these stories were gathered. Some were recorded as memoirs or diary entries while others have been compiled as family histories to enlighten later generations, but the majority of the accounts had been stored in the memories of the Chinese Guyanese and it took just a small amount of prodding for me to liberate these treasured recollections. In the process I have been told of experiences that run the full spectrum of human endeavour. Several people were in the armed service participating in the various wars of the 20th century – from World War I to the Gulf Region battles – and some of them endured great loss as a result of those conflicts. Some have served within the palace walls of Her Majesty Queen Elizabeth II and others have served time within the walls of national detention facilities. A significant number have made strides in medical practice, becoming pioneers in performing heart operations, heart/lung transplants, orthopedic procedures and enabling public health reforms. At the same time, numerous other Chinese Guyanese have made their contributions in less prominent roles as mechanics, store clerks, taxi drivers and more. Such diversity is representative of a cross section of any selected migrant group. Their stories came to me through personal interviews, letters, faxes and emails. Indeed, the internet era has greatly facilitated the exchange of information that enabled this collection to be compiled.

I am very grateful to all those who have contributed their stories, and I do know that there are many similar and equally enticing tales that have not been told here. Perhaps this recounting can provide an encouragement for others to record their own life experiences for posterity, because a fuller accounting and a clearer understanding of first generation immigrants are frequently lost with the passage of time.

The stories are arranged in more or less chronological order so that the effects of the changing circumstances over the years can be seen in a timely context. These accounts are not just about the famous and wealthy but rather descriptions of the experiences of people of varied economic and social backgrounds who became new immigrants in a different country. Although I am aware of Chinese Guyanese migrants who have gone to Australia and Brazil and to Yemen and Zimbabwe not all of the known destination countries are presented in these accounts. This is because some potential contributors have felt that they did not have much of a story to tell or that their own achievements were not significant enough, even though I would beg to differ.

In collecting these stories based on a common theme of Chinese Guyanese migration the definition of an immigrant in this book is taken in a liberal sense such that there is no specific time period for residency or achievement, e.g. attaining citizenship. The connecting thread is that each contributor has Chinese Guyanese roots and has gone to live and work in another country as the next step in their personal development. Their stories describe both triumphs and trials although, by and large, the Chinese Guyanese have managed to prosper in the places that they have chosen, becoming essentially citizens of the world.

I feel fortunate to have been able to gather stories about Chinese Guyanese who have gone to China, their ancestral home. Their accounts describe the experiences of living in a changing China during recent decades, starting with life in pre-Communist China, surviving through the Great Proletarian Cultural Revolution, then experiencing the opening of contacts with Western society and finally witnessing the furious changes brought about by modernization as the 21st century approached. Even as this book goes to press the changes of today's China have pushed these accounts into the realm of "past history." It is a far cry from the situation in the 19th century that caused Chinese to migrate to a place half a world away – a place that became a new homeland and produced descendants who would later become Chinese Guyanese rovers to many countries.

Slow Boat to China

James Chow

James Chow, born in 1894, was the fourth of eleven children of David and Emily Ewing-Chow. David was a devoted Christian and several of his children followed his lead in propagating the teachings of Christ. James studied law at Cambridge University and was admitted to the bar in mid-December 1916. He then wanted to go on to study medicine, but his father sent him a cable: "Come home." In Georgetown, he found that his father had already prepared an office for the new lawyer, complete with desk, chairs, document trays, typewriter, bookcase with glass doors, as well as a room for the office boy. It was no wonder that the cable had urged James to return. Although disappointed, he accepted his father's decision and, for the next nine and a half years, James practiced his profession doing Chamber work and civil cases.

In 1923 David Ewing-Chow suffered a stroke and his health deteriorated rapidly. Before he died he repeated his hope that all his children would do their utmost not to stay in British Guiana. Sometime in 1925, James's sister, Mary, who had studied nursing in England, was invited to go and practice her profession in Shanghai. It was through Mary's connection that James received an offer to teach English and History at the London Mission College in Shanghai. He was preparing to leave the colony when his mother suffered a stroke and died. James settled her estate and financial matters and then, in December 1927, he set sail for China.

* * * * * * * *

I sailed away about two days before Christmas, believing that God was going to guide me all of the way to do His will and not my own selfish will. After the usual farewell to the family, I was taken by some of the members of the family to the ship. The ship moved away slowly to sea and took a day and a half to get to Trinidad, where we spent the morning, and set out at night for the next port, Barbados. We arrived on a rainy morning, so no one went ashore; soon after, we went to Grenada and other West Indian islands, and we reached our destination, Halifax, which was now transformed into an entirely new Halifax with more modern and higher buildings and better berths for ships of bigger size, as, after the war, population and business increased, which made for the extension of the city and suburbs.[1]

Our ship arrived after dinner, and went to its berth. We were hustled on to the CPR[2] train, which set off for Montreal, where we went through the Customs, and the Immigration authorities' checks, for there were many Chinese 2nd or 3rd Class passengers from Dutch and French Guiana returning to China, so a special guard was to be amongst us (although I was a 1st Class passenger), and would hand us over from one guard to another, first at Toronto, and then at Winnipeg, until we got to Vancouver and on to the ferry for Victoria.

By the way, on the long voyage from Georgetown, British Guiana, from the 1st Class deck I noticed about 16 Chinese passengers on the lower deck looking very miserable, so I went to find out the cause. They said that they were not accustomed to the food on the ship and did not feel happy at all. I told them to wait and I'll see the purser to find out what can be done about the matter. I explained to the purser the situation, and I suggested that he can arrange with the chef of the kitchen management that a certain amount of eggs, vegetables, rice, meat, fish etc. could be given daily to the group of Chinese passengers, who would cook and wash up after every meal, either before or after their ship's scheduled meals. The purser immediately realized their problems, and promptly made the arrangements for the foods, etc. to be given out daily at a certain time, as he himself knew about Chinese food, which he often tasted at Chinese restaurants, so the group of Chinese passengers were happy, thanked the purser, and expressed their gratitude to me.

Thereon I used to see them, chat with them, and learnt from one chef from Bermuda working for a millionaire – who owned a fine building,

---

1   A considerable section of Halifax was destroyed when the *Imo*, a Belgian steamer, and the French ship, *Mont Blanc*, accidentally collided in Halifax harbour on 6 December 1917, as the latter vessel, loaded with explosives tried to enter the harbour. It created a fire that resulted in the largest man-made explosion before the nuclear age, taking the lives of over 2,000 people and destroying some 326 acres.

2   Canadian Pacific Railway.

and had to entertain a number of friends who spent the holidays at his house – that the chef had to leave the work, although they paid him $600 a month with a return fare with room, board plus tips. This was because he found the work too hard, as they used to call on him to have a meal at uncertain hours in the early morning, after midnight, or for a late "brunch," and for tea with Chinese side dishes. He felt his health was being taxed to the utmost, and so resigned the job after two months, so he was going home with about $1500, including tips. He warned me to be careful of the persons, well-dressed, meeting passengers on board in Shanghai, inviting them home or to a hotel with only one purpose – to rob them.

He ended up by presenting me with two pairs of socks and a number of photos, knowing I was unmarried, of young ladies belonging to his family in Shanghai and Canton, which of course I could not refuse, as it would be against "Chinese custom." To crown it all, the news that I was on the train apparently had gone ahead of me, for I was greeted by about 4 or 6 Chinese, who said that they were friends of the chef or others of the passengers on the ship, and presented me with several kinds of Chinese cakes and sweets at two or three stations where we stopped, namely, at Toronto, Winnipeg, Calgary, and of course Vancouver, but what would I do with these presents? I thanked the various givers, took a few small dried nuts and fruits and told them to share the balance of the gifts among the children of their clubs.

Departing on the train from Montreal, I was in the 1st Class carriage. At noon, the lunchtime (to the Canadians, the dinner time) came, so I went to the dining compartment, when I was shown the menu. I ordered soup, trout, steak, and apple pie. The waiter seemed surprised, but I was in for a bigger surprise, for when the soup was brought, it was in an extra large soup plate, and I took only about 8 or 10 spoonfuls of the soup. The waiter then brought two trout, about 12 inches or thereabouts without the heads, fried with a lump of butter on them. It was delicious, and supposed to be "fresh caught." I ate and enjoyed one, then the steak was brought in – it was about two or more inches thick and about 5 x 3 inches in length and breadth, along with two or three kinds of vegetables; I could only eat three of four mouthfuls of that, tender and juicy as ever. Then I looked aghast at the apple pie, which was a quarter of the pie, filling almost the whole plate on which it was served. I took about three small helpings, mostly of the fruit, calling that meal the greatest surprise of my life, costing me about ten Canadian dollars with a tip for the waiter who smiled his thanks.

At the two large stations, at Toronto and Calgary, two new guards took over to see that none of the Chinese passengers escaped from the train and disappeared into the blue, as several, posing as students, had done that. So the government made the CPR post a bond of $500 for each such passenger who got into Canada by such means in order to make a livelihood. I observed at two places, where there were two cemeteries, which we passed, that some passengers stood up and saluted, explaining to me afterwards they were paying tribute to the many Chinese labourers who gave their lives in building the railway across Canada.

At Shanghai there were no Customs, nor was there any Immigration officer at all to delay us, when our old friends Dr. S. Hsia, his wife and her brother, Dr. W.S. New, and my sister Mary met me. They took me in a car and drove me to their mother's home, Mrs. New's, in Bubbling Well Road, which was supposed to be the terminus or boundary for the International Settlement. On my leaving the pier with my friends, I noticed some long seats or benches on the Bund and written on the back were these words, "Chinese and dogs not allowed here." I thought that was funny, as rich Chinese would hardly go to the Bund and the chair coolies can't read English, nor can their dogs. However, I noticed that after a riot, or other incidents over some wrong done elsewhere, the writing on those chairs was painted out; likewise, those on the various park benches.

I was taken to Medhurst College. At first it was expected that Rev. Box was to give me a bedroom at his house, but for some reason that was not done. Eventually, I was given two small rooms among the boys' dormitories, one for a sitting and dining room with a bed, and the other room was for a wash-stand and a commode. I did not mind that, as I was accustomed to roughing it. Then I was told that I would be paid two hundred and fifty dollars (Mexican),[3] in other words US$125. This was really a shock to me, of course, but Dr. Hsia told me that I could have

---

3   The Mexican silver dollar was an international standard in the late 19th century, and was still popular currency in China, and Shanghai in particular.

teaching jobs at another college or university. Well, I was a bachelor and did not mind.

I was to teach 16 hours a week, and take care of the students along with another teacher in doing early morning exercises. I would cook my own breakfast of buttered toasts, two to three eggs, and coffee in my room at 6:30 a.m. After the drill at 7:00 a.m., the boys had breakfast at 7:30 a.m. in their dining room, but teaching began at 8:15 a.m., after morning prayers and announcements. There was a break of 15 minutes to play, then studies resumed to 12 noon, when lunch would be served. I lunched with the boys, but ate little, as I had to rush away to teach at two places, one at the Chich Tze University, about 20 minutes run by the rickshaw man, and then another in the city at the Chinese Chamber of Commerce College. Students in the class at Medhurst College were about 30, at Chich Tze University about 34 to 40, and at the Commerce College about 40, so that teaching English, especially English composition and essays, in all three places entailed hard work. For reading and correcting essays I was paid double, it's true, but the work was arduous, so I had to make corrections while traveling by bus or rickshaw and between hours when not teaching the boys. The College bell for lights to be switched off was at 10:00 p.m. sharp, just the same as the bell would ring in the morning at 7:00 a.m. for drill.

The school playing fields used to be a large swamp and had been filled up so the surroundings and school compound were extremely damp, and with the old windows not being fitted properly, or shrunk with age, there was always a draught, so that in winter the bedroom and school rooms were damp with cold. Nevertheless, I enjoyed the teaching, and especially the boys, who were very serious at their work; but what used to surprise and worry me was that a boy of 15 years or 16 years would be called home on a Friday, get married on a Saturday, and by Sunday evening (or, if the boy lived far from school, on Monday morning) he would be back in class. So wherever I went to teach, I would condemn "early marriages," especially because they used to be an expensive affair as both heads of the family often had to spend a great deal – those who came to the wedding were numerous, for a boy in one village would, through a marriage-match, chose a girl from another village, not of the same surname. Expenses would be so high that money supplied by the family chest had to be borrowed at a large percentage of interest. This practice I also condemned. Now Chich Tze University was near to the Mayor's office in the City Council, and I had a friend, a Dr. Lowe, who was a physician to Mayor Wu Teh-Tseng (whose clerks were in my English class). So between the students and the doctor, my ideas were no doubt made known to the mayor, and he issued an order that whoever wanted to be married must apply at the Mayor's office and have the couples placed on the list. On Sunday of every week or fortnight he would marry 12 couples at one time at his expense at a tea party and each couple would be given a certificate with his signature along with those of the parents and the couple.

One day, I heard and saw a man pitifully weeping over a basket of eggs, some of them broken and contents spilled on the ground. I was so deeply moved at his predicament that I dived into my pocket and gave him a silver dollar. I walked away quickly from the sad scene, but after walking a little distance away I saw the man quickly putting the good eggs back into his basket with a policeman threatening him with his staff. I had walked about two blocks away, when a man, who had seen what I did, told me that were I to go five blocks further I'd see another man with his upset basket of eggs tearfully carrying out his "profession." I was a wiser man from that day.

I started out by saying that I went to live in one of Mrs. New's houses. She was a sister of Mrs. Soong, whose eldest daughter married Dr. Sun Yat-sen, the first president of the Republic of China. Another daughter married H.H. Kung, reputed to be descended from the sage and philosopher, Confucius. He became Minister of Finance under Gen. Chiang Kai-shek. The last daughter Soong Mei-ling, a Wellesley College graduate, married Gen. Chiang Kai-shek, to the great disappointment of her mother (as well as that of Mrs. New and Mrs. Wan, her aunts) as the general was married already and had his wife living in Feng Hwa.

One day, I happened to visit a lawyer, Dr. H.C. Mei, who was a Masonic brother. I was the first master and chief founder of the Lodge and we named it "Amity Lodge." I also visited another lawyer, Mr. S.Y. Yeh, whose son I taught, in the same building as Dr. Mei, and between the two offices was a Chinese lady dentist's office. I asked my friend Mr. Yeh who this lady dentist was. He said that he did not know her personally, but heard that she had come from Hong Kong and took her dental degree in the USA. At the next fortnightly Lodge meeting, Dr. Kwok and I met and she told me where her clinic was – next to the bus stop at Dinty Moore's Restaurant, famous for its corned beef.

A fortnight later, I found that one of my molars had an abscess and my gums were swollen, so I thought of Dr. Kwok. It was a Friday afternoon; after teaching I made an appointment by telephone and she said she would see me if I got there within an hour's time. She took an X-ray of my tooth, had it developed by her assistant, then after five minutes or so, showed me the film, pointing out that the roots or prongs had grown inwards. After an injection and waiting a few minutes, she pulled out the tooth quite easily, but a part of the prongs had broken off and would have to be extracted. It was a long process – for me at any rate – as she tried to take out the remaining portions by little bits. It seemed like hours to me, but, really, it was about 25 minutes. The pain was bad because the injection of the drug (cocaine) was beginning to wear off. I got up from the chair but felt shaky, so I sat down in the waiting room and chatted for a while. Then I paid her her fee, but not until she gave me 12 tablets to take every four hours. These helped a lot. I boarded a bus, paid my fare, and meant to get off at Chao-Fung Road and then take a rickshaw to my college. I had fallen asleep, however, and went past the place I was to stop. I was awakened by the conductor who said, "Aren't you getting out?" Then I became aware that I was at the terminus. I bought a ticket for Chao-Fung Road and he looked at me as if I were "one of the drunks, as usual."[4]

---

4 Dr. Dorcas Kwok performed another noteworthy extraction which she later described to her children. One day a person came to her office accompanied by several well-armed guards. It was General Chiang Kai-shek and he requested that all his teeth be pulled because he was suffering from serious gum problems. Dr. Kwok complied but her patient began to bleed profusely. She felt that she would be in great danger if the general encountered more serious medical setbacks or die as a result of her actions. In desperation she summoned the help of a few other dentists in the building and together their efforts managed to stop the bleeding. In retrospection Dr. Kwok surmised that Chiang Kai-shek would have felt more comfortable going to a female dentist because of a lesser likelihood of her being involved with the ongoing civil conflicts. If Chiang Kai-shek had chosen a dentist who was opposed to his party and policies, the events of Chinese and world history could have taken quite a different turn.

I was asked to spend the Summer holidays at a mountain resort up the Yangtse River. The trip up the mountain was very exhilarating, as the air became fresher as we went higher; every short turn unfolded different kinds of trees. Each chair was accompanied by an extra coolie, who would change places with one of the tired chair-bearers until the other coolie got tired, when his place would be taken by the one who had dropped out. This went on until we got to what is known as the "half-way" house or hut. Here there were other chairs with their chair-bearers who were calmly taking a whiff from an "opium pipe" for which, of course, they paid a lot to the keeper or owner of the miserable but warm hut. After 15 minutes' rest, the chair-bearers returned to their passengers' chairs accompanied by another coolie who was fresh and ready for the final climb to the top, which was a bit dangerous in parts.

James Chow in traditional Chinese outfit. *Ming Chow.*

After the Summer holidays I phoned Dr. Kwok's office, but her office boy told me that she was in Hong Kong for two weeks' vacation with her parents. I had recently bought an old two-seater car – a Wolseley – from an English Army officer who was going back to England. It cost me two hundred dollars. When we next met at our fortnightly meeting, I asked her if she would go to tea with me. After a slight hesitation she said, Yes. Then I said I would meet her at the Palace Hotel, at the corner of Nanking Road and the Bund, after 4:00 p.m. when she closed office, and after tea I would drive her home in my "old jalopy." We met and had tea in a corner overlooking the Bund and we got on pretty well, so I was bold enough to ask her to tea at the Cathay Hotel the next afternoon at the same time. The Cathay Hotel was directly opposite the Palace Hotel and was supposed to be the best hotel in Shanghai. She accepted the invitation with a smile. On parting, I said, Why not let's have tea again in the Cathay Hotel, as the music there is so good? She accepted with a little eagerness, so on the way home I said to myself, If she is not too high-hatted to be seen driving with me in my old beaten-up car, she must be a sincere sort of girl.

I decided to go to Peking where my brother Robert was. He had left Hong Kong after passing his first year medical examination but decided he wanted to do the Lord's work with "The Little Flock" with Watchman Nee, a Fukienese. As the leader of that group, he had studied at Yenching University while taking "Kuo Yu" or "Mandarin" in the Peking Language School. In his spare time, he would read portions of the New Testament in Chinese and try to remember the characters and their meaning. It was a slow process, but he made progress quickly, and, by meeting many students, he learnt many Chinese idioms and phrases. On the sixth morning, I got a cable from Nanking, the Legislative Yuan, of which the Vice President of China was Dr. Hu Han Min. He invited me to join their committee to help "codify" the Civil Laws of China, to take notes, etc. for translating into English what the committee decided, after collaborating with various law experts, both Chinese and foreign.

I immediately took a first-class ticket on the first train but, at the next station, we were turned out of our compartments by the officers under Chang Hsueh Liang, son of the warlord, Chang Tso Lin, so we all went into the dining car. I had to sleep the first night on one of the dining tables with my knees drawn up. Anyone who passed by touched me, so I could not sleep. Fortunately, they all left the train at the next stop, and "good riddance" to them.

I was appointed as First English Secretary to this legislative body under the vice-president, and was given a Yuan badge and insignia to be worn on my lapel. I was assisted by a Chinese secretary, a Mr. Chang, a law graduate of the Philippine islands, who accompanied me back to the hotel to do our part of translating into English each section, as it was passed by the Committee. I worked under pressure in the heat for nearly seven weeks after which I told Dr. Hu that I had to go back to teach. He said I could run up to Nanking on weekends and alternate with Mr. Chang. That was arranged until the whole code was completed and translated into English. It was finally perused carefully by Dr. C.L. Hsia before being sent on the printers, Kelly, Walsh & Co.

Returning to Dr. Kwok and myself, there was a sequel to those three

THE CIVIL CODE

OF THE

REPUBLIC OF CHINA

Book I . . General Principles
Book II . . . . Obligations
Book III . . Rights over Things

TRANSLATED INTO ENGLISH

by

CHING-LIN HSIA, M.A., B.SC., PH.D. (Edin.)
Member of Shanghai Bar Association
JAMES L. E. CHOW, B.A. (Cantab.)
Member of Shanghai Bar Association
Barrister-at-Law.
YUKON CHANG, B.SC.

Preface by
His Excellency HU HAN-MIN
Member of the National
Government of the Republic
of China
President of the Legislative
Yuan

Introduction by
Hon. FOO PING-SHEUNG
Chairman of the Foreign
Relations Committee of the
Legislative Yuan
Chairman of the Civil Codi-
fication Commission

SHANGHAI:
KELLY & WALSH, LIMITED
HONG KONG : : : SINGAPORE
1930

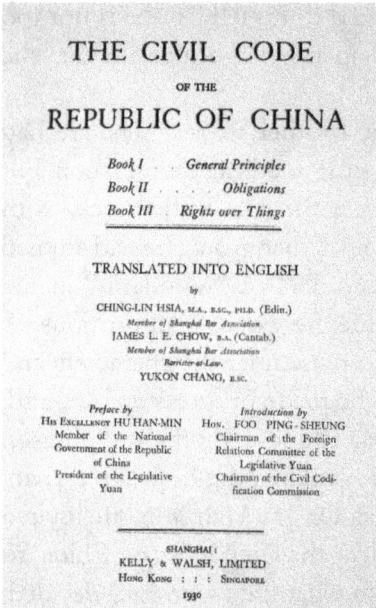

First page of *The Civil Code* for which James Chow participated in the translation. *Trev Sue-A-Quan.*

tea engagements with her, because a few days after each tea I received three Police Notices one after another, charging me for parking my car on the "No Parking" side. I immediately wrote in reply that, as I was not too long in Shanghai and only recently acquired the car, I was unaware of the "No Parking" notice and apologized for my mistake. I thought I would have to pay a fine, but I heard nothing more about the matter, so it pays to be honest. I afterwards told Dr. Kwok about it and we laughed over it. She then suggested that if we were to go out again, that we should go to some other place, less conspicuous. I agreed to her suggestion. Later I found out that both of us were lonely and were in love with each other, so we agreed to be engaged, provided her father gave consent, and that if we were to marry, we must do so in a simple ceremony, quietly and without fuss, to which I agreed. She got a reply from her father that she could be trusted to know her own mind and make her own choice, but that she should be sure that I was not a married man for I told her I was nearly 36 years, and it was unusual for a Chinese not to marry before that age. My passport, however, showed all was correct. Her father said he would come with others of the family to Shanghai, on his way to Peking and Pei-Ta-Ho. Three weeks or more before they were to arrive, I went to the British Consulate and applied for a licence to be married and the notice was posted up at the Consulate that we would be married on 13 September 1930.

We all first went to the Consulate to have a civil marriage there with Dr. C.L. Hsia as one of the witnesses, and then proceeded straight to the Union Church to have a church wedding by the Pastor. The wedding dress was white silk and lace, and I had a light grey suit made for the

James Chow and his bride
Dorcas Kwok. *Ming Chow.*

occasion - a very simple affair, according to what I believe, and to which Dorcas fully agreed.

After my wedding, my brother, Joseph, wrote from London to say he would arrive very soon to stay with us. I was able to get Mr. P.Y. Tang, a prominent factory owner, to promise to find a job for Joseph on his arrival. Mr. Tang knew Sir Robert Calder-Marshall, the President of the British Chamber of Commerce very well. Sir Robert, on hearing that Joseph was a Cambridge graduate, became interested about finding a job for him. He finally succeeded in getting him a position as salesman-clerk in the Chinese section of a large oil company, the Asiatic Petroleum Company, receiving the salary of a Chinese, which he accepted of course, but another surprise followed after this.

A cablegram was received saying that Rachel (my sister) and Charles (my brother) were on their way to Shanghai, and would arrive within two months. I contacted a Mr. Sam Chang, who was assassinated by the Japanese later, as he used to write articles attacking the Japanese action in China. He was able to get Charles employed as an accountant with the same insurance company with which he was employed, as Charles had an Accountancy Certificate from the London School of Accountancy.

Joseph and Charles had made arrangements to rent a room in a boarding house next to us, while Rachel occupied our top bedroom, but all had their meals with us. Joseph used to miss dinner frequently, as he was quite serious about his girlfriend, whose Chinese father or English mother had at first opposed the "match," but the young girl, only 17 years, was as strong-minded as the mother, and refused to listen to reason. Finally, the father consented and both became engaged and later got married quietly, without telling us until the deed was done.

Rachel and Charles felt a definite "call" for them to go to Peking and join "The Little Flock" there. Rachel, a dressmaker, had no trouble in obtaining a job to look after the linen and clothes department and also do "social work" at the Peking Union Medical College (PUMC) founded by the Rockefeller Foundation, whose president, Dr. C.U. Lee, a British-trained doctor, was known to her and the family, for he often came to dinner with us in British Guiana.

Robert, knowing about cars, etc., was able to go on a trip during holidays with old Dr. Stuart, a missionary, and be responsible for the driving and repairing of their truck, which was filled with bibles and portions of the Old Testament and the New Testament. These they would distribute to the nomadic tribes of Inner Mongolia. Many a time they used to sleep on the large kangs (cement beds) in inns,

Joseph and Margaret Chow on their wedding day. *John Chow.*

heated from below, on which about eight men or more could sleep. They could hear the men, bandits really, saying, They are not rich, but good men giving us books without charge and teaching us about God and His Son, Jesus. Robert learnt a great deal from that trip and from the members of the various tribes about their customs. Above all, he learnt from old Stuart how to approach and deal with these tribes. He lost, however, several teeth from eating too much of their sweetmeats, as approaching some people who waved their hands over their trays, they would see swarms of flies being driven off from the cakes and sweetmeats, etc. that they were selling. As they were hungry, they would buy some, praying before they ate, thanking God and asking the Lord to protect them from harm.

To return to Joey and Margaret, the latter suffered from a spinal injury and got worse in spite of drugs and medical treatment. Joey and she thought that the only thing left was prayer. Formerly, both were "in the world" dancing and enjoying what they considered to be the "life,"

James Chow (standing 2nd from left) and his wife Dorcas Kwok (seated 3rd from right) in the company of literati and foreign-trained scholars. *Ming Chow.*

but now the Lord brought about a wonderful change. During the war, they began to meet those who were believers in prayer and miracles. They met with others to pray for healing, while at night both prayed for healing without drugs, confessing their faults, and called upon the Lord to hear their cry. The Lord did hear and helped, because the pain gradually eased and within a short space of a few days, Margaret was completely healed and began to put on weight: from 90 lbs. she went to over 110 lbs.

At about this time, the Japanese started a second but massive drive on Shanghai, and, in the north, towards Peking. Their attack by the army and navy with their heavy artillery and airplanes on Shanghai continued day after day. The Japanese acted quickly by taking over all British and American businesses in Shanghai, and put the personnel and their citizens into prison camps. My brother Joseph, who worked with Asiatic Petroleum Co., a British subject of Chinese race, was not put into prison camp, but was allowed to go free to do what he wanted, provided he wore a red armband given to him. Of course he had to leave his job but, as a salesman, he knew to whom he sold quantities of gasoline, etc. and where they were kept. So he was able to get the gasoline quietly sold to various purchasers and in that way made a commission and was able to keep the family.

On the other hand, when I heard the big explosion by the sinking of the U.S. gunboat *Panay*, I had no idea that it was war, so I went to work as usual, but when I arrived I found the Japanese, along with Bishop Yu (who was the Chairman of the Bible Societies) in the Bible House. Now a collaborator, he pretended that he was protecting the interests of the Bible House. I was told that I was no longer employed. I asked for a letter of confirmation from him. He wrote: You are forthwith discharged as from this date. He signed it and I accepted it and left the Bible House after serving the best years of my life – almost ten years, with a curt dismissal.

The next day after my dismissal, I went to St. John's University where a Lodge brother, Dr. Sung, was the president, as I knew they were short of teachers after the Americans were sent to "camp." I began teaching on the same day, getting a salary which was adjusted from time to time with the devaluation of the Chinese dollar, so that each month's salary lasted us no more than 20 days. As a result, in due course we had to sell whatever articles and jewelry we had of gold or silver, bit by bit.

During the Japanese occupation we ran short of food and had to live on rationed rice and beans on many a day. From my experience in the First World War, we made a box lined with cotton-wool and straw and left a hole in the middle large enough to hold a large pot of boiled rice and beans. This was covered with a lid and heavily lined with cotton waste so that the pot could be kept warm for lunch and also dinner, as there was no longer any gas supplied to anyone.

After the Japanese surrendered, I continued teaching, but was invited by my Oxford friend, Mr. S.Y. Yeh, to join him in his office to do his work along with two other lawyers, locally trained, while he went to Peking to have a holiday for six months. I was able to build up the practice, as my partner unfortunately used to neglect his work because of the opium habit. Work came in a wonderful way, through God's help, insomuch that we were remunerated with business, and fees came in, especially as the businessmen knew of my part in the codification of the

Civil Laws of China. The business was prospering until the Communists became a threat to Shanghai, as they had already occupied Wuhu. My wife and I packed up a few necessities, for I was advised to leave for Hong Kong by steamer, which we were able to board in spite of the large crowd evacuating for Hong Kong. Although we had booked and paid for a First Class cabin, we were shuffled into a Third Class cabin as some official and his family took our cabin and occupied it.

I was invited to see Dr. Katie Woo, the principal of St. Paul's College for co-educational boys and girls, to go and teach at her college as she and her brother, Dr. Arthur Woo, had been contemporaries of mine in England. As I was an M.A. of Cambridge, I was given a senior teacher's salary. My brother Robert and his wife Ruth were still in China, and they left for Singapore just two weeks before the Communists came to power. Robert was fortunate to get a government job as a teacher and later became Superintendent of Teachers on the strength of his being in Hong Kong for the first year medical course, and at Yenching for one year on some other course. Charles was in Hong Kong at the time, preparing a hymn book for "The Little Flock." When he completed it, he came to say goodbye as he was returning to Peking. He said, I must return to Peking, I have a wife, Esther, and the children there. At the end of the war, Joseph, his wife Margaret, and their children went to England as they were British subjects and had the right to be repatriated there. After seeing many of the cities in England and having preached at several meetings and groups, they decided to return and open up a little church in British Guiana.

While teaching in Hong Kong, I got in touch with Bishop Hall, and I attended classes under him, as I wanted to be trained for ordination. I taught a few years at St. Paul's; I enjoyed my teaching there, as all the students were so keen to learn and to help each other too. I took them out at summertime to visit the boys and girls in homes and orphanages for the street waifs. In Hong Kong, through prayer, we felt led by God that we should leave at the end of June 1952, soon after the final examination and the handing in of the results and marks of the students and classes I taught. We were able to book tickets on 30 June.

Being Civil in Engineering

William Manson-Hing

In May 1997 Trev Sue-A-Quan visited with William Manson-Hing, who was resident in Vancouver, Canada. At 85 years of age William was of sound mind and memory. His only handicap was that he was completely deaf in his left ear and retained only about 10% hearing in his right ear. Our exchange was conducted at a high volume level along with much scribbling on paper to clarify the items. Otherwise he was in good physical shape and he kept himself fit by swimming frequently in the community pool.

* * * * * * *

William's grandfather, Mun Sun-hing, traveled to British Guiana aboard the *Mystery* which arrived on 9 June 1861 after a 97-day voyage originating in Hong Kong. He was only 12 years old and allotted to Helena, a sugar plantation in East Coast Demerara. When he reached adulthood Ernest – the name that he was given – married Emily Lee a local girl of Chinese ancestry and he was employed as a driver (the supervisor of indentured workers) on Plantation Hope, East Coast Demerara. It was there that the first of 13 children was born in 1879 and he was named William Mung-chung Mun-Sun-Hing. Ernest ventured into shopkeeping and settled in Plantation Farm for a few years but eventually moved to Georgetown in the late 1880s. His descendants are known by the surnames Man-Son-Hing and Manson-Hing.

William Mung-chung learned about business operations in his father's shop and then became a clerk at John Tat Co. where his prospered so well that he later bought over the company. He then branched out into other lines of business – hardware and lumber trading. He succeeded in these ventures to the extent that he became the exclusive authorized provider of hardware supplies to Dutch Guiana, the neighboring country to the east. This monopoly brought William great wealth and importance in the Guianas. On one occasion he was aboard a ship headed for Dutch

Guiana and on the same ship was the governor of that colony. According to protocol the governor was supposed to be the first to disembark and the rest of the passengers had to wait until the appropriate formalities were completed before leaving the vessel. William had an important contract to sign with the deadline fast approaching. He spoke to the captain who in turn informed the governor that Mr. Man-Son-Hing was a key man in securing the country's hardware supplies and that he needed to get off in a hurry. With the governor's permission William was able to break the standing protocol.

In the late 1890s William married Elizabeth Samoi but the marriage was not a happy one. It turned out to be a tragic one when Lizzie died not long after the birth of their short-lived second son in 1899. William found a new marriage partner in Emilie Marietje Felixyalh, a Chinese girl from Dutch Guiana. They were married in December 1902 at St. Saviour's, the church that was built by and for the Chinese Anglicans in Georgetown, and enjoyed a happy life together.

Wilfred, the elder son from William's first marriage, grew up in an environment of relative wealth and enjoyed the many benefits that money could bring. His father held the hope that his first-born would go to study medicine in Edinburgh, with this university having a good reputation as well as being less expensive. However Wilfred has little interest in studying and did odd jobs when he felt like it. Actually, he had become infatuated with a girl named Rhoda Lee and was determined to marry her. Rhoda's mother was of Indian descent and William was not in favor of Wilfred's intended marriage and threatened to cut him off from any financial support, although he conceded that he would let Wilfred have accommodations in one of the units in a building complex that William owned. When Wilfred went ahead and put love before riches his father disowned him. Two years later William died but he had made prior provisions that his fortune would be passed on to his second wife Emilie and her children.

Emilie bore five children with William and they were named Walter (1904), Winifred (1906), Waveney (1910), William (1912) and Wanda (1922). William Junior recalled that his father jokingly said that by having everyone being named W. Man-Son-Hing it created a good excuse for reading one another's secrets.

Walter was another son who lived off his father's wealth. He was placed in a private school but he was not keen on studying. William sent him to England for further education but Walter became more interested in extra-curricular activities. He was a motorcycle fanatic and this led to his death in a motorcycle accident in 1928. William grieved for this eldest surviving son with whom he had placed so much hope.

Winifred, Emilie's second child, was also enrolled in a private school. She was sent to England to continue her studies but was called back in 1939 to run the family business. The Second World War was in its early stages and the Netherlands passenger ship *Simon Bolivar* on which she traveled struck a German mine 25 miles off the coast of England on 18 November 1939. She was rescued from the chilling water but did not survive the ordeal.

Waveney was yet another child who was dispatched to England to study. There she met and married Kuo Yao who was sent from China to England for education. Yao's family lost their fortune in the upheavals in China during the 1930s and he became dependent on Waveney. They moved to British Guiana but Yao did not feel at home there and the marriage broke up. Waveney died in London in 1996.

Wanda, William's fifth and last child with Emilie, married Alvin Duval, an American who served in the Armed Forces. They settled in Houston, Texas where she died in 1993.

The fourth child of William and Emilie was William Junior. From a young age he was fond of books and eager to acquire knowledge. This made him a good student and he did well enough in primary school to be granted a government scholarship to complete his secondary level education at Queen's College, a prominent private school for boys, where he studied from 1923 to 1929. This enabled his father to save some $5000 in tuition fees. William then boarded a ship to take him to England for higher education. Four days after the ship set sail his father died. He had been suffering from diabetes and this incurred much discomfort and pain. Although insulin had been discovered earlier in the decade this medical treatment was not yet widely available to meet the needs of diabetic patients around the world. He was aware that the disease would cause his demise and he told the young William that it would likely be the last time that they would see each other as they parted company at the ship's dock.

William was accepted at Imperial College in London in 1930 and he received a B.Sc.. degree in Civil Engineering in 1933. He found that the British were rather snobbish and rather envious of him being financially well-off. Because of this William deliberately went to buy himself a Riley sports car as well as a rigger which he would row daily on the River Thames for exercise, going about 12 miles on weekdays and up to 20 miles on weekends. There was another motive in William's pursuit of this on-water physical regimen. His rowing activities fulfilled the qualification for him to be accepted as a member of good standing of the Imperial College Club. There were ample bathing facilities in the clubhouse and this was the only place he could find where he could enjoy the comfort of a lovely hot water bath. The physical exercise built up his strength and stamina and he would sleep like a log under the open window of his dormitory, even in the depth of winter.

William was the only one in the family to complete a university education and after graduation he set out for Malaya and was employed there by the Public Works Department. Over time he became recognized by his peers as a competent engineer. However this evaluation was not embraced by his superiors who were concerned about his forthrightness in dealing with ongoing situations and assignments. William found that he was consistently being passed over for promotions. On one occasion he asked for a loan to purchase a car but his superior refused to help. On hearing this William promptly went off and bought two cars for $12,000 in cash and he had the message conveyed to the superior that he could have bought two more cars.

William eventually found out a more sinister reason for his being overlooked. There was a lot of graft and payoff going on at the Public Works Department and William was indignant about these underhand dealings. In one particular project that was budgeted at 14 million dollars there was so much money being shifted to line the pockets of his superiors that the contractors were forced to cut corners and use inferior materials as well as unacceptable building practices. William wrote several memos to point out the deficiencies and stated that the building would be unsafe. These letters were of course ignored by his superiors. On the contrary he began to receive threats to his life, but he dismissed these as grievances and felt that the matter could and should be resolved in a civil manner. One day William was at the work site and had just stepped away from the building when a length of steel angle girder measuring 6 inches by 6 inches came crashing down near his feet. He looked up and saw the perpetrators scurrying away.

The falling girder was no accident and William knew to expect a bigger and more serious confrontation. Some time later he was approached by a gang of three men. The leader tried to deliver a blow but William let fly with a quick kick to his groin. The attacker collapsed with his arms draped over William's shoulders and William delivered several telling blows to the opponent's abdomen while receiving some hard hits on the head from the other henchmen. With the leader of the thugs in distress the others called off their attack. William emerged the victor in this encounter but the blows he received caused significant hearing loss that remained for the rest of his life. William later found out that his attacker had died and an inquest was held. One man gave the opinion that the victim was overcome by William's fitness and superior boxing skills. Another gave the suggestion that the deceased man was suffering from some prior ailment or disease. William felt that a third opinion was probably the correct one and that the victim was winded and in such poor physical condition that he could not sustain a fight. At the inquiry it was indicated that the attackers were gang members, like a Malaya Mafia, and a verdict of self-defense was declared. Shortly after the opening of the 14-million dollar building – when equipment was being moved into the premises – it collapsed, sinking to its foundations.

When it became evident that William was being repeatedly passed over for promotion some questions were raised by government officials. The head of the Public Works Department somehow managed to deflect these queries but one day William happened to see that his confidential file was lying on the desk of his superior. He took a glance and noticed that the department head, Mr. N., had claimed that William was suffering from serious mental disturbances, which in recent months had become more severe. This came as a real shock to William and he was furious. He was determined to make a response although once again he felt that the matter needed to be handled in a civil but firm fashion. He wrote a letter to an even higher superior in the government hierarchy in which he lambasted the department head for his gross incompetence while pointing out his excessive capacity for lies, libel and liquor. William indicated that all the graft that Mr. N. had been receiving was merely going to quench the man's thirst for alcohol and that he had little qualification for being head of the department. As a result of this furore the government superiors had to choose between holding an inquiry or having the department head resign and return to England. Mr. N. chose the latter course but shortly thereafter he applied for a posting to another location. This move prompted an investigative hearing. William expressed the opinion that Mr. N. was definitely unfit for re-admission into the Public Works Department. This opinion prevailed and Mr. N. was rejected. Not long after that he died of cancer.

The nefarious matters at the Malaya Public Works Department still continued and William found that he had become the principal target and named as the person who was incompetent. The failure of the multi-million dollar building was said to be directly attributable to William. An inquiry was called and in his defense William claimed that he had sent memos to his superiors pointing out the unsafe practices and dangers involved. However, no copies of such communications could be found among the office records. It was then that William went home to check the little cedar storage box that he used to put away his important papers. This habit of putting away items of value was one that he had learnt from his father and the box was one that gave off a beautiful fragrance. After presenting his copies to the board of inquiry William was delighted to hear the words: "Mr. Manson-Hing, you are completely exonerated."

WILLIAM MANSON-HING
March 6, 1912 – November 20, 2004

Civil Engineer William Manson-Hing.
Louise Manson-Hing.

In His Majesty's Service

Marian Sueafatt, née De-Wever

On 22 June 1945 I returned home to London after being evacuated to Somerset to escape the bombing and rocket raids that threatened several major cities in Britain during World War II. This was a month and a half after victory in Europe was declared and I was a schoolgirl at the time who was only too glad to be reunited with my family after five long years of dodging the threat of the German bombs. I soon found that our home had become a gathering place for some servicemen from British Guiana because that very weekend some of them arrived on leave. Among them was Duke "David" Sueafatt, an engineer with the Royal Air Force, a dashing young man to whom I was instantly attracted. I also admired him for enlisting to serve his king and country. It was my father, David Arnold De-Wever, who had met the younger David at Trafalgar Square on VE Day and amidst the throng of jubilant, shouting celebrants he ran into some men who wore flashes on their shoulder sleeves displaying the name "British Guiana." My father had been born there and was so delighted at meeting fellow Guianese that he invited them to his house where my mother cooked curry and rice, much to the delight of the guests.

My ancestral connections to Guyana go back many generations through aboriginal peoples. The Fourth Hereditary Paramount Chief, Amorotahe Haubariria (Flying Harpy Eagle), of the Eagle Clan of the Arawak tribe was my great-grandfather. His daughter, Princess Marian the Luckie, had been adopted by Rev. William Piercy

The Harpy Eagle. Sacred Messenger of the Great Holy Spirit. *Damon Corrie.*

Princess Marian of the
Arawaks. *Damon Corrie.*

Austin, the Anglican Bishop of Guiana, who later became Archbishop of the West Indies. The bishop baptized her with the name Marian Luckie. In the late 19th century Vivian Arnold De-Wever, who was born to a well-off Dutch family, decided to seek his fortune in British Guiana. There he married Marian in 1896 and they had seven children, six of whom survived to adulthood.

In 1921, His Royal Highness the Prince of Wales (later to become King Edward VIII) paid a visit to British Guiana. A ball was held to honour the occasion and Mr. Vivian Arnold De-Wever and his wife Marian were invited to join the colonial socialites. The governor of British Guiana, Sir Wilfred Collett, introduced Marian to His Royal Highness as "Princess Marian – daughter of the last Arawak King." The Prince of Wales requested that this princess be seated close to him. It was from that moment of public recognition of her being a hereditary noble that the Eagle Clan Arawaks (who never previously accorded high ranking females of the nobility with a formal title) forevermore applied the title of Princess to her.

My father was born in Essequibo in 1908, the second child of Vivian and Marian. Grandfather Vivian decided to move to Barbados and in 1925 was joined by Princess Marian and their six surviving children. My grandmother found that an extremely prejudiced attitude prevailed against non-whites in the colony and she was no longer considered to be a socialite and a respected descendant of an ancient nobility, merely a "Jungle Indian." Her children grew up hearing white Barbadian neighbors admonishing their children not to play with those people because they might eat you.

When my father turned 18 he was taken to Britain by his father and left there to fend for himself since he was considered to be an adult. He was provided with only three pounds in his pocket. In 1928, Princess Marian died in Barbados at age 49, overcome with grief resulting from the treatment she received in Barbados and the abandonment by her husband. Meanwhile, in England, David Arnold found it very hard to

David Arnold De-Wever, Faithkeeper of the Eagle Clan Arawaks, 1908-1995. Photo taken in the 1940s when he visited the Mohawk Tribal Nation, Trois Rivieres, Quebec, Canada. *Damon Corrie.*

survive, living essentially from hand to mouth. One day he was sitting in Dreamland Fun Park, a popular seaside amusement park in Margate, looking very disconsolate when a lady came by and asked what the problem was. He explained that he had not eaten for quite a while. It so happened that the lady was a pastry chef and she took him to the restaurant where she worked and arranged for him to have a meal. It has been popularly said that the way to a man's heart is through his stomach. Margaret "Peggy" Skillen, who was born in Cumberland to an Irish father, was already married but obviously very skilled at cooking. Her offerings nourished their friendship and eventually they married and had five children, making us princesses in the hereditary Arawak royal lineage.

When my sister Patricia and I were about to start school way back in the 1930s my mother went to enroll us at a nearby private school. The headmistress told my mother that if these children were Italian, Roman Catholics, or Jews, "I cannot have them in my school." My mother looked at her and said they are none of these, adding that our father was from British Guiana. She asked my mother, "Where is that?" In response my mother queried whether she is a true headmistress because if she teaches children she should know geography. The headmistress then wanted to know if my father wore native clothes and walked around without shoes. My mother stared at her and said, "I would not think of sending my daughters to your school because first of all I don't like your attitude. GOOD MORNING!" She left the headmistress standing with her mouth agape. That put her in her place.

Medals and awards given to David De-Wever for heroic acts and service in the Royal Merchant Marine in the North Atlantic, the invasion of North Africa and the invasion of Sicily during World War II. *Damon Corrie.*

David De-Wever's life took a turn for the better and when World War II broke out he served with distinction in the Royal Merchant Marine. He was a part of the Allied invasions of North Africa and Sicily, and for his brave actions in these theatres of war he was awarded six medals of valour. It was a moment of great rejoicing when VE Day was declared and David found himself facing another David, also from the land of his birth, and started chatting. David Sueafatt had enlisted with the Royal Air Force (RAF) in 1943 when he was still a teenager in British Guiana. He sailed to Britain on the *Windrush*, a ship that ferried several thousand recruits from the Caribbean to join the war in Europe, accompanied by three other enlistees: his cousins Ivan Tsoi and Whitty Loi, plus three others – Joe De Freitas, Samuel Vieira and Clinton Wong. David was posted to an RAF camp at Wilmslow and later moved around to various military camps across the country as the war effort required. He trained as an aircraft mechanic although he never really discussed with me the exact nature of his work with the RAF. Most likely it was the maintenance and repair of aircraft and other machinery on the base.

However he would jokingly say, I was a pilot and shot the Germans. On one occasion he was reprimanded for not saluting an officer properly. He was asked, "You call that a salute?" and sent for disciplinary action. He was required to peel potatoes for the canteen. When the officer in charge came by and saw a collection of marble-sized potato nuggets he queried David as to what he was doing. David replied that he had not been taught before to peel potatoes and he kept peeling and peeling. On another occasion he shared barracks with an airman who never got up to use the toilet at night. The fellow would use a tin hidden beneath the blankets to collect his discharged fluids. One day David said, I'll sort him out. He then made holes in the tin. That night the airman carried out his usual routine but this time the liquid all went into his bed. He shouted, "I know the #&%@ who did this. You'd better watch out." However it probably was just a vocal threat because nothing happened to David and the perforated tin certainly cured the nightly performances.

One day David got terribly ill, struck down by an aneurism. It was not the first time that this problem had affected him and on previous occasions he got medical attention from the RAF doctors who managed to provide relief. However this time the situation was serious and he required emergency treatment. He was rushed to the Manchester Royal Infirmary where Professor Jefferson, who had returned that very day from a holiday in America, was summoned to do an operation. As a youth of 10 years, David had been play fighting with other boys using sticks and was struck severely behind the ear. The blow he had received now turned into an emergency life and death situation. Dr. Jefferson had to do an incision from the back of David's ear down to his neck and managed to correct the medical problem. When he awoke from his anesthetic-induced sleep his first words were some expletives and "I want ice water. I want ice water!" I was informed that this was the first operation of this type performed in Britain. David remained hospitalized for some 8 to 9 weeks and gradually the hair on his shaven head grew back. He was then taken to our home in Islington for recuperation. My mother was the main person nursing him back to health and I was glad to provide whatever care that I could. From the first time we met I had the feeling that David was the one for me but he already a girlfriend. But as he recovered at our house we were able to be together and developed an attachment to each other. After regaining full health and returning to his RAF duties we would correspond regularly and this then became an exchange of love letters. He would always sign off his letters with "Sealed with a loving kiss," and "P.S. I love you." My letters to him were equally passionate. David would come to our home whenever he had leave and our relationship flourished. In 1947 David had to return to British Guiana to be demobbed and to get his official discharge papers. He then came back to England in May 1948 and we were married in 1950.

David's ancestry can be traced back to 1861 when his great-great-grandmother Lo Shee arrived with her husband and children as immigrant labourers aboard the *Chapman*. They were allotted to the sugar estate at Ogle on East Coast Demerara. Lo Shee's grand-daughter Mary U-Hing married Matthew Wong and it is from this branch of the family that David and his cousin Whitty Loi are derived. A daughter of Matthew and Mary, named Eveline, married John William Sue-A-Fat and they had four children with my husband David being the eldest. Actually, David's father was adopted by the Sue-A-Fat family and the biological ancestor is named Tsoi-A-Ho. Not much is known about the circumstances of Tsoi-A-Ho's demise and the adoption of his children by others. The children carried the Sue-A-Fat surname but David himself later pondered whether he should change it to Suefat but opted instead for the spelling Sueafatt, perhaps because he was not keen on having "fat" in the family.[1]

David found it hard to get work in England after the war. He once went for a job taking along a job application that he had picked up at the Labour Exchange. When he got to the place of employment the person interviewing him was in the process of taking down all of David's particulars when he looked up and saw the boss himself shake his head. David asked the employer to fill out a form so that he could take it back to the Labour Exchange and post it as a job already taken. The man said, I can't do that because the job hasn't been taken. So David told him to

---

1   Having the Chinese name Fat is not uncommon in China and is associated with prosperity. The Cantonese New Year greeting, Gong Hay Fat Choy, literally means "Wishing you happiness and much wealth," or in more colloquial terms, "Be happy, be wealthy."

put on the form the reason why he won't be employed: Tell them it's because I'm a foreigner, the same #&%@ foreigner that helped you win the war. In filling out application forms David would put in big capital letters: CHINESE WITH A GOLDEN SKIN. I used to laugh at his doings because he was always so jovial. David had to settle for jobs in iron foundries. He did this until early 1949 and then decided to move to London. The employment situation there was no better and his non-white features did not help him. He eventually was able to get a job as a metal polisher. Then in 1952 he found employment as a jointer's mate at British Insulated Callender's Cables Ltd. He worked hard and took exams to become qualified as a jointer. David sat further exams to become a first-rated top jointer. On one occasion he was working on cables when an engineer came on the job site. The engineer bypassed David and went to one of the mates and starting asking about the project. The mate said, I don't know anything about this job; David's the jointer . . . ask him. So the engineer said, What . . . that Chinese man is a jointer? He came to speak to David and David was reluctant to talk to him initially but he eventually did so. But back at the office David reported the man's attitude. He was really vexed and never minced his words. He became experienced in dealing with all manner of cables including oil- and gas-filled cables. His job took him to Portugal, as well as to different parts of the British Isles. He also was sent to Australia and New Zealand where he spent nine months on projects including the laying of an undersea cable. He was asked if he wanted to be qualified as an engineer with supervisory responsibilities but he turned down the offer saying that he preferred to work alongside his mates. He retired in 1986 at age 63. We were out one day doing some shopping and walked past an old man who spat and said, so and so foreigners. David swore back and responded, Where were you when your Nazi cousins were bombing the hell out of you? You see, he had an answer every time.

David did not take part in any special activities. He would go to the dog track, place a bet at the bookies or drop a few pounds at blackjack in the casino. But he provided adequately for his family and we were not in need. Whenever there was a dance for ex-servicemen he would take me along for a night out. A night of dancing was also an occasion we enjoyed when a West Indian dance was put on at the Caribbean clubs in

London. In addition we loved to go to the movies together. He had a quick sense of humour and used to call me Buck Banana or Buckie. In 1996 he took me to Guyana and we stayed there for a few months. He found Georgetown to be much grimier and unruly than when he had left in 1947. We went to the Sea Wall where the locals would fly their kites at Easter and David recalled that as a youth he used to make kites for sale to earn pocket money. The Sea Wall was also the place that many courting couples would take a stroll or sit in order to be caressed by the cool breezes and each other. David passed away in 2004 by which time we had shared more than 50 years of loving relationship. He was my Duke and I was his princess.

David and Marian Sueafatt. *Marian Sueafatt.*

Lawyer in Singapore

Elma Thwaites née Hoalim

In May 1859 the *General Wyndham* arrived in Georgetown with 450 Chinese immigrants. Among them was Ho A-lim, an 18-year-old labourer from Pok Loh, Guangdong Province who was allotted to Blankenburg estate, West Coast Demerara. He became known by the name Thomas Ho-A-Lim and took Mary Chung Shee as his wife, with whom he had ten children but several of them died at an early age. One of their sons, Philip, was born in 1895 in Leonora, not far away from Blankenburg. He studied law and found himself in Singapore when the Pacific phase of World War II erupted.

* * * * * * *

When we lived in Georgetown, Pops was a bookkeeper. He had one suit and mother used to wash his shirt every evening and whiten his hat and shoes with Blanco when he came home and iron his suit and shirt every morning so he always went to work clean. We did not have a lot of money. My grandmother Mary did not want anything to do with him after he married my mother so he had to make his own way in the world to show his mother that he could do without her money. He used to make extra money by playing dice with his friends. He practiced and practiced all the time until he became the best at it and no one wanted to play with him any more. He also used to give talks and plenty of people would gather to listen to him and so he earned some money to support himself and his family.

Mother was Portuguese. Her parents and her mother's mother, whom we would call Avo, the Portuguese name for grandmother, came from Madeira, which is an island off the West coast of Africa belonging to Portugal. Mother's name was Amelia Faria. Her family called her Melia but Pops called her "M" which was short for Emily. She was born on 1 January 1894. When mother took up with Pops she was very young. She did not want to go to school . . . she wanted to be with Pops and greatly admired him. He was always talking and would tell her of the things he wanted to do with his life, how he was going to get on and she was thrilled with it all. She left home and they lived together. This was a way of life in British Guiana in those days. People were poor, food was scarce and there was little to look forward to in life. Pops and mother finally got married and they had a total of nine children but most of them died in infancy. Only my elder brother Philip, my younger sister Joyce and I survived. Mother loved animals but she hated cats because one of her babies had died because a cat slept on his face. But she loved dogs and children. Mother was the kindest and most loving person there was. She was always helping someone and people would tell her their sad stories of their lives and she would listen for hours. So she was a good listener and that was what Pops loved as he always needed to have a listener as he never stopped talking!

Pops did not have a lot of money in those days as his mother had chased him out when he told her he was planning to get married. Grandma Hoalim did not want her son to marry a non-Chinese . . . she wanted Chinese grandsons. A funny thing, when she was living out her final days it was mother who looked after her. Her daughter, Rosaline, had gone to live in Malaya and her others sons were not married. Mother dropped everything and moved to live in Leonora and looked after the shop and my bad-tempered old grandmother!

Grandma Hoalim. *Malcolm Thwaites.*

Pops applied for a job with a lawyer named Luckhoo. Then he got a job at Prestons at $40 a month. There was a man there named Boyd. Pops decided that he wanted Boyd's job so he made himself indispensable and worked hard and did Boyd's job also. It worked and he finally got Boyd's job. He only mixed with clever people and in the evenings he would ride his bicycle to the sea wall and discuss politics and other things with his friends. Once he went up the Essequibo River to look for gold. Five of them were in a small boat, which overturned. Pops clung on to a sack or something and was later rescued but the others drowned. He never did that again.

1922 to 1928 was an exciting part of Pops' life. He set up with a group of friends to give a talk on life after death. Plenty of people turned up to listen and a crowd was on the bridge and it broke. The people demanded their money back. Grandma wanted Pops to be a priest as she was a Christian, but he wanted to be a lawyer. Finally she relented and gave him US$15,000 and he went to England to study law. He left his family with Uncle William to look after us as well as mother's family. We children became Roman Catholics because my mother's family was Roman Catholic. In the Roman Catholic school I was called Marian Lydia because Avo had me baptized a Catholic and gave me the name Marian Lydia Hoalim. When Pops came back on his holiday he hit the roof and had me baptized in the Protestant Church as Elma Hoalim. Whenever Pops came back we had to go to a Protestant school where I was called Elma Ho Ah Lim. So I shuttled between the Catholic school and the Protestant schools depending on where my father was at the time. So there I was not knowing my own name and at times getting into trouble with the teachers because I would not answer to my name.

After my grandmother died in December 1929 Pops came back from London. He had done a three-year degree course in 18 months and he was on his way. He sold all the shops and took us all by ship to London. Uncle William came with us. It was sad leaving my mother's family in British Guiana and we did not know if we would ever see them again. It was in 1932 and off we went. The ship stopped in Madeira and we visited mother's family in their home. We never saw them again either. In London I attended the Maida Vale High School. Philip went to the Polytechnic and Joyce went to a primary school. After a year or so Pops decided he wanted to go back to British Guiana but first he would call in at Penang in Malaya to visit his sister Rosaline. We set sail by the French ship *Andre Le Bon*. But in Penang Auntie told us that the Japanese had invaded China and were in Shanghai so Pops decided to go down to Singapore and wait for the Japanese to be defeated in China. In actual fact, the Japanese defeated the Chinese and four years later bombed

Pearl Harbor on 7 December 1941.

Pops joined the Prinsep Street Church and he used to give talks there. He made friends with a few young men especially Charlie, Big Boy and Heng, all of whom remained his friends until they died. He also met Song Ong Siong, a lawyer, who invited him to join his legal firm, which Pops of course did. He worked hard and never stopped reading his law books and became well known in Singapore because he seldom lost a case. He made a lot of friends among whom was Mr. Lee Chin Koon, father of Lee Kuan Yew who became Singapore's Prime Minister and later led Singapore to its independence.

Every Sunday a Chinese man used to come on his bicycle with a large bundle at the back of his bicycle. He would spread out the things he was selling – tablecloths, bed sheets, etc. – all from China. His name, he told her, was C.K. Tang and he was going around selling this to make a living. Mother was so sorry for him and always bought things from him even though she did not need anything. She used to put them into a cupboard and later during the Japanese Occupation I would at times sell these things to buy food. Little did she know that Mr. C.K. Tang would become a multi-millionaire and own one of the biggest department stores in

Amelia Hoalim with her daughter Joyce. *Malcolm Thwaites.*

Singapore. C.K. Tangs is still flourishing and the company even built and owns the Dynasty Hotel next door.

Early one morning we were awoken by loud noises. It was 8 December 1941. We did not know what it was. The bread and the newspapers were late but when they came we heard that the Japanese had bombed Singapore and destroyed many buildings in the city area. Many people were killed. Pops went down to his office later and discovered that it had been hit so he had to move to another place. Then the Japanese landed in Alor Star to the north of Malaya. The British sent two warships to fight them but both ships were attacked and sunk. It was a big set back for the British in Singapore. They had been so very confident of licking the "little yellow one" and now the British Army were daily retreating south as the Japanese bombed and shelled them.

The British thought the Japanese were coming by sea. Instead the Japanese came walking down the Malayan peninsula, killing, raping and destroying as they came. Penang was captured and the great exodus to Singapore started. We lived in Katong near the sea and the British soldiers came and told us to pack a few things and get out as they still thought the Japanese would attack from the sea. All the big guns pointed to the sea. In actual fact we moved to the front line without realizing it as the Japanese were coming down Malaya. When they reached Johore they started bombing and shelling Singapore and we were in the thick of it. There was panic in the city. Dead bodies were everywhere with no one to bury them. People were digging holes in their gardens to bury the dead in front of their houses. No one knew who they were but if you had a garden you buried them or lived with the stench.

Mother, Philip and Pops stayed with Mr. & Mrs. Schubert and their son Carl in Lincoln Road. I had just given birth to a tiny baby girl and stayed in Norfolk Road with Lee Chin Koon and his family. Without knowing it we left our safe home in Katong and went to live in the most dangerous part of Singapore, being the front line as the Japanese moved down Bukit Timah Road. We lived in the air raid shelter and shared our space with any soldier who came by. The bombing and shelling were continuous. Then one day the shelling let up for a while . . . the British surrendered on 15 February 1942 and the bombs and shells stopped coming. But the Japanese soldiers were there and the soldiers were given three days freedom of the city as a reward for capturing Singapore. Three days of looting, raping and murder. I was hidden away so they could not find me but they came into the house and demanded watches, Parker pens, money and food. By then everyone was willing to give them anything they wanted as long as they went away.

I did not have news of mother and Philip for a few days and I sent my husband, Denis, to see if they were alright. He came back to say the house had taken a direct hit, there was blood everywhere and no one around. I began to panic. I wanted to be with my mother. Denis said there was no sign of the dogs also. I sat down and cried and cried. Then Lee Kuan Yew (who later became the Prime Minister) went out looking in the nearby hospital. He found Mrs. Schubert and mother there. They had been wounded. Mrs. Schubert lost a leg and mother had a lot of injuries. There were no doctors or nurses in the hospital – all had run away after they heard that the Japanese had gone into any hospital they came across and bayoneted anyone they found there. Mother had been hit on 14 February 1942 and Pops brought her to Mrs. Lee's house where a bed was set up for her in the garage. She was in great pain. I did not know then that she had cancer of the liver and had an operation for that in October 1941. When she had the operation no one told me what her ailment was . . . I suppose they wanted to spare me. It was only years later, long after the war, that Philip told me that mother had cancer. But now she was in pain and had a doctor to look after her. He gave her morphine to ease the pain – it was all he could get. She used to throw her arms and legs over the side of the bed and moan, Oh God. It took the doctor, Philip and sometimes Pops to lift her legs and place them on the bed, they were so heavy. The doctor kept saying he did not understand why she did not die, her limbs were dead but her heart was still keeping her alive. My mother was taken to the Kandang Kerbau Hospital nearby but the place was in shambles. Doctors and nurses had run away. People were lying on the floor as there were no more beds, the Japanese were bombing and shelling all the time and the area around the hospital was full of deep craters from bombs and shells.

One night I had a dream that mother was waiting for a priest. I told Mr. Schubert, who was a Roman Catholic, and he said, My God, why didn't I think of that. He went down to the Cathedral of the Good Shepherd but the priest refused to come. My mother had been excommunicated when she married my father, who was a Protestant, but for the rest of her life she did her best to bring us up in the church. She used to say she was going to the market on Sunday and ask her driver to leave Joyce and me at the Roman Catholic Cathedral of the Good Shepherd. Then she would pick us up after marketing. In October 1941 Joyce had gone to Melbourne (Australia) to study at the Emily

McPherson School of Domestic Science so she was not with us during the war. She could not study for the Senior Cambridge as her eyesight was bad and the optician could not give her thicker lenses so she worked on Pops until he let he go to Australia, so Philip and I were the ones left in Singapore during the war.

The priest said mother had been excommunicated and he could not give her the last rites. Mr. Schubert argued and pleaded and in the end threatened to leave the church. The priest finally came with a little altar boy. He blessed my mother, anointed her with oil and prayed for us. Then he said, Mrs. Hoalim, I am going to say the Act of Contrition. If you can hear me, say it after me. And he said sentence after sentence very slowly with a pause after each sentence. When he was done she gave a great sigh and never moved again. Mother died early the next morning, 18 March 1942. The priest refused to come to the burial ceremony. I told him it was not his job as priest to sit in judgment of my mother's soul and he should have faith that even with her last breath God had forgiven her for her sins. But he did not come. My father said a Protestant prayer over my mother's grave but she is buried in the Roman Catholic side of Bidadari Cemetery. I never went back to the Catholic Church and became a Protestant and I have been so ever since.

We were often short of food but Philip and Pops gave us as much as they could and I sold my clothes and household articles to buy food. Once he brought a pair of rabbits to us. He said they multiplied quickly and would be a good source of meat. They did multiply quickly but we did not have the heart to kill and eat them. We had an Alsatian called "Duke" and he used to sit and watch the rabbits and if one dared to escape Duke would pounce on him and break his back. So Duke had rabbit for dinner quite often. Pops used to ask to be paid in rice and other foodstuffs when he did a case for anyone because money began to have no value.

Three and a half years of the Japanese Occupation came to an end and the British came back to Singapore. But things had changed and people began to think in terms of independence from British rule. Pops was the first to start a Party to work towards independence for Singapore. He called his party the Malayan Democratic Union and he was the president. Other parties joined in. I remember a few of the names in the MDU: Lim Kean Chye (my cousin) and P.V. Sarma among others.

Pops became very well known in Singapore. He had a big car with a flag on it because he was the president of the MDU. The children were not allowed to touch his car. I remember that my son Malcolm (Butch) was scolded once because he rubbed his hand over the bonnet and Pops thought he was scratching the car. Pops became very important. Once I was walking along Mountbatten road on my way to Katong and Pops passed in his car. He did not stop.

Pops always wanted me to be a lawyer and trained me for it. He said I would have to be a good lawyer – the best in Singapore. So from an early age he began to prepare me. He wanted me to read only school books and books on Literature. Then before I went to bed I had to write in an exercise book the stories I had read, the people I had spoken to, the conversations, the times of the conversations, etc, etc. It became so that I would lie awake for hours after going to bed, going over in my mind what I had written and worrying if it was correct because every Sunday

Elma Thwaites.
Sandi Wong-Moon.

he would take the book and question me on it. And I had to reply straight away.

I did not become a lawyer. I rebelled but Philip went to England after the war and studied to become a lawyer. I went to England and studied singing and youth work. During the Japanese Occupation I discovered that I had a high soprano voice so I joined the choir of St. Hilda's Anglican Church. I came top in all my exams in London on the History of Music etc. and in Swansea University where I studied philosophy, psychology etc. as part of the youth work I was doing. I had to study why young people do the things they do and why they rebel against adults. I came to understand myself in Swansea University but Pops was not interested in my results because I was not doing

Philip Hoalim, Jnr.
Sandi Wong-Moon.

law. Philip passed his Bar exams, married a Penang girl who was also doing law and they both came back to Singapore. I came back to Singapore and became a teacher and at least I was doing something I liked to do. I taught English and Literature at a Secondary School in Singapore and I was happy. Pops washed his hands of me but up to the time he died and when he could no longer speak he would still wag his fingers at me and I knew that he was still telling me, You could have become a good lawyer.

Obituary for Philip Hoalim
from a local newspaper.

We record with sadness the passing of a distinguished lawyer - PHILIP HOALIM SNR. – on the 24th July 1980 at the age of 85. He was born in British Guyana (now the Republic of Guyana) on the 29th August 1895 and had his early education there. B.G. being a colonial outpost he spent his youth prospecting for gold and other minerals in the vast hinterland. Later he was articled to the firm of a very prominent and outstanding solicitor in the country, Robert Dinzey, who saw tremendous potential in him and got him interested in the growing political movement of the Negroes and Indians against British colonialism.

Due to his political involvement at the time, Dinzey subsequently advised him not to remain in the country but to become a barrister before becoming a politician. He left for England and joined the Middle Temple – passing his Bar Finals in 18 months and was called in absentia. Dinzey died whilst Hoalim was in London and that made him decide to go to Africa (Kenya) where he had several good friends. However, he was persuaded by his sister, the late Mrs. Lim Cheng Ean, to visit her in Penang before deciding to settle elsewhere.

Mr. Hoalim arrived in Penang in 1932 and found it to be a small island and the handful of lawyers there were family solicitors. He realized that he was not cut out to live a protected legal life under the sheltering wing of a brother-in-law who had a good practice. So he made up his mind to migrate to Shanghai. He booked his passage for China but on arrival in Singapore he was met by an elderly Chinese gentleman (probably informed by his sister to intercept and offer the restless young Hoalim some sound advice). The gentleman was the late Sir Song Ong Siang and the offer was to try his (Sir Song's) legal office for 6 months and if he still wished to go to China after that Sir Song Ong Siang would not stand in his way. Mr. Hoalim not only stayed on in Singapore but later assisted Sir Ong Siang and the late Revd Murray to teach English at the Straits Chinese Reading Club in Prinsep Street where he took the Senior classes. Two years later he became a partner in the office of Mendis and Ahlip and in 1939 he opened his own firm under the style of Philip Hoalim & Co. and established the present system of using personal names to represent legal firms rather than practice in office in a personal capacity and individually.

He devoted his time purely to his law practice and as described by an old legal associate . . . "he had a stern countenance but he was a defender of the underdog and a man with a fiery temperament." He never invited partners to join him and he was strict and exacting not only to his chambering students and legal assistants but also unto himself for he never relaxed from his law to the very end of his days.

He not only had a successful legal practice but he became the firebrand leader of the earliest political party after the Second World War. As Chairman of the Malayan Democratic Union he fought the British bureaucrats tooth and nail and championed the cause for the Asian. However the MDU folded 3 years later soon after the precipitous action of the Communist Party to violence which brought to an end Hoalim's efforts for national unity and democracy for the new Malayan Nation. In retrospect his efforts were the forerunner of the future national movements for independence and democracy both in Singapore and Malaysia.

One interesting encounter he had before leaving Penang in 1936 was with Sir Cecil Clementi who was then the Governor of the Straits Settlements. Mr. Hoalim had crossed his path in B.G.

when Sir Cecil was then the Colonial Secretary. There Sir Cecil had made a speech in the Legislative Council in B.G., which had raised an outcry among the indigenous people and Mr. Hoalim had identified himself with the local population in the outcry. Sir Cecil asked Hoalim in Penang to promise that he (Hoalim) would not get involved in politics in the Straits Settlements or in Malaya. Mr. Hoalim so gave his promise. But when the Japanese Occupation ended, to Hoalim the OLD ORDER was also over and he considered his pre-war promise to Sir Cecil no more binding.

In his time he created a few legal milestones. However his last case was ironically his own matter concerning his beloved island – Pulau Tekong Kechil – which was compulsorily acquired by the government in 1968 and not disposed of till 1979 and which kept him from retirement till the disposal thereof by the Privy Council in 1977 on points of interpretation and in 1979 on adequate quantum of compensation offered. Eventually he won on both counts and received the handsome sum of $1.5 million – no more no less as he had envisaged from the start.

Philip Hoalim, Snr. *Malcolm Thwaites.*

Recipe for Adventure

Laura Hall

Phyllis Laura Lee[1] boarded an airplane for the first time in 1954 and flew from British Guiana to London Heathrow. She was leaving behind all that was familiar to marry a man she barely knew in a distant land. At least that is how I as her daughter interpreted the event. After my father died, I asked my mother how she could have been certain that he would actually marry her once she arrived. She gave me one of her black looks. As children we recognized this as a sign to retreat from the impending storm. She shouted at me with great irritation, that it had never occurred to her, "your father was not that sort of man."

Of course Phyllis was certain about Philip, or she never would have set foot on the plane in the first place. She had never traveled outside of British Guiana, even so, British culture did not seem so alien. In school she memorized the names of the kings and queens of England and Great Britain and read the works of Shakespeare, Charles Dickens and Jane Austen. She saw the English countryside in movies, great castles and country houses, and a fog-swathed London. Britain was after all "the mother country" to her colonial subjects. More important to her decision to board that plane than these abstract connections to "England" was her faith in the Englishman who had asked her to marry him, a young geologist Philip Kenneth Hall.

Philip had been recruited by the African Manganese Company, a subsidiary of Union Carbide, to examine the extent of manganese deposits in British Guiana. Like many companies operating in the colonies, they frowned on their employees fraternizing too closely with the locals. Temporary relationships with women were tolerated but permanent unions were discouraged. Philip met a vivacious Chinese woman, Phyllis Lee, at the photography counter of Bookers Department Store in Georgetown. She turned down his requests for a date informing

---

1   Phyllis Hall née Lee is a descendant of Isaac Fung-Teen-Yong. She passed away in 1999.

him that he would need the permission of her father. Alexander Lee, a shopkeeper at Diamond Estate, informed the brazen young man that Chinese girls did not go out with Englishmen. Given the reputation of the expatriate bachelors he had good reason to deny the geologist's request to date his youngest daughter.

Philip was undeterred by Mr. Lee's rejection. After each prospecting trip to the interior he returned with a bag with rolls of film. Countless mundane and identical photographs of forest, rivers and camps were of dubious scientific or aesthetic value and served one purpose only. Each roll of film was a return ticket to the attractive Chinese girl at the photography counter — once when he brought the film to be developed, and again when he returned to pick up the order. A month in the interior could provide a month of opportunities to meet Phyllis.

Phyllis Lee, photographic service attendant at Bookers. *Laura Hall.*

Once he proposed marriage, the Lees accepted him as a future son-in-law. They acceded to his request to take Phyllis to England to be married there. Having seen the marriages of six of his own children, Mr. Lee reasoned that it was only fair that Philip's parents get to enjoy the marriage of their eldest son. The fact that Phyllis's brother Johnny had recently moved to London and was himself about to be married there gave the family some comfort. On hearing news of the engagement Philip's employers informed him that this ill-considered action would impede his advancement with the company. He was swiftly dispatched up the Mazaruni River in the rainy season, a difficult assignment in the dry season, but treacherous when the river was high. This did nothing to dampen his ardor. They underestimated Philip Hall who liked nothing better than a field assignment with a touch of danger.

Discovering the Mother Country

Philip brought his sister, Dorothy Walker, or Dolly as the family called her, to meet Phyllis at Heathrow airport. The taxi ride back to London was a comic encounter of cockney and creole with Philip translating between the two versions of the "mother tongue." Phyllis imagined everyone in England spoke with the same clipped Standard English of the British expatriates in British Guiana. However the Hall family of Dagenham, like most residents of the council estate, were recent migrants from the East End of London, homeland of the cockneys. Philip, the exception, had cast off his accent as he climbed the educational ladder and traveled far from home. Further exposure to the natives of the Mother Country forced Phyllis to revise many of her preconceptions about the British. Bathing habits, English houses and cooking practices were just a few of the new experiences.

Phyllis first resided with Betty, her brother Johnny's fiancée. The two brides-to-be shared a bedsit in north London.[2] Her first bath was a revelation; when it came to bathing, the British were surprisingly undemanding about the quality of their amenities. All the residents of the building shared one bathroom with a bathtub. Baths were not officially rationed but the ritual required to take one was enough to deter residents from indulging too frequently. A coin inserted in the meter provided a certain amount of electricity for lights, heat and cooking; or gas for hot water in the case of the bathroom meter. Following Betty's instructions, Phyllis armed herself with a supply of coins, fed the meter, waited for the tank to heat up, then ran her bath. Sitting in a tub of hot water was a novelty for the girl from Diamond but after soaping herself all over she realized that she was now soaking in a tub of dirty water made scummy by the hard water of the London system. Obviously a rinse was in order. Stepping out into the hallway in her dressing gown with another handful of coins, she refilled the meter ignoring the indignant glares of the other residents patiently queuing for their turn. It was Saturday night, bath night. Being British they did not complain.

The wedding was a modest affair arranged by Dolly who was married only a few months before. At Phyllis's request, Philip set aside his long-

---

2　Bedsits or bed-sitting rooms were furnished rooms in subdivided houses, a cheap form of rental accommodation. They usually consisted of a bed, a sink, and some kind of primitive cooking appliance. Separate toilet and bathroom facilities were shared by all the occupants of the house.

Bride and groom flanked by Philip's parents and Phyllis's brother Johnny & wife Betty. *Laura Hall.*

standing atheism and agreed to be married in church. A reception and lunch at a local hotel followed the ceremony, all attended by the Hall family, Johnny and Betty, and a few of Philip's friends. Photographs of the happy event were dispatched to the family in British Guiana and the occasion duly noted in the *Daily Argosy*.

Residing with her in-laws was an educational experience for Phyllis, particularly in culinary matters. British cuisine of the 1950s was impoverished by the years of rationing and economic hardship during, between and after two wars. Years of deprivation had nurtured a suspicion of "foreign" ingredients such as garlic or basil. Ivy Hall, Philip's mother, could be described as a plain cook. Keen to ensure that her son should be properly fed, she instructed her daughter-in-law in the preparation of his favorite dishes such as steak and kidney pie. Ivy was unaware that he had developed a preference for the tinned version produced by Fray Bentos during his bachelor days. Like most Guianese women, Phyllis was an excellent cook. Her repertoire of dishes included all the Guianese ethnic food traditions, including "English" but she had never cooked English food in the manner of her mother-in-law. She related how she watched in horror as her mother-in-law placed a joint of pork in the oven without one bit of spice, not even salt. Vegetables were treated no better, submerged in boiling water until color and flavor were diminished.

Phyllis's first attempt to introduce Philip's family to Guianese food was not well received. The newly weds had set up home in a small flat in the nearby town of Ilford and she was eager to repay her in-laws many kindnesses with a meal. She could have cooked an English meal better than most English housewives but at Philip's insistence she prepared a Chinese meal. This required no small effort on her part. Ingredients such as ginger and garlic could not be found in the high street supermarket. Several train trips to London's Chinatown and hours of preparation resulted in an exotic feast of wonton soup, Chinese style chicken stew and more for her new family. Much as they loved their new family member, the Halls could not overcome their natural resistance to the strange smells, textures and tastes before them. Philip's parents, Phil and Ivy, along with his sister Dolly and brother Brian, poked at the food on their plates leaving most of it uneaten. Only Dolly's husband Stan ate everything heartily and for that he earned Phyllis's enduring affection. She reserved her fury for Philip for what she considered to be a misjudged attempt to show off his bride to his family.

Philip was still employed by the African Manganese Company who dispatched him to Sierra Leone soon after the wedding. He returned shortly when the company reneged on their promise to allow Phyllis to join him. He then accepted a job offer with Site Investigation Company, to work in Iraq. Wives were apparently welcome there. Philip went in advance to secure housing for the two of them and the baby on the way. When he departed for his job in Sierra Leone Phyllis found herself alone in the flat at Ilford. In no time she packed her bags and was on the doorstep of the Hall household in Dagenham. Dagenham, part of Greater London, was and is the site of the largest council housing estate in the U.K. Built by the government after the First World War to be "Homes for Heroes," the terraced houses boasted electricity and gas, indoor bathrooms and toilets and gardens. The bath was an improvement on that of the bedsit, no coins or meters were involved. This modern appliance was heated by means of a gas-fired copper boiler in the kitchen, the heated water was then hand pumped up to the unheated bathroom. The only heat in the house was the coal fireplace in the living room. Small electric fires provided temporary heat in the other rooms. Despite these shortcomings, she preferred the conviviality of her in-laws home to the luxury of her own flat and bathtub.

The Hall family accepted Phyllis wholeheartedly from her first arrival. Dolly made the arrangements for the wedding celebration, having recently planned her own wedding to Stanley Walker. She also took Phyllis shopping for clothes appropriate for the English weather.

The Guianese girl had arrived wearing sandals and owning nothing warmer than a thin blue cardigan. Finding clothes and footwear to fit her diminutive Chinese sister-in-law proved to be a challenge. Fortunately Phyllis was a natural seamstress who had observed her older sister Marie, a professional seamstress, and then taught herself to sew. She would examine the cut of a fashionable dress that she admired in the department store and then, without the assistance of a pattern, work out how to make it at home. She surprised her older brother Archie, the family's science prodigy and future nuclear chemist, when she asked his advice on doing a geometric cut for a complex style she wanted to replicate. He recalled that she was fifteen at the time and he was unaware that she had any sewing skills.

Phyllis was delighted with the wide choice of styles in the English shops but most of the clothing was too large for her petite form. Undeterred, she bought and altered some items, others she made from scratch. Shoes, a size too large, were stuffed with tissue paper. For outerwear she was determined to have a swagger coat, a flared style of the 1950s, and something that she could not make herself. She bought one that she liked which came down to her ankles and cut it down to size.

Her brother-in-law Brian, a teenager at the time, took great pleasure in walking down the High Street with "the most exotic woman ever seen in Dagenham." The first time she saw snow she borrowed her mother-in-law's boots, put on her new coat and walked for hours enjoying the white flakes that swirled in the air and was soft underfoot. Mr. and Mrs. Hall expressed no misgivings over their son's marriage to a Guianese woman of Chinese heritage. When told of the engagement his father commented that he always knew his nomadic eldest son would marry a foreigner. Philip senior was a grouchy and often ill-tempered man who had few words of praise for those closest to him. With the arrival of Phyllis the family noted that he became amiable, almost cheerful. Few could resist her sunny nature.

Iraq

Baghdad in the 1950s was a bustling metropolis with a large British expatriate community, a legacy of longstanding British interests in the region.[3] In British Guiana, Phyllis and her family had little to do with the expatriates. Here in Baghdad she was part of that community by default, though she still felt like a stranger among them. Philip too with his working class origins did not feel entirely at ease among them. They did not join any of the clubs frequented by the British in Baghdad but they did gradually acquire a small circle of friends from among the other geologists and their wives.

A few months after her arrival in Baghdad, Phyllis gave birth to their first child, Laura. The mid-1950s were a relatively peaceful period in Iraq and medical facilities were as good as any in England. I was born at St. Raphael, a hospital run by French and Iraqi nuns of the Dominican order, and one of the few hospitals to survive the looting after the initial weeks of the U.S.-led military invasion of the country in 2003.

Far from any family support, Phyllis had to rely on the sisters at St. Raphael and her own experience of helping to raise her nephews and nieces in British Guiana. Philip, who had no such experience, purchased Dr. Benjamin Spock's latest book on raising babies and read it from cover to cover.[4] Dr. Spock no doubt had advice on travelling with an infant but could not have anticipated the idea of embarking on a four-month camping trip to a remote region of the Middle East, by Land Rover and mule train with a baby of ten weeks. His famous admonition to parents to "trust yourself" no doubt appealed to Philip who expressed no doubts then, or even in later years, about the wisdom of taking his family with him on a geological field trip to Kurdistan in the far north of Iraq. This was a period of relative calm in the tumultuous relationship between the Kurds and the government of Iraq.

The trip was documented in a handsome green and white embroidered bound album, the only album my father seems to have had the time to assemble in the course of the family's global travels. Each photograph

---

3   Britain had been involved in Iraq since the First World War when it was part of the Ottoman Empire. Baghdad was invaded in 1917 to protect British oil interests. In 1955 Iraq's government was headed by a British sponsored monarch, King Faisal II. He was overthrown and killed in 1958.

4   Benjamin Spock published *Baby and Childcare* in 1946 and *A Baby's First Year* in 1954, both bestsellers. His approach to childcare, treating children as individuals, was considered revolutionary at the time.

is held in place by the precisely glued corners and described in his neat handwriting:

July 1st 1956. My camp at Kara.

July 22nd 1956. Resting at spring above Bektar.

August 27th 1956. Leaving Kukerri. Laura in sling.

November 1956. Kurdish children and policeman at Bakarman.

November 1956. On a roof at Aqra

The album documents two trips, each two months in length, between July and November 1956, to dozens of villages in remote regions of Kurdistan.[5] For Phyllis these first treks with Philip were memorable. She recalled the Kurds as the most hospitable people they encountered over Philip's long career as a geologist. A hospitality all the more poignant given the extreme poverty of most of the Kurdish villagers they encountered. Being then in my infancy, I retain no conscious memories of Kurdistan but I have reconstructed fragments of the journey from my parents' stories, photographs and home movies.

Philip's assignment was to produce the first geological maps of Kurdistan. Once outside of the major cities such as Mosul, the road network deteriorated with the altitude. In the most mountainous areas the only reliable means of travel was by mule. A team of mules carried the Halls, the Arab assistants, the cook, Kurdish guides, and all the food, tools, camping equipment and other provisions necessary for the lengthy expedition. Philip carried the tiny baby in a sling that hung from his neck in front of him, leaving his hands free to hold the reins of his mule. His experience with live animals was confined to the chickens that he raised for eggs during the war. One mule, sensing Philip's inborn suspicion of most domestic animals, or, prompted by an unnecessary prod from his heels, took off at a gallop. Clutching his baby with one hand and clinging to the saddle with the other, Philip managed to avoid the indignity of

---

5   I have followed my father's spelling of the names of places and people in the photo album for this trip. I have not been able to locate most of the Kurdish villages that he names on a map. They may be misspelled or too small to be designated on most maps. Thousands of Kurdish villages were destroyed and hundreds of thousands of their inhabitants killed by Saddam Hussein's government between 1987–1989 in what is referred to as the Anfal. The campaign is well documented in a report by Human Rights Watch, *Genocide in Iraq: The Anfal Campaign against the Kurds, 1993.*

being deposited head first into some bushes. Thereafter he treated his mule with caution and respect.

Phyllis, whose only riding experience was on a bicycle over the flat terrain between Diamond and Georgetown, adapted quickly to the demands of riding a mule. She commandeered a pair of her husband's trousers and using her skills as a seamstress adjusted them to her size. Riding experience was not necessary, the sure-footed animals knew the paths better than the riders which was reassuring on the slippery narrow hairpin paths carved into the sides of mountains. Leading the train was Philip's Kurdish guide, Abed Saala, a short stocky man, who invariably appears in photographs with a cigarette hanging from the side of his mouth. Abed was his guide, guard, translator and intermediary on this and all of Philip's journeys to the region.

The Kurdish men who accompanied the couple across the mountains were perpetually armed. Iraqi Kurds had struggled for autonomy since the beginning of the century; from the Ottomans, then the British and the regimes that they installed in Baghdad. Later it would be the Baathist governments. In a photograph Phyllis poses cheekily with a group of Kurdish men. Their poker straight faces do not betray what they think of the young woman in their midst. At her side is one of their Enfield rifles, almost as long as she is tall, she wears a cartridge belt at her waist. The pants in this picture are not Philip's but a pair of the Kurdish

men's baggy pants that she has acquired and altered to fit. On her feet is a pair of klash, lightweight flexible Kurdish shoes made of cowhide and knitted cotton and ideal for traversing the mountains.

When possible they camped by a river for ease of access to a supply of fresh water. Sometimes they camped near a village. On such occasions it was the custom to seek the permission of the headman or mukdar who usually insisted they join his family for a meal. At the home of the host Philip and Phyllis would be taken into the separate quarters for the men, and the women and children respectively. In the steep mountain villages the stone houses protruded from the hillsides, small cubes perilously piled on top of one another. The interiors of the homes were simple with earthen floors and mud plaster walls. Traditional carpets and floor cushions woven by the women were the only furniture and adornment.

For Philip in the men's quarters there would be an extravagant feast of lamb or goat and piles of rice and wheat. Phyllis experienced a much simpler feast with the women. Some ground meat and wheat with some vegetables but delicious all the same. From the moment Phyllis entered a room the baby would be taken from her and passed around, the object of curiosity and admiration. As was their custom, they cradled the baby's bottom in the palm of the hand and passed the upright wobbly infant from person to person. Healthcare in that part of the world was non-existent. Respiratory diseases and skin infections were common and many of the children had eyesores, an indicator of trachoma. Yet it would have been supremely insulting to decline offers of food or requests to hold the baby.

Philip routinely carried packs of British cigarettes as gifts for the Kurds they encountered. Benson & Hedges and Dunhill were the most coveted brands. On several occasions he was called upon to use his geological skills to help find a new source of water for the villagers. Village life was not possible if a well or spring dried up. At one village he reported with regret that he could not locate any promising sites for a new well. His men asked what had happened to his water finder. They pointed to the compass that he always carried with him and which they assumed was his water divining tool.

Phyllis found her own way to reciprocate, usually with food. At one village, the mukdar sent his youngest son to watch over Phyllis and the baby while Philip and the men were off working. This was not a welcome gift. Camping with a baby generated a lot of work. Nappies had to be washed and baby food prepared. Their own clothes needed mending and laundering. She also helped prepare the evening meal. She asked the cook, the only member of the team to remain at the camp, what might be done with the young man? The cook, ever attentive to an opportunity to vary the camp menu, suggested that she ask him to shoot some birds. In no time he returned with a dozen pigeons that would be a tasty surprise for the hungry team when they returned.

Phyllis wanted to repay the mukdar for this and other generous gestures with a sweet treat. They had limited provisions but the cook could spare her some flour, sugar and oil. He provided a headcount of twelve for the mukdar and his sons. Later in the evening she sent the cook to the mukdar's house with a platter of a dozen freshly-made hot doughnuts. He reported to Phyllis with regret that he had undercounted the number of sons by one. Thus the sugary foreign delicacy was distributed to all but the youngest son. Kurdistan was my mother's first adventure with my father. They were to have many more throughout his career as a geologist but whatever the circumstances she always cooked enough for an army.

Sierra Leone

After completing his contract in Iraq in 1958, Philip returned to Sierra Leone, this time with Phyllis, Laura and the most recent addition to the family, Susan. Russell would be born there some years later. Philip was now a civil servant employed by of the Government Geological Survey in the capital, Freetown.[6] In Sierra Leone he developed his specialty, the exploration and evaluation of diamond and kimberlite deposits. Philip continued to take his family with him on trek whenever it was feasible, by

---

6   Sierra Leone was a British colony until independence in April 1961

Land Rover with the occasional perilous river crossing in a dugout canoe.

Phyllis, a naturally social person, was adept at making friends. As the wife of a field geologist who spent one month out of three away from home, friends were vital. Fellow West Indians and other Britons were always

Phyllis with her children Susan and Laura in Sierra Leone. *Laura Hall.*

among her friends of course, but she was also drawn to those who were marginalized by the exclusive British expatriate culture of Freetown. There was Barbara, a German doctor whose qualifications were not recognized by the medical authorities, and her shy British husband; an Anglo-Indian family who ran a business and more importantly from the children's perspective, had a swimming pool; and naturally she befriended any Chinese person who crossed her path. Though she spoke not a word of Chinese and they spoke little English, especially the women, food could be counted on to ease communication. A team of Taiwanese farmers on an agricultural mission invited the Hall family to delectable feasts of Chinese food. A doctor from Hong Kong and his family visited whenever they were in the capital. They were stationed at a small town in the interior, surely one of the loneliest postings. When Philip's treks took him in their direction he made sure to take a detour to bring them Chinese foodstuffs from Phyllis.

One of Phyllis's most memorable catches was the crew of a Korean fishing trawler who had the misfortune to be stranded in Freetown when their vessel broke down. Philip's month long treks to the interior were nothing compared to their yearlong sojourns at sea far from their families. Phyllis met two of them in the supermarket and invited them to tea one Sunday afternoon, adding that their friends were welcome.

Uncertain of how many were coming, she prepared cakes big and small, plain and chocolate and a variety of sandwiches. A van arrived with a dozen or more Korean men. They might have had a dozen words of English between them. The cakes and refreshments were eagerly consumed but their greatest pleasure was simply being with a family. They each competed to have their photo taken with the children, Laura, Susan, and now baby Russell.

I imagine that somewhere in Korea a retired seaman has a photograph album of a fishing voyage halfway around the world and an unplanned visit to Sierra Leone. There are photos of the crew standing awkwardly with plates of cake in their hands and, in another photo, the funny Chinese lady who invited them to tea next to her English husband. The seaman's favorite photo is the one of himself squatting with the three Hall children, a souvenir of unexpected hospitality in a distant land.

Swiss Movement

Janet Signer, née Wong

I was born in Georgetown in 1936, the fourth child of Reginald and Clarice Wong. My father was a land surveyor and my mother a schoolteacher before she got married. They lived in a modest house on Crown Street, in a middle-class neighborhood of Georgetown and raised all their children there. I attended Bishops High School and, like many of the local girls, joined the workforce after obtaining several passes at the "O" Level exams. I was employed as a secretary initially at the British Council and later worked at a bank and then an insurance company. I began dating a young man who did not meet the approval of my mother, and she packed me off to London.

My brother Gerald was studying civil engineering in London and it was with him that I stayed initially. One of the dream occupations as a girl growing up was to become an airline stewardess, but in my case it didn't work out. I took on a more down to earth approach and Aunt Elsie Luck was helpful in getting me into an exclusive school to become a seamstress. The school attracted a number of hoity-toity people who were as stuck up as the needles they wielded. I got fed up with both the sewing and the school and decided to pursue my greater interest in languages.

I enrolled in the Regent Street Polytechnic to learn French, Spanish and German, all at the same time. Having a background in Latin, I didn't find it too difficult to cope with these three languages although German was the most challenging one. Even so I found that there were some similarities in German and Latin in grammar and sentence structure, which made things easier for me. I enjoyed learning these different languages and my enjoyment increased even more when I developed a friendship with a young man from Switzerland. Alfons Signer was a bank employee, working in the stock brokerage department, who came

Janet Wong (2nd left) with other members of Guyana's Women's Hockey Team about to fly off to compete with Trinidad and Jamaica (1956). *Janet Signer.*

to the polytechnic to improve his English, which was already quite good. I decided that it would be good for my German if I were to go to a German-speaking environment and I wrote to my mother to explain that I would like to move to Switzerland. Her reply was that no such move would take place unless I became Mrs. Signer. Alfons and I considered the various options and we decided to get married.

When we moved to Zurich we spent the first three to four months in a small rented apartment. It was essentially one large room, and the kitchen and bathroom were shared with the landlords. We had to insert coins into a meter to get gas heat. The owners did not have other people in their family and they did not use the kitchen very much so essentially I could use the kitchen whenever I wanted. This worked out all right because Alfons came back home for lunch every day. The bank owned apartment buildings and the employees were given first choice on them when they became available. So not long after, we were able to move

Alfons and Janet Signer on their wedding day. *Janet Signer.*

into a self-contained one-bedroom apartment.

When we were settling in to our new accommodations and life together, Alfons was summoned to go off to military training, mandatory for every Swiss male between the ages of 20 to 42. The initial basic training would last for three months, then a refresher course would be scheduled periodically – annually in the first few years, and then every two or three years subsequently. The militiamen would go off to various camps in the countryside and mountainous areas. I understand that there are some mountains that are hollowed out and ready to deal with any national emergency, being equipped with medical supplies, food and water. The workplaces were obliged to let their employees go off to these training sessions. There was no way to escape military service, and those who missed or dodged their obligation would be fined. Every man would have a rifle and ammunition at home, but the ammunition would be sealed.

With regard to medical services, I feel that Switzerland has a very good health care program, provided mainly through company insurance plans. After the birth of a child, someone would be assigned to come for two weeks to help in the care of the newborn and the mother, providing various services including shopping, cooking, cleaning, washing and whatever else was needed in getting adjusted to having a new member in the family.

The vast majority of Swiss wives remained at home taking care of family and household matters. In those days the prevailing attitude was that wives ought not to be working. I found that the Swiss people, at least in Zurich, were very conservative and continued in their traditional ways and habits. Although I was obviously an "import" they did not go out of their way to find out more about me, or where I came from. Switzerland is the home location for several important organizations, including the United Nations and the International Red Cross in Geneva, and the Olympics in Lausaunne, but the ordinary citizens in Zurich remained rather insular in nature, in keeping perhaps with the way that the privacy of bank accounts are meticulously guarded. Swiss bank accounts have gained the international reputation of being hidden, secret dealings. This plus Switzerland's neutrality in the major wars has worked well for Zurich, the country's financial center. These days, things are a lot different and there is a more open attitude among the people. However, the right of Swiss citizenship, which I received with my marriage, is no longer automatically extended to spouses.

The central location of Switzerland made it easy to access other European countries, and vice versa. Many products from nearby countries were easily available and Alfons was the owner of a Peugeot, BMW and Alfa-Romeo at different times. German cars were known for their quality and were popular in our area, and so too were Volvos. We took trips to various parts of the country, but that would not take much time because it required only about two hours to drive from the northern to the southern borders of Switzerland, and perhaps three and a half hours going from east to west. For our vacations, we would typically go abroad, such as to the western coast of Italy and also to Spain where we could enjoy the beaches.

Our first trip on vacation together exposed us to the Swiss custom of running on time. We planned to go by train that was scheduled to leave shortly after 6:00 a.m. and so we arranged for a taxi to pick us up early in the morning. Hauling our luggage to the street, we waited for the taxi, but it did not show up. Through a hurried phone call we learnt that the taxi could not come and that another would be dispatched. But we could not wait any longer and we flagged down a passing taxi and rushed to the station. However, as we arrived at the platform the best we could do was wave bye-bye to the train as all we could see was its back half as it departed from the station. We were still able to get to our destination on the same day but we had to break the journey. The first train would have had better connections, and taken us to Genoa where we would have caught another train going down the coast. Instead, we arrived at one station in Genoa and had to go to another railway station, then wait for the next available train.

Precision is indeed a familiar word associated with Swiss engineering and technical equipment, particularly with the manufacture of watches. Watches with "Swiss movement" (the driving mechanism for the timepieces) were regarded as setting the highest standard in the industry. For many decades Swiss timing was used at the Olympic games. Several brand names, such as Omega and Rolex, have become associated with both accurate timing and luxury, well before the advent of quartz crystals. The fine engineering skills cultivated by the Swiss have been duplicated in other fields, including medical instruments and precision tools.

The Swiss name has also been associated with another product that has become well known in many countries – cheese. However, while there are many kinds of delicious, and exquisite, cheeses made in Switzerland, none of them is known as "Swiss cheese." You would have to know the variety or specific name of the cheese – perhaps Appenzeller, Gruyère, Tilsiter – and not all of them have holes in them. In the northern section of Switzerland sauerkraut and pork hocks were popular dishes, just like in Germany. One of the local specialties is polenta, made out of corn meal and typically served or cooked with other items, particularly cheese.

There is another specific item that is eaten in the days just before Lent. It is a crispy pastry, rather like a thin pancake, that is fried and served with icing sugar. It is associated with fastnacht, or night of fasting, although the fasting actually starts on Ash Wednesday. So in the few days up to Fat Tuesday there is a karneval. It would be celebrated in different ways across the country; the guilds, e.g. the carpenters or plumbers, would parade in colorful costumes. Actually fastnacht officially begins at 11:00 a.m. on the 11th day of the 11th month, November, when there would be group of enthusiasts parading and beating drums. However, this moment marked only the beginning of fastnacht and there were other occasions, particularly Christmas and New Year, that would intervene before the bigger pre-Lenten karneval. It was a distinctly Swiss variation of Mardi Gras. One of the many spring celebrations that Zurich is famous for is its historical Sechselaeuten (ringing the bells at six) with parades, the burning of "Winter" and guild ceremonies in the evening. This celebration dates back to the Middle Ages. The "Boogg," a straw snowman, representing Winter, is placed at the top of a huge bonfire, filled with fireworks. As guild members ride around, the bonfire is lit at the stroke of six. As the fireworks explode, the crowd anxiously waits to see what the forecast is. If the straw man burns up quickly it means winter is dead and over with and if it takes a long time to burn up it means that we would have many more wet, cold days ahead.

The Swiss also have a distinct set of playing cards that start with ace, king, queen, jack and down to six, i.e. there are no cards from two to five. These jass cards are played in a manner similar to whist or bridge, with bidding. In one variation, the six can be designated as the highest card and ace the lowest. Jassen is a popular card game that I found enjoyable to play. This card game, knitting, crochet and embroidery, were some of the popular activities for Swiss housewives. Another was singing and yodeling, especially as participants in choirs, of which there are many.

The Swiss Alps provides an excellent setting for winter sports, but we didn't go in for any of the mountain-related activities, only a bit of skating, especially after our two sons were born. There were enclosed rinks as well as open-air areas for skating. During winter Lake Zurich would freeze in places and the thickness of the ice would be tested before people were allowed to venture on the ice. On occasion the temperature would be so cold that the whole lake would freeze over and the citizens of Zurich would set off to work with their skates and skis, and not have to rely on the ferries or trams. In the summer months the lake became a popular place for recreational boating, with various watercrafts being used, including a two-seater boat in the shape of a swan that would be propelled by pedal power. It was fun for both children and adults.

At home, we spoke English and that's what the children learnt until the age of five when they started at kindergarten. Children would begin primary school at age seven and continue for six years and then they'd attend secondary school for another three years of compulsory education. About a half of the school leavers usually would go on to vocational schools where a combination of theory plus practical on-the-job experience would be acquired. These produced skilled craftsmen, in trades varying from carpentry to finances. Our elder son, Philippe, had an inclination to do cooking, so he worked for a chef while going to school. There's a very renowned school of culinary arts in Lausanne and we reserved a place three or four years in advance and put down a deposit. But when it was time to go Philippe said, I'm not going. So we lost our deposit and he just did his apprenticeship and took the tests afterwards to get his diploma in cooking. Our other son, Alex, did a business diploma. He worked for an office – finance, insurance – as well as attend business school. When they reached the age that they needed to serve in the military, they went off, like their father, to the various training camps. It was either that or leave the country; and if you were to return, the obligation to serve still remained. That was the Swiss way.

Another area of essentially compulsory participation was in the Swiss style of democracy. For ages men were the only ones who could vote, but in 1971 women were also given voting right for federal elections, although there are a few cantons, or electoral areas, where women cannot vote on local issues. The urge to participate was backed by the fact that you could be fined for not voting, at least in past days. Switzerland is a democracy in the real sense of the word because you had to go and vote for everything that there was to be decided. If they wanted to build a school somewhere, you got your voting card. I can remember getting voting cards for selection of teachers. If a teacher needed to be hired in a certain school in your area a vote had to be taken. This could be for a primary teacher, or any other teacher, not just a specialized one. As long as there are three people interested in the job, you had to vote. Each parent of children in that school could vote whether they wanted this or that teacher. If they were going to build a street somewhere in your district, you would get information saying they're planning on doing this, do you approve. If the citizens voted against it, they couldn't do it. There weren't any canvassers or promoters, you just got a sheet of information about the issue and the candidates for election, with background information on each of them. This method of exercising democracy is one that sets Switzerland apart for others in the world.

Diplomats and Diplomas

Ivy Gee, née Ho-Yen

I came to the United States in 1948, as a result of my husband's (Chih Yuan Yu) transfer to the consulate in Houston, Texas. He was then the chancellor at the Chinese consulate in Georgetown, representing the Republic of China, governed by the Kuomintang Party. We made a holiday itinerary on our way there, visiting relatives in Trinidad, Tobago and Jamaica. The first stop in the United States was Miami. I can still remember how almost childishly impressed I was with the myriad display of city lights, as seen from the airplane above and I had to write home to tell of that. This was, after all, my first trip abroad!

Chih Yuan, who adopted the English name Alfred, had a brother who was in graduate school at the University of Maryland, so we caught a connecting flight to visit him. The brother, Yi Yuan, was well liked by many of the professors and a few got together to give a tea party for us. It was a wonderful afternoon, and the professors showed a great delight in listening to me (a Chinese) speak with an "English accent" and they kept engaging me in conversation, which I thoroughly enjoyed. Of course I didn't think that was anything unique, because, after all, I grew up in British Guiana and attended schools with teachers from England. On the other hand, I knew almost no Chinese; one of my brothers had realized that the spoken Chinese we were learning was not grammatically correct and decided not to learn it at all! That probably set the example for me.

That done, we went on to visit New York and Washington, D.C., in all their excellence, scenic and political. From there, rather than flying to Houston, Texas, we decided to take the train to see the sights of the countryside. As countrysides go they come in all varieties, picturesque and less so. Since the trip was from the North to the Deep South, we passed through all kinds. As we got nearer to Houston, more or less called "East Texas," and I looked out on that stretch of land, I got a horrifying feeling too hard to describe. The houses (if houses they're called), along the railway route looked like large wooden boxes scattered hither and there and I thought, Is this where I'm heading to from British Guiana? WHY NOT NEW YORK OR WASHINGTON?!

Anyway, pretty soon we got nearer to civilization as such, and Houston was beautiful, though very much smaller than its BOOM of the succeeding years. But in 1948, the war was over and housing was in short supply. Our consulate was regally sized, but incoming members who worked there had a great deal of difficulty finding housing facilities. The first two months we were house mates with a local American Caucasian family. We found this arrangement through the classified section of the paper and were located on the outskirts of the city. Soon thereafter we were able to move to a small apartment nearer to the consulate.

However, as many Guyanese who have moved to the U.S. or England will attest, it is a fact that ... *you have to do everything for yourself.* No pampering or domestic help of any kind, though of course, in the service of a government, there are enviable privileges; but this period, too, happened to be soon after the World War when international relations were being reshaped!

The folks back home were amazed when I wrote to tell of many of the things I did to give our apartment a brighter look. I discarded the pitiful-looking drapes and the awful rug, made new curtains, in brighter colors, and painted both the walls *and* the floors! In contrast, when we lived in British Guiana, a brand-new duplex was built and furnished for the vice-consul and chancellor. The car and a chauffeur were available to the members of the consulate; we had not only a gardener, but also a cook and a maid, who also shopped at the market for each day's meal.

But parties and galas were in abundance, even in Houston, since consulates and embassies are famous for these. I, admittedly, was quite pampered, being the youngest among this accomplished group – a diplomat by marital association. But how did I get to be a member of this rather elite setting? Simply said, I met the chancellor of the Chinese consulate at a party. But this is a story from British Guiana, where nothing is simple!

Welcoming parties for the consul and vice-consul and their wives were normally held in Georgetown, the capital. The West Coast Demerara Chinese community wanted to be a part of these celebrations. Therefore, when Chih-Yuan Yu (Alfred) arrived as the new chancellor, they quickly voted to have the welcoming festivities on the West Coast, at the spacious house of my uncle, F.A. Lewis, a prominent and successful businessman.

The event was to start at 2 p.m. In order to coordinate arrival time with the ferryboat schedule, we invited the consular staff and dignitaries to have lunch with us at noon. Lunch was a bountiful and authentic European affair, served by two of our most experienced butlers. This was then followed by the 2 p.m. welcome, of which the West Coast Chinese were justifiably proud. The celebration continued well into the evening with dancing to the accompaniment of a live orchestra! Only a few from the consulate had to leave to catch the late afternoon ferry. And news from the "grapevine" over the following week was that the chancellor had "fallen in love at first sight!"

So on some Saturdays, the chancellor would make the long trip by ferry and train over to the West Coast, for a two-hour visit, which would consist of a high-tea and conversation. I was also frequently invited to functions in the city. Now there were many other young women in our community, whose mothers were heard to say, Why isn't the chancellor dating the other pretty girls? However, the rumors were that during consulate business, the chancellor was heard to ask, Have you met Miss Ho-Yen yet? She is quite a charming young lady. And what was the attitude about a local girl marrying a Chinese diplomat? Proud, indeed. There were many parties, the town was truly "abuzz." And the newspapers had a field day.

The wedding was an elaborate affair. The city provided honor guards to the church ceremony. We also had a Chinese ceremony hosted by the consul, in the Chinese Association Hall attended by both Chinese and non-Chinese Guyanese, and the Chinese dignitaries. The reception was a sumptuous and authentic Chinese wedding banquet, followed by dancing into the dawn! As if all were saying: This is Our Party!

We then rode in a surrey to our honeymoon site; this wonderful start was followed by a gift from the governor: a week's stay at his country home with the use of his entire staff! The beach was at our doorstep, and was refreshing, invigorating, and totally inviting. We were also able to dine with family friends, who lived in the area and were the local physician and his wife.

This would be a good place to describe British Guiana in the 20th century. I lived there at a time that the population had made the transition from being immigrants coming as indentured servants to immigrants coming on work visas. Emigrés came from Britain, and Europe as well as China and India. Though each race had their distinctive customs and communities, the immigrants did not stay confined to their groups of origin. The 20th century blossomed in British Guiana with a blending of these varied groups. This then evolved into interactions based more on interests rather than ethnic origin. This was the Guyana in which I grew up. And I rather naively thought that the entire world was this way!

I went to high school in Georgetown at Bishop's High School, one of the secondary high schools in Georgetown. (It was the school for girls; Queen's College was the boys' school. Central High School was a co-ed school.) However, I lived in West Coast, Demerara, and some of my high school friends would come to spend time with me, for in addition to companionship, they got a change from the city. We were not all of the same race but we were oblivious to this. In addition we were also invited to European parties. I mention all of the above because of an awkward awakening that I had shortly after moving to the States.

I hadn't paid much attention to the fact of segregation in the South, until one of those dear high school friends, who was black, wrote that she would be on an extended vacation and would be able to spend a few days with me. Now I was in a quandary. How could I tell this friend who had spent so much time in my home in B.G. that she was not welcome in my home in Texas? Would she react by thinking that Ivy had become a "high hat?" On the other hand if I did invite her to my house, would I be "crucified" by my neighbors, or even worse, be in trouble with the law?! I asked my sister who was still in Guyana, to explain racial tensions in the South ahead of my letter, which made it more personal and more easily understood. All went well with the visit, as my friend was able to stay with relatives who were also in Houston. But it is with a sense of great sadness that I remember the state of racial relations in the U.S. in contrast to British Guiana in the 1950s and the risk that it put to our long-term friendship.

But back to Houston in 1948. Half a century ago, Houston was not a large metropolis, but it was taking root. The Ship Channel was being enlarged to allow larger merchant ships to enter and sail in towards port. This was completed around this time (1948-49). Boats and luxury ships were all in celebratory regalia. Members of consulates and embassies play a large part in such, for after all, much of their duties are intertwined with trade. Subsequently, the most luxurious of the ships was used as the vessel to sail out along the channel and back. On board, the cream of the crop of society was on this momentous trip, and I was among the floating cream.

I didn't lack for conversation, and both men and women surrounded me with compliments; I seemed to remind many of the women of their youthful days and they would tell me about them, so I began to truly believe that I was a charming and intelligent person. The attention given me was very flattering and I cherish those moments. I should also say that the meal and service were "top-notch!"

By 1949, the war between Communist China and Nationalist China had come to a conclusion. Members in Chinese consulates and embassies all over the world had a reduction in their salaries, followed by recall to Taiwan, since the Nationalist government did not have adequate funds to maintain the diplomatic missions. By this time we had one child and preferred to remain in the U.S. However, Alfred spoke only simple grammatical English and had administrative skills limited to the diplomatic setting. My own experience was in grocery and merchandising. These were not skills that transferred well into the local job market and after much thought, we finally bought a Dairy Treat in a small town near Houston. At this time it was a relatively new thing to sell soft ice-cream through a window. The store was across from the high school and we lived in the house behind the store. The house was separate from the store and had a yard with a lawn and a very large pecan tree!

We then had one daughter and a baby on the way. We managed this for a few years during which time we had our third child ... now there were two girls and one boy. We had moved from Houston to Pasadena, Texas where I became active in the Episcopal Church, teaching Sunday school, and we were among an extremely wonderful group of friends.

Yet soon the government sought to enforce its regulations and since we were obviously not American citizens we were told that we would have to leave. Subsequently we applied for exemption from deportation. Letters "flew in" on our behalf and we received exemption.

However, the novelty of this type of ice-cream service wore out, and the business, which was initially highly successful, took a turn for the worse. We sold the store and moved back to Houston believing that in the larger city there would be more promising opportunities. Now Alfred was frequently out of town in an effort to gain employment, but unfortunately without much success and our liquid assets were dwindling. To ease our situation my brother took care of traveling expenses for me and the children to go visit the family in British Guiana while Alfred could look freely for work. So it was to Jamaica, Trinidad and B.G. we went. (Remember? It was B.G., Trinidad and Jamaica when we left B.G. eleven years earlier!) I had two brothers and a sister in B.G. and a brother in Jamaica.

The brother in Jamaica was "self-taught" after getting only a primary school education. His endeavors in Jamaica advanced him to the position of manager of the Crown Life Insurance Company, with headquarters based in Canada. (Jamaica was within the group of islands called the British West Indies, as England still had an empire that was on the brink of extinction.) My brother was an extrovert by nature and we thoroughly enjoyed the luxuries of his lifestyle. Besides having an elaborate abode, he had the services of a cook, a maid, who also served as a butler, a chauffeur and a gardener. He and his wife had two adopted children. He also has a daughter from his younger years. Our trip then continued on to B.G. through Trinidad where we were able to visit two half brothers.

My sister had a "dry goods" store and also sold groceries in Uitvlugt on the West Coast, Demerara. My other two brothers lived in Georgetown; one was the Head of the Forestry Department, having studied in Trinidad and Canada. The other was the Government Analyst, which is equivalent to the Head of the Food and Drug Administration and had received his FRCS degree in England.

Our children and their cousins enjoyed the togetherness and had great delight in playing cricket or at least attempting it (a game they did not know about in the United States). I really was back in British

Guiana as I had "promised" when I was leaving that many years ago. The outpouring of joy was rather overwhelming among my family and friends, with their kids and with my own. Parties were in abundance.

It was still a semi-primitive life style on the West Coast. In Uitvlugt, where my sister and husband had their store, the living quarters were adjoined to the shop and water was stored in large vats (rain barrels) so it had to be taken to the living quarters in buckets. One day, my four-year-old was being given a bath by the maid (being bathed by someone else was also a new experience) and as she stood on the concrete floor, the maid dipped from the bucket to pour water on her. I heard her tearfully cry out, "I want to take my bath in Texas!" not realizing how far away Texas was! Or DID SHE!? Amazingly, this may have been the sole objection by any of the children during the trip, as they were extraordinarily well behaved during the entire six weeks!

On the return trip home, we stopped at Montego Bay, where one of the attendants came to me saying, We have to change your schedule to leave the next morning because there are some others and the plane is full. Said he, We will pay for your night's stay in Montego Bay. I answered in half-anger that I won't deplane and that I had three children, and had booked a schedule that would take us home without spending a night away from home, and I'm surprised that you should ask me such a thing. We went home on our schedule.

In the meantime, Alfred had no reasonable success. Tensions grew over the years, making life chaotic; the situation became impossible and ended in our divorce. In fairness to Alfred, his difficulties probably lay in that his background as a foreign diplomat did not prepare him for work that was available in the U.S. However, prior to the divorce, I did attempt to complete a program in medical technology. As we did have young children, one would think that he could help care for them by not going out of town. The hours were long and we lived on the opposite end of Houston from the medical center, making the commute one hour each way. The youngest was three years old and arrangements for a sitter were not successful, so my oldest, Pam, held down the fort, at age eight, until I got home. After they were in bed, I studied late into the night to be able to complete that day's assignments. Academically, I was doing quite well, and I was even asked by the faculty to have lunch with them on a regular basis! Pleasing as that was and in spite of my love of the material, I had to give up the program when I noticed that Pam was sleepwalking and realized she had been given too much responsibility... an opportunity lost. I have often wished that I could have completed that course.

To earn some measure of livelihood I worked as a cashier in a grocery store. It was there that I met Jimmie Gee and we were married in 1962. Jimmie was a WWII veteran in the U.S. Army. He had come with his family to the U.S. from Canton at the age of 13 and grew up in San Antonio, Texas. He legally adopted my three children soon after our marriage and it was his strong desire to encourage them to achieve a higher education. Indeed they were already highly motivated. Prior to our marriage I had needed to direct the children from work, whether it was homework questions or settling arguments; the new marriage also allowed me to stay at home. We had hoped to have a child together, but were not able to conceive successfully.

Jimmie had an outgoing personality and no formal education. He would describe himself as a "Jack of all trades." He was manager of a meat-packing company, owned by a Caucasian-American, and manager of a poultry company, owned by a Chinese-American. He began visiting the grocery store sites, to make collections, and this became a regular assignment as well. These visits were both social and business and allowed him to converse in Chinese as most of the owners of these stores were immigrant Chinese. Houston had become a popular city for Chinese immigrants, because of its warm climate, and the growing economy, and the rapidly growing population.

We attended Chinese Festival Days with full-fledged Chinese banquet meals and I am sure that I was regarded as an "odd-ball" in this group. After all, how could there be any Chinese person, who could not speak Chinese!? Indeed, I felt as the odd woman out, and wished that I could communicate. On the other hand, I did also think that they (the group) could have tried harder to adopt the language and customs of this new country, rather than trying to create a closed Chinese enclave. We did attempt to have the children learn the Chinese language, but the teacher was a volunteer and was teaching to a class in which the students already spoke Chinese. As there was no accommodation for students who had no knowledge of Chinese, our three lost the opportunity to learn the language. However, I learned to cook Chinese food, from Jimmie, who had owned and run two restaurants in France and Germany after WWII. And he taught this to the children and to the grandchildren as well! So all was not lost, and if you want a true feast, have a Chinese roast duck cooked by any member of this family!

All the children excelled in school, each winning awards in both scholastic and athletic fields. Debbie, the youngest was chosen as the student intern to visit the nation's Capitol for a week at which time they were inundated with the workings of politics. Because of various accomplishments, she earned a place in "Outstanding Teenagers of America." She graduated from Yale University and attended University of Texas Medical School in San Antonio where she received her MD. She is now a psychiatrist in Albuquerque, NM.

Victor won scholarship awards and was selected Outstanding Senior Boy. His scholastic ability was well known and his awards were numerous. Representative Bill Archer from Texas nominated him for West Point and Senator John Tower, also from Texas, nominated him for the Air Force Academy. He chose the Air Force Academy.

Pamela, the eldest, seemed as if she could not help being the vanguard of her siblings, and how well and without fanfare she did it! When we attended her university graduation, where she received her bachelor's degree, summa cum laude, from the University of St. Thomas, in Houston, the audience had been asked to hold their applause until the end. Just before her name (Pam's) was called, the President of the University said, "You do not need to hold your applause for this student." Proud Parents? Wow! She went on to medical school at Baylor College of Medicine and is now a physician specializing in Obstetrics and Gynecology.

But life is not always rosy. A sad and unfortunate realization was the discovery, while our son was at the Air Force Academy, that he suffered from schizophrenia. My son's illness was a great drain upon me. I recall an incident during this time; one daughter was attending Baylor College of Medicine, our son was at the Air Force Academy and our youngest was at Yale University. Such accomplishments make parents rather proud and happy. So, on the back of our car window, the appropriate car stickers were proudly affixed. The names of Baylor, the Air Force Academy and Yale were all on that window. Then, as I recall it, came the "bombshell" (the diagnosis of schizophrenia).

Soon after, in tears, I went to the car and painstakingly removed every letter! For me there has never been healing, but one must move on. This would have been in the mid-70s when we were still living in Houston. And what was I doing through these years?

I walked, I ran, I biked, I played tennis and I attended classes at the University of St. Thomas. Time to do some of these was lessened or halted when I helped care for our first grandchild, who was born in 1978. The parents, my firstborn, Pam and her husband, Steve, were both doing their residencies and they had opted to take the same days "on call." Otherwise, they'd hardly see each other in such a hospital rotation.

Jimmie and I thoroughly enjoyed this time as my granddaughter was precious and a pure joy. We would drive 45 minutes to the kids' house, fix breakfast for ourselves, allowing Pam and Steve to leave by 6 a.m. to get to the hospital. Then I would drop Jimmie at work and go back to our house with my little granddaughter for the day. One of her parents would then drive over to get her and return to their home.

I was also associated with the program of Literacy Advance. Believe it or not, many adults and some high school juniors and seniors lacked reading comprehension. We met in nearby public libraries, one student at a time. During this endeavor I had seen successes and failures. The television crew came occasionally to document some of these events. One of the students had never had reading lessons before and had obviously never gone to school (we had different levels of teaching). Her level of understanding and retention was admirable, she could almost retell the whole bit of a given article or story. One day I wanted her to say what would be the equivalent to the headline of an article. Invariably she'd tell me the whole bit. So how could I get this across? I came up with . . . Imagine you are going to board the bus, you see one of your friends and you want to tell her about this, but the bus is about to leave . . . remember? . . . what do you say to her? *Bingo!* She got it right on.

We "teachers" were royally thanked by the Houston Community College System with a bountiful and truly delicious dinner. The administrators gave high praise of our efforts, successes and dedication.

We were a large gathering and reveled in the atmosphere of appreciation. That was sufficient for me. However the speaker continued with a proposal to recommend that future participants in the program be given a tax deduction in order to encourage others. This to me was contrary to volunteerism. It appeared to me that those who would not necessarily be true to the spirit of the program would take part only for its benefits. I guess I'm odd, but that was why I did not continue. A celebratory dinner party to show appreciation would have been sufficient for me.

Suffice it to say, Jimmie and I were very attached to our granddaughter and vice versa. Her parents had completed their residencies, Pam in Ob-Gyn and Steve in Urology, and then accepted positions in Spokane, WA. It was decided that we should make the move too. Therefore a year later, in 1982, we arrived in Spokane to be reunited with this part of the family. Soon after our arrival, we learned that our granddaughter would soon have a baby brother. Eight days after his birth, my grandson had his brit milah; and included among the guests were my close high school friend and her husband: Megan and Bertie Allsopp, now of Vancouver, British Columbia. We chatted and chatted and chatted! I had an embarrassing moment. Our spare room had a trundle bed, and as Bertie fixed the set to the larger size, something slipped! Wow, down it went. Now tell me, what hostess wouldn't be embarrassed![1]

In British Guiana, Megan, Enid Yhap and I were best friends; we usually, and sometimes shyly, called ourselves the "True Trio." Years later we three met again during Expo 86 in Vancouver. It was my second visit to Megan. I also was lucky to get together with Esther and Lawrence Yhap, as well as Enid and Clement Yhap. We Guyanese are a unique people!

I love to travel. I recall the simplicity of the ancient Mayans in the Yucatan Peninsula, east, and the stark poverty of the Seri Indians in the west (Mexico). I have visited the Mayans; the calm and acceptance of their lifestyles were evident. I visited their ruins and their temples and

---

1   Bertie Allsopp recalls that the date was 1 September 1983 and he was glued to the television absorbing the news that Korean Flight 007 had been shot down over Soviet airspace. During the night he reacted to a nightmare induced by the air tragedy by sharply kicking out his leg thereby causing the downfall of the bed. In the morning US Army veteran Jimmie Gee reacted nonchalantly to the incident.

I cannot really describe my feelings, only to say it was as if I had made a pilgrimage to a life of hundreds of years ago, as told by the stories left there. The Seri Indians seem to survive on the mere fringes of their struggles. They never had art lessons, yet produced art objects in various forms and media – amazing. I was the youngest among the Elder Hostel group from the U.S. and maybe that was why I was chosen to be the Chairperson. I thoroughly enjoyed that and was rather a "busy bee," with charming results. We all admired our sponsors and since it was basically a learning experience, we were very attentive. (I still have artwork from there that the Indians carved from the wood of their ironwood trees.)

I have been disappointed on missing two major trips: 1) China: the Tian An Men Square outbreak caused us to cancel, and 2) the 50th anniversary celebration of WWII in France. Why? An almost inexcusable reason, we didn't foresee how quickly and early accommodations would be booked up! . . . and Jimmie had fought in that war, storming the coast of Normandy at Omaha Beach on D-Day! However, since two brothers and a sister were living in Great Britain, Jimmie and I traveled all over England, Scotland and Wales in the 1980s. A particularly exciting part was crossing the Menai Strait, and climbing up the short but difficult hill to Anglesey, the outermost, uppermost part of Wales, all the way up to the lighthouse! It was really a great view and a great feeling to be way up there.

Additional travels were to France, twice, Switzerland and Italy. Most of these trips were gifts from our daughters and their husbands. Nice, isn't it? My youngest daughter, Debbie Christine Gee, is a psychiatrist in Albuquerque, N.M. She recently received the distinction of becoming a distinguished Fellow of the American Psychiatric Association in 2003. Her husband, Bobby Hung-Jeh Wang, has an MD and MBA and works as a computer consultant, with connections around the States and overseas.

Steve and Pam continue to practice their specialties, urology and ob-gyn, full time in Spokane and are very active in the Spokane community and in synagogue life. The grandchildren are both young adults now and attend universities. Shayna graduated in 2000 from Yale University and worked for three years in New York City, for the Lower Manhattan Cultural Council and for the Silk Road Festival in Washington, D.C.

with Yo Yo Ma. Her interest in the violin, and Middle Eastern and Mediterranean music have led her to pursue graduate studies at the University of Chicago, where she has started the first year of a five year PhD program, having won a full fellowship in the department of ethnomusicology. Joshua is in his second year at Brandeis University studying European cultural studies, with an emphasis on Russian and Jewish literature. He spent his first year after high school in Israel, studying at Hebrew University and working on a kibbutz. He is also an avid cellist and skier.

So besides helping with the grandkids when they were younger, what did I do? I was an arbitrator with the Better Business Bureau, and an active member of the League of Women Voters. I continued to play tennis until my mid-60s. I received my bronze Life Master in duplicate bridge and have competed in many tournaments in Idaho, Montana, Seattle, Portland, California and Hawaii (twice!). For such a recreation in competition, I have received some awards – that was fun!

But my son's condition, (Victor), has always been a cloud over me. Then, in late 2003, Jimmie died. He had a funeral that was both Chinese and military. I was given a flag and "Taps" was played. I am now struggling with new emotions.

It is said that time heals, therefore on that I depend. There are clouds and there are rainbows.

China Mission

Li Bixia, Zhou Hong and family.
Translated by Liu Yan

David Ewing-Chow was a devout Christian and when he was nearing death in 1927 he expressed the hope that one of his eleven children would preach the Gospel in China. Several of them attempted to carry out their father's wishes but, because of the language problem and ongoing changes in China, just one – the fifth child, Charles – succeeded.

Charles Ewing-Chow was born in 1904 in Anna Catherina, West Coast Demerara, British Guiana. He had a talent for music. At the age of eight, he gave a performance on stage playing the piano. It was said that when he played, all the neighbors would open their windows to share the sweet music. He once said, Humming birds will come from South America to listen to my playing. During his teenage years, he studied at The Royal College of Music, London, majoring in Music and Accounting. He entered the international piano competition for North American students twice, and won a gold prize each time, at the age of 16 and 17.

* * * * * * * *

Charles was not first person in his family who came over to China to preach the gospel. Before arriving in China he went to Europe to look for various works of music to add to his collection. He acquired a lot of treasured musical works . . . Beethoven, Schubert, Chopin and others. Following in the path of his brothers and sisters, Charles landed in China around 1935 to make his father's wishes come true. His sisters, Rachel and Mary, and his brothers James and Robert were already in China. Charles worked in the Shanghai Customs Office as an accountant and did not preach the Word of God at that time. After a while, he went to Beijing to carry out the project that God gave him. It was difficult for him to communicate with people around him because they couldn't understand his English and halting Chinese. But he continued to go to church regularly. He believed that Jesus was aware of all of this and He

On the left is Rachel with Robert's son Daniel, born in 1935. On the right is Robert with the Pan family in Hong Kong in 1937. From right: Peter, Jnr., Dr. Peter Pan, Mary (Robert's sister), and Alec. *John Chow.*

would help him preach the gospel to the Chinese people. One day, when he was preaching, he said, Everyone needs to be baptized ("shoujin" in Chinese), to be reborn after death. Everybody needs to share in the death of Jesus, and be resurrected by God. Belief in God is the only way to be transformed. A person is never by himself, alone, but joined with the spirit of Jesus. At that time China was impoverished and living conditions were harsh, so the people were eager to find a saviour. Among the listeners was a lady named Li Bixia who was moved by these words, so she went to shoujin after the meeting. A few days later her aunt and uncle said that Kangyao Chow (Charles) was in need of someone who is good at both Chinese and English to help him to preach in China, and maybe Bixia is that person. That night, Miss Li prayed before God and got the inspiration that Charles is exactly the man suited to be her husband. Later, they came to know each other and fell in love.

Miss Li was a first class medical doctor who studied at New York State University. She had suffered an acute bout of pneumonia when she was 40 days old. Her father's friend Dai Desheng was a famous Western-trained doctor who was also a preacher. He told Bixia's mother to put her in a wooden basin with warm water, and every half an hour take out

Li Bixia at her graduation.
John Chow.

one gourd of the cooled water, and replace it with hotter water. Her mother prayed for her for three days and nights until she recovered. Her parents felt indebted to God so they persuaded her to become a Christian. Li Bixia also resolved to become a pediatrician.

There's a moving story about Miss Li's parents. Li Bixia's grandfather donated to the church all his fortune, his house and the property where the church was built. The church held on for about 60 years in China (1864 - 1925). After that Miss Li's grandfather went to Hui'an city to live the life of a pauper. There he made friends with another Christian whose surname was Zhang. Because Mr. Zhang was a fisherman he would regularly sell fish in the front of Li's house. As the days went by they got to know each other very well. Later, their wives got pregnant at almost the same time. They were very excited and made promises to each other according to an old tradition that if they were to have one girl and one boy, they would be married when they grew up or else be sisters and brothers. The two children are Li Bixia's parents.

In the summer of 1937, Charles Chow and Miss Li went to the British Embassy in Beijing. They wanted to get married, but according to policy of that time, the two betrothed people had to be of the same nationality. Charles was a British citizen, having been born in a British colony, and Li Bixia was entitled to become British through marriage. However, they both decided to become Chinese nationals. But several days later, when they came back to pick up their documents, they got a surprise when passports were issued to them as British subjects. When they asked the officer, they found that a mistake had been made. In those days, most Chinese people wanted to go abroad, attempting to get away from war, hunger and poverty. The officer could not recall any previous request to change from British citizenship to Chinese and had misunderstood the instructions. The officer promised to remit the entire

Wedding of Charles Chow and Li Bixia. *John Chow.*

fee they paid for their passports and put out a public notice of amendment. Li Bixia wanted to argue with the officer because she really wanted her husband's nationality to be Chinese but Charles didn't blame him for the error. He told Li, Let's face reality; it's God's intention. On the 30th of June, they pledged an oath in the embassy. The next day, a big religious wedding ceremony was held at a building on the street where the foreign affairs department was located. The couple lived a happy and comfortable life for a short time after the wedding, since their well-off relatives gave them lots of furniture, carpets, a piano and also a big apartment in the foreign affairs district. Mary was quite a rich woman, so she gave the new couple all the expensive stuff.

In 1937, Mrs. Li took the name Esther, given to her by Charles. She told Charles, When I was a child, I dreamt of spreading the Word of God to the inner regions of China, like Yunnan, Gansu, Xinjiang, Nei Meng. This was because Dai Desheng, who had saved her life when she was 40 days old, had established the inland Church of Jesus. Charles responded, If you think you can do it, why only think about it … do it! This was at that time of the 7th July Incident.[1] The Union Medical Hospital where Li Bixia worked was closed, so there was nothing to stop them from embarking on their great missionary project. They sold all their furniture, piano and other possessions and prepared to go to Yunnan Province. But the Japanese army had destroyed the railways. So they had to go there via Hong Kong, Vietnam and Burma, which were colonies of England and France at that time. Their British passports helped them to pass through smoothly and they regarded this as a

---

1   In 1931 Japanese forces invaded Manchuria (north-east China) and established a puppet state there. On 7 July 1937 a minor clash occurred between Japanese troops and a Chinese garrison at the Marco Polo Bridge located between Beijing and Tianjin. The incident quickly escalated into general hostilities between China and Japan, marking the opening of the Pacific phase of World War II.

wonderful testimony that God had prepared the very things they needed most!

The moment they arrived at Yunnan, the president of Hui'an Hospital, who was a classmate of Charles's 3rd brother at Cambridge University, visited the couple and told Charles, I need your wife to be the main provider of essential services in my hospital. Esther refused and stated, I am meant to spread the gospel here, not be a doctor. The president said, I also am a believer in Jesus Christ. Besides, healing illness and preaching the Word of God are both in the service of God. Just ask God if you should do this or not? Give me your answer tomorrow. Of course, God wants to save all people who are suffering. Li Bixia received the guidance she sought and the president gave her advance payment for the first month in her role as the vice-president. At that time, they had only a few yuan left. God gave them care once again.

At Kunming, they gave birth to a boy, and named him Mengyue Chow. Unfortunately, he suffered from dysentery when he was three years old and passed away. They were also blessed with Mengzhao (Paul) and Meng'en (Mary) Chow; Meng'en's name was later changed to Zhou Hong.[2] After Yunnan, the family went to Ganzhou in Jiangxi Province.

In 1944, the fourth girl, Anna, was born. They next went to Meixian in Guangzhou Province, There, they gave birth to their last child Mengxuan Chow. Later they left for Shantou, another city of Guangzhou Province, where Li Bixia established a medical clinic with funds donated by herself. (Li Bixia worked as the president of a girl's middle school, where Bixia herself provided all medical appliances, including a microscope)

During all these years of travel, Charles Chow was essentially a househusband for most of the time. He nurtured all the children at home.

Charles Chow's family in Tian An Men Square, Beijing. *John Chow.*

---

2   The pinyin spelling for the Chow family name is Zhou.

In order to deliver the Word of God he didn't mind doing even menial work. Around 1948, before the liberation of China, the Communist Party gave all foreign embassies a circular, declaring that all capitalist citizens needed to get out of China. Charles left for Hong Kong, for fear of political or religion persecution. Li Bixia went to Shanghai to have a hysterectomy. That was really a difficult time for them. Charles bought a boat ticket for Li Bixia and all the family to go to Hong Kong, and from there to British Guiana, but she persuaded him to come back instead. She pleaded, You said that you would settle down and preach the gospel in China, how can you give up half way? A policy was enacted by the government promising that there would not be any religious persecution. Feeling that there was nothing to be worried about, Charles came back and they lived in Shanghai at the Fuyin Bookstore. There, Charles embarked on an ambitious project – writing piano accompaniment for 1,052 Chinese poems and hymns. Part of this was based on Western music he had collected during the time he lived in England, as well as

Paul and his father Charles Chow (1963). *John Chow.*

Negro spiritual songs, Italian folk music, and others. He chose to set music to appropriate selections from the vast array of Chinese poems. Others he wrote and composed by himself. To do a better job Charles bought many treasured musical records, such as the works of Beethoven, Schubert, Chopin, and others. His collection was published and translated into many languages to be sold abroad. However, he never put his name to his creations or translations, feeling that he was doing this work in praise of God.

Around 1956, during the purges,[3]

---

3   The Hundred Flowers Campaign of 1956 (Let a hundred flowers bloom: let a hundred schools of thought contend) encouraged Chinese citizens to criticize government policies and programs, attempting to gather input so as to correct mistakes. The resulting millions of letters overwhelmed the authorities and the campaign was brought to a quick halt, followed by the persecution of many intellectuals, the main advocates for change, as rightists and counter-revolutionaries.

the manager of the Fuyin bookstore was framed as a rapist and imprisoned. Then the bookstore was closed. The Chinese Central Conservatory of Music, which at that time located at Tianjin, invited him to teach piano there and he accepted. Because of the language problem, Charles worked just as a lecturer and not a professor, but he placed no great importance on this. God was always in his heart and that gave him the greatest pleasure. He got along quite well with his students and always taught them English after class. He gave them the affection of a father.

In 1964, Charles retired. The Great Cultural Revolution then broke out in 1966. During the following ten years Charles did not encounter much calamity because he was already retired, but many of his colleagues were persecuted. His nephew, Li Xizhong, who was 13 years old, led a group of little Red Guards to Charles's home and cut his leather shoes into pieces, as was encouraged by the Sijiu Movement.[4] What hurt him the most was that his son Mengzhao (Paul) Chow forced him to sell all his manuscripts to the waste collectors, to be turned into pulp, while his classic musical phonograph records were thrown out as rubbish. Charles couldn't hold back his tears every time he recalled this.

One day, people of the building administration came to their house and asked for the document showing title to the property. Charles's mother-in-law knew that they won't return the material once they took it away, so she didn't get it out from their stashed belongings. The people were so angry that they kicked the old woman until she was black-and-blue. Charles's mother-in-law fell ill from then on and died three months later. During that time, Charles looked after her with great care, just like a son, even though this mother did not like her son-in-law before he had married Li Bixia, since she believed that a preacher was nothing but a sophisticated beggar.

---

4   The "Destroy the Four Olds" movement was aimed at getting rid of old ideas, old culture, old customs, and old habits. Western suits and dresses were considered to be aspects of bourgeois decadence.

Life in Israel

Sally Bors, née Evan-Wong

"Why on earth do you want to go to Israel?" a colleague said at my going-away office party. "You're Chinese, born in British Guiana. You live and work in London. You've married a Hungarian. Now you're leaving us for Israel? What on earth do you want to be – a walking United Nations?" My reply to that query then (and now) was, "Heaven forbid!"

It was Gregory's idea to try out life in Israel. From birth practically, he had been enthralled by the thought of creating a Brave New World there. "Follow your dream," I've always said. On reflection though, following someone else's dream could be foolhardy. Would builders, dedicated to carving out a New World for themselves, welcome an outsider like me barging in, especially someone who had a perfectly good ready-made world of her own elsewhere? Gregory's coup de grace settled the matter: "When will you have another opportunity to witness the Birth of a Nation? If you don't like it, we'll leave."

So, we sailed away from London on a cargo ship destined to collect oranges from Malta, Cyprus and Israel. Our fellow passengers, keen to escape the horrors of the English winter were taking a round trip cruise through the Mediterranean. We got off at Jaffa Port.

Our ship, much too big, was obliged to anchor outside the harbour. Transshipping us and our luggage off the boat, into a launch and on to dry land generated some excitement, but hardly comparable to the challenge of descending from a paddle steamer into a wobbly Amerindian canoe – the obligatory practice on jaunts with my father up the Essequibo River in British Guiana. Once on land, more echoes of childhood greeted me. There on hedges or by the roadside, grew with brazen nonchalance Hibiscus, Oleander and Flamboyant trees! I had completely forgotten them. "Ha!" I thought, "I know those trees. Just like home! No problem coming to grips with life here." I was completely wrong.

In 1964, Israel lacked flats for rent, telephones, cruising taxis, supermarkets, white bath towels, adequate public transport on weekdays and any at all on Saturdays. Worst of it all, it was impossible to express shock or lamentation at these hydra-headed obstacles that kept popping up. The Hebrew word for "frustration" didn't exist in 1964. The language had been dead for two thousand years. It took another couple of years after our arrival before the Hebrew word for frustration (tizkul) was invented. Thus from the outset we were obliged to gear ourselves, wordlessly, in Robinson Crusoe survival mode. But we were never actually reduced to tracking down footprints in the sand. Oddly, a Good Man Friday seemed to materialize whenever the situation got desperate.

Desperation befell me the very next day. We settled in a modest hotel in the suburbs and in the morning set off for Tel Aviv to hunt, Gregory for a job and me for a flat to rent. We agreed to meet and review the state of play in the evening at the home of parents of a school friend of Gregory's – perfect strangers to me. As I tramped around empty streets in fading light looking for their address, a sleek, black limousine drew up and its driver volunteered to help. He turned out to be a diamond merchant from Holland and didn't know the district too well, but he methodically drove around until he found the right street and number, escorted me to the flat, checked that the occupants were indeed Gregory's friends and disappeared before he could be properly thanked.

My report on the day's reconnoitering was grave. I'd learned the country's building programme at that time was aimed at housing three types of people: hotels for visitors, hostels and subsidized flats for immigrants arriving under the auspices of the Jewish Agency, and houses/flats for rich individuals with sufficient capital to purchase them outright. Flats for rent were non-existent. We, freelancers, were doomed apparently to fall between the cracks.

It was a frail looking creature who prevailed over our housing problem – the toughest one we ever had to face. "NOTHING is impossible!" she chirruped. She came from one of those unpronounceable places in Central Europe where she'd learned eight languages rather well but, as she said, only spoke five of them fluently. She was a friend of a social worker I'd come to know during my job-hunting phase. She doubted I'd find a job in my field without spoken Hebrew and prescribed weekly Hebrew conversation with her at her home to supplement the efforts of my ulpan (school teaching Hebrew free of charge to all comers). Our talk often became so absorbing, the conversation degenerated into English and I never did master Hebrew, but I learned about buying the lease for a key-money flat.

My indomitable friend helped me unearth one, perched precariously as an afterthought on top of a ramshackle building right in the centre of town It was barely affordable for people like us, destitute of capital, and the neighbours were unpromising. All other flat-owners in the building had lived there so long they hated each other and never spoke. They peered suspiciously out of their doors at each passing footstep. (In the early days of Israel's history, flat owners were collectively responsible for the maintenance of the public spaces of their building, roof, stairways, lobby, etc. Some housing committees worked well, others degenerated and owners developed deep rooted suspicions of one another fearing the other might be trying to pull a fast one over them.) We, naïve newcomers, persisted in greeting each head as it popped out of its door. Our neighbour in the flat below ours finally broke down. Unasked, she became a faithful watchdog, meticulously reporting who had ascended our section of the stairway when we were out. Perhaps it was a good thing. The door of our flat never would close properly. In any event, we lived there happily and safely until the advent of high-rise buildings which spoilt our view. Reluctantly, we moved to more modern accommodation with a front door fitted with a triple lock where we were ultimately burgled.

Like flat hunting, landing a job was also a long and lucky story. I went to talk with a professor of psychology at the Hebrew University in Jerusalem. He was surprised to see me and asked how it was I came to have a name like Bors. I launched into my usual spiel. The name was Hungarian, meaning "pepper," NOT the marvelous large green, red and yellow kind . . . an assumption I myself had first made. It was only after marrying Gregory, I had sadly discovered the name meant plain pedestrian black pepper. He heard me out patiently, then said, "Yes, I know. I'm only surprised YOU do!" (He was a Viennese Hungarian, as he later on explained).

He, like everyone else I'd met in my field, gave me a list of possibly useful names to contact which ultimately lead to my researching street corner youth gangs in Tel Aviv. My fellow and senior researcher was a sociologist from Bar Ilan University. His family had lived for several generations in Jerusalem and had had simultaneously a rigorous religious and secular education prior to his national army service. He was my handy, inexhaustible, patient source of information for Jewish religious practice both ancient and modern. Each morning I could rush to him for background to all the burning issues currently plaguing Israel society in the newspapers that day, such as: Who is a Jew? How to define a bastard? His exposition on the latter proved a boon to Gregory, who would casually drop it into the conversation whenever an opportunity arose, stunning listeners with his Judaic erudition which was otherwise non-existent.

Five years flew by and Gregory was assigned to go to Switzerland for a couple of months to help computerize the Zurich branch of his bank. I needed a valid passport. In 1964, British citizens entered Israel without a visa. If I remember aright, I think Immigration didn't even bother to put an entry stamp in my passport. Since then, I'd only used my passport when shopkeepers panicked on seeing a cheque book rather than cash.

"Either way, it's going to be a bureaucratic hassle," said Gregory. "Apply for Israeli citizenship and a passport. Use the Israeli passport to travel now and citizenship will enable you to vote in National elections later on. Renew your British passport when you need it." But I never did renew my British passport. Through the mail, I received an Identity Card and a nice letter signed by the Minister of Interior himself congratulating me on becoming an Israeli citizen. Since then I've traveled everywhere without impediment simply with an Israeli passport to the astonishment of those Israelis holding dual passports. For my part, I'm astonished they find keeping two valid passports worth the trouble.

Nowadays tourists, business people, pilgrims from all over the world arrive in Israel. When Gregory and I came in 1964, I think I was the only Chinese living anywhere in the whole country. I suspect most people were intrigued and went out of their way to be helpful. Someone once ran after me and asked breathlessly whether I was from China? She was extremely downcast when I said, "No." "Oh," she wailed, "I thought you were Chinese. I am Chinese!" I looked at her doubtfully. She was a tiny redhead. I learned from her there used to be a group of Russian Jews who settled in Harbin trading in furs. She had hoped for a little nostalgic chat about the land of her birth. On the other hand the name British Guiana has only rung a bell to Israelis three times in all the forty odd years I've been living in Israel. The first time occurred after Jones, the "revivalist" leader persuaded his flock to commit mass suicide in the interior of Guyana. The last two occasions were recent: a podiatrist, originating from Brooklyn, not only pinpointed the precise geographic location of Guyana, he could even cite the exact date of the Jones mass suicide. It all happened when he was swotting for his final medical exams. A security guard at the airport was delighted to discover from my passport I had been born in Guyana which he had visited. (After national service, young Israelis often take a year or so off wandering the globe to exotic lands before settling down to further study or work).

I think though in Israel I have earned more undeserved brownie points for being Chinese than unadorned British Guianese. I suspect that people here are much kinder and more tolerant of my mistakes than they are with each other, because seeing me they assume I'm a foreigner, which is not wholly true. I have now lived 43 years in Israel – more than half

Sally and Gregory Bors out hiking by the Yarkon River (2003). *Sally Bors.*

of my life – and though my ancestry is Chinese, I am only able to say, "Happy New Year" in Cantonese, a phrase for which I have so far not found much use. In recent years, Israelis occasionally greet me with "Nee How" to which I smilingly reply, "Shalom" in the hope it will forestall further untoward demands on my Chinese.

Songs, Strings, and Steel

Trev Sue-A-Quan

My parents were not affluent, and both worked hard to accumulate sufficient funds to send their three children to university. My father was the proprietor of a rum shop while my mother did catering (pastries, cakes, black pudding[1]), as well as running a small guesthouse, providing accommodations mainly to British expatriates working in Georgetown. These were not very prosperous enterprises and, in 1960, my parents left for Trinidad where they took over the management of the branch of the winery that had been started by my uncle, James Sue-A-Quan. I remained with my uncle to complete my secondary school education at Queen's College.

Our 3-bedroom house at the corner of Smyth and Hadfield Streets. The ground level, previously open, has been converted into guest rooms for rent. The front garden provided vegetables and flowers (~1958). *Peter Lam.*

---

1 Black pudding is a local favorite consisting of rice or sweet potatoes seasoned with thyme and basil (married-man pork) and mixed with blood (pig's or cow's) and stuffed in sausage-like fashion into the small intestines from pigs. The 2- to 3-foot lengths of boiled black pudding is typically enjoyed with a sour, or a tart-flavored condiment.

In 1963, I took the "A" Level examinations at a period when the country was at the crossroads in its destiny, the previous year being one in which civil disturbances, fueled by political and racial prejudices, racked the country. In February 1962 a general strike by workers was in progress and after rumours spread of people being killed and injured by the police the downtown area was affected by rioting, looting and arson. From my bedroom window I witnessed the shooting of Superintendent McLeod as he led a group of policemen in full riot gear, including gas masks, in an attempt to disperse a disobedient crowd. The superintendent died a few days later from the single shot to his abdomen. The climate of uncertainty and instability caused many to consider leaving for other countries that could offer a more peaceful or prosperous future.

In British Guiana, it was ingrained in people's minds that Britain was the "Mother Country." After completing high school it was the "natural" next step to go to Britain to become qualified in a profession based upon higher education. I was the last one in my immediate family to leave, when I departed for Trinidad in August 1963 for a vacation. There I met Winston Akong, an engineering student at the University of Birmingham, where I had been offered provisional acceptance pending satisfactory results from my exams. I flew to Britain in anticipation.

My brother and sister were already enrolled at Edinburgh University studying medicine and mathematics, respectively. I was there when I received news of my passes in Chemistry, Physics, Pure Mathematics, and Applied Mathematics, and I proceeded to the University of Birmingham. My digs was a room in a house owned by the parents of a physics professor from Trinidad who was of Chinese heritage. There were less than two-dozen students from the West Indies who came from British Guiana, British Honduras, Jamaica, and Trinidad and we found a commonality in the Birmingham University West Indian Society (BUWIS). We would gather to lime around and gaff, particularly about cricket, at a time when the West Indies team was a dominant force, with multi-talented Garfield Sobers and stroke-making Rohan Kanhai on the attack, while the tricky tosses of Lance Gibbs, along with the double-barreled deliveries of Wes Hall and Charlie Griffith, backed up by an acrobatic Deryck Murray, scattered wickets. But we felt that we needed some more action than just claiming spectator association with world-class players.

The decade of the 1960s was a time when the Caribbean nations were clamoring for and achieving independence from Britain. The British began to see a large influx of off-color folks in their neighborhoods and there was a certain degree of resentment about such developments. We students felt that we should try to offer some cultural and social insight into the West Indies. At first we tried to hold a social event with West Indian foods as the main attraction. We posted signs and promotions about our feast. Various individuals were assigned the tasks of shopping for supplies (meat, chicken, cassava, plantain, etc.) with which we would try to make West Indian style curry and metagee.[2] Without accomplished chefs in our pack, the effort was not what one would classify as a treat, especially when the chicken was one that would more properly be termed "ol' fowl," acquired because of its low-priced status. We were not far wrong in claiming that the lowly dish had an acquired taste. The party venue was the meeting room of the university's chapel (which had a kitchen) and we waited for the uninitiated to arrive. We waited . . . and waited. But besides the handful of die-hard English students dedicated to promoting international relations, no one else put in an appearance and we were left with substantial amounts of leftovers that we had to divide up and distribute among ourselves.

In our midst was Gordon Rohlehr, a bass singer with a wonderfully deep voice with whom I had appeared in earlier days in leading roles for the Queen's College production of Gilbert and Sullivan's *Pirates of Penzance*. We both were in the Queen's College Male Voice Choir, and I had been a choir member since joining the school in Preparatory (Prep) Form. There, Lynette Dolphin was the class teacher and capable music instructor who could readily tell who in the class was a warbler and who a garbler. She was the one who encouraged a few of us to form a musical group to enter the newly-introduced category – Guyanese folk songs – at the local Music Festival. Singing was one of my favorite things and St. Saviour's Church in Georgetown provided a suitable venue for such vocalizing, whether at regular Sunday services or at special events, such as weddings. I was also a member of the Goodwill Choir that sang

---

2   A dish consisting of root vegetables and chunks of meat cooked in a coconut broth.

Stan Ridley (Pirate King), Trev Sue-A-Quan (Frederic, the Pirate Apprentice) and Aubrey Joseph (Ruth) in the Queen's College production of Gilbert and Sullivan's *Pirates of Penzance* (1961). *Guiana Graphic.*

Christmas carols from the roofs of department stores to the audience lining the streets.

At the same time, the influences of American pop music took hold through such artistes as Elvis Presley, the Everly Brothers, and Chuck Berry, making the guitar a popular instrument. I taught myself a few chords on guitars owned by cousins and friends and after a while I decided I wanted my own instrument. I began saving money earned from helping at my dad's rum shop, delivering my mother's delicacies, and doing other errands. I found out about a local guitar maker and when I visited his workshop I was delighted to learn that he was beginning to make a new batch of guitars. Over the next days and weeks I was a regular visitor and saw the guitars taking shape. Eventually he told me that the guitars would be ready in a couple days after allowing the varnish to dry properly but I realized that I would be short of the $20 needed to buy the instrument. I had my eye on a particular instrument and rushed over to plead with him that all I could manage was $18. Whether my plea or my persistent appearance was the deciding factor, I cannot say, but he let me have the glistening guitar at my lower offer. I happily rode my bicycle home that day with the guitar slung across my back and for the next while acquired sore fingers and calluses, but with pleasure. In my later teenage years, I was seduced by the electric guitar, but this was definitely beyond reach, more than what I could accumulate in allowances and errands. So I decided to make my own instrument and did so, fashioning it out of a solid block of crabwood. It was painted black. Since the electric guitar relied on an amplifier rather than a sound-box, the only critical item was to align the frets properly. Working with a mathematical formula derived from physics theory I was able to make a guitar with a fretboard that was even longer than that on a conventional guitar. But the greatest delight was that it actually worked. I took the guitar with me to England.

At a meeting of BUWIS in October 1964, at which 13 students attended, it was Gordon's suggestion that we start a folk song group. At our first gathering, eight of us tried to sing, but it was obvious that considerable practice would be required to transform a motley group into harmonious songsters, particularly when some were hardly able to carry a tune. Fortunately, Winston Akong also knew to play the guitar, and together we provided some musical direction for the din. We three were the core group and we were joined by Bobby Huggins-Chan, Keith Jeffers, Irwin Lett, Chris Lihou, Ken Warner and Aman Young-Hoon (all from Trinidad), Bertie Bascombe (Guyana) and Aggrey Burke (Jamaica), whenever they had the time and inclination. We named ourselves the West Indian Folk Singers and built a repertoire of songs from Guyana and the islands. These were not the songs made popular by recording artistes, such as *Banana Boat Song, Jamaica Farewell*, and *Island in the Sun*, but rather authentic Caribbean folk melodies, including *Missy Las' She Gol' Ring, Lisa, Satira Gal, Ganga Money, Sweet Madeline, Sly Mongoose, Yalla Gal*, and more from Guyana; *Every Time Ah Pass, Mangoes*, etc. from Trinidad, plus some more from the other islands that Gordon had learnt. We tried to get together at least once a week and worked hard on straightening out the notes that were being produced from some participants. Then we moved on to getting harmony in the group, i.e. tonal harmony. Our first public performance was at St. Martin's Hall in downtown Birmingham. The evening program offered poetry reading, short stories, recorded folk songs, and a few live performers who played guitar and sang, but without much enthusiasm. We were the last act. After our first song there was thunderous applause. It took us completely by surprise, and perhaps it was the contrast between our light-hearted song and the sedate tones of the previous offerings. Besides, the majority in attendance were West Indians who were resident in the city. We performed four more songs that had the audience clapping and stomping. It was an amazing initiation for us West Indian Folk Singers, and there was even some fellow that said afterwards that we should make a recording!

Each of the student societies in the university was allowed to use the Debating Hall in the Students Union for one night each year so as to promote its organization, and it could be open to the public. From sheer ambition and guts the West Indian Society decided to host a hop – a dance that we called Caribbean Night, featuring a steel band and folk songs. It would take place in early December 1964. We hired a steelband, actually a small group of players with a few pans, and they were scheduled to arrive at 7:30 for an 8:00 p.m. start. However, in not unusual Caribbean manner, they trickled in at 8:15 and took a half hour to get set up. Musically, they weren't very good either but the crowd, mainly West Indians from the community, enjoyed the rare chance to have a jump-up. Our folk song group went on stage at 10:30, during the band's break, and we had to stand behind the pans with no microphone. The situation was far from ideal and our voices carried a short distance to a small number of disinterested listeners in the front of the hall.

At the next meeting of BUWIS we pondered sponsoring conferences, lectures, and debates on West Indian affairs but felt that we would not draw sufficient interest, and such activities could easily consume our meager financial resources. The suggestion was made that we start a steelband. We figured we could do no worse than the band we had at Caribbean Night.

The West Indian Folk Singers continued their singing ways and were invited to various functions, socials and church groups. We also added calypsos and popular Caribbean melodies including *Big Bamboo*, which, although well received by the student body, was not performed for church gatherings. We were even featured on a program with the Ian Campbell Folk Group, a professional group with recorded songs, but we were the sideshow to their main act. However, there was someone in the audience who heard us and invited us to perform in Handsworth. We were flattered to receive such attention but the invitation did not materialize into an actual event.

The word went out that we were in search of steelband instruments to start up a student band and in February 1965 Ken Warner was told by the steelband leader that we would be given two pans. A few days later we collected two first (tenor) pans and a second (guitar) pan. One of the first pans had a crack in the center and produced rattling tones, the other was half in tune, and only the second pan appeared to be in reasonable shape. No wonder they wanted to give the pans to us – they were close to useless and perhaps regarded as sufficient to meet educational purposes.. Relying on our guitar-playing skills Winston and I took the initiative to try and get the better of the pans. It was hard slogging indeed, especially trying to get the notes on the pans in tune. Notes were "crossing," some dull sounding, others tinny. The layouts of notes on the two tenor pans were not the same and on one pan a couple of important notes in the musical scale were missing altogether. With a hammer we bashed and bashed but could not make the pans match up. We realized that we needed to get some other pans. Ken managed to contact a representative of Texaco and secured the promise of a few brand new drums. They arrived in May.

We managed to contact a Trinidadian, Roy Jacobs, who used to be a pan-man and he agreed to help us along. We bashed away at the drums to make them suitably indented. Roy informed us that his own band had broken up and that he had previously secured engagements at various places, and he wondered whether we could get ourselves into playing shape to fulfill those commitments. That really made us double up on the bashing. Then we discovered that the Texaco-donated drums were of the wrong type – the metal was too thick and not flexible enough. As a result they tended to split when beaten too much. But they were acceptable as bass drums because the depth of the indentations were minimal. These drums had two rings that bulged out from the sides, but there was another kind of oil drum with multiple, closely-spaced, corrugated ribs and the latter was the preferred drum, as far as musical potential was concerned. Now that we knew what kind of drums to look for we trolled the city's back alleys and industrial factories, searching for old drums, and begged for them if they looked unused and in decent enough condition for our needs. We even fished one out of a river when it was spotted stranded on the bank awaiting an appreciative owner. Then Roy went to work marking out the sections for the various notes and we took over with hammer and nail to punch the perimeter of each note with a line of indentations. The backs of the notes were then beaten to push out the raised and tuneable bumps. We also started a bonfire at the back of the Chemical Engineering department and heated the pans, then pulled them off and quenched them with a bucketful of water. On other occasions we used a blowtorch to heat up the pans, although this was not ideal especially during the cold weather. Roy did the tuning of the pans. The workshop of the department was where frames were constructed from which to hang the pans, using 3/8-inch pipe with threaded ends, connected with pipe elbows, as well as with some welded junctions. The frames were designed to have disconnecting sections so that the various pieces could be laid flat for storage and transportation.

We knew from the beginning that we were a small-time operation and we had to scramble to find enough enthusiasts among our few West Indian students to form a band. There were some who had other things on their mind – like wanting to study for a university degree. Then there were those who couldn't tell a note from a goat, or carry a beat, or even bleat. But a core group started to form. I took on the first (or tenor) pan. Ken opted to try with the second pans. Because of the limited size of the group we needed to maximize our sound production and he learnt to play with four sticks, two in each hand, so that he could play full chords. The notes had been purposely laid out to place harmonizing notes close together. Irwin kept rhythm with the "two-note," a small sized drum with the top surface divided into two unequal parts to produce two different-sounding thumps. Winston practiced on the cello pans, and Gordon tried his best with playing the bass pans. But while Gordon was a pro at English and an excellent choir singer, the dexterity and coordination required for swinging around and striking the notes spread out on four big bass drums presented quite a challenge. I myself had some problems mastering the tenor pan. My tremolo technique was not good and hitting the right notes was literally a hit or miss adventure.

We were a band of noisemakers and I left for a vacation in London, but when I returned I was greeted by a most pleasant surprise. The band members had improved their technique, especially Gordon, who was swinging away smoothly with his arms with hardly a look at the notes he needed to strike, booming away with consistency and rhythm. It was the turning point. We tried to gather as often as we could, at least once a week, to rehearse in the Music Room of the Students Union. It was a lot of work trying to get a bunch of guys (most with no experience in playing any musical instrument) to become a coordinated and pleasant sounding unit. We students practiced on our own, but Roy would join us with his own tenor pan as often as he could manage. We mastered a growing collection of songs and felt proud of ourselves. Roy had an English pal, Bill, who owned a drum set (traps), and with whom he would play on stints, and Bill became part of the group.

Our first engagement was in early October 1965 at a function in Wolverhampton. Well-attired gentlemen in formal wear with bow ties, accompanied by ladies in long, fancy evening dresses, arrived. The booking had been arranged by Roy, and he took the lead on the tenor pan to present a variety of calypsos and Latin American rhythms. I took up the maracas that night. After the first number, there was polite applause, but after a few more songs the people got up and got into the swing of things, moving in good rhythm, so much so that the floor began to undulate with the beat of the music, causing the glasses of champagne to shift around on the tabletops, with the bubbly liquid quivering and bubbling even more. It was a good indication that the session was going well. There was tumultuous applause when we finished at 1:30 a.m.

For the next two months until mid-December we were requested to play steelband and sing folksongs at 14 functions, mainly for various university student societies, several of them for charity. It seemed as if we were performing almost every Friday night. We were willing to play with no pay at some events in order to give the band exposure, and to get ourselves practice and experience. The reception seemed to follow the same pattern – initial curiosity about the unfamiliar sound, but once some dancing started it quickly developed into a rollicking good time.

We now needed to choose a name for ourselves. Roy used to play for one of the many "All Stars" bands in Trinidad, and was insistent that we call ourselves All Stars, and so it was that the BUWIS All Stars came to being. We painted the drums in red and black – the colors of the Trinidad flag – with the playing surface polished with black shoe polish to prevent rusting. We then painted on our name: BUWIS All Stars. Roy's wife, Doreen, got some heavy, bright red material and fashioned some blazing uniforms with two vertical black stripes. Stars never blazed so brightly although the designation was certainly debatable . . . and none of us know how to read music, only trying our best to play it. But, for sure we were getting better as we went along.

Early on 17 December we set out in two vehicles for Plymouth, some 200 miles away where Roy had been hired to play for the Royal Naval Engineering College's Christmas Ball. There were several bands booked to play in various rooms, and we were scheduled to alternate our performances with the Royal Marines Sextet in the "Caribbean Room" between 8:30 p.m. and 1:45 a.m. We found that it was easy to play for the room-full of sailor boys (and admirals) because we could carry one tune for 10 to 15 minutes non-stop with great appreciation from the enthusiastic dancers who were jumping in fine style. In fact, at the midnight break, when the sextet took over and began to offer the quickstep and foxtrot the revelers quickly stepped out of the room in a trot such that after 25 minutes there were only two couples left. And, shortly after, they too drifted away. The sextet decided to pack up for the night. We set up at 12:45, a quarter hour before our scheduled time, and before our first song was over the room was again packed with people. We continued playing until 2:30 a.m. for the appreciative dancers.

We were provided with sleeping accommodations in the dormitory. The next morning a voice called, "Good morning, sir. It is now 7:00 a.m." The phrase was repeated until it registered in my brain. "If you are interested, breakfast is at 7:30." Although I appreciated the courteous but unexpected treatment, I decided I wasn't interested, and went back to sleep until 10:00 a.m. Later on that same day we had to go to another naval college to play, this time at Dartmouth. The reaction was not as good as we had received at Plymouth, because the people would rush away to various famous bands whenever they were scheduled to perform in other halls. We played from 9:00 p.m. to 2:00 a.m. taking occasional breaks to indulge in the crate of beer, bottles of whisky and rum (one of each kind) that we were allotted for the nine of us.

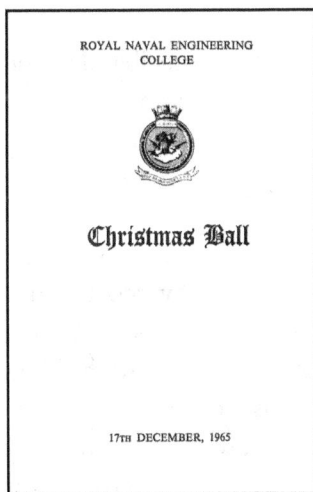

ROYAL NAVAL ENGINEERING COLLEGE

Christmas Ball

17TH DECEMBER, 1965

Programme for the 1965 Christmas Ball at the Royal Naval Engineering College, Plymouth. *Trev Sue-A-Quan*

PROGRAMME

THE CARIBBEAN ROOM	GREAT HALL
Dancing from 8.30 p.m. – 1.45 a.m.	8 p.m. – 10 p.m.
to the	BUFFET SUPPER
TRINIDAD ALL STARS STEEL BAND	*to the accompaniment of*
and	THE ROYAL MARINES ORCHESTRA
THE ROYAL MARINES SEXTET	
	10.30 p.m. – midnight
	CHRIS ALLEN AND HIS BAND
LA DOLCE VITA	
	midnight – 12.30 a.m.
THE ROMEO BERTI QUARTET	CABARET – CY GRANT
and	
THE COLLEGE JAZZ BAND	
	12.30 a.m. – 2 a.m.
9 p.m. – 1.45 a.m.	CHRIS ALLEN AND HIS BAND

Our group was featured as the Trinidad All Stars Steel Band and allocated to The Caribbean Room. *Trev Sue-A-Quan.*

In 1966, we continued to present our folksongs and steelband music for various functions. In February, the Cercle Français asked us to play for their society's celebration. It was held in a house and the pans occupied a significant portion of the small living room. It meant that the rhythmic dancers were closely packed together while they gyrated. We played until 1:00 a.m. and generated much enthusiasm from the students of French. When the party ended, we went to get our overcoats from the bedroom upstairs and noticed a couple holding hands. This was not an unusual sight because this couple would be seen always holding hands as they walked on the campus. But there was a different twist this time. The girl was sitting at the foot of the bed and, with one hand, was clutching a dress in front of her naked body, while her boyfriend sat beside her, holding the other hand. The spectacle took us aback until we noticed that there was some activity in progress on the floor beyond the far side of the bed, and realized that the seated couple was just patiently waiting a turn. We were aware that the music of Pan could affect animals,[3] but were not aware of the full potency of our pan music. But these were the days of Make Love Not War, and university students were vigorously carrying out the movement – in various ways. It was an interesting climax to our performance. C'est la vie.

For two years, I had been taking part in the University Carnival, a fund-raising event for charity in which students went on the streets in costume attempting to liberate a few pence or shillings from the pockets of the general public. For 1966 I felt that we could have our own float and join the parade in grand style. I thought up a cricketing theme, especially with the West Indies team being on tour in England. We had a prelude to what might happen when we were invited to join the Sutton Coldfield Carnival as part of the International Friendship League's entry. The float was decorated with large travel posters showing various exotic travel destinations the world over. Our band stood on the deck of the truck and we hammered out our music as we went along the parade route, while coins galore were tossed in our direction. At the close, we were awarded third prize in our section (the adults) and invited to play for the mayor and his entourage.

The University Carnival parade was on 25 June 1966. Large flatbed trucks were made available to the various societies and decorated to present an appropriate theme. We decided to mount a huge blackboard against the back of the cab of the truck in the form of a cricket scoreboard plus a set of stumps at the back end of the flatbed. The open deck would then be available to set up the band. We then had a crowd of followers dancing behind the float, including a dozen and more family and friends who came from London. We had prepared placards for them to wear around their necks depicting various cricketing happenings. On the truck sat Perry Christie,[4] a student from the Bahamas who had his leg in a plaster cast, having suffered an athletic injury during a triple jump competition. His placard said: Leg Break. Near to him was a glistening toilet bowl: clean bowled. Walking behind the float was Get-fui Hew, an already short fellow from Jamaica, who was wearing track pants in such a way that the crotch was at knee level and appropriately named

---

3   "Panic" is derived from this Greek mythological figure, a fertility deity.

4   The Hon. Perry Christie became the third Prime Minister of independent Bahamas in May 2002.

One of the Birmingham University Carnival floats in 1964. *Trev Sue-A-Quan.*

short leg. A mannequin leg (obtained the previous day from a department store) dangled in front of another dancer on the street, leg before. A double-layered arrangement of umbrellas carried by another reveler provided extra cover. One of our female participants wore an obviously pregnant frontage to indicate maiden over. Another pregnant performer, who carried a baby doll in her arms, displayed the placard: Second Slip. Then there was their male companion wearing a long ladies' undergarment – caught in slips. There was silly mid-on, whose midriff was a collection of odd paraphernalia. Meanwhile, the band played on, thumping out a heavy jump-up beat as we wended our way along the parade route in downtown Birmingham. We were delighted to see that many of the coins thrown our way were of the silver variety rather than copper. There were many flashing cameras among the spectators but none of us captured the event for posterity.

The BUWIS All Stars performed at other functions, and went again to Dartmouth Naval College in July for the graduation celebrations. We were even invited to perform for the touring West Indies team – a function that was held in the church hall of St. Ambrose Church. Knowing the venue a few days in advance we tried our hands at playing the Nun's Chorus, which didn't sound too bad. Because of a clash in engagements, the only players from the WI team who were able to attend were David Holford and Rohan Kanhai. We did meet with Lance Gibbs on another occasion, when Aggrey hosted a dance at his flat and the famous spin bowler appeared.

When we got started with the steelband, we had set a fee for performing, which increased as our talent and exposure grew. Since the group owed its existence to the Society, we decided to give BUWIS half of our proceeds. Soon we found that the Society's bank balance was growing at a significantly rapid rate, more than we were capable of spending on any worthy cause, such as covering the expenses for a fancy dinner for its members. So we voted that BUWIS would be counted as the equivalent of a playing member when the proceeds were divided evenly. But this still meant a windfall for the Society. Eventually we decided we would give BUWIS an honorarium for each paid performance. We players of course enjoyed the benefits of the earned money, which changed from shillings to pounds, to add to the meager funds provided by hard-working parents or conservative research grants.

For some of us students the need for extra funds ranged from a mild necessity so as to maintain an acceptable level of living to a bonus that could provide a degree of luxury, such as a trip to the Continent. My own needs fell somewhere in the middle and I sought employment during the vacations. During Christmas break of 1963, I signed up with the Post Office. After receiving instruction on how to separate the letters and insert them into the appropriate pigeonholes based on address, I took up my mailbag and was guided to the streets where the letters were to be delivered. I was somewhat puzzled that at such a time of rush for the Post Office my mailbag was only half-full, such that I was done with my route in short order and then had to return to the mail processing office to stuff more pigeonholes for letters destined for other routes. Another surprise was that I hardly bumped into anyone on the assigned street, and the only real show of activity was from a dog lurking behind the mail-slot, eagerly waiting to deliver the mail, and other bits, personally (or rather, dogmatically) to its mistress. My instructor did caution me about this possibility, along with the advice that one's fingers should never enter any slot no matter how inviting. It was only after several years had passed that I learnt the reasons for the lack of activity on that street . . . it was renowned as the main avenue of the Red Light district in Birmingham, with activity arising during the night hours. No wonder I encountered a very drowsy lady when I once had to deliver a parcel that was much too large to pass through the slot and I had to knock.

The next summer I had a working vacation in London, taking employment at the famous department store, Selfridges, on Oxford Street. There, I was an assistant in the carpet section, helping to move, roll and fold back carpets for the customer to view and make a selection, then wrapping and hauling the carpets and rugs to the shipping area.

On another summer vacation I joined the Midland Red Bus Company as a bus conductor, collecting fares. On the employment application form was a line that asked about skin color. This was the first time that I had encountered such a query, and I naively interpreted it as a question of complexion. I looked at my hands and thought that they looked pretty pale, especially considering that the summer sun had not yet left its mark, and so I wrote "Fair." After reviewing the form, the tutor vigorously crossed out my entry and inserted "Dark." He himself was of Indian ethnicity and I didn't question his action. I figured that he must know the ropes around here, and, in any case, he was the boss in this situation. He then gave me a test on my ability to deal with the British monetary system consisting

Bus conductor for Midland Red Bus Co., Birmingham in 1966. *Trev Sue-A-Quan*

of pounds, shillings and pence. Various additions and subtractions were among the host of test questions. I did not reveal that I had just qualified with a First Class Honors degree in engineering. My objective was merely to get the job for a few weeks in order to accumulate some funds to let me go touring Europe later that summer.

During 1966 we tried to upgrade our steelband pans. Roy drove a few of us to a junkyard to see if we could turn trash into treasure. We did locate a few useable drums and I remember that visit only too clearly because I stepped on a loosely balanced piece of metal and it rotated and clobbered

Trev Sue-A-Quan and Robert Huggins-Chan, B.Sc. graduates in Chemical Engineering (July 1966). *Trev Sue-A-Quan.*

me squarely on my shinbone. The pain! Even though we gathered an odd collection of non-matching drums, we managed to get enough of them to start bashing. We put in a lot of effort into getting the pans prepared, acquiring blisters, sore muscles, cuts and bruises. But these were temporary inconveniences, and nothing in comparison to Gordon's setback . . . he lost his hearing in one ear from the relentless pounding of metal.

Roy once again got an invitation to play for naval students, this time at Dartmouth for the annual Christmas Party. We found it difficult to arrange transportation. We looked for a van to rent but found that they were all taken by the General Post Office to deal with the Christmas rush. We felt that the only viable option was to buy a used van and dispose of it afterwards. A Ford Thames van with two bars on the roof (exactly what we needed) was seen at a car dealership. A decision was made to use some of the Society's funds (which by now was sporting a healthy bank balance). The van was a rust bucket that had seen better days, and in fact, much better days. When we drove away, the gear changing was so difficult that we drove it back. The mechanic tested it out and fortunately encountered similar problems as we had just experienced, and so he greased the gear linkages that reduced the problem to a reasonable state. The van cost us 75 pounds sterling. And it bore a licence, good until January. We hurried to install a long roof rack, made from Dexion (slotted angle iron) to hold the large-sized bass and cello drums, eight in total. It was 1:00 a.m. when I got to bed.

At 5:00 a.m. the very next day, Saturday 17 December, the process of gathering the band began. We then set out for Dartmouth and arrived at mid-afternoon. We played in a room decorated like a jungle with trees on which there were real oranges, bananas, limes etc., and coarse netting inter-twined with bamboo stalks. We did find the arrangement a clever design. We were also allotted two cases of beer and two bottles of rum. We played from 9:00 p.m. to 2:00 a.m. and the music was well received. By now we were seasoned musicians (although not because of the rum) and it was "just another event" for us. Before we went to bed we pondered whether we should keep the van to use for other engagements. However, if we kept it, the users, as individuals, would have to pay for the maintenance, operating costs and licensing.

The next day, after returning to Birmingham, we went to Roy's house to enjoy curry and roti prepared by Roy's wife. Roy mentioned that he could get engagements in Switzerland, as well as other places across England. He had promised a Paris date a year before, which was inconvenient for us because of exams, and in any case the inquiry did not materialize into a definite offer. The long rides to Dartmouth plus the over-ambitious expectations were getting to us and we decided to drive the van to London for Christmas and see if we could sell it off. Then on Monday when I went to the taxation office to change registration I learnt that the previous owner had revoked the licence and asked for a refund. That meant that we had driven around the country the past weekend in an unlicensed vehicle.

In London I had to arrange for some help to improve the gear linkages, adjust the brakes and carburetor, patch the radiator hose with tape, sew up some torn sections of the upholstery, hit out some dents, remove the most obvious rust, etc. Actually, the only thing that looked presentable was the new licence on the windscreen. Winston and I went to a few car dealers and the van produced some raised eyebrows and stiffer upper lips. One dealer took one look at it and, without even peering inside or taking it for a test drive, said that we would be very lucky to get £55 for it. It was a shock to us. We didn't try our luck any further. We felt the van was in better condition than when we bought it. It took us safely back to Birmingham, although the heater failed near the end of the journey, and from thenceforth it was always a cool van.

Roy decided to set up his own new steelband and our band now consisted entirely of students, which we called BUWIS Steel. We added new songs to our repertoire such as the new tune by the Beatles, *Hey Jude*, played to calypso beat. British rock music was the rage of the world at that time and it was not within our faintest consideration to challenge that dominance. But we did get our few minutes of fame when BBC Radio approached us to do a taped session, including an interview with Winston, which was broadcast three days later on the Home Service. The recording was re-broadcast several days later and the representative from the BBC said he wanted to film us for television, and even offered us £12 to do the piece. We were hesitant, the sum offered being small compared to what we would bring in with a regular engagement, although the performance would be only a few minutes. But we relented, and set up our band at the BBC recording studio downtown. We had to do several takes because of miscues both on our part and on the camera operator's part. The next day we were given four minutes notice that our TV performance was going to be aired as a news item. Winston, Ken and I, along with Ken's wife, Orella, rushed over to the Students Union just as Winston appeared on the TV screen in the interview. Our two songs then followed. I do recall that we were in the middle of a huge crowd of students in the Common Room watching the telly as our band came up on the screen. I was able to recognize our faces but others in the crowd did not, or else were more eagerly awaiting the football results, than to be concerned about the curious beating of pans or the appearance of foreign faces and music.

Our bookings for events kept us busy with practices and performances. We appeared at a variety of events, including Civic Ball, pajama hop, concerts, student society functions, masked ball, skating rink, dance halls, private homes, and barnyard dance. Eventually, the main members of the band graduated and moved on. New recruits were hard to come by, and although some did try to develop pan-playing skills, the level of enthusiasm was not the same. The steel pans began to collect dust. There was no need to keep the van, which had already recouped its initial outlay and was getting more and more costly to keep on the road. It had taken us from Edinburgh in the north to Plymouth in the south, but it was now consuming excessive amounts of fuel, oil and personal funds, especially my own, being the principal driver. By this time a leaky valve stem on one tire required that air be added every few hours; no two tires were a matching pair and the spare tire was completely flat. After advertisements placed around the university campus for a cheap, cheap vehicle went unheeded, I sold it for a few pounds to a junkyard where it joined its counterparts that had produced the start for our steely band.

Leaving the Cold, Taking the Heat

Michelle Lam (née Lemay)

In June 1943 Cary Aubrey Lam was born in Georgetown to Kenneth and Viola Lam. The Lam family was well known from Ken's trading and import business, particularly with Ovaltine, the beverage for which Ken's father, Michael Lam, had become the commission agent many years earlier. Viola was also well known in her own right through her hairdressing salon. Cary grew up in the environment of successful middle-class family and attended Queen's College. The family members were active supporters of St. Saviour's, the church that had been established in the 19th century to serve the Chinese congregation that embraced the Anglican faith. At an early age Cary had expressed an ambition to become a missionary. His mother advised him that people would not listen unless something was offered to them first. She felt that he could perhaps fulfill his missionary urge in a more practical way by becoming a medical doctor thereby providing service to the community by his actions. Cary followed his mother's guidance and gained his medical qualifications from Edinburgh University. He started his internship in England and then decided to immigrate to Canada.

* * * * * * * *

Cary Lam continued his internship at St. Boniface General Hospital in Winnipeg. I was a student nurse at the same hospital and we met at a dance in February 1969. We were both residents at the housing facilities in the hospital compound, he in one wing of the building and I in another. We would meet in the cafeteria shared by all the hospital personnel and also at social events. It was a whirlwind romance and in October 1969 we were married. It was quite a challenging turn of events for a prairie girl who had decided to take up nursing as an avenue to adventure. Little did I know then that Cary's daring spirit would take us to situations filled with enough adventure to last a lifetime that, in some cases, came awfully close to coming to a fatal conclusion.

After doing a year's work as an intern and gaining his full MD

Newlyweds Cary and Michelle Lam set out on their married life together. *Cary Lam*

qualifications Cary decided to specialize in pediatrics, but in the following year he gave up this quest. He felt that when it came to applying his medical training for the benefit of the public he could accomplish just as much as a General Practitioner than pursuing another 3 to 4 years of study to become a specialist. This was typical of Cary's nature – he did not have the urge to acquire a higher academic status and more degrees that would give him a string of letters behind his name. Then he got to know a senior doctor at the University of Manitoba who was active in northern medicine. This doctor was recruiting and overseeing other medical personnel to practice in Churchill, the remote town on the shore of Hudson Bay in the northern part of Manitoba that had been established as one of the fur-trading posts in bygone days. Later on it also became a military base, a weather station, a hub for the traffic on the Hudson Bay and a focal point for naturalists seeking to learn about Arctic flora and fauna. By the time Cary decided to accept the posting to Churchill we had become parents to our first son, Ian. The three of us set out on this northern adventure not knowing exactly what to expect but full of enthusiasm to meet the challenge. Cary was one of three doctors who served at the hospital located at Fort Churchill, the military base a few miles from the town of Churchill itself. The community consisted of a few thousand people connected with the military plus civilians resident in the Churchill area. It was certainly colder than in Winnipeg and we found winter quite challenging especially when we had to dig into huge mounds of snow to uncover the antenna of the car in order to determine where it had been parked. At the same time there was some shelter from the elements because there were enclosed walkways, called tunnels, connecting the various buildings including the hospital and the residences for the medical staff. The resident doctors provided basic medical services to the Inuit people (Eskimos), military

A weather balloon about to be
launched. *Cary Lam.*

Churchill endures subarctic weather
with long very cold winters. *Cary Lam.*

personnel and town residents. The doctors would also be flown out to
Baker Lake, Repulse Bay or Chesterfield Inlet if a medical need arose
there. On occasion, perhaps once a month, a specialist would be flown
in to Churchill to deal with specific ailments. Most of the medical needs
were to treat respiratory problems, including coughs and colds, accidents
(sometimes from coming out on the losing end of an encounter with a
polar bear), and alcohol-abuse problems with some of these resulting in
fights or domestic disputes. Cabin fever, or restlessness and irritability
resulting from close confinement for an extended period of time, would
affect locals as well as some of the seamen who made the long journey
to get to Hudson Bay. Depression would also afflict some residents as
they endured long wintry nights with up to 20 continuous hours of
darkness.

In the summer the extended hours of daylight brought its own
problems in sleeping and dark curtains had to be hung up to bring the
day to an earlier close. It was also the season when mosquitoes would

Medical services to Northern communities were
provided by plane. *Cary Lam.*

become oversized
marauders and so
numerous that they
seemed to be a shower
of rain. They took any
and every opportunity
to attack exposed
flesh. Cary got himself
a bee-keeper's helmet
with its protective net
to fend off the winged

The Lam family adjusted well to local conditions. *Cary Lam.*

terrorists. Even with the threat of attack Cary would be willing to go for a swim in the lake in the summer, but that required that the time between the stripping of clothes and entering the water be reduced to the bare minimum. In the remote area there was not much to do; the bowling alley and movie theatre offered limited entertainment. Sometimes we would drive our car (which had been shipped in) for a few miles along the one road leading out of town. We could also watch the periodic launching of weather balloons that drifted high into the sky. Despite its isolation Churchill was visited by Her Majesty Queen Elizabeth in July 1970 to commemorate the 100th anniversary of Manitoba joining confederation. We were able to see her when she went to Fort Prince of Wales, located across the mouth of the river. Another visiting dignitary was Jean Chretien who was then the Minister of Indian Affairs, before he became Prime Minister of Canada. Cary met with him on that occasion.

Despite its remoteness and lack of activities we adjusted to life in Churchill and enjoyed its charms whenever they occurred. We were offered polar bear to eat and although it looked like a beef steak it had the flavor of fish. We were cautioned never to eat the liver because it could cause acute toxicity and even death from hypervitaminosis A. Polar bears have a much higher tolerance than humans for Vitamin A which is soluble in fat and can occur in very high concentrations in the bear's liver. We really enjoyed caribou meat which had a wholesome taste. Canada goose had a rather gamey taste and although the bird is fairly large in appearance there would not be a lot of meat but a significant amount of bones. On the other hand ptarmigan, a member of the grouse family and the official bird for Nunavut, had a lot more flesh and was delicious. The color of the feathers on this bird would change with the seasons with a brown texture in the summer while in winter it would be totally white with feathers extending all the way to its claws. Arctic char was another favorite of ours and very tasty and fresh. One of the staples in the north was bannock which looked almost like a plumped-up pita bread.

We befriended Brian Ladoon, a naturalist who became a self-made specialist of Artic wildlife. The area was the breeding spot or a migratory stop-over for hundreds of species of birds. We would go out on the tundra and he would point out the delicate birds and the tiny colorful flowers that appeared in springtime. Migrating geese and ducks would flock to the area as the weather grew warmer. The aurora borealis in the night sky brought a dancing spectacle of light and color. Beluga whales were plentiful in the river and sometimes a narwhal with its distinctive pointed tusk would appear. Seals could be seen dipping in the bay and in winter they would be the prey for polar bears that would lie in wait on the snow and ice, each with a front paw covering the black nose that could otherwise betray its presence. There were so many polar bears in the area that Churchill became known as the capital for polar bears. In the late fall and early winter thousands of tourists would flock to the area to see these magnificent beasts in their natural surroundings. Everybody had to be cautious and go by car even if only to get to the nearby school or make a trip to the commissary in case a polar bear might suddenly appear from the high snow bank. The culture and practices of the Inuit had their own charm as they performed throat singing, drumming and rhythmic dancing or went about on dog sleds. Cary and I enjoyed and appreciated these aspects of Churchill and I admired how he, a person born in the tropics, was able to adapt to the situation. We spent a year there and then felt it was time for a change.

In an entirely different part of the world Dr. William Close (father of award-winning movie actress Glenn Close) was practicing medicine in Africa and was the personal physician of Mobutu Sese Seko, president of Zaire (now the Democratic Republic of the Congo). When the Belgians had granted independence to Zaire in 1960 they essentially packed up and departed, leaving the country without a viable infrastructure, schooling and services. Mobutu became the leading figure in 1965 and under his direction the Mama Yemo Hospital was built in the capital, Kinshasa. It was the nation's largest hospital and was dedicated to Mobutu's mother. In order to get the hospital functioning Dr. Close went on a recruiting drive in the U.S., Canada, Belgium, France, Iran and other countries to find suitable medical personnel through FOMECO (Fonds Médiceaux du Congo). Dr. Cary Lam, having survived the cold of the Arctic, perhaps thought that an African experience would be just the thing to thaw him out. He made the decision to go to Zaire.

Before going to Zaire it was required that Cary gain a working knowledge of French and a crash course was arranged in Paris. We first stopped over in London, where Ken and Viola were now resident, and they let us have their Volkswagen camper, one with a pop-up roof. We then drove to Paris and headed for the camping grounds in the Bois de Boulogne, the huge green park (865 hectares) located in the western part of Paris. Since we arrived in winter there was no problem getting a camping spot and from there we were able to travel around on short excursions and return to "home base." While Cary went off to study French at L'Alliance

A campsite in the Bois de Boulogne became our home in Paris. *Cary Lam.*

Française, I took Ian on visits to museums, tourist sites, les bistros, etc. We went skiing together at Les Deux Alpes which offered many groomed slopes and a vertical drop of some 2,300 metres. This was quite a contrast to Clear Lake outside Winnipeg which was essentially a glorified molehill by comparison although it was the place where we first learnt to ski when we were courting.

Cary's intensive course lasted six months and he was a quick learner, ready, willing and able to try out his newly-learned language skill on me. Magnifique. We then went back to England, returned the camper, and made a shopping trip to Marks and Spencer to accumulate what we felt would be needed for the two-year commitment in Africa. We bought numerous light clothes, shorts, shoes, backpacking equipment and the like. We then flew out to Zaire. It was 1972.

We landed safely in Kinshasa but our suitcases did not appear. Somewhere along the way our bags were lost. A couple days later they were delivered to us, but when we opened them they were only half full – apparently the people handling the luggage decided to liberate all of our newly-acquired stuff. Cary took the loss philosophically, saying that the new owners were probably more in need of the items that we were. Housing was provided for us as well as a car that carried a FOMECO licence plate. Actually, we had been promised a nice house suitable for a family in a gated community but instead were allocated accommodations intended for singles in the Minibal hospital compound. We did have a private guard posted outside. He would sleep or take naps in a low-slung chair, low enough that his hands were able to touch his machete lying beside the chair.

It took some adjusting to get used to conditions in Kinshasa. We were told that we had to have a houseboy . . . it was what was expected for the respected doctor from abroad and it also provided employment to a local person. We would invite the houseboy to share meals with us but this made the fellow feel very uncomfortable. On one occasion Cary invited a number of local nurses to a party at our home in order to create some rapprochement, stimulated by music and food. We were in a rush to get prepared and I took off my wedding ring as well as a diamond ring and gold bracelets from Guyana. When the party was over I discovered that all these jewels had disappeared. Once again Cary let his generous attitude prevail saying that those who took the valuables needed them more than we did. There was one male nurse, Jean, who was kind to us and willing to make friends with us. He would take us on occasion to local places and popular sites, and asked us if we were interested in some local food which he could bring for us from his home. We accepted his offer and he treated us to mouamba chicken, the national dish which is cooked in flavorful palm oil and served with pili pili made with hot peppers and crushed palm nuts. The orange color of this dish stood out in sharp contrast to the green saka saka, consisting of ground cassava leaves cooked with palm oil and peanut paste. Another delicacy, the pièce de résistance, looked exactly like juicy, plump, fried maggots. Cary, the eternal adventurer, had a taste and felt it was nice enough such that he indulged himself with the treats, while I declined. They indeed were fried grubs.

We were able to visit several beaches, mountains, jungles and waterfalls, including Ruwenzori National Park. When on safari we were cautioned to remain either in the vehicle provided for tourists or else in a circular hut with a grass thatched roof where we would spend the night. One night we were awoken by loud noises, grunting, huffing and heavy breathing and the hut began to shake. This continued for a short while and we three nervously wondered whether our hut of mud and straw would be knocked down. We had no idea what was causing the disturbance but shortly afterwards we looked through the narrow window and saw a departing bull elephant with a very prominent and eager appendage showing that it was in heat. The elephant had been rubbing against the hut. The park provided us the opportunity to

While on safari we spent the night in huts made of mud and straw. *Cary Lam*

Lions were a common sight on safari. *Cary Lam*

experience typical African wildlife in natural surroundings and the place was rich with game – hippos, baboons, rhinos, flamingoes, lions and many more.

In Kinshasa we had to shop for food regularly and on Cary's days off we were able to get around town together. On one occasion Cary took a photo of a plush residence. Shortly after doing so some men approached and asked what he was doing and commanded Cary to turn over the camera. They explained that the taking of photos of the president's residence was not permitted. This came as news to us, both the prohibition on taking photographs and the fact that it was the president's home. We were hustled off to the police station and interrogated all afternoon.

There was a river beach in Kinshasa but we didn't see anybody swimming. Cary felt that this was such a waste of available facilities and he asked why nobody went swimming in the river. The answer was: Les crocodiles. But this did not deter Cary's spirit of adventure. After all, back in Guyana it was not unusual to go swimming in waters in which piranhas abounded. Cary was in the habit of pushing the envelope and after all he could see no crocodiles around. So off we went for a swim, but not long afterwards we noticed in the distance a dark bumpy object floating on the surface of the water. On closer observation we found that it was floating in our direction. We decided we had better depart the scene tout de suite.

Cary worked in the emergency department of the hospital. It was a hectic situation there and more like a triage centre. Supplies for performing medical procedures were not always available. Surgery would occasionally be done without the aid of anesthetics and the people took this stoically, knowing that that was the ongoing state of affairs. Most of the ailments were common ailments – fevers, coughs, wounds, infections, intestinal worms, diarrhea and, interestingly enough, vitamin A deficiency caused by malnutrition. Also evident were tropical and water-borne diseases: malaria, dysentery, snail fever (schistosomiasis), elephantiasis, etc. Sometimes people would be lined up for blocks waiting to get in to receive medical attention. On occasion Cary would have to stay at the emergency department continuously for several days and the staff provided for his needs. The patients meanwhile had to have their family and friends bring them food and drink and take care of their laundry.

One day, maybe about a year after we arrived in the country, someone came barging through at the emergency department seeking immediate attention from the attending doctor, who happened to be Dr. Lam. Cary asked him to go to the back of the line and wait his turn. Then a nurse came up and said, no, no, he is the vice-president. With the situation now a little different Cary examined the little boy that the vice-president of Zaire had brought and felt that it was a situation that required attention by the pediatrician. The child had been taken to witch doctors and was not doing well. In the hospital his condition showed little improvement in the few subsequent days. Then the vice-president suddenly showed up and took his son out of the hospital, perhaps to take him once again to witch doctors. However, the boy died apparently from a ruptured appendix that had festered and left too long before the child had been brought to the hospital. The vice-president issued an arrest order for Dr. Lam and the pediatrician. It was apparent that the two doctors were being accused as causing the boy's death and the consequences of such charges could even be fatal. Cary telephoned me from the hospital and said that he would not be able to come home and that I should prepare our passports and essential things in case we needed to make

Cary worked at the Mama Yemo Hospital in Kinshasa. *Cary Lam.*

a hasty exit from Zaire. Cary was interrogated the rest of the day and released at about midnight. It was a harrowing experience. The fate of the pediatrician was not made clear to us even to the day we left the country.

As the end of the two-year contract approached Dr. Close asked Cary if he would be willing to stay a while longer to provide medical services in a remote area, in essence to work in the bush. Once again the missionary spirit in Cary got the better of him and he agreed to extend his stay. We stocked up with cans upon cans of mackerel, Spam, corned beef as well as bags of rice and other dried goods. We were taken by boat to Bolobo, up the Zaire River. We found ourselves in an isolated village with no electricity, shops or built-up roads. We were provided with a western-style house, the largest one in the complex. The houses had been built by missionaries for their own use and in fact the other eight houses were currently occupied by missionaries. What a turn of fate it was for Cary to find himself in a circumstance that saw his youthful ambition become a reality.

The villagers treated us with kindness and respect. We were able to get fresh fruit and fish. On one occasion a nurse brought us some mushrooms and the three of us enjoyed the meal, Cary in particular, having eaten the most. That night we were stricken with the effects of

Our residence in Bobolo had been built by missionaries. *Cary Lam.*

severe food poisoning, and all of us were vomiting along with diarrhea and painful cramps. It was like a merry-go-round at the single bathroom, one after the other, and definitely no fun. Dr. Miatudila, a local black doctor who had trained in the U.S. came to see us and a nurse was assigned to stay with us overnight. Out in the remote jungle there was little that could be done to get additional help. If any of us became severely dehydrated Dr. Miatudila could have provided an intravenous drip but other than that it was a matter of waiting and hoping for the better. Fortunately, our own bodies did the healing but after that we were very cautious about eating unknown mushrooms, no matter how appealing they appeared.

One night we heard raindrops hitting the roof but it was not the rainy season. In the morning we stepped outside and found a carpet of torn leaves scattered on the ground below the huge tree outside our bedroom. The tree was almost completely stripped bare of its green foliage and infested with grubs. It dawned on us that the raining sound we had heard was that of falling bits of vegetation – the bits and pieces that had escaped the jaws of the voracious grubs. When the children realized that an overnight windfall had come to the village they scrambled up the tree to collect the grubs in order to make a tasty meal.

Grubs made a tasty meal for the villagers. *Cary Lam.*

Once a month a supply of goods would be delivered by plane, for which the runway had to be cleared of grass manually. Our Christmas cards arrived in February. In the village there was a little boat with an old motor. Cary and some others tinkered with it and managed to get it working. Cary learnt that a Canadian International Development Agency (CIDA) worker was stationed downriver in a village where there were plans to erect a school. We had received this information from either the people on the hospital boat or from the talking drums that the locals used for communication. The villagers there were being taught to make bricks

A huge statue in Kinshasa pays tribute to the talking drums. *Cary Lam.*

for the school and Cary felt that it would be worthwhile exploring the possibility of also building a clinic or small hospital. He wanted to see the prospects for himself and decided to make a trip personally to meet with the CIDA worker. The boat was loaded with a few supplies and we three Lam family members set out on our journey with a bon voyage send-off from the villagers. The Zaire River is very wide and the opposite bank could not be seen as we rode in the boat. Cary skirted the nearby bank and did observe some signs posted in the river but he did not know what they indicated. The next thing we knew we were stuck on a sandbar. We spent some time struggling to get the boat free but to no avail. As nightfall was approaching we decided to pitch tent. We barely got it set up when darkness came and the mosquitoes descended on what they must have sensed were easy pickings. By this time we had used up our supply of fresh water and the evening meal consisted of a mixture of dry oatmeal, powdered milk and brown sugar. It was the best we could do under the circumstances.

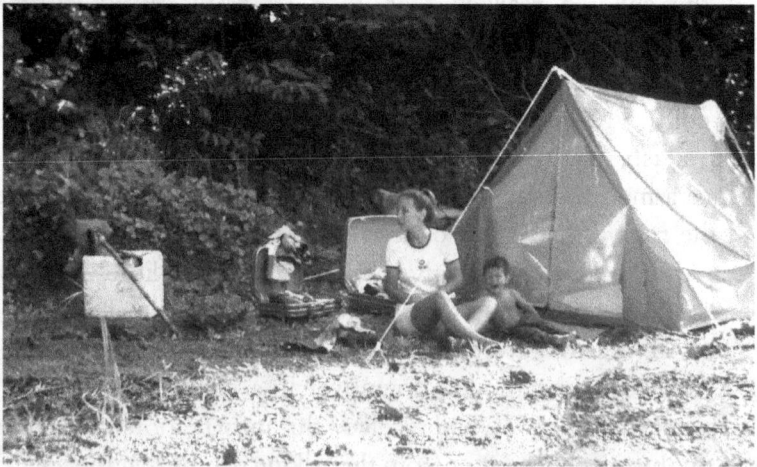

A hastily-erected tent became our shelter from swarms of mosquitoes. *Cary Lam.*

The next day we found that the boat had become unstuck and we were able to continue on our trip . . . until a cotter pin broke and we had to paddle to the nearby shore. We were literally in the middle of nowhere and had a sense of impending doom. I tried to take care of Ian as best I could. Then, somehow or other, we got the feeling that we were being watched. We looked around and saw a number of eyes peering at us from the bushes. They were children from a nearby village and they led us there. We were treated with kindness and provided with food. Somehow or other Cary managed to make a makeshift replacement for the broken cotter pin and once more we continued on our journey.

We needed to cross a wide lake, Lac Tumba, and we were told by the villagers that flash storms were a frequent occurrence. However, it was a bright day with no threatening clouds in the sky and Cary assured the villagers that things would be fine. We set out on the most direct course to Bikoro and at about 3:00 p.m. when we were in the middle of the lake the wind began to pick up and waves started to rock the boat. We had our life jackets on and Ian was as quiet as could be, probably sensing that his parents were facing a difficult situation and needed no distraction. As we continued across the lake heavy rain came down and lightening flashed everywhere. I had to keep bailing the boat as Cary steered the best course he could in the raging wind. When we reached the shore we were glad to have arrived safely and began to pitch our tent not far from the edge of the lake. Some village people appeared and advised us not to stay there. However, reflecting on the kindness we had received from the folks in the previous village Cary felt that we should not impose on their hospitality and told the locals that we did not want to be an inconvenience for them. We thus settled down for a night of much-needed sleep. Through the night the storm continued and grew worse but we were so tired that we went off to sleep.

In the morning when we unzipped the tent we found ourselves surrounded by a huge crowd of Africans. Then we saw our boat and it had been picked up by the surges of waves and deposited on top of some tree stumps a significant distance from where it had been originally tied. It was then that we understood that we were being warned of the power of the storm and the locals were waiting from the break of dawn to see if any living creature would emerge from the tent. When they discovered that it was Le Docteur in their midst we were led to the village with great pomp and ceremony. The CIDA representative showed the foundations of the school and explained that funding did not come through to complete the project. Now he was teaching them how to grow food using crop rotation, irrigation and the like. The villagers picked the best of the crops, slaughtered the chickens and made the finest meal that they could for us. There was music and a procession to accompany the feast. It was a very moving gesture considering that these remote villagers subsisted on manioc and edible leaves. The next morning the winds died down and we made our return journey to Bolobo, this time without incident.

In the village there was an old beat-up truck and once again Cary's urge to tinker got the better of him. Eventually he managed to get it going and he decided to teach the houseboy how to drive, much to the detriment of the cleared grassy area (lawn equivalent) on which the lad made unplanned excursions. Cary wanted to drive over to another village to get some fresh meat, something that we had not eaten in quite a long while. Over there a white Belgian man had settled with his Congolese wife and started an experimental farm to raise zebu cattle. This type of animal was better suited to the hot and humid conditions of the tropics than the dairy or beef cattle commonly found in developed countries. Cary acquired a young zebu and brought it back on the truck. One of the villagers then set about slaughtering the animal. A piece of meat would be cut off and plopped onto to grass. The villagers would then get a piece they wanted. The delicacies were saved for the important people in the village – the eyes for the village chief and the tongue for the doctor.

One day we got news that the father-in-law of the Belgian farmer had died. A large wake was held in front of the exposed body. The villagers danced and sang songs while the women went about with bare breasts as a sign of respect. There was considerable wailing from the attendees and we learnt that if the wailing was deemed to be insufficient or lacking in sincerity then the wailers might be accused by the witch doctor of being responsible for the death. The Belgian man came to visit us and stayed a while or he too would have come under suspicion of causing his father-in-law's death. He was advised not to leave the country in case any explanations were needed from him.

After spending six months in the bush Cary fulfilled his contract and his mission. Cary appreciated the experience in Africa. It matched his outlook of wanting to help people while challenging the odds in the spirit of adventure. He enjoyed what he was doing and lived life to the fullest. In the two and a half years in Zaire we had encountered numerous death-defying experiences and we felt that it was time to move on. We departed Bolobo by plane leaving everything we owned behind. At the Kinshasa airport Cary gave away the coins he had in his pocket to the various attendants as tips. However, he decided to keep a few as mementos of his stay in Zaire. The airport was a high security area and there were many alert eyes around. Soon Cary was approached and asked whether he had any coins in his pocket. Cary knew all along that there was a prohibition on taking local currency out of the country, but in his usual habit of living on the edge he thought that he get away once more with his luck. The questions continued: who are you with, where are you going, why are you keeping money? I was frightened that at the very last moment we would be detained in Zaire, and even charged. Eventually, after what seemed like an extremely long time, Cary was required to surrender the few coins before being allowed to leave. Half an hour before the scheduled departure we hurried to board the plane that took us out of Africa.

Turtle Trail

Maxine Everson, née Chung
and
Jackie Balls, née Chung

Before World War II Louis Chung had become a familiar name in Guyana because of his expertise in taking photographs and his photo studio was recognized as one of the leading ones in the country. His interest extended beyond family and individual portraits because he was an adventurous person who loved taking pictures of the outdoors, the countryside. He took some magnificent photographs of Guyana's interior and especially of the Kaieteur Falls by taking a trip in a tiny plane and hanging out of the window with his waist strapped to prevent him from falling out as the plane dove into the gorge and then climbed above the more than 700 feet sheer drop of the waterfall. The photos turned out very well and caught the attention of many people. It was through such experiences that Louis was commissioned by the U.S. military to take photographs of their air base. The U.S. military installation had been set up through an Anglo-American agreement in which America supplied material support to Britain before the attack on Pearl Harbor drew the U.S. into the war. A photographic record of the air base was needed but before Louis could do so he had to sign a declaration of secrecy to protect the photos from falling into the wrong hands.

Louis gained extensive knowledge of Guyana's interior – the forests, savannahs and rivers – and he was instrumental in bringing Hollywood to Guyana. The MGM film studio wanted to make the romance movie named after the novel *Green Mansions*, in which the leading actor, Anthony Perkins, flees from political persecution by going in the jungles of South America and stumbles upon an innocent and sheltered plantation owner's granddaughter, played by Audrey Hepburn. The film was directed by Mel Ferrer and released in 1959.

Although he was very successful in his photography business, to the extent of winning several awards, including from Thean, Louis wanted to pursue his real interest – ichthyology. He already had developed a hobby of collecting and raising tropical fishes and in about 1947 he set up a freshwater aquarium to be used for the import and export of tropical fish. The fish farm was the largest one in South America. He would bring in reef fish from Brazil and Peru and export these and other local fish species to Europe, North America and other regions. The farm tanks provided a major means for holding stock because it was not possible to go out into the rivers to gather fish during the rainy seasons. The fish farm, located not far from the air base, became popularly known as Chung Creek and was a place where locals would go for picnics and swimming. It was convenient to be located near the airport, through which the imports and exports could be expedited. Louis also pioneered the practice of shipping fish packed in plastic bags, with oxygen added to the water to reduce the death rate of the fish. The oxygen came from tanks that were purchased from a local air separation plant. Louis also managed to discover a new species of fish in the Upper Mazaruni River. He was given credit for this in one of Axelrod's books of fishes.

In 1973, the government under Forbes Burnham no longer gave permission for fish to be exported. Louis and his wife Winnie got wind of the impending prohibition when they were vacationing in the Caribbean. Louis was in contact with another Guyanese who was also exporting fish and, through implicit reference and coded language, Louis understood that the business operations in Guyana were in jeopardy. So Louis and Winnie decided to abandon everything in Guyana and to remain in the Cayman Islands. Louis knew that he could get Burnham's ear, and indeed could tell him a thing or two about the negative impact that the export restrictions would bring. However, Louis thought better of doing so and instead, with only the clothes with which he and Winnie were traveling, did not return to Guyana. There were significant assets that were abandoned – the fish farm, which was fully stocked, several vehicles including large trucks, and all the ancillary equipment.

The government restriction of certain exports was another aspect of the trade policy in which the importation of various products was also curtailed. Many items that had been brought in from abroad were banned in an effort to promote local products and enterprises, thereby stimulating employment as well as the national economy. Apples, raisins and walnuts were some of the items on the list of banned imports and their prohibition affected a program that Louis Chung had initiated. For the Christmas holidays he distributed these and other foodstuffs to the local Amerindian children located in the interior of the country, from upstream regions of main rivers to the southern interior of Rupununi. The gift items were taken there by plane, canoe and backpack as the different locations required. Some two to three thousand children were able to receive the holiday packages that were prepared and wrapped by the Chung family members but the program had to be terminated. In the government's thinking, if the children could not get apples every day, why should they be getting them only for Christmas?

When Louis and Winnie got the message that Guyana's government controls would become even more restrictive they essentially decided on the spot to test the waters of the Cayman Islands. It was not as abrupt a relocation as it might appear because their daughter Jackie was already resident on the island colony, with whom they were staying for the Christmas vacation. In addition Louis and Winnie were the directors of Mariculture Inc., based in Grand Cayman. This had come about through a situation that unfolded a few years earlier, in 1970. It was early in that year that four Americans and a Caymanian visited Louis and Winnie Chung's residence in Guyana. The Americans were the president and doctor from Mariculture Inc: USA, a consultant and a scientist who had invented a machine to cut the grass underwater. The team wanted Louis Chung to coordinate an expedition to collect wild turtles and their eggs and apparently the visitors were recommended to Louis because officials in Guyana's government were aware of Louis' expertise with fishes. Louis and Winnie found Mariculture's mission of breeding turtles in captivity for human consumption to be very interesting. Upon agreeing to undertake the expedition, Mariculture's president invited Louis and Winnie Chung to become Directors of Mariculture Ltd Cayman along with Dr. Grimmer, a retired scientist who was then living in West Bay, Cayman Islands.

It was going to be a difficult and hazardous journey to the North West area of Guyana, but arrangements were made by Louis who was

Turtles at Louis Chung & Sons Ltd Fish Farm await shipment. *Maxine Everson.*

Loading a turtle on a chartered plane to Grand Cayman, 1970. *Maxine Everson.*

familiar in jungle life, having explored many uncharted rivers. The team was fairly successful and brought back some adult turtles – Logger Heads, Hawksbill and Kemps Ridley, the smallest and rarest sea turtle, and thousands of eggs that most probably had other species. The turtles and the eggs were kept at Louis Chung's Fish Farm until they were flown from Guyana to the Cayman Islands. Arrangements were made for an associate's company plane captained by Captain Andy Anderson to fly from Miami to Guyana, then to Cayman Islands. In addition, the plane brought in the Styrofoam boxes to be used for transporting the eggs, this being the safest and best way.

The logistics of moving the turtles and eggs, first by steamer from the North West territory, then by truck from Georgetown (Guyana's capital) to the Fish Farm, coordination of forklifts/trucks to take the turtles from the farm to the airport to be loaded on the plane were daunting, but everything went smoothly considering the long and tedious journeys. To prepare the turtles for the flight from Guyana to Cayman Islands, Louis Chung personally fed the turtles with water from small bottles to which baby nipples were attached. The turtles were loaded on their backs on the plane and then tied in place so that there would be no shifting in flight. Coordination was again important and Mariculture was advised of the flight departure and estimated time of arrival in Grand Cayman. The flight arrived as scheduled at the single runway and a small building that served as the airport in Grand Cayman at that time. Mariculture's team advised Louis Chung how pleased they were that the turtles arrived

Louis Ching (right) with a manager at Mariculture Ltd. (1970). *Maxine Everson.*

in good condition with just a few broken eggs.

The Chungs were kept abreast of the progress of Mariculture farm. However, in mid 1971 they received an urgent message asking them to visit the facilities in Grand Cayman on their way to Florida. The Chungs were met by Dr. Grimmer who still lived in West Bay. They were entertained at one of the few restaurants on the island and stayed at the Royal Palms. The Chungs were driven to the farm where they met the doctor who was in charge of the farm. Adult turtles were being kept in ponds on the eastern side of the island since the farm was trying to give the turtles an environment that was conducive to the turtles. On the west side of the island there were hundreds of young hatchlings of different size in circular holding tanks. Winnie Chung who had extensive experience in handling millions of aquarium fishes shipped to North America and Europe was not very pleased with what she saw. She told the doctor bluntly that they had a bunch of sick turtles and recommended medicating them with potassium permanganate. It appeared that the Farm was in financial difficulties and it was disheartening to hear this from the doctor who had devoted a part of his life to such a worthwhile research.

Within a year after their visit to Grand Cayman, Louis and Winnie Chung received an invitation to appear in Atlanta, Georgia before the United States Fish and Wildlife Service to hear

Turtle farm tanks at Salt Creek, Grand Cayman Island. (1970). *Maxine Everson.*

the senator from Florida explain the new law to protect endangered species and to prohibit the importation of certain dangerous species into their country. This law covered not only aquarium tropical fishes but also turtles. There were several delegates from many countries as well as key United States tropical fish businessmen in attendance to hear the United States' proposals since the outcome would have an adverse effect primarily on the tropical aquarium fish industry. After the senator's disclosure, Louis Chung spoke about aquarium fishes, those that were truly dangerous and endangered, and he also spoke about the breeding and rearing of the turtles in the Cayman Islands. He gave an invitation to any member of the United States senate to visit his fish farm in Guyana and in addition, he would take them to Grand Cayman to show them proof of how turtles could prosper under properly run farm conditions. This offer was not accepted.

The United States made sweeping changes to fish and wildlife policy, with a total ban on the importation of turtle in any form into their country. It then lobbied that the ban become a worldwide one by major countries of the world, which is still in effect today. This decision by the US Fish and Wildlife Service contributed further to Mariculture's difficulties. In 1975 Mariculture's interests were sold to the Cayman Island government and its name changed to the Cayman Turtle Farm. It has now become one of the primary tourist attractions with new and larger facilities under construction in the wake of Hurricane Ivan in 2004.

The pioneer of the relocation of the Chung family to the Cayman Islands was Jackie, the youngest daughter of Louis and Winnie Chung. She was a young lady living in Georgetown when she caught the eye of Peter Balls, the

Reconstruction underway in 2006 at the Cayman Turtle Farm following the destruction caused by Hurrican Ivan in 2004. *Trev Sue-A-Quan.*

manager of Barclays Bank, who was sent to Guyana from Britain on a tour of duty. After they were married, Peter and Jackie lived in several islands in the Caribbean – Jamaica, Barbados, St. Vincent – before Peter was transferred to the Cayman Islands in 1972. In those days, Jackie, as the wife of the manager, was traditionally expected to be a person who did not seek employment and a lady with a presence in the community, if not of leisure. Jackie became involved in the Drama Society, a non-profit organization promoting the arts, helping with the choreography. Jackie's interest and ability in ballet were made known to the Caymanian community when the profiles of the bank manager and his wife were made public. But it was a friend whose child had nothing to do for an extra-curricular activity that became the initial spark and in 1973 Jackie was asked if she would be willing to teach ballet. Jackie had been trained in ballet by Ivy Campbell in Guyana and was on the verge of going off to join the Sadler's Wells Company in England when she opted instead to become the bank manager's wife. Jackie knew that her husband's appointment in the Cayman Islands would be for only two years but she decided to take on the challenge of starting a ballet program.

Starting off with about 36 children, classes were scheduled twice a week at the Catholic school in George Town. Initially a small classroom was used and a few removable bars installed on the walls for the children to hold while practicing ballet movements. Later, as the interest in dance grew, a larger classroom was put to use, followed by the library and then, in 1998, Jackie's own studio was launched with a sprung floor installed especially for dancing, as well as mirrors. Classes were ongoing from Monday to Saturday in ballet, jazz and tap dancing for three-year-old children to adults, with two hired dance teachers. By 2004 the enrolment reached 174 students. For 26 years Jackie taught all the classes, but she now lets her teachers do dance instruction while she focuses on the choreographer, adding character to the performances. Obviously, Jackie had found her calling and it was so much to her liking that she decided to stay more than two years in the Cayman Islands.

Many significant achievements were made over the years by Jackie and her students. She is one of four people responsible for writing the dance curriculum for the government and was given a recognition award for promoting dance in the Caymans. Adjudicators from other Caribbean islands and North America have been brought in to judge dance presentations and Jackie has organized several troupes to go abroad to New York, where several awards were won. One of her students became the prima ballerina for a company in England and others have gone abroad to study dance, some with scholarships that Jackie was able to obtain from local corporations and businesses. On the island Jackie has put on performances including an adaptation of the Nutcracker Suite, which she named the Christmas Fantasy, and a gala performance celebrating the 30th anniversary in 1992 of the Cayman Islands separation from association with Jamaica. Rather than having annual shows Jackie would stage a major show only after she considered that her dancers were ready to give a first-class performance. This approach allowed the children to focus on their regular schoolwork without distraction. Letters addressed to "Miss Jackie, Cayman Islands," would be correctly delivered to her studio. On occasion, tourists on cruise ships have asked for Miss Jackie and the taxi driver would know exactly where to take them.

In addition to operating the dance studio, Jackie opened a gift shop of sorts that also sold a few pets and pet products, primarily tropical aquarium fish. Her interest in this field was apparently in the family genes, taking after her parents' successful venture in Guyana. In fact, Jackie was not the only one because Maxine, the eldest daughter of Louis and Winnie Chung, also tried her hand at fish farming in the Cayman Islands. This was after her parents had decided not to return to Guyana and Maxine and her husband, William Everson, undertook the responsibility to sell off the Chung residence – at a considerably depressed price. Only a very small number of family and friends were aware that the family was leaving for good, the impression having been given that the family was going abroad for a vacation. In 1973, a few months after her parents landed in the Cayman Islands, Maxine and her family arrived there. Initially Maxine decided to set up a fish farm in Newlands, east of the capital George Town. It turned out that the quality of the water was not good and within a year the venture was a failure, with a significant amount of investment going down the drain.

Maxine then decided to go seek her fortunes in the finance industry, having had secretarial and accounting experience at Royal Bank of Canada in Guyana. She eventually worked in the banking business for

23 years and retired as the manager of one of the corporate managers in charge of forfeitures. While her venture into the financial world has been successful for Maxine, she credits her work with the Special Olympics as her most rewarding and enjoyable activity. She first became involved as a volunteer with the local organization and now serves as the local fund-raising director for Special Olympics Caribbean, with 23 participating countries.

The concept of the Special Olympics began in 1962 when Eunice Kennedy Shriver opened her home as a day camp for people with intellectual disabilities. In July 1968 Chicago hosted the First International Special Olympics Games. The 2003 Special Olympics World Summer Games were held in Dublin, Ireland in June of that year. Some 6,000 mentally challenged persons from 132 countries attended including a contingent of 11 from the Cayman Islands, and one of the Caymanian sprinters recorded the fastest time for his group. Because of the mental disabilities of the participants in the Special Olympics a greater degree of attention and supervision have to be provided and Maxine derived the greatest satisfaction by being able to give the required help and support. While Maxine has been putting her efforts to the Special Olympics her sister Jackie has been making recordings for the blind. Their interest in helping the less fortunate could be considered a family trait because her father Louis was actively involved in the Lions Club International – a commitment that started in Guyana – and in the Cayman Islands he became its first director of Caribbean origin. Maxine and Jackie have also become lay preachers for their respective churches and their devotion to their Christian faith has been a major aspect in their lives.

The care that the two sisters gave to others also extended to the family. After Louis Chung died in 1985 they thought of getting their 79-year-old mother to take up painting so as to keep her occupied. Winnie had never held a paintbrush in her life but decided to have a try. Art has been a tradition in the Chung family. Maxine used to paint eggs and one of Jackie's paintings graced the walls of Government House. Winnie started using water colors and then moved on to oils and mixed media producing a unique style that received praise from a professional Canadian artist. "Don't ever change," he told her. She made paintings on wood and T-shirts and specialized in doing beach scenes. Maxine decided to set up a shop downtown to sell her mother's paintings as well as a variety of items geared towards the tourist market – a tourist trap. Winnie's paintings are now all over the world, each signed by a large "Wini."

In early September 2004 the residents of the island were made aware that Hurricane Ivan was headed their way. There was enough time for those who wanted to leave the island to do so. Boarding a chartered flight organized by Goldman Sachs', her daughter's employer, Maxine managed to take her family, Winnie included, to New Jersey. They evacuated on the day before the hurricane hit, leaving the tourist shop to face the rage of the storm. Fortunately the swirling winds struck the northern coast first and George Town, on the south shore, was spared from the greatest impact. The damage to the tourist shop was not as severe as that suffered by Jackie's shop, where she found that a flood of water still remained, knee deep in height. The water ruined 80% of the stock and destroyed the floor of the nearby dance studio. After the storm had passed the clean-up operations went on for days, with Jackie and her husband wiping, scrubbing and sweeping from morning to night. The walls were soaked with a mixture of seawater and sewerage and proved to be an ideal growth medium for mold in the hot climate, requiring endless hours of repeated scrubbing. Many articles including gifts and toys had to be dumped and the garbage bags were tagged with a note that advised: "Sewerage soaked – do not touch," to deter children from searching the bags. Jackie gave candles to the Red Cross to provide light while the electricity was out of service.

The material things – the store, goods, dance studio – were eventually restored by the first week of December, and it was about that time that electricity was restored. However during the period of uncertainty following the hurricane it became a nerve-wracking experience trying to establish communications with the outside world. All contact with the island was lost. The island's highest point is only 60 feet above sea level and the water surge whipped up by the ferocious winds well exceeded that height. For some seven hours radar systems were unable to pick up any signal being reflected from the island. At one point photographs taken from satellites were unable to detect any sign of land where the Cayman Islands should have been. Maxine was unable to contact anyone on Grand Cayman Island. She tried using the telephone, internet, and cable to get in touch but no avail. Eventually Jackie was able to charge up her cellular phone using a car battery and for a brief time managed to get a signal that put her in communication with Maxine. After five days of complete silence Maxine got tremendous relief just to hear Jackie's voice. Even those who remained on the island were unable to find loved ones for quite a while. Immediately after the worst of the hurricane had passed it was noted that the roof of Jackie's home was in danger of collapsing and she was ordered by authorities to evacuate the house. In the middle of the night the drive that ordinarily would take five minutes by car turned into an agonizing crawl that went on for two and a half hours. Meanwhile, her son had gone to stay with friends to ride out the storm in a less dangerous location and there was no way of knowing the fates each of the other. He searched for his mother far and wide and even posted her photo on the internet as a missing person. It took three agonizing days before he was reunited with Jackie.

The days after the hurricane were ones of basic survival. Fortunately, there were few deaths during the storm but there were some who succumbed to heart attacks and emotional stress in the cleaning-up operations. It was a trying time for all, a time of survival. The banks allowed only $100 withdrawal in cash. People had to line up to get food and there was a ration of one gallon of water and a loaf of bread per family per day. Getting these meager supplies required some three hours of waiting in line. Barbecue pits and grills were heavily utilized with plenty of wood available from the trees that were wrecked by the storm. Amidst all the wreckage strewn all around the Caymanians went about trying to put their lives back in order. It was a time of simplicity, a time when people showed care for one another. In the darkness of the night it was like going back to Nature – no noise pollution, no light pollution. When electricity was restored the glare of the lights as they came on felt like a rude interruption to the peaceful atmosphere. But, from another point of view, it was like waking from a nightmare. All members of Chung family survived and, in the way they had overcome obstacles in the past, they went about paving the way for a better future.

Learning to Handle Hot Things:

Reflections on the Chinese-Guyanese diaspora

Jennifer D. E. Wong

Images

Through a window, the fronds of a solitary palm tree wave against a cerulean blue sky. In the painting, the window is framed by dark grey planks. The fronds are many shades of green; the trunk is hardly visible; it's the clacking swish of the blades in the sea breeze that you hear. The sea is not far off; it'll be another grey line, beyond the mudflats, on the other side of the pitted and worn seawall. I can smell the salty brine. As the brushwork is vigorous, rapid, assured and the layers of paint thin, so the palm tree looks insouciant: a simple poem stroked out of basic matter: a tree in the wind, planed wood, the sky.

The artist was my English uncle, Peter. He also sketched Stabroek Market stallholders in pen and ink, and painted large female nudes that used to show to advantage in the ballroom at Arvileen. They lined the painted wood panelled walls of this immense room with its expanses of polished floor, swiped by two hammocks, which would swing free when we pushed each other to see how high we could go. The casement bay windows would be open and sunlight streaming in with the sea breeze and perhaps a lazy marabunta or two. It was a room I loved. At one end, a niche held bookshelves on three sides, and a red couch with throw pillows to curl up on and read. Facing this bohemian and artistic arrangement were a couple of large yellow and turquoise striped Morris armchairs, a rattan recliner in the corner. The ballroom is also the backdrop for the settee, in tropical wood and rattan, again, with a trio of children sitting on it in white organza flounces.

Peter was part of the exotic life of Georgetown, only sixty miles down the river from where I lived. It was a day-long ferry boat ride away, on the steamer we'd take at least once a year for the dentist, another uncle, but my father's this time. Peter's wife Pat was definitely exotic, a trim dancer with black hair in a long ponytail hitched high on an exquisitely moulded Nefertiti head: porcelain and kohl. Loops of gold, flash of earrings. She wore mules that clacked provocatively, was a choreographer and dancer, dashed around town in a yellow Volkswagen bug, with a reputation for driving recklessly. Peter did not drive, and Pat used to drop him off every day in High Street where he worked as the harried manager of the last remaining family business which sold Archimedes motors, fishing rods and other assorted sporting goods.

"Diamond Prospecting," a sketch by Jennifer's uncle Peter Andersen (c. 1968). *Jennifer Wong*

Peter's palm tree painting recalls Matisse in its characteristic use of a window to frame a view. I like Matisse – I like the demarcation of the inside looking out, the interiors are like secure shelters, yet the spirit is taken out to another horizon. It is an attraction of opposites. I myself create such shelters but they feel transitory, as waystations, to be created only to go beyond. On the other hand, I have often felt my place as if I were on the outside looking in at warm lit rooms that others call home.

Peter, so I imagine, could see the palm tree from his studio window in Kitty. The studio was in one of the disused rooms — formerly where horses were stabled, I believe — underneath the rambling family house, built in the 1930's by RV, as the family calls him, my grandfather Robert V. Evan Wong.

The painting itself has a simple frame in an unknown dark tropical wood, which gives perspective and depth to the minimal subject matter. The frame is intact; the wood has not split. Such cracking and splitting has often been the fate of other wooden artefacts from Guyana, like my mother's purpleheart ashtrays, or our Ho Shan Buddha which used to preside over the dining room buffet. Ho Shan is the laughing Buddha. His statue has ivory teeth set in an open generous mouth, long-lobed ears and high, rounded polished pot belly, sleek carved curved barefeet, draped loins.

I note that tropical wooden artefacts do not travel well to climates where the humidity is less than 80%. Whenever I return to the tropics – Martinique, Abidjan — I rediscover an intensity of memory and sensation that assaults when you step out of the aeroplane's cold air-conditioning into that enveloping, torrid heat, sauna-like. Even early in the morning when it's freshly opened, like a pawpaw (papaya) sliced with a squeeze of lime, the dew starts to steam and the close mugginess and humidity are soon enveloped in a hot, bleached sky. Sweat is always a film on the skin. I see the same muggy sky as in another oil painting of two cane-cutters hacking at head-high cane with machetes, a line of dark bush on the horizon. The horizon is banded with bush and jungle, the odd flowering tree yellow or flamboyant red standing out like a cauliflower, in the same way as the Demerara River, when you took this waterway up from the coastal lowlands and mud of the Dutch colonial dyke-built and reclaimed flats, through the bush on either side of the riverboat bow's ripple, up into the heart of the continent.

The Palm Tree is a large painting, almost a metre square. It has been awkward to transport to all the places where I've lived, from Mackenzie to Toronto to San Francisco, across the deserts of New Mexico in a drive-away car to New York, and from there to here, to Paris. But I have wrapped it carefully in brown paper and bubble wrap and cord, fashioning a handle to carry it on planes as cabin luggage. I could not have left it behind me: it has become iconic, reminding me that the "past is not dead; it is not even past."[1]

Other icons and ritual settings

In my childhood in Mackenzie[2] inland on the banks of the Demerara, we celebrated Christmas. Pine trees were not imported for decorative purposes (as they were in Jamaica), rather the Demerara Bauxite Company provided its expatriate community with flat-leafed trees, spray-painted with aluminium and firmly anchored by the Stores' carpenters on cross stands, secured by guy wires. Silvery bushes made a special time out of those weeks, when there would be dancing at New Year's to calypso bands, and basins of rum eggnogs on Boxing Day. It was a sensuously different time of year. New dresses, the gala and play the schoolchildren put on would be other highlights. Apples would be imported from Canada, individually wrapped in indigo-coloured tissue paper, like gifts. They came set on a cardboard tray moulded into cups, like the egg cartons used by the cheese and egg man at my market here in France. My mother, who was Canadian, would work with the local ferns and casuarina boughs, transforming them into Christmas bowers decked with bright coloured glass baubles. We would give them to her bridge partners. Our childhood gifts often came from Evan Wong & Sons: bicycles, snakes-and-ladder board games, bows and arrows out of fibreglass. Before, my brothers had been content to bend a supple piece

---

1   William Faulkner, cited in the preface to Peter Carey (2002) *True History of the Kelly Gang.*

2   This bauxite-mining town was renamed Linden by Forbes Linden Burnham in a moment of self-aggrandisement; Burnham became the first president of a newly independent Guyana in 1966.

of stripped wood into a bow and sharpen sticks with penknives to make clean smooth arrows to go shooting lizards.

Jennifer's elder sister, Linda, aboard the *Nomad* in front of the Evan Wong house at Mackenzie. *Jennifer Wong.*

Christmas was a celebratory interval, a strange adaptation of essentially northern rituals translated into a tropical reality. It was a time overlain with excess, staying up until dawn to catch the sunrise on the sandhills. The first time that I stayed up all night was an Old Year's night, pulled by the dream of dawn on the horizon ...postponing sleep, partying all night, diving into the pool to chase the cobwebs, time extended with more music, wafting on willpower, no known ending. The first Christmas tree I made in France was also spray-painted, orange, a leafless branch stuck in sand and hung with tangerines tied on with blue ribbon, the shades of a mandarine tree under cerulean skies. I will still stay up all night to watch a new year's first dawn, preferably to look upon a river or water, luminosity and reflections changing even as you gaze.

Our schoolteachers came from Canada. They were buxom blondes and nervy brunettes, young bachelor women, a strange hybrid and transplanted species, from a place where rivers froze, where a mysterious cold would make sharp noses red and drippy, sting ears into numbness. Where they ate potatoes. Where milk did not come as powder in a drum, or as evaporated Carnation in cans. Christmas cards were a highly displaced element, either engraved biblical scenes or banal snowy landscapes, leafless white hillsides with sleds and children in wool toques sliding, or cosy hearthfires with stockings. Nothing at all like our lazy overhead fans, slowly stirring liquid air, or our lush yard where we would play on the sandbank by the river amid the dry silk slurry of bamboo, and where Cheu-Leen, my Chinese grandmother would tend the fragrant gardenia and blushing hibiscus, keeping a wary eye out for the odd skittering snake.

Mackenzie was a physically-segregated town: the expatriate, mining engineers and managerial personnel lived in the Camp, with its golf course, club and pool, while the indigenous inhabitants lived in the Village and worked in the bauxite and alumina plants which created a smoke-belching zone separating one part of town from the other. The commercial centre was Cockatara – a few concreted streets, the market beside the river, the stelling for the riverboat from Georgetown, the cinema, Sprostons' department store, and a barren square — a wasteland of tufted grass — with dirt paths winding across it to the fly-infested meat stand in the market where whole carcasses of beef swayed from hooks at Persaud's. Like the trip to Georgetown, even going down to the market was redolent with sights and smells of a foreign and exotic expedition. The smoke from the bauxite plant, I noticed, always drifted downriver over Cockatara and Wismar, and not up Watooka way. Among the fleet of corials taxiing across to Wismar, boys would swim and play in the river because they had no pool. But there were less piranhas down by the market because of all the boats, the gas in the water, the sewage too, I imagine. There were rum stalls at the market, men hanging about in worn, khaki pants. And bright printed cotton fabrics on huge rolls, like piles of logged lumber; a white-shirted clerk, usually Indian, would flap them out and down to be measured off on a notched wooden counter with a yardstick nailed along its inner edge where the customer could witness the deft gestures and rhythms, the swag from finger to finger.

Other voyages

We first left Guyana when "The Troubles" began in 1962. "They've burnt down half of Georgetown," went the rumour. I remember seeing flames reddening the sky from the breakfast room window at Arvileen, where I must have been visiting Uncle Peter and Auntie Pat. Steps would have been taken to hustle me back up river to Mackenzie where there was less danger — a new and strange feeling that threatened our heretofore carefree existence.

We left one September night some six months later on the night tide in a bauxite freighter, sailing first to Chagaramus (clouds of ochre dust and cranes) in Trinidad to top up the holds.[3] We were following the same path as that pinkish ore that kept Mackenzie on the map. It made its way across the Gulf Stream, up the grey choppy St. Lawrence River to the mill-town of Arvida and its smelters in energy-rich northern Quebec. A sea voyage, I see in retrospect, has slower transition value than air travel. You contemplate the waves furling from the bow for hours, looking for the flying fish, feeling queasy with the heave, lap the deck, walking the mile of the transoceanic crossing. But even with time to make the transition, I felt the rupture keenly.

The ship ploughed slowly up the majestic Saguenay Valley between steep, forested escarpments at sunset. The cliffs and rock falls gleamed misty silver, the sun catching the white statue of Marie Madeleine, arms outstretched like the Cristo of Rio, on a sheer rock wall high above the river, another river, black, still, deep, cold, maybe salmon or trout, no pirae (piranhas) or corials or water-skiing here. A silent gliding canoe of the *courrier des bois*, or the Micmacs. "This is Canada! Quelle grandeur!" I was stung by excitement, anticipating the new life in a place where there were seasons, transition, a harbinger being the nippy air of autumn that cooled our necks and made foreheads ache slightly. The pressure, the lack of humidity, was different. My mother had made us flannel jumpers, which were unaccustomedly heavy and vaguely scratchy. Under them my sister and I wore lambswool twin sets, in lemon yellow for her, forest green for me. The palm tree days were transformed, a layer of memory had been woven.

---

3   Bauxite ore boats left Mackenzie 3/4 empty to be able to pass through the Demerara's mouth where sandbanks were a barrier to fully loaded ocean-going ships.

Dutiful Chinese daughter

My father taught me a few things. He used to say, "Always keep your options open." Also, "Never travel with more than two suitcases." Like many Chinese, my father enjoys gambling and card games: he taught me to play poker and blackjack. The one book he gave me was his copy of "The Poker Game Complete," 1956 edition. When I leaf through it — the faded bluish-grey binding crumbles at the spine — a parchment-coloured loose page falls out: they are notes typed on my mother's manual Olivetti summarising his "system." I am honoured to be the caretaker of book and notes. This is one way that I show the respect to my father that a dutiful (Chinese) daughter should.

I think of myself, when the ethnicity issue arises, as half-Chinese, but aside from a tug of curiosity about things Chinese, I espouse few Chinese traditions. It was my mother in our family who was the bearer of traditions and stories too, and these were of fields and bulls, barefoot schools, the weekly bath in tubs in front of prairie homestead houses. She learned to cook Chinese from the domestics in her mother-in-law's house — in Arvileen, of the polished ballroom floors and jalousie-striated light in amber bands — where the young married couple first lived when my Dad returned after engineering studies in Toronto.

Ancestors and precursors

Christine's parents had been immigrants: an English schoolteacher and a Danish farmer, who had eked out a living on Saskatchewan's prairies during the Depression. I find it an odd wrinkle in the scheme of things that this schoolteacher, my Canadian grandmother, re-emigrated to China in 1952. Once an M.P. for Canada's largest constituency and the third women ever elected to the federal parliament, Dorise Nielsen had needed to go "where the revolution was really happening." My Dad's ancestors came from China to Guyana in the 1860's, but he has never expressed much interest in delving into our Chinese origins. He will name for me the various bauxite mines where he worked — Maria Elizabeth, Three Friends, Topira, Nieu Harden, Montgomery — where we used to expedition on weekends to swim in the creeks, to see the draglines, to climb and dig in the sandhills created by the removal of the overburden.

My father sent me a story about the mines, and the history of their names. "The mines were all named after the local name for the area. Each of these was at one time an operating agricultural estate." In a way, it was no surprise that the story evoked rivers, bush, *métissage* and not so surprisingly, the English landed gentry way of life in the 19c:

> The three friends were Spencer, Blount and Patterson, who fought against Napoleon. Spencer's daughter, or maybe granddaughter, Maria Elizabeth, was a lady of legendary strong mind and independence. She was educated at the Ursuline Convent and in England, but was not accepted by English society because her mother was Amerindian. She lived in a huge house on Maria Elizabeth estate, complete with several grand pianos. The house was long gone by the time I was there.
>
> The locals spread many rumours about her, which had no known basis in fact. She supposedly had many lovers. Once a year she was said to have loaded a huge raft with produce, skins, etc., and floated to Georgetown. After a period of wild parties, she would return to her mansion in the interior, and the landed country life.[4]

How very different a life a century makes! My father now lives in Massachusetts. He is a retired GTE VP, now finished with the frequent international transfers of multi-national executive life (he himself has moved a lot, from Guyana to Hawaii, to Massachusetts to Silicone Valley, and back to New England: his first marriage to my Canadian mother did not survive this corporate nomadism). Now he has remarried Katy, from the rainy Northwest with her own century of Polish heritage, and settled in a condominium development for adults in Middleton. Here the lawns, landscaped to billiard table perfection, are watered every morning by the automatic sprinkler systems whose operation comes under the Condominium Regulations of Communal Spaces. His life seems at once more modern and more regulated than mine is. He lives in America, I live in the Old World, and there is the Atlantic and say, two centuries between our points of historical reference. But paradoxically, perhaps

---

4   Evan Wong, e-mail, end-Nov 2003.

for the constancy and stability yet within the embrace of fleeting modern life (an ironic contrast) I enjoy visiting him. The feel of a touchstone, something akin to home arises, I am sure, more from a familiarity with him and his outlook than from any particular affection for suburban Middleton, MA, a rural suburban township near Salem, home of Witch Trial hysteria, and seafarers to the West Indies and China, but where woods, coastlines and clean shopping centres could just as easily be near Seattle, say, in the Pacific Northwest. Nonetheless, I love how Evan puts on a party to celebrate visits: he mixes up a crystal jug of mean rum swizzles when the sun goes down and plays calypso tunes on his organ. I shake the maracas. Like me, my father imbues significance in objects: that authentic Guyanese swizzle stick — it looks rather like an instrument of torture — that he found after long searching, for example, is a token of his past; he associates it with one of his few stories, "On Sundays, your grandfather would have his cronies over for lunch and a rum swizzle party; the secret ingredient is the Angostura bitters."

Traditions

I myself have not carried on this tradition of rum swizzles. When in France, do as the French do: my rum is from Martinique and with cheese, I drink St. Estèphe. The traditions or rituals around food and drink and celebrating that I now follow are, for the most part, French. I do have a wok and whatever I cook in it, I eat with chopsticks inherited from my mother who became a student of Chinese civilisation and was to visit her mother there (my father did not go with her). From our Guyana days, I've also inherited the brass elephant bell, which Flourie used to ring to announce meals. When I use it to call my own family to dinner, I always remember how it would peal out through the screened galleries of that large airy house and across the lawn as far as the riverbank where we were playing, sand, bamboo, the Demerara River running clear brown, like tea, or rum. The bell bongs now through hewn stone walls of an old dwelling built before my ancestors came to Guyana from Canton. I came to France seeking the traces of more history, identifiable traditions evolving more slowly than in North America. When I hiked along a Roman paved road on a ridge in central France for the first time, my imagination had reeled with a sensation of wonder at such craftsmanship enduring over centuries. Sandaled centurions would have marched these very slabs, and here was I, also in leather sandals, treading the very stones, with the odd purple spring crocus nudging through the interstices. The relative permanence of man-fashioned stone was a heady discovery. Lichen worked so much more slowly to efface the mark of man than the omnivorous cycle of the jungle's green rhythm of exuberant growth and decay or the wrecker's ball in American cities. If this was only one of several pull factors, as important or more so was a push factor: a gut dissatisfaction with compromises I would have to make with the possibilities offered by the American dream where I felt commercial objects, machines, consumption, mythmaking by media, and the needs of a nombrilistic, superpower ideology dominated the sense of man and history of his products.

My father's choices to move were bound up more with his work, while mine are made on another basis. He has developed a different tradition of nomadism, continued now in his mobile home, driving south with his GPS system, and west to California, golfing along the way, gambling in Las Vegas, and north to rainy Washington state then through the Montana badlands back to puritan New England. In the last few years, he has spent Christmas on the road, easy riding.

Jennifer's parents on Spadina Road near the University of Toronto (1950). *Jennifer Wong.*

Shifting

Since the first rupture — the bauxite boat exodus to Canada — I have felt as if my life foundations shifted, the constancy of place was broken, and thereafter I would continually and consciously examine my connections to places, weighing them in the web, net, the gathering and the balancing act. Not just to place, other sorts of bonds link me to the rest of my globe-scattered family, bonds arbitrarily tied at birth.

The move was, although I didn't have much beyond an overwhelming impression of the new and different, a turning point: a tectonic shifting in my take on the world. Since it also coincided with the self-consciousness of a pre-adolescent, this shift was also an awakening; I began to have a (self-)conscious viewpoint and define my "identity" whereas before, in Mackenzie, I had been merely a child, blithely given over to activities or desires of the moment: whether shooting arrows at watermelons in the patch where the crabgrass gave way to bush, or examining, with gleeful repulsion, the toads flattened and dried like pancakes on a griddle of the baking macadam road.

My life as a nomad, a wanderer, had begun. Nominally, I have dual nationality and have kept my American green card valid (in case) which gives me bureaucratic stakes in several countries. Bruce Chatwin, the English writer with a history of leaving his mother country to travel in exotic places, impressed me deeply when I read one of his reflections on the natural state of humans.[5] Small children, who from the earliest times of hunter-gatherers, were transported on their parents' backs, continue to have their cries calmed by being carried and walked. The rhythm of steps, the moving, is like music, inducing a natural feeling of well being. It is perhaps no accident then, that, often in a train between Paris, say, and London or Amsterdam or the Cantal — I feel gladdened, hopeful, in the best of moods: being neither here nor there, just moving — in between, uprooted — to the swaying rhythm and hum and rush of a high-speed train. Over time and through the vicissitudes of my displacements, I believe that the sense, desire (almost need) of movement has become part of me: it's forever in my "flesh and blood, skin and bones."

~ ~ ~

Arvida, Quebec, was a small provincial town. It had only one office building housing the town hall and municipal library, a hotel, a cinema, two schools (the one run by the Roman Catholic nuns was to ever remain mysterious), a red-brick (RC) church, and one clapboard rooming house where we stayed when we arrived. I would marvel at the pink chenille bedspreads, so sophisticated when compared to our beds at home where nights were so mild that only a sheet was needed. Life in Arvida I perceived as sharply different from life "before," and although

---

5   Bruce Chatwin (1985), *Songlines*.

I accepted and enjoyed it as children do all new experiences, it was tinged with the struggle to make the best of challenges, to make a path through whatever life circumstances would then dictate. The snow was dirty and tired looking in spring. We walked to school along streets like those in the Dick and Jane schoolbooks. The sand we had in Arvida was underfoot, but we did not play in it. It was a utilitarian, urban amenity matter, sprinkled on the streets with salt after winter blizzards, making them gritty under your heavy-soled winter boots, when the streets dried after snowmelt.

Water strategies

Northerners couldn't swim worth beans; swimming was like second nature to us "jungle bunnies." At an end-of-summer swim meet, I won a trophy, had churned up the laps like a seal and felt powerful. On the strength of this brass-winged statue, and to make my mark in the new land, I decided I would shine as an athlete. The gym teacher put my sister and me on the high school basketball team even though we were not yet in our teens. I'll always be grateful to Mr. Lee for the sweaty sports experience of women playing on parquet, cinder tracks and fields, in shorts, in tanksuits, in pools in locker rooms, and otherwise physically exerting themselves. In movement, working up a sweat. This is possible even when swimming laps, say a couple kilometres.

I was very conscious of the differences between our family and the others, the Rogers, Nichols, McCleods and Tremblays. We had a Chinese name. Tommy Andrews, in a defensive schoolboy gesture, launched an ugly nickname for me, Wongy-Pongy. The name stuck. When the kids would taunt me with the nickname — yadda yadda! — I was very hurt, offended, shocked and could only mumble how unfair it was and set off for home, alone, saddened, smarting with the rejection. In the cruel community of children, I hadn't made it. I was not like the others but somewhere out there on the fringe, beyond the pale, outside looking in.

We were poorer than other families. My Mum used to save on food bills by serving oatmeal porridge for breakfast. Dad turned his hand to carpentry work in the basement workshop, designing and building a family-room sofa and a bin for apples. He was after all an engineer, and knew shopwork.

I determined to do my bit and crown the family name with honours. As well as showing astounding physical prowess (a female Tarzan), I would be smarter than everybody else. I became a serious pupil. Academic recognition, then a compass point of pride with me, was later to fade as an aspiration during university years, when I discovered conviviality, and say, fencing, city streets and cinema. I made the greatest effort in French where I trailed lamentably behind my fellow students who had been surrounded by this second language from their earliest years. This confrontation with a different language gave me a sense of accomplishment in a mysterious new domain. No doubt, it stoked my interest in other languages, the Latin, later the Spanish, German, Arabic, Serbo-Croatian, Portuguese, Chinese, and odder ones yet, Walpiri and Welsh, that cropped up in my later pursuits in theoretical linguistics.

In Paris, I was to study at the university, finding there was an added benefit in meeting people with whom I shared interests and so a way to develop a milieu in another new country. I had met Rouben one night in the streets, in front of a Latin Quarter metro station. There had only been five people in the cinema, re-run of a disturbing Polanski movie. He had offered me a coffee, I had blurted out that I needed human warmth, not coffee. He smiled and shared a cognac.

Merely adopting my husband's friends would have made me feel like a parasite, as if my connections with people were not really mine. Although I was fairly comfortable speaking French already, I did have to work hard to feel I was expressing myself adequately in language. I kept a notebook for new words and expressions in my bag, and assiduously picked out unknown expressions, looked them up in the dictionary, tried to incorporate them in my speech or writing. Avidly scanned and compiled and reflected upon were sources like news-papers, ads in the metro, French cinema, books from stalls in at the market (along the Seine the famous stalls were too expensive and very picked over), friends' offhand speech, the radio. "Was that *zarbie* you said?" Ah, inverted syllabic slang from *bizarre*, popular among youth.

And solecism; or egregious?[6] Challenges for most people, so to

_____

6 **adj. 1.** outstandingly (outrageously) bad; flagrant: *an egregious lie.* **2.** *Archaic.* distinguished; eminent [c16: from Latin *égregius* outstanding (literally; standing

enlighten and incorporate, I find for the former, having footnoted the latter for the non-lexicographically challenged:

The non-standard use of a grammatical construction; any mistake,

incongruity,

absurdity.

A violation of good manners,

[c16: from Latin *solecismus*, from Greek *soloikismo*s, from *soloikos* speaking incorrectly, from *Soloi* an Athenian colony of Cilicia (Anatolia) where the inhabitants spoke a corrupt form of Greek]

I relate to the idea of a colony but am sceptical about the value judgement carried by such a thing as a corrupt form (I'd give it a status of *patois*). Colonies like languages are made from transplanting cultures. So I played Scrabble in French, in English, in both. Win some, lose some. I feel myself hybridising daily, sometimes with a rapidity of a plant unfolding its first bi-valved leaves in spring. Accepting the soil and water creating the *va et vient* between cultures.

There is the lure of worlds and cultures more ancient still: *spem in alia numquam habui* (I never had hope in any other...), a 40-voice motet, involving 8 choirs sung by the Tallis Scholars, composer Thomas Tallis doing a capella plainchant in c16. In the company of music, and strangers, I go forth.

Sometimes the task is overwhelming and I retreat from word-mongering, taking refuge in making images, painting and sketching and collaging: portraits of people in the metro, leeks and flowers in still life, window frames, scenes from photographs of friends I met in San Francisco, and still more or less know where they are, and if they have had a child. Expressing connections, peeling away and laying down threads, or layers, shiny as mica, or looping silk.

Transformations

In 1965, my parents returned to Guyana, my Dad accepting a corporate policy proposal to be the new Personnel Manager at DEMBA,

---

out from the herd), from *é-* out + *grex* flock, herd], in *Collins English Dictionary*, London & Glasgow: Collins, 1986.

charged with recruiting programs for more Guyanese personnel to run the company. We kids were sent to boarding school in Canada for the next five years, going back to Guyana in the summers and at Christmas. The long plane trips in noisy BWIA planes, through Antigua, Barbados, Trinidad to Timehri, also contributed to my nascent nomadism and the expectations that to be on the move, to travel, brought that sharp tingle of anticipation, on the cusp of discovery. The rupture that I had initially felt was like a scar, but I was transforming such leavings and arrivals into positive experiences.

In all trajectories across continents, books have also been companions. If my painting of the palm tree has gone with me, so has my library, stashed in a large and sturdy canvas bulk-book bag from the Post Office. I must have read V.S. Naipaul's *The Enigma of Arrival* at least four times.[7] *Adrift on the Nile*, by Naguib Mafouz attracts because of its title and evocations of rivers and movement, houseboats with balconies moored on idyllic currents.

Boarding school in St. Thomas, Ontario, was a very schizophrenic existence – on the one hand, I was a model schoolgirl in that small town, WASP-dominated, practically rural experience where autumn meals could be fresh corn and ripe tomatoes, all we could eat. On the other, I was a carefree summer teenager, in another small bush and jungle town of latent cleavages, rebelliously smoking "555" cigarettes, hanging out with the gang of other adolescents all home just for another endless summer, for some water-skiing, adventures in rum, waiting out torrential rains huddled in the speedboat, listening to music in the nights or watching the moon on the sandhills.

At school, a privileged and protected environment, I learnt little about Canadian society at large. It's indicative of my ignorance and naivety that I later found myself at the University of Toronto for no other reason than that it was the Alma Mater of my school principal. At the university, I would ask friends, "So what does it mean to you to be Canadian?" More often than not, they had replied, "Well at least we're not American!" I thought to myself, "Canadians define themselves by

7 Naipaul left his native Trinidad on a scholarship to England; a novelist, he has extensively written of his travels back to the Caribbean, to India, Africa, and the Southern U.S.

what they are not, not by who they are. Not positively, but negatively. How dialectical!" If I was to figure out what being Canadian was all about, I concluded that I also had to get to know Americans and the US of America. In 1971 I had made my last return to Guyana to stay with my sister for a few weeks. My father had decided to leave again, under more personally directed political pressure, I felt, the year before. Burnham had asked him to be President of the newly nationalised entity that was to become Guybau, but he had refused a position that risked being political. Indeed, a behind-the-scenes approach was made to Evan because he was one of the few Guyanese-born engineers at DEMBA with practical and management experience of the bauxite and alumina producing operations. The milieu I had felt was home – the Mackenzie expatriate community – was disintegrating. I clearly saw that Guyana was over for me, I would have to make a life in Canada. Or elsewhere. Disappointed in my university milieu, I decided to live and learn without being defined by an institution. I would be a "starving student in a garrett in France for a year." In those folkloric times, friends jammed on guitars singing ballads "from a ship a-sailing" – a song of leaving, and all that one can do is send back, not even bring back, "Spanish boots of Spanish leather." I worked double shifts during the summer, put my finger on the map of France and went to spend a year in Toulouse and hitchhiking Europe, to learn and use the various lingos in real life and not just from textual evocations of rivers in Flaubert and Beauvoir or of guitars under orange blossoms in Garcia Lorca. The plunge into another highly civilized and old culture was a great shock but I soon fell under the charm of that French provincial town, its combination of immediate sensuousness of place but over the long term skein of time, rendering a density and complexity I hadn't felt in Guyanese jungles or Canadian hinterlands. Although it took me three days to figure out how to order a ham sandwich in a café and I was appalled at French Turkish toilets on the landing, I was living a continuous adventure as I walked on old rose-coloured stones beside the Garonne, noted the exuberant statuary on fountains in squares, shared a cider with an old peasant, and dawdled over a café in a slower rhythm, hailing friends who went by. In the spring I left with a backpack, breadknife in a sock, one book "The Greening of America," a cape to wrap up in sleeping out under the olive groves near Cordoba, and a police file (for attending a student strike planning meeting). I ran out of money in Ibiza.

A decade later, at the American Embassy in Toronto, I first had to swear I had never been a card-carrying communist. This was an indelible introduction to Reagan America and a history of extremes, oppositions and to highly differentiated regions. Los Angeles, where I first lived, made a keenly visual impression. The palm trees were stiletto-thin, feather dusters against a movieland blue sky. There were the days when the brownish pall of pollution would hang immovable, trapped in a climatic inversion, over the spaghetti tracing of the highways. I read Raymond Chandler's novels, following his seedy detectives from Pasadena, and the art deco offices of central LA out to the beach houses of Santa Monica. I drove those itineraries a lot – urban design "windshield surveys" – also seeking the vibrant murals in the Latino and industrial quarters. I had known when I came to the US that I was transient: I'd give America a chance, say, five years. It resembled a road movie from the start, Ventura Blvd., Las Vegas, neon. Burger stands. Twenty-four hour life à la Raymond Chandler, and then modernised. Still gritty.

Rental cars from airports were also a *passage obligé* in discovering America. I travelled, doing field research in different towns and states, meeting Americans in vastly different landscapes: the lumber company towns of the Pacific Northwest; the blackjack dealers and MGM casino employees in Reno, NV where life was glittery, fast-food, on-the-go 24-hours round; the hardy single mothers living among the broken-glass-strewn sidewalks of tough neighbourhoods in Oakland and Berkeley.

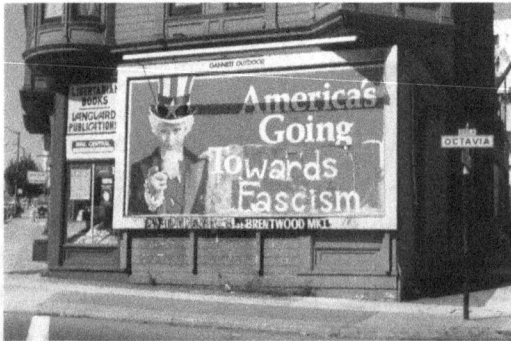

Altered billboard in San Francisco (1983).
Jennifer Wong.

I also read Kerouac, of course, and after a spell with my parents in Silicone Valley, moved to San Francisco's Mission district, the city's Hispanic neighbourhood. I had a house-warming party in my new apartment, and my father was nervous about coming, wondering if his car would be vandalised. He had integrated the suburban fear of the inner city, an unattractive paranoia that I would come to struggle against myself.

In San Francisco, I would go to hear Berkeley poets do readings at coffeehouses and listen to jazz in North Beach. One particular poem on salt and earth and journeying, was to inform my choice for another change of country. I also tried to be a leftist militant, a hopeless effort during the Reagan era, if ever there was one. But I did feel part of the Bay Area community whose political effervescence suited me. As in Toronto, I joined community groups working to improve the quality of local urban life. In our gentrifying neighbourhood, a collective of self-identified militants and artists did street theatre, mounted campaigns against advertising pollution, slum landlords and American hegemony. In the end, it was the pervasive sense of violence stemming from the rawness of social cleavages in American society, and that consequent sense of paranoia that I did not like and could not become accustomed to. Canada, I had found, did espouse different values, a greater tolerance of diversity; it had a slower creative rhythm that was not driven by the individual's need to make it and get ahead. There was a leftover flavour of paternalism and other fealties, of older, less utilitarian social relations that had been attenuated but that had survived colonialism through till 1867 and beyond. The US, on the other hand, after gaining independence a century earlier, had presented no barriers to rampant, expansionist capitalism. So in Canada, I had not felt that product obsolescence and innovation were the built-in motors of life in the fast lane (LA) or its reaction, an opposite current valuing "alternative life-styles," where you were laid back and ate whole-grain bread (Marin County).

Roots and seeds, stone and wood

I have some friends from that time who I see for dinner when they come through Paris. Vicki is Eurasian (I identified with her). The summer I returned to California to explore the New Mexican desert and its horizons, we brunched together at their home in Menlo Park. They had a house and a round, granite table (both California architect-designed) with a built-in lazy Susan, which swivelled to offer us the granola and fresh bran muffins. I loved the way Vicki had incorporated this "tradition," materialising her roots. Or seeds.

From her example, I now aspire to emulate that table in some way, perhaps in the old barn on the plateau that we've bought in rural Cantal. Just as, I aspire, one day, to sewing up the silks my grandmother sent from China into cheong sams and jackets with frog fastenings. But these remain aspirations. For sure, the ephemera of garments is more to my nomadic tastes than rural landownership, a current adventure I am trying on for size but which I feel vaguely uneasy about. Does it fit? Was I ever meant to own land and "settle down?" Especially now, after a first visit to Singapore where I was delighted to be surrounded by Asian faces, people who looked like me. The feeling right in this place astonished me, not different, not a stranger. Although I've never felt the need to give a large place to my own ethnic identity, but only to indulge in tokenism (how could it be otherwise in my family where things Chinese had already been so attenuated?), I am now finding that the charm of the Orient beckons strongly. But then, I also dream of a banana-thatched hut, perhaps in the Maldives, a melting pot of cultures in the middle of the Indian Ocean where I would feel the buoyancy of the sea, and the sand between my toes. Where clothes are light, cotton, minimal, tie-fastened, not the heavy woollens pullovers, layers, and polar tech bundling of the north.

What does one make of origins and traditions? You cannot change where you were born, grew up, circumstances which were beyond your childish control. Adult, you do make conscious choices in rituals, traditions, how you make your path, where you live, what you construct as a connection, or a memory. Every year I make ritual pilgrimages to build stone cairns I've built in the woods here to commemorate people who have died elsewhere.

The idea of home is an abstract concept which goes no further than something obscurely tactile. I'm ok with a good night's sleep. Sometimes I feel like a motherless child, a rolling stone, a leaf on a breeze, a kite flying high. Dominique says this is natural as I have no motherland or fatherland (as opposed to nation). Although there be indeed the baggage, the two suitcases, books, paintings, and other visions and mementoes of landscape: shells, driftwood, rocks, and postcards.

~ ~ ~

I usually travel in Europe to see art exhibitions, or visit with friends and relatives, and walk other streets or moors or forests or beside rivers, fantasising on whether I could ever live there, and perhaps develop habits, routes to walk, observations to make, images to transform into connections. It is not necessary to drive here. I like this. In LA you had to adopt the vehicle, the highway and its billboard perceptions. Here in Paris and suburbs there are old stones which recall other, by-gone natural harmonies: flowing river and light through the trees, an industrial smokestack, a 18th c. collective laundry (*lavoir*) or 19th c. Zolaesque linen-drying building, the tracery of train lines and freight elevators, canals, less and less trafficked, but still functional.

Drawing horizons

So I muse on the wood and stone configurations of where I am. In the fall, there is the golden birch leaf, which sails down on a breeze against an indigo sky. In the springtime, the almond tree flowers first, white powdered and dappling. In the jungle, there is a scrap of leaf on the rum-brown current of water flowing. And so by a Baudelairian *correspondance des sens*, I also remember with delight the luscious taste of morning mango chunks and the new day's heat, but there are no seasons, it is only day or midday or late afternoon or dusk. At teatime my grandmother would recount stories of her white gloves left at the Governor-General's house one other civilised teatime in another age of *politesse* and tradition. The ritual of having a cuppa is English, albeit. And at dusk, there would be the dense ringing of insects, the jabbering roar of a collection of green parrots nesting for the night in palm trees. There are sunsets. I feel like a nomad, but not of tents, of a higher technology age where the hiking boot is on a par with train schedules and internet access.

~ ~ ~

There are still horizons, rivers, salt, earth but while I feel grounded, it is not by roots but rather by seeds. Their growth may be discovery, and they can be carried on the air and windblown, or drift like a coconut to another island. One hand in my pocket and the other one giving a high five. I have become a French citizen because I wanted to be able to vote, participating in the political, adding my voice to, say, a democratic tradition where participation rates reach 90%. The sociological idea of "belonging to a community," has not had an organic evolution with me but has always been a specifically voluntarist step. In France, I was attracted to the community of this squat, then about 100 people strong, people who shared a concrete interest and who worked hard together to protect and change their living space in ways they wanted. I thought it would be an experiment in building something together, enjoining social relations through our activities making our own (semi-)urban space. A long-distance ten-year love affair with Rouben, whom I had met on another summer visit to France and was a first generation squatter, was transformed into a bureaucratic status of concubinage (only in France!) until I needed working papers and felt the easiest path was through embracing the institution of marriage. So, as comrades and neighbours, we have battled eviction notices, strung electricity lines, learned masonry, put in plumbing and built stone walls for flowerbeds in the courtyard. Renovations to roofs and facades in what used to be condemned housing have been won, as has the fight to transfer ownership to an appropriate social housing company.

We go to market on Saturday and afterwards, have a coffee or a *mauresque* (long drink of ice, barley water, *pastis*) and meeting up with five friends, we talk of places south: Avignon, the state of the wisteria, Aix-en-Province. We decide to have a potluck picnic on Christopher's terrace for no other reason than that we're enjoying each other's company. In the sun, on the café terrace, but the café will close as the market winds down. This is very French – an occasion for good food and drink and sociability – will be very gastronomic, as there are pickled *pâtissons* (custard marrow *Br*, squash *Am*) from Poland. And homemade cider from Sylvie's mother's place in the country. Christopher has a sprawling herb garden, the sun swings around through the bamboo; we finish the goat cheese with olive oil and fresh thyme, celebrate Didier's secretive 50th birthday, and young Pierre suggests we sing, so we do. John Lee Hooker on the disc player is also easy to sing with. Rising from lunch as the rays decline, we pick up Zacharie from his soccer game, and *la posture se défait*. Back home, we help Guy Pat put up a new parasol in some, modern, bronzily translucent material, and then it's almost time for another *pastis* in the courtyard, as the sun sinks behind the red-tiled and zinc rooftops over the garretts, studded with chimneypots. Back in Canada, my sister will think of me as a *bohème*.

~ ~ ~

The birth of my son did physically "fix" my domicile more. He is a boy with a complex heritage: he walks to school on cobblestones, takes subways to visit his French grandmother who was born in Romania and had married first a Palestinian, then an Armenian. I'd always thought I'd get married on some border station, if for no other reason than for the romance of it, the story it would make, and possibly – here's the pragmatism – also for the visa. I was going to give France and its old stones at least 10 years to see if the notion of "roots" would take, and now find it's been 20 years that I've lived in the same house, and it still feels like seedbeds rather than old oaks, like bamboo with rhizomes. Children are definite rhizomes: they grow as you add nutrients, rather than change the soil, so there's an impression of stability and its particular joys. I see the complexity added by another person, a whole other variable in any decision making, such as to travel. I have made sure that he knows how to pitch a tent, use a knife, shuffle cards, prefer reading in English, express early memories, love mango, fish and swim. Complexity, I have learned, its different pacing and solutions, has a way of inducing a longing for insouciance and for being other places.

It was tiring at first, to speak only English with my son, and to have to switch to French at the dining table, in order to speak to his father. Now I am used to that and am glad that my son has been bilingual from birth, and does not have to go through my own travail with the language of the place where I now live. I still have to rehearse a conversation with a bureaucrat. My paper archives (X-rays, jottings, letters, university degrees I've collected) have also accompanied me, in those two suitcases. They have grown to include tax returns and wage slips as I ensure minimal material needs, working as a lexicographer, a lifeguard, a journalist, urban planner and office manager, a researcher, conference organiser and translator. It has certainly not been a devotion to a calling or profession that has provided any constancy. I market adaptability and rigour. But

French friends view my take on labour mobility and the overcoming of borders that are barriers to it, as eccentric, I suppose. They look askance, express astonishment, but do not attempt to persuade me otherwise. At a meeting of our Philosophical Pizza Association, we debated the notion of l'Etranger and I learnt that in English we would translate this with variable nuances: stranger, outsider, foreigner, alien; and derivately: unauthorized, odd, unknown, not a member, uninvolved, unfamiliar, not mixed up. The tension in the existential questions of to belong or not, to what degree, on which life axis, is irresolvable and bring new discoveries. This is what I am learning to savour in the handling: it makes for a hot, generative flow giving universal energy from the yin and the yang, earth and sky to the body and an alertness to the spirit. At some moments, a lucid aphorism or other folk wisdom inspires. Such has been Julia Child's advice to makers of food: "Learn to handle hot things. Keep your knives sharp." As my friend Yola has said, "You cannot change the wind, but you can change the set of your sails," or less metaphorically, "The call to abandon illusions is the call to abandon a condition which requires illusions."

I feel as if I sit somewhere upon a web, new strands continually woven as people shift and change, as objects and places endure, are transformed, and wear out. Time's patina. Memory's caress. Freshness of a new day early morning. Grasping the ex-colonial expatriate dilemma, like a nettle, if you squeeze hard you don't get stung: the flavour is made up of a life, looping, weaving, sensing. An eye to the past, making a way forward, it is not linear although there is a definite sense of journeying and challenge. How hard it is to describe dappled things, the play of light and shade and the transitions in between, let alone render the effect on the path, in paint! I never got to eat a Chinese prune in Singapore, and wonder when I'll be that way again. First perhaps I shall plant a rice paddy or water lily pond on the plateau where the endless skies at dawn are streaked lilac on the horizon, and a bounding and loping across a field resolves itself into a fox.

FAST PLANE TO CHINA

Trev Sue-A-Quan

In 1963, after arriving at Birmingham University in England, the overseas students from various countries were hosted for several days of orientation in one of the student residences. We were provided with guidance about settling into the city and university, including finding places to live, and participating in sporting, social and extra-curricular activities. We were taken on visits to a few places, including an institution that cared for handicapped persons, and Cadbury's factory where chocolates from the production line could be sampled. On one evening there was a formal dinner at which we were greeted by place settings consisting of a dazzling array of cutlery. Not many of the foreign students had any idea of what should be done with such an impressive collection of implements, and we had to follow the lead taken by our instructors in selecting the correct piece of silver. The university had only in recent years begun to allow foreign students to take the regular three-year course for a bachelor's degree and this initiative was still under evaluation. Previously, a preliminary year was added on to even out the differences in standard of education and English ability among the foreign students. While passes at the "A" level were an indication of academic ability, we were all required to attend a welcoming lecture by the chancellor and write a summary of his presentation. This determined whether the students would be enrolled in a three- or four-year program.

I was an undergraduate in the Chemical Engineering Department and qualified in 1966 with a B.Sc. degree (1st Class Hons.). At my graduation ceremony, I was surprised to see my name listed on the program as the recipient of the Neville Moss Memorial Prize (a modest monetary award) for being the outstanding all-round student in the Chemical and Electrical Engineering faculties. In reflection, I deduced this was because of my involvement with folksong and steelband activities, as well as being the goalkeeper on the university's 1ˢᵗ XI field hockey team. I opted to remain at the university to obtain a Ph.D. degree and successfully passed my examination in December 1969. Later in that same month I immigrated to Canada where, based on the promotional information available, the standard of living appeared to be better than in Britain. I had already secured my landing papers in advance in anticipation of this move. The transition was made easier because my brother, an orthopedic surgeon, was already living in Toronto, and I was able to find shelter with him. As it turned out, I received an attractive employment offer from Amoco Oil Research & Development in Whiting, Indiana, essentially an industrial suburb of Chicago, Illinois where several oil refineries, heavy industries and manufacturing companies were located.

I took up residence in Chicago and settled into a comfortable lifestyle because of my status as an unmarried person, living in a bachelor apartment, coupled with a relatively high salary. Within months of my arrival came the surprising news that the U.S. table-tennis team had visited China, at a time when no diplomatic relations existed between China and the U.S. This ping-pong diplomatic overture was followed three months later by a secret visit to Beijing by U.S. Secretary of State Henry Kissinger. A year later President Richard Nixon paid a visit to China. These developments in world affairs caught my eye.

Up to this time, my knowledge about China was minimal, and basically was what the western countries and politicians wanted to portray about China – an undemocratic, communistic, mysterious place that harbored intentions of burying the West; in essence, nothing less than a backward, good-for-nothing country run by dictators. Although my ancestors originated from that place, they had left more than a century ago and, except for its culinary delights, I currently felt little connection with China, emotionally or culturally, because of my Western education and upbringing. When I was in the Mother Country – Britain – I did meet with Chinese students from Singapore, Malaysia, Hong Kong and Taiwan but their sentiments towards Red China were either antagonistic at worst, or indifferent at best. After mixing with folks from Pakistan, Thailand, South Africa, Rhodesia (now Zimbabwe), Turkey and others, I gained some understanding that each place had its own set of difficulties, both internally and in relation to other countries. While still an undergraduate,

I decided that I ought to seek out some of the handful of students who had come from China. However, before I could put my plan into action, they were all recalled because of the huge political movement known as the Great Proletarian Cultural Revolution.

The Cultural Revolution was still in progress when President Nixon went to meet with Chairman Mao Zedong. Whenever any program appeared on the television about China I tried to see it. The messages from the media were mixed or superficial. There were mild apologies for the western portrayals of Chinese being like Charlie Chan and Foo Manchu, while at the same time showing that the similarly-dressed Chinese masses appeared like blue ants, impoverished and backward, having to manually haul simple, overloaded carts. American reporters could gain very little information about China from the man-on-the-street, and while there were long-term foreign residents available, the information gleaned from them tended to be interpretations that were not much different from official Chinese sources. Diplomats, businessmen and reporters from several countries, such as the United Kingdom, were sought to get their perspective. But even after all this, China still remained an inscrutable place.

However, it was through this rapprochement that my appetite was whetted and I attended presentations by the U.S.-China Peoples Friendship Association (USCPFA), which sought to promote people-to-people ties and understanding of China. Films and talks describing how the Chinese were coping on their own through self-determination and sheer physical exertion were impressive. There were books from China but inevitably they bore a stamp on the inside front cover stating that the material was considered by the United States government and security agencies to be not in conformity with U.S. goals and values. It was a wordy statement that conveyed the message that the book was anti-American, and no doubt deterred a number of potential buyers from fear of having subversive literature in their homes. After all, the McCarthy era was only one generation before.

The USCPFA was run by volunteers, and after realizing that there was much more for me to learn about China, I decided to join, and eventually I became an active member. The Association attracted people of all stripes. There were some who belonged to left-leaning as well as communist parties (official or underground) who hoped that the USCPFA could serve as a means for understanding, and even accepting, the Chinese revolution. Then there were business people who were eager to capitalize on the almost one billion Chinese potential consumers who were obviously deprived of many material necessities. The Christians joined the Association, with faith and hope that the heathen in China would see the light; the Buddhists at the same time were interested in getting closer to a major center of their religion. There were tourists, eager to climb the Great Wall, and also those with school ties, who wanted to teach the Chinese a thing or two about the West. Also attracted were local Chinese holding high expectations for China's future, and well as non-Chinese who were more interested in China's past.

The USCPFA was granted the privilege of organizing a limited number of tours to China, hosted by the Chinese People's Association for Friendship with Foreign Countries. This represented a significant breakthrough in establishing people-to-people contacts. It was through this arrangement that I visited China in November 1974 with 23 others. We entered via Hong Kong and traveled north by train, stopping at various cities on the way to Beijing. The visit was quite an eye-opener for me. Obviously we were shown the sorts of facilities that would showcase China – factories, communes, kindergartens, schools, hospitals, sports facilities, etc. But what made a greater impression on me was traveling in southern China, in and near Guangzhou (Canton). There, I saw donkey-hauled carts, lots of bicycle traffic, punts transporting farm products, fishermen with cast-nets, peasants working in rice fields, ferries taking traffic across rivers, canal networks with many raised bridges, dams and dikes, palm trees, bamboo, sugar cane stalks, and more. All of these sights looked so familiar to me from my youth. The red soil, typical for that part of the country, was also reminiscent of the burnt earth that was used to make roadways in Guyana's countryside. I had left Guyana eleven years previously but it seemed to me that I was having a flashback experience. It would take more than eleven more years for me to discover that my ancestors came from this very region. But right there and then, it felt close to home.

I made another tourist trip to China in October 1976 and it happened to coincide with the downfall of the Gang of Four.[1] Our tour group was in Nanjing at the time and, overnight, fences and walls were plastered with posters and cartoons denouncing the Gang of Four. There were parades and rallies that attracted tens of thousands of people at a time. There was some concern whether the tour could continue but our hosts reassured us that our trip would proceed as planned. In Beijing, the one obvious feature that was not seen two years earlier was an abundance of soldiers, standing in pairs at street corners, armed with sub-machine guns. China was going through a political upheaval, one that eventually led to a greater parting of the Bamboo Curtain, and allowing more exchange with the West.

The minister in charge of Overseas Chinese relations issued a call for Chinese abroad to go to China to help in reconstruction, now that the Cultural Revolution had been officially declared to have ended. This made me seriously consider the possibility of going to China and I wrote to the Friendship Association in Beijing, indicating an interest in putting my scientific training to use in China if a suitable opportunity presented itself. By this time I had accumulated almost eight years of research experience in various aspects of fossil fuel upgrading, and was able to achieve a significant research breakthrough in gasoline refining that resulted in a U.S. patent. (Patents in Europe were also granted for this technique). My financial situation was secure and I enjoyed the high standard of living that America offered.

In late 1978, I received a letter from the Friendship Association stating that the Coal Science Research Institute in Beijing was interested in my joining that institute. I then made plans to go to China. One of my last activities with the USCPFA was attending an official dinner reception in Washington, D.C., for China's paramount leader, Deng Xiaoping. The news of my decision to go to China came as a shock to my parents who were retired and resident in Montreal, where my sister lived, but they made only minimal efforts to block my way, although they did ponder whether I was doing the right thing, because China was such

---

1   In an internal political coup, the radical Gang of Four, consisting of Jiang Qing (widow of Mao Zedong) and three other government ministers, was arrested and convicted of "anti-party" activities. This led to the eventual reinstating of Deng Xiaoping as China's supreme leader.

an unknown place to them.

I took a jet plane to China, landing in Beijing on 16 April 1979. At the airport I was met by Cadre Li Changkui from the Institute as well as by John Swaner, a member of USCPFA of Chicago, who had earlier been accepted to teach English at the Foreign Trade Institute in Beijing. We headed off to the Friendship Hotel, where all the foreign experts were housed. The Friendship Hotel had been built for experts from the Soviet Union who had been sent to help China in the 1950s. After a rift developed between those two countries because of differing views on how to implement Communist ideals, all the Soviet specialists were withdrawn in 1960. I was assigned a one-bedroom unit, which also had a small living room and washroom.

Meals were provided at a common dining hall where a small selection of main courses was available, perhaps four or five items. My institute paid for the meals and it soon became apparent that there was a gross overestimation of the capacity of my digestive tract. The portions were more than ample, with the amounts on the side dishes alone equal to a full meal. The dining hall was the area that the foreign experts, primarily English teachers, met, chatted and socialized. John was already an established figure and introduced me to various people from all over the world. On occasion we would be joined by some of the China "old hands," who had been living in China for three or more decades. It was through their intervention that my meal portions were reduced, because they could converse fluently with the attendants in Chinese.

Before leaving the U.S., I had purchased a set of Mandarin tapes and instructional books, published in Beijing. However, I did not have sufficient time and dedication to get very far in the courses. I also took along with me an English-Chinese dictionary of technical terms. The entries were translated into both Chinese characters and into pinyin, the standardized method of writing Mandarin using the alphabet. In fact, it was the pinyin system that permitted me to speak Chinese, because pinyin has no irregularities of pronunciation, unlike English where a simple word, such as "bow" could be enunciated in different ways, rhyming with either "dough" or "cow." Where the problem arose was in using the correct tones for the words. An incorrect inflexion of the word "mai" (pronounced "my") could change the meaning from "buy" into "sell," which could have dire consequences for a businessman or stock trader. Fortunately, at my Institute, there were various translators who were available to assist me.

The need for their help was quickly apparent when I was told that a National Conference on Coal Utilization would be held in Lanzhou[2] in June, a mere two months after I arrived, and I was being encouraged by the Institute leaders to make a presentation. I decided to take up the challenge and wrote out a technical paper in English. The translator then converted it into Chinese. She then read the Chinese text to me and I transcribed it into pinyin. The pinyin version was then typed out and the next step was for me to add the appropriate accent marks to indicate the four tones in Mandarin, utilizing superscript symbols: ¯, ´, ˘, and `. This required that the translator re-read each word individually so that I could determine the correct tone and assign the corresponding symbol. Then she had to read once more, sentence by sentence, so that I could add notations linking associated words, so that the flow of words would not become a monosyllabic staccato. It was now necessary for me to practice the presentation. About this time, Barbara Mutu, an English lady who was introduced to me by John, thought that she could be of help. Barbara had been teaching English in China for more than a dozen years and was impressed that I would want to give up a good life in America to try to do something for China's development. Among her students in one of her English classes was a girl she thought would be of benefit to me.

Barbara invited Cao Xiaoli to her apartment at the Friendship Hotel. Xiaoli was an attractive young lady who was also impressed that I was so noble-minded, seemingly like a swallow returning to look for its nest, while accepting an obvious lowering

Barbara Mutu was the go-between who introduced me to Cao Xiaoli at the Friendship Hotel. *Trev Sue-A-Quan.*

---

2 Lanzhou is an industrial city in Gansu Province, located on the old Silk Road, some 28 hours by train from Beijing.

in my standard of living. She admired my determination in wanting to contribute to China's improvement.

With less than a month left before the national conference Xiaoli and I got together on a few occasions to rehearse my presentation. We went to a park where, at an ancient pavilion halfway up a hill, I addressed the trees and she corrected my faults in pronunciation and tone. To the few who meandered by they no doubt must have thought it an odd experience to happen upon a technical talk in the middle of a recreational area. At Lanzhou, the coordinator of the speakers called me up to the podium and, glancing over at my unfamiliar pinyin text peppered with handwritten notations, told the attendees that he didn't know what language I would be using for my talk. Fortunately, it appeared as if everyone understood my improvised Chinese.

I chose to conduct research in catalytic steam gasification of coal, a new field of study for the Institute, and was assigned two engineers and a technical assistant. We essentially were starting from scratch, and conditions were a far cry from the new Amoco Research Center in Naperville, Illinois, that I had left, which had won awards for state-of-the-art laboratory design and facilities. We collected various pieces of available equipment while I had to design a water delivery system, improvised from glass vessels and tubing, and fashioned by a capable glassblower. For analysis of gas products, we relied on decades-old techniques. Nevertheless, we went about our research in a systematic way and, within a short period, were able to get some encouraging results.

By this time the Institute had assigned a small apartment to me, across the road from the research center. It was located on the fourth floor of a six-floor walk-up building and consisted of a bedroom some 7 feet by 11 feet in size, a marginally larger living room, tiny kitchen, washroom with a sit-down flush toilet and enamel sink, plus a small balcony. The kitchen was equipped with a flat stone platform at hip height on which was a two-burner unit that utilized piped fuel gas. The apartment was built of concrete with walls covered by yellow-tinted whitewash. The bare floor needed to be mopped with regularity to remove the ever-present Beijing dust, brought in from the deserts and loess plains by westerly winds and joined by the particulates generated from the tens of thousands of coal-burning stoves in homes, institutes and factories throughout the city.

As the heat of summer approached, I was shown how mopping served to cool the house, by allowing ample amounts of water to remain on the floor to evaporate. There was no washing machine and I had to purchase a wooden corrugated washboard and large basin to wash my clothes by hand. As a luxury, the bathroom

I was assigned an apartment on the 4th floor of a six-floor walk-up building next the Coal Science Research Institute. *Trev Sue-A-Quan.*

was rigged up with an elevated water tank and, by improvising a gas line using a rubber hose leading from the kitchen, hot water could be obtained after the gas burner was transferred from the kitchen to a rack below the tank. I made improvements to the setup by attaching a glass tube so that the water level could be seen. The only way to control the water temperature was to leave the burner going for a certain time, and, if the water became too hot, cold water had to be added to the tank. A simple showerhead was attached to a tap on the side of the tank. Used water ran off into a drain-hole that was an integral part of every apartment with a cement floor. I was also granted one other luxury – a double bed, which, according to hearsay, was provided only to married couples. The bed consisted of a metal frame that supported a few wooden planks, with a thin cotton-filled mattress (more like a quilt) placed on top. On a scale of hardness, it would have been difficult to find a bed with a firmer consistency. A mosquito netting, suspended from the ceiling, was acquired after a more-than-desired amount of blood had been withdrawn without permission by the nighttime pests. In the stairwell of the apartment, there was a light socket on each level, with a pull-string. However, many a time, the bulbs were missing or broken and both residents and visitors had to make their way in pitch darkness, using their feet as their sensors in going up and down the stairs. Actually, this was not an uncommon situation in many apartment buildings, although it did present a tricky exercise for me when I ported my bicycle up or down the stairs. Despite the apparent starkness of the apartment, the accommodations represented a level of comfort that was better than what the majority of Beijing residents had at the time.

The lack of "modern" facilities was not a great concern for me. When I accepted the invitation to come to China, I asked for no special privileges, and wanted to share the prevailing living and working conditions of Chinese citizens. However, I did buy an 18-inch color television set (shipped from Hong Kong), a distinct luxury when the vast majority of people had no such gadget in their homes, or else a 14-inch black-and-white set, at best. The Institute leaders did try to make things as comfortable for me as was within their control. I was paid 250 yuan per month, considerably higher than the 50 to 80 yuan that scientists were paid. Cadre Li, who lived two floors above me, on the sixth floor, was my designated assistant for worldly matters. He accompanied me when I went shopping for clothes, pots and pans, bicycle, radio, etc. and arranged for tickets to the cinema, theatre and soccer matches. He spoke no English and was one of several political cadres at the Institute. In essence, he helped to smooth the transition that I was going through, taking care of mundane matters and procedures. He apparently was also

taking care of other matters, because I later learnt that there were a number of potential marriage candidates eagerly hoping for an opportunity to get at Dr. Su. But Cadre Li did his job well (or too well) and he did not arrange any encounters with matrimonial intent, giving me a chance to get settled first.

It was very fortunate that Barbara had introduced Xiaoli to me so soon after my arrival. Besides being a great help in my technical presentation, she was an eager listener and our languages undoubtedly took great leaps forward as we met regularly.

Xiaoli's ancestry had some

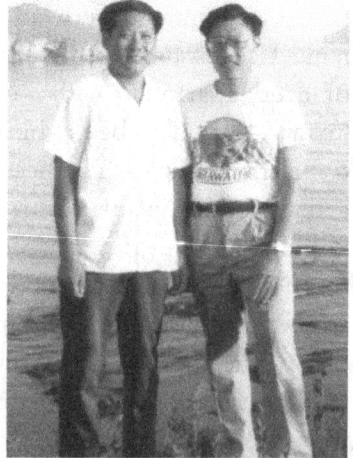

Cadre Li Changkui was my assistant in getting settled in China. *Trev Sue-A-Quan.*

connection outside China because her maternal grandmother was born in Yokohama to a Cantonese family that had emigrated to Japan and started a restaurant business. Her grandfather was a graduate from Tokyo University in Social economics. Xiaoli was familiar with the concept of 19th century Chinese indentured labourers traveling abroad and had written a paper about the Chinese who had gone to work in the sugar canefields in Hawaii. This accumulation of knowledge came through her own initiatives and this determination and quest for knowledge had served her well. When the Cultural Revolution was launched in 1966 she was a promising student in a well-known middle school and her formal schooling came to an abrupt halt. The youth of China were called upon to roam the country and learn from exposure to the lives of others. She traveled to several provinces for a few months and was fed and clothed by the locals. Various daily-need supplies were loaned to the visiting students by military units and civilians with promissory notes indicating that the items would be returned in due course. These paper promises were to be turned over to the schools from where the roaming students originated but it is difficult to say how many were dutifully submitted. With youthful exuberance Xiaoli enjoyed her travels that took her to historic temples, soaring mountains and revolutionary sites.

Because members of her family had overseas ties and intellectual achievements Xiaoli was not "red" enough to be accepted as a member of the Red Guards that engaged in eliminating bourgeois habits and old-style mentality while promoting class struggle. However, she did witness some of the excesses that the Red Guards brought upon the populace. Some of her own teachers were hauled before a crowd and denounced by their own revolutionary pupils. They were humiliated with trumped-up charges and had ink poured in their eyes. In her neighborhood some people disappeared and the screams of others could be heard as they endured beatings that left them close to death. Chairman Mao had declared that only 10 percent of the people were in fact bad elements. At every institution, factory and office there were gatherings to try to determine which ones among themselves were the evil 10%. The Red Guards visited Xiaoli's own home and searched for incriminating materials. By this time precious family photographs as well as valuable gold coins had already been pushed through cracks in the floorboards into the dust below, indeed into the dust of history. The family was spared from harm but only after Xiaoli bravely removed some "large character posters" in the nearby street that denounced her mother. In the morning light the questionable accusations evaporated.

In September 1969 Xiaoli along with hundreds of thousands of youths in the big cities began their journey to the countryside in accordance with Chairman Mao Zetong's proclamation to "go down" to the countryside to be re-educated and learn from the peasants and workers. At the army camp in Inner Mongolia she was required to cultivate the land, raise pigs, and make bricks. She endured the piercing cold and the dusty air for almost two years. During that time she held faith that knowledge and education were important and would secretly read novels by foreign writers such as Balzac, Dickens and Pushkin. Sometimes this meant reading by candle light under the blankets - a dangerous exercise intellectually as well as physically, which resulted in a blackened face in the morning.

Because her mother suffered from severe rheumatoid arthritis Xiaoli was granted permission to return to Beijing to help in caring for her mother. Xiaoli was assigned to a job in factory making semi-conductors and remained there for seven years. During this time she quietly devoted herself to learning English, with the help and encouragement of a few fellow workers and neighbors although the majority of the workers at the factory considered this an exercise in futility. Then, in 1976, came a series of events that steered China on a different course. In January Premier Zhou Enlai died. An earthquake of magnitude 7.8 struck Tangshan in July and significant tremors were felt in Beijing, 149 km away, such that many residents in the capital city decided to sleep in tents outdoors for the next while, including Xiaoli's family. These events and especially the Tangshan disaster that killed hundreds of thousands seemed like an ominous portend. Then in September Chairman Mao Zedong passed away. Shortly thereafter the Gang of Four was overthrown.

A year later, in 1977, schools reopened and examinations were held for those wanting to enter university. There were thousands upon thousands of candidates who wanted to gain university entrance, Xiaoli among them, but only a small percentage could be accepted. Chinese, mathematics and foreign language were among the subjects under examination. Xiaoli was able to obtain sufficiently high marks that she could be accepted to a top university. However, there was an age restriction with those older than 24 years considered as undesirable material for university studies. She was assigned to Beijing Normal College to be trained as a teacher of English. She resumed her classroom education in 1978, twelve years after it was so suddenly interrupted by the decree from Chairman Mao.

Not long after I arrived in Beijing I was taken to a somewhat overused black-and-white movie which concluded with two butterflies emerging from a tomb. This seemed to be an unusual story to me but Xiaoli explained that this was one of the Chinese classics dating back to the Tang dynasty. With an outcome comparable to Romeo and Juliet the two young lovers, Liang Shanbo and Zhu Yingtai, find their dreams about to be shattered when Yingtai's father arranges for her to marry a rich but unimpressive man. The young lovers make a mutual pledge of eternal love but Shanbo's health deteriorates and he dies. On her marriage day Yingtai is prevented by fierce winds from continuing as the wedding procession nears the tomb of her lost lover. She goes to pay respects at the tomb, and it suddenly opens with a clap of thunder. Yingtai immediately plunges in and soon two butterflies emerge.

It was obvious that my awareness of Chinese history and customs was severely limited but Xiaoli was a veritable fountain of knowledge and through her I got to know about the Monkey King, Nezha, Wu Song (who kills a tiger with his bare hands), fox spirits and much more. The Cowherd and the Weaver Girl was another legendary love story but one between a fairy maiden who descends to Earth and is wooed by a mortal. The Goddess of Heaven in an angry fit over their union draws a line in the skies – the Milky Way – separating the lovers who are allowed a reunion once per year on the seventh day of the seventh month, which can be seen when the stars Altair and Vega are poised high in the summer sky. In addition to literature, Xiaoli was also fond of poetry, music and dance and not long after we met she composed a poem about me entitled, "The earth is calling you back."

She taught me that I didn't have to go into a detailed explanation if someone asked, "Have you eaten?" or, after seeing me carrying parcels, "Been shopping?" or "You went out?" These expressions were merely the Chinese form of greeting in the same way that "How are you?" is not an invitation to describe one's current ailments. I was not warned in time to prevent a diplomatic incident that questioned my character. It is the custom (especially for children) to politely refuse when offered a gift. One day I was visited by three children in the neighborhood and I served them some candy. They of course refused. I placed the tray of treats before them and picked one for myself. Later I became aware that I was considered selfish and perhaps miserly. I was then informed that the correct procedure was to persist in offering the candy despite the refusals and only after the third time would the offering be accepted. Thousands of years of history and traditions required more than a crash course but I was obviously in capable hands with Xiaoli and her instructions and guidance were most welcome.

Our meetings grew more frequent and we grew closer in our relationship. I noticed that there were many people using umbrellas for shelter in the heat of summer. In fact, a significant number of couples seemed to be strolling at the back of the Gu Gong (Palace Museum, formerly called the Forbidden City) with raised umbrellas, even though the sun had already set and there was not a cloud in the sky. Xiaoli explained that in the busy, densely-populated capital, there were few places that couples could find privacy, and the umbrella became a practical cover in such time of need. For me, it was a pleasure to try out how this technique worked, with a beautiful girl being the most needed component. (It is also worth noting that the umbrellas in use were of regular size and not outsized golf umbrellas.) In the heart of this ancient city we strolled on the same paving stones on which millions of people had trodden (or been trodden upon), and we saw our paths merging.

In October 1979 Xiaoli and I became engaged and I informed my family in Canada. Cadre Li was also brought up to date on the developments and he apparently did what was considered appropriate – an investigation of Xiaoli's background. He cleared her for our proposed union, and at the same time cleared his list of potential candidates. To make our marriage official, we rode our bicycles to the registration bureau on 8 November, with Cadre Li accompanying. Standard questions were asked of us by an official who sat at a plain wooden desk – name, workplace, etc., and whether each of us was single and a willing participant. We signed our names, and departed with the certificate. Registration was only one aspect of becoming married. It was also necessary to have a reception, and only then would the marriage be recognized. On Saturday 24 November we received colleagues at my Institute, with groups of twenty or so coming in rotation to crowd into our living room to meet the happy couple while asking probing questions about how we met, or else having us sing a song. The guests were treated to tea, candies, peanuts, melon seeds and cigarettes. On the following day, my 36th birthday, we held a reception at

Our wedding portrait in typical Chinese style.
Trev Sue-A-Quan.

the Friendship Hotel with a large number of the foreign experts and old China hands attending. I had retained my British citizenship, even while in the U.S., and not long after we were married we went to the British Embassy where Xiaoli was registered as a British subject and had to swear allegiance to the Queen.

Products in China at that time were not abundant. We had a book of ration tickets to get rice and flour from a nearby depot, as well as coupons allowing us a small bottle of milk per day. Meat was also rationed and Cadre Li's wife would let us know when pork was scheduled to arrive at the neighborhood shop where she worked. As winter came closer, Cadre Li asked how many cabbages we would be needing. Xiaoli explained that the wintertime ritual in Beijing was for each household to stock up a huge pile of cabbages to provide the only source of fresh greens. While the outer leaves of the cabbage might dry up over time, the inner core remained intact and "fresh" for consumption. We decided to order 150 jin – 75 kilograms – and piled them on our balcony, where they occupied a significant amount of available space. Actually, the amount we bought was much smaller than what most families would get for themselves.[3]

---

3   It was not unusual for families to buy 500 to 1,000 jin of the inexpensive long-stalk cabbages, to last through four wintry months.

Tons of cabbages are brought into Beijing by cart to provide residents with a supply of vegetables to last through the Winter. *Trev Sue-A-Quan.*

The reason for taking such a small quantity was that, as a foreigner, I carried a "Special Privilege Card" which allowed me into the Friendship Store, a place normally reserved for tourists, diplomats and high-ranking officials.

There we could get other kinds of vegetables, such as carrots, celery, potatoes, tomatoes, radishes, as well as a better selection of fruits and meat. The Friendship Store also stocked a full range of consumer goods – towels, clothing, bicycles, toys, batteries, household items, artwork, carpets, etc., – that could also be purchased in regular stores all across the city. The one big difference was the service provided by the store clerks. At the Friendship Store the attendants were generally polite and attentive to the needs of the customer. However, the regular department stores were populated with some indifferent clerks who cared not a hoot if you bought an item or not. Sometimes a pair of them would be chatting at the far end of the counter and a significant amount of hailing would be required to gain their attention.

The Friendship Store became the source of a novel imported item – motor scooters (mopeds) from Japan – and I went there to buy two of them. Xiaoli was still completing her studies at Normal University, which was at the other end of the city, so the scooter came in handy to get around a little faster. We bought safety helmets and during the winter we would be amply cloaked with coats, gloves, and long scarves to protect ourselves from the chilling wind. We would use the scooters to venture further than we would normally have done on bicycles, although we had to monitor the gas gauge closely because there were only a limited number of gas stations in Beijing. We were provided with coupons to buy gas even though we would be buying only a gallon at the most. We stored the scooters in one of the research rooms at the Institute, which was at ground level.

The existence of the Friendship Store was an overt display of discrimination practiced in China. Ordinary Chinese citizens had to deal as best they could with ration coupons, long line-ups and an insufficiency of goods, with patience being a necessary attribute. The extension of privileges to high-ranking officials provided these VIPs with the ability to maintain a somewhat higher standard of living. At the same time it was assumed that people from abroad could afford to pay a higher amount for some goods and services. As one example, two-tiered entrance fees were instituted for the parks and ancient palaces, with different booths set up to sell the same right of entry to locals and foreigners, separately. The guards at the gate would keep their eyes open for those people they felt, because of either attire or mannerism, were not local Chinese. Because of this, Xiaoli would be the one to buy the cheaper entrance tickets.

One of a pair of Yahama scooters that extended our range of mobility in Beijing. *Trev Sue-A-Quan.*

Even so, there were occasions when the guard would challenge Xiaoli, asking what kind of person I was as we walked in together. Since my ability with Chinese was sufficient to understand the query, I would quickly interject, "What kind of person do I look like?" and continue to walk past his stunned countenance. Overseas Chinese were frequently caught in this form of ethnic scrutiny. One of the popular derogatory remarks was to call someone a "fake Overseas Chinese," meaning that the speaker felt that, in observing some aspect of dress or materialism, it was a China-born resident pretending to come from abroad by behaving in an ostentatious fashion. Such remarks were heard when we rode our scooters around Beijing.

Another gadget that we acquired was a telephone in our home. This privilege was usually reserved for high-ranking officials and army officers, but now phones were being made available to ordinary citizens, at a cost of some 3000 yuan for hook-up. My Institute was able to obtain a connection as a branch circuit, but which required new lines to be run to the apartment. The cost for us was 400 yuan. This was a great convenience, because the only other way to phone others was from the office during work hours. At the unit (apartment building) that Xiaoli's parents lived there was one telephone at the gate of the compound serving more than a hundred households. If a phone call came in, the gate attendant would go near to the appropriate building and shout out the name of the family (or unit number) and the party in question would go out to the gate to take the call. The quality of the telephone connections left much to be desired, sometimes requiring so much shouting that I would wonder if any phone equipment was needed for the other party to hear the caller. One "modern" offshoot of having a phone was that we began to get nuisance calls. The phone would ring, usually at lunchtime, but whoever was calling never spoke a word. We tried to get the Institute to trace the calls but this was unsuccessful. The phenomenon lasted a few months.

Our son David playing with the telephone. *Trev Sue-A-Quan.*

One day in 1980, I saw in the *Beijing Evening News* a photo of a Chinese person with a steelband pan. This of course caught my attention and I telephoned the person in question. He explained that he had seen and heard a steelband that was on tour, most likely part of the entourage during a visit by Dr. Eric Williams, prime minister of Trinidad. He was fascinated and decided to start his own made-in-China steelband. He fashioned the pans himself and, after much experimentation to get some instruments that produced acceptable sounds, he started a band. I invited the fellow to my apartment and a few days later he showed up with a rusty tenor pan. It was apparent to me that his pan had some shortcomings. The indentation was too shallow to produce a thin enough surface necessary for the high notes, and although the bumps did emit various notes they were rather clunky in nature. He explained that his dream was to visit the Caribbean, particularly Trinidad, and so he was glad to learn that I hailed from that part of the world. He told me that his band would be playing at a concert in a few weeks and wondered if I would attend. I accepted and he said he would get me tickets. I didn't try playing his pan because the notes were laid out in a pattern of his own choosing and I wasn't captivated by the less-than-melodic sounds produced from striking the notes.

The bandmaster informed me that he didn't have a collection of steelband music. In fact, neither did I, but his enthusiasm prompted me to call the Guyana Embassy. I spoke with Maureen Fraser, the Econonic, Trade and Cultural Officer, and was invited over to visit her and her husband George. We reminisced on people we knew in common from Georgetown, and I was lent a cassette tape of steelband music. I made a copy of the tape for the Chinese pan man and called to inform him of my efforts. He didn't express his feelings one way or another but on learning that I now needed four tickets he said that he would get them for me.

On the day of the performance, my wife and I joined Maureen and George to head off to the grand sports stadium where the concert was being held. We found ourselves in some of the higher elevation seats, some distance from the center where the performers went through their acts. There were Chinese instrumental bands, dancing and singing. We waited patiently for the much-anticipated steelband. As it turned out, it was the very last act. Out came the various pans and they were set up just like a normal West Indian steel orchestra. Then the band played. It was not any tune that was recognizable as having a West Indian origin. And rather than the syncopated beat of a calypso that would produce the fast-pulsating "ka-CHING-a-ling" rhythm, the band played with the emphasis on the last beat, resulting in a more pedantic "ka-lunk-a-DUNK" lilt that was appropriate for the northwestern region of China (Xinjiang Province), where the influence of Middle Eastern culture had penetrated along the Silk Road. It would appear that the music man had brought one of his prototype pans when he had visited my apartment, because the sounds coming from the pans at the concert were quite good; the music was not unpleasant, just unfamiliar. When the few tunes that the band played had ended, there was minimal applause. I reckon

George and Maureen Fraser, Guyana's Econonic, Trade and Cultural Officer, at our apartment. *Trev Sue-A-Quan.*

that the Chinese masses may have felt that the music was not unfamiliar, just unpleasant.

We were glad to have had the opportunity to hear the band and I tried to contact the fellow to give him the cassette tape and some advice about the rhythm. But my calls went unanswered. I don't know if he felt that I was just pretending to know about pan and really was incompetent to play anything on the instrument that he had spent countless hours trying to make. I rather suspect that he may have learned that I was a "foreign expert" and those were times when Chinese citizens' contacts with foreigners were regarded with some suspicion, or fostered with caution. If that were really the case then the fact that I had gotten the Embassy of Guyana involved must have caused him real concern. In any event, I did not hear from him again and I never learnt the fate of the budding Chinese home-grown steelband, nor that of the innovative pan man.

In 1980, my parents and two aunts made plans to visit China for the first time. Xiaoli and I went down to greet them in Guangzhou (Canton). She remained there while I crossed over to Hong Kong to meet the family. There, as wedding luxuries, I bought two Citizen wristwatches as well as a refrigerator, which I requested to be shipped directly to Beijing. We took the train to Guangzhou and stayed at one of the hostels belonging to the Ministry of Coal. These accommodations were modest in price but also modest in amenities. One aunt had caught a cold on her way to China and found that the squat toilets were below her comfort level, and so she returned to Canada. The rest of us traveled north by train, visiting Shanghai, Suzhou, and Nanjing on our way to Beijing. Their visit to China was a somewhat rugged but enjoyable experience and my parents were appreciative of the opportunity to see the land of their ancestors.

It was in the land of our ancestors that my interest in family roots began. Before leaving Chicago, a cousin, Delbert Sue-A-Quan, paid me a visit and handed me a document of great significance. Knowing of my imminent departure for China, he gave me a copy of the contract of indenture for our great-grandfather, dated 1873. Delbert thought that this material would be of interest to me. It clarified several things, one being that the family surname is Su, and that great-grandfather was one of the thousands of Chinese who were introduced into Guyana to work on the sugar plantations as indentured labourers. Furthermore, he was accompanied by his wife, and a nine-year-old son, my grandfather. From the Chinese characters on the document it became apparent that

Trev's parents in Suzhou.
Trev Sue-A-Quan

it was from grandfather's full name that the family surname Sue-A-Quan was derived. I went to the Beijing Library and noticed that it carried a few books in English relevant to Chinese immigration in the 19th century. One was entitled "The Chinese in British Guiana," by Cecil Clementi. It was published in 1915, but even after so many years the book was in excellent condition, apparently not having had many hands touch it.

There were several other "Returned Overseas Chinese" of various ages, mainly of Taiwanese origin, who had also decided to go to China. The government created an association for Taiwan compatriots and although I did not belong to that category, it was the closest fit that could be found for me. The association was provided with tickets to concerts, plays and receptions, such as for a grand celebration at the Great Hall of the People for National Day. Our group was also taken on vacation to various places – Beidaihe (the seaside resort nearest to Beijing), Chengde, an ancient imperial city during the Qing dynasty, Qingdao, the important port city of Shandong Province. At these outings we were accompanied by various attendants who made arrangements for our accommodations and sightseeing. They also encouraged us to put forward opinions on how to make China a better place, a better society, playing a more important role in world affairs. Invariably, the response we gave was to pursue the

Chengde, 230 kilometers north-east of Beijing, was the summer resort of Qing dynasty emperors. *Trev Sue-A-Quan.*

course of modernization as vigorously as possible, through which an improvement of the economy and people's standard of living could be realized. Whether or not these opinions were heeded by the authorities is not public knowledge.

Changes were coming about in China. The blue "Mao" jackets worn by every male began to give way to color and style, with TV personalities and political leaders appearing in Western-style suits with ties. Change for women was also in progress, with more varieties and colors of dresses, and less rigid hairstyles. An English language newspaper, *China Daily*, was launched, signaling a greater openness to foreigners and foreign affairs. Many Chinese used this paper to try to increase their English skills and vocabulary. Ration coupons for cotton cloth were no longer needed and rice coupons also became a thing of the past. More products, and a greater variety of them, were appearing on store shelves. The stretchable plastic mesh bags that the residents commonly carried around to hold their purchases would quickly be filled. Artisans appeared regularly in the neighborhood, singing out the services they provided – sharpening knives, or repairing punctured pots and pans. The pop-rice seller found ready customers among the children who delighted in watching him place the rice grains into a sealed pot, which he then rotated above a portable gas burner until the grains popped. The lid was then

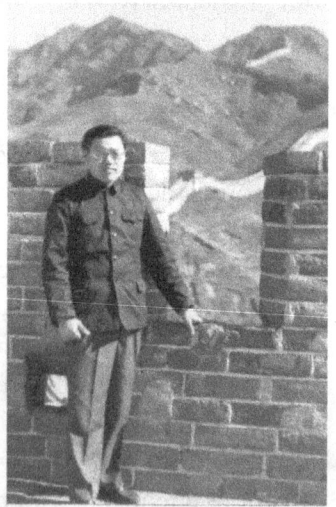

In China the "Mao" jacket is known as the Sun Yat-sen jacket. *Trev Sue-A-Quan.*

opened into a cloth bag, giving off a loud bang – this was the Chinese variant of popcorn. Hawkers would come by regularly, selling peanuts or tofu from trays mounted on the back of their bicycles. Liquefied petroleum gas, supplied in short tubby canisters, became an available alternative for cooking in household kitchens, and gradually replaced the polluting and inefficient coal-fired stoves. Privately-run restaurants were opened, some of them utilizing former bomb shelters or even the tiny living rooms of the operators. At street corners, individual bakers sold their bread and pastries from three-wheeled pedi-carts. Other sellers offered books, soap, yogurt, or other miscellaneous items.

A new self-service store opened at the major intersection near our home. It was such a novelty that there were long lines of people waiting to get in. However they soon discovered that the products available were mainly canned and bottled foods that could be purchased anywhere, although on occasion there would be batches of vegetables, fruit, pork or belt fish that provided some choice for the customers. The only really novel thing about the store it was the elimination of the rude attendants. But even the clerks at the regular stores were now admonished to be polite and attentive to customers. Not far away from the neighborhood self-service shop, a "free market" opened up for farmers to sell their produce. This was a much more interesting place to buy foodstuffs. There were live chickens and ducks, eggs, fruits and vegetables in good supply, spices, peppers, plus candied fruits, and roasted sweet yams, taken hot from the barrel of coals. Housemaids, many from the countryside of Anhui Province, became commonplace, attending to the needs of busy working couples, doing the cooking, and taking care of infants. Household gadgets and luxury items such as washing machines, fridges, and color TV sets appeared on the market. Construction of tall buildings was going on all over the city, for hotels, business offices and apartments. Roads and overpasses were being built at a furious pace. Japanese cars and trucks, particularly Toyota and Nissan models, started to appear in significant numbers. Grass was planted in many parks, looking initially like lonely patches set in a chessboard pattern; the intent was to beautify the place and reduce airborne dust. Maxim's de Paris offered haute cuisine, not far distant from – and somewhat over – the enshrined body of Chairman Mao Zedong at Tian An Men Square. More airlines were granted landing rights in China and a large number of tourists streamed into the country. Billboards advertising imported products appeared along the streets, and a number of films from abroad were being shown at the cinemas, after being dubbed with Mandarin voices. Many more translations of books by foreign writers could be bought.

There was an increased interest in non-Chinese things and English quickly overtook Russian as the preferred foreign language. Some of the members at my Institute wanted to improve their pronunciation and a small coaching session was organized. We used a textbook called English 900, created in England and containing 900 sentences with increasing degree of difficulty, accompanied by explanation of the use of the words and sentences. For many Chinese, there were definitely some combinations that were difficult for them to master, such as the "th-" sound in "there," or properly pronouncing words beginning with the letter R. Among the learners was a fellow from Guangdong Province who would say "sh-" for a word starting with "s-." In this way, "socks" would become "shocks," and "said" sounded like "shed." This became a big problem when he needed to say, "Please sit." I carefully enunciated the words, and repeated them for him: "sit . . . sit . . . sit," but his response was a determined effort that had more to do with a certain consequence of sitting. I also was asked to coach a group of four recently-graduated teachers of English at the Institute of Chemical Technology, where Xiaoli was assigned to be a teacher. She was included among those students in my special class. We discussed both historical events and current affairs, although I tried to stay away from topics that had a political bias either towards the West or towards China. The important thing was to discuss the use of language and the meanings of words in different contexts.

In my own sphere of activity, some good results were obtained in the research work. A new type of catalyst was created that was considerably better, and less expensive, than the most active catalyst acknowledged for coal gasification. We continued to work on refining the process. Eventually we reached a stage where some generalized announcements could be made about the new development. In the changing environment of more openness in China, the Patent Office was reactivated and my engineering assistant and I went there to explore the possibilities of applying for a patent. To make things clear, I asked her to explain our achievements while I waited a short distance away. While the Patent Office was physically open, it appeared that minds there were still closed, because my assistant was asked why we wanted to have a patent, and whether the real motivation was to get an excuse for me to go abroad.

Ways of thinking in China were still rather restrained and this became apparent in the way our new scientific discovery was received. I requested that the next step be pursued, requiring larger and more expensive facilities. This was acknowledged but my project was regarded as too novel a proposal and the long-term plans could not readily accommodate such a late entry. It was already four years since I arrived in China and although some pieces of equipment were being collected to continue further research, it seemed as if the project was being hindered from lack of political and administrative support. The inertia, or lack of it, was dragging my research to a crawl. The established engineers in the institute would have been risking their careers if they were to support my newfangled process which, admittedly, needed considerably more research and expenditures before it could become commercially viable, if ever. Instead they backed ongoing research on more established gasifiers, including ones that were invented prior to World War I.

In February 1983, the Vice-Director of my Institute and I paid a visit to the U.S. on a scientific investigative tour. We attended a conference on instrumentation and I visited various companies active in coal research to exchange ideas and be updated on research developments. One such company, SNC, one of the largest Canadian design-engineering companies expressed interest in taking my catalytic gasification concept to the next stage – a pilot plant that would be set up in Canada.

Towards the end of 1983, my father suffered a stroke, his second, and Xiaoli and I felt we ought to go to Canada as soon as we could. With a family that now included a son, born in February 1983, we applied to the Canadian Embassy for the necessary immigration papers. On 16 April 1984 we left China via Hong Kong and took a jet plane from there to Canada, by way of Chicago. It was five years to the day that I had spent in China.

Practical Accounting

Joe Pierre

Frederick "Joe" Pierre was born in 1928 in the North West District of British Guiana and grew up with his grandmother, Maria Chan-A-Sue, who was one of those who took care of Joe after his mother died when he was just 3 years old.

Even before emigrating in 1973, Joe spent his adult life working for different foreign companies based in Guyana, gaining experience that continued to be a great asset in Canada.

* * * * * * * *

I started school in October 1939 in the North West, but only attended 2½ years of elementary school. In July 1942 I managed to achieve the primary school-leaving certificate at age 14, the highest level of education available in the countryside at that time. I began to work as an assistant to my cousin Sonny Chan-A-Sue in his general store, while my grandmother Maria instilled the value of hard work. This was at Mabaruma, and I after that went to Georgetown in March 1944 in search of a job.

Wilfred Golding Stoll, my second cousin, was then the chief accountant for Bookers Timber Company Ltd. and he got a job for me, at $20 a month, to work as a general clerk at Wineperu (win-e-PEA-roo), some 30 to 40 miles upstream from Bartica on the Essequibo River. The Second World War was coming to an end and I was penniless when I went up there. Stoll suggested that I improve myself by taking postal tuition lessons from abroad, as he himself had done through the Bennett College based in England.

At Wineperu I was doing the bookkeeping work, as well as running the ration store. Even though I was just out of school, I had some experience from working at Sonny Chan-A-Sue's shop, the only general store in the region. In those days in a Chinese-run shop, especially in the

The Chan-A-Sue family shop in Mabaruma. *Joe Pierre.*

outlying areas, you had to give credit – allowing customers to charge their purchases on account, and receiving payment later. We kept a notebook for each person that we gave credit to, such as the doctors, nurses, District Commissioner, policemen, clerks and many others. They would bring along a written slip, and we would write up the items they required in their respective passbooks, file away that slip and then at the end of the month they would come and pay after we showed them the passbook. It was a debit and credit system, and that's how I got my first basic knowledge about bookkeeping. While I was working in the general store in my earlier days, my aunt had to go off to help out when Sonny was in the orange fields and on the farm and I would be the one to help to write up the books. So when I went to Wineperu, I knew quite well what debits and credits meant.

In 1946, Stoll became the Commissioner of Inland Revenue. He sent me one of the accounting journals that he used to receive through being a member of the accounting association. He was the first Guyanese to be qualified as a Certified and Corporate Accountant, a stage below the Institute of Chartered Accountants. Stoll recommended two schools to me – one was the Metropolitan College in St. Alban's, England and the other was the School of Accountancy in Glasgow. With so many ships being sunk during the war, we used to get a ship arriving in British Guiana only once a month. So I decided that if I wanted to get through the courses quickly I would have to take the elementary stage of bookkeeping, commercial arithmetic, as well as business machinery and practice from the Metropolitan College, while, at the same time, taking the advanced accountancy stage from the School of Accountancy in Glasgow. It took me about two years because I might send off about 6 to 8 papers to be marked before I could get back the corrected results from an earlier one. There was nobody around with the knowledge

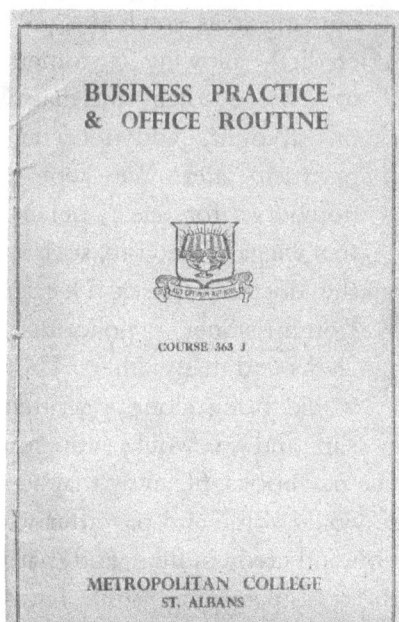

BUSINESS PRACTICE
& OFFICE ROUTINE

COURSE 363 J

METROPOLITAN COLLEGE
ST. ALBANS

Course manuals from St. Albans Metropolitan College consisted of mimeographed sheets of typewritten text. *Joe Pierre.*

to guide me, so it was very, very difficult to understand where I was going wrong. Yet I was getting about 96% in the elementary course, and in the second one – the more advanced course – I got somewhere around 80%. One of the problems I had was how to arrange a balance sheet. In the English system you had to list the liabilities first, on the left hand side, and on the right hand side you would write down the assets. You put the fixed assets first, then the current assets in order of convertibility into cash, e.g. cash on hand, then stock in trade, book debts, and investments. Ten years later I went to work at Fitzpatrick, Graham & Co., the only firm of chartered accounts in the colony, and I appreciated the experience of the correspondence courses. One problem I had was in transactions of stocks and bonds. Having never gone to high school I didn't learn any Latin, so I didn't know the difference between "cum div" and "ex div." When you buy cum div it means that you are entitled to the accrued interest or income on those stocks or bonds up to the date you're buying it. So therefore you had to make a journal entry treating the accrued dividends or interest as income and debiting back that amount so as to get the true capital cost of the asset; otherwise you would be overstating the value of the asset, and understating your income.

The courses cost me about $300, including books, and there were some real difficulties. When the marked papers were returned to me, addressed to British Guiana, some of them were sent by the U.K. Post Office to Guinea, in Africa, and then they were redirected to me. There were no gas lamps available when I was studying and so I had to study with a bottle lamp – essentially a bottle with kerosene and a wick made

View from Wineperu, overlooking the Essequibo River. *Joe Pierre.*

from newspaper or a piece of cloth – and try and do as much work as I could during the day, after I had finished doing company work. This was the situation at Wineperu and Arawai, both located some 150 miles up the Essequibo River. At Arawai, conditions were worse, because the logging workers' campground had moved about ten miles down the creek and I used to see them only once a week. I, and a 12- to 14-year old black boy from Buxton, who used to cook the meals and help me in the shop, were the only ones there. This lasted for about six months until one night a huge jaguar came and snatched a stray dog that had liked to come near the shop for safety. I was too young to be permitted to own a firearm and immediately after that incident I requested a transfer or else I would quit. A temporary supply store, with living quarters, was set up at the workers' camp and I worked there until the area was cleared of all the previously-cut logs.

The job at Wineperu and Arawai was with Bookers Timber Company Limited. They were the suppliers to the British admiralty, the major buyers for the war effort, and would haul greenheart piles and huge hewn square timbers. It was primarily a log trade. I had to record all the measurements and calculate the cubic contents because the truckers were paid according to the cubic foot, or the lineal foot for piles. Later, I was in charge of the Machine Utility Stores where they had the tractor spare parts, fuel, etc., and I used to go around and make myself familiar with the items. We had logging trucks, Caterpillar tractors, International tractors, and so forth, so I learnt the names and functions of the various replacement parts. I could tell you what a clutch throw-out bearing was, a clutch pressure plate, high-tension coil, distributor cap, rotor, spark plugs, and so on. After four years at Bookers, I quit the job, at the end of 1948.

Before WWII, Wilfred Stoll had been employed by an American company, the Greenheart Lumber Company, in the lower Essequibo River. When it became time for him to sit the final accountancy exam in Georgetown the company refused to give him time off, so he quit the job. He felt it was racially motivated, but he never took any real malice against them. In those days, the prevailing attitude was: If you black, stand back; if you brown, stick around; if you white, you all right. After passing the exam, he applied to become the chief account for Bookers Timber Company and was offered the position at $98 a month. Meanwhile, the wharfinger, Ferdie Glasford, who was of fair complexion, was getting $120 a month. That's why Stoll quit and he went to work for the government for over $140 a month after an advertisement was placed for the first time in 1946 for Senior Income Tax Inspectors.

When I left Bookers Timber Co. in 1948, I applied to the Colonial Development Corporation,[1] which had just bought out E.S. Sills' timber operations at Manaka (man-AH-ka), closer to the mouth of the Essequibo River. The finance director for CDC was a chap named Cecil Yarnton Mills. He took me on because I had the experience that they wanted for running the supply stores and so forth. The stores were in a complete mess. Mills visited Manaka shortly after I arrived and I brought to his attention that there were no records showing quantities or values. He agreed with my assessment and decided to start from scratch. So we piled up the items in the middle of the store and with Mills holding a pad of paper in his hand, I told him what the items were as well as the quantities. Mills was so impressed, he right away told the manager

1   The Colonial Development Corporation was founded in 1948, with its board members appointed by United Kingdom's Secretary of State for Foreign and Commonwealth Affairs. The purpose was to assist economic development in underdeveloped countries by making investments into developmentally sound business enterprises that would contribute positively to national development.

to raise my pay by ten dollars a month, and appointed me Head Stores Clerk.

In 1949, the CDC acquired the entire logging operations of Bookers Timber Company Ltd. at Wineperu, an area of some 1,200 square miles and known as the Bartica Triangle, and also the sawmills at La

Logging operations at Wineperu.
Joe Pierre.

Penitence, in Georgetown, and Stampa Island in the Essequibo River. Also in 1949, the CDC appointed Steel Brothers & Co. Ltd. as managing agents of CDC's timber investments in British Guiana. This English transnational company's main interest was in the Middle and Far East, involving the extraction and milling of teak logs, primarily in Burma before that colony became independent. A local company, British Guiana Timbers Ltd., was incorporated. In 1951, after spending millions of dollars at the Manaka site on extending the rail line and building extensive housing and facilities for both executive and subordinate staff, Steel Brothers recommended to the CDC that the Manaka timber concession would not be a financially viable operation, and that it be sold to A.M. Fredericks Ltd. so that they could concentrate on developing the Bartica Triangle while a modern band-saw mill was being built at Houston, East Bank Demerara. After the Houston mill was completed in early 1954, the La Penitence mill was sold to Toolsie Persaud for $70,000. Before the end of 1958 both Fredericks and Persaud became millionaires from the very favorable deals they were given by Steel's executives, causing the local workers to say, CDC stands for "Cash Don't Count."

After the Makaka operations ceased in 1951, I was sent back to Wineperu as Head Stores Clerk, under Steel Bros. I was amazed at the dramatic changes that had taken place since I left in 1948. From a few huts at the riverside, it was now a modern village with hundreds of houses and infrastructure facilities in the process of construction. At Manaka I had a staff of two persons and now I had 20.

Steel Brothers & Co. was paid 3% on the money they spent in addition

A welding plant mounted on a railway car used by CDC at Manaka. *Joe Pierre.*

to a management fee, which, I think, was about 10,000 pounds sterling per annum. The result was that they bought a lot of white elephants, things that even a visiting World Bank representative told them were a waste of money. All they knew about was how to extract teak in Burma, India, and Thailand with elephants and the wood would float. Greenheart and most of the hardwoods in South America do not float. They brought in a lot of machinery and trucks that were a complete failure. Eventually, after several years of continuous financial losses, the CDC, in 1955, sent down Gwyn Bowen-Jones, a Welshman who was a Certified and Corporate Accountant from their British Honduras Fruit Company operations. The forest manager for Steel Brothers, Jack Barnard, who was half Burmese and half white, treated him like the plague and he left me to take him around the forest operations and explain the forest accounting system. In those days they used to keep the forest accounts in Georgetown and it took six months before the forest manager could know what his costs were. I took Bowen-Jones around to wherever he wanted to go, and answered his questions about the forest extraction system, how we dealt with stores, etc. When Bowen-Jones went back, he wrote a scathing report, recommending that CDC cancel the management agreement with Steel Brothers and retain just two guys, the Wineperu forest manager, Barnard, and the forest manager in Georgetown, Philip Howe. Bowen-Jones also said that I was capable of producing the forest accounts within days at Wineperu, which proved to be right, because we set the cut-off date for accounting purposes at the 26th of the month, and by the 1st of the following month the forest manager knew what his costs per mile were, and for each stage – felling, trucking, tractor hauling, and at the inland beach, plus what it cost FOB loaded on the pontoons. The

result was that after six months
into the year, I was instructed to
prepare the working estimate for
the following year based on that
first half-year, for it to be sent
for approval by CDC's offices in
London.

Bowen-Jones said that under
the old system all the accounting
information given to the forest
manager was historical whereas
with the new cost-accounting
system transferred to Wineperu,
management would be able to

Joe Pierre in front of his residence at
Wineperu after his promotion to executive staff. *Joe Pierre.*

pinpoint within days where problems were occurring and could take
corrective measures much earlier. In particular the downtime for tractors,
trucks and machinery was significantly reduced. After my first year with
CDC, we started to make a profit. And that's how I got my first bonus.

After working for Steel Bros. for about five years, I decided to apply
for an overseer's position on any of Bookers' sugar estates. Bookers
asked Barnard for a reference, but Barnard wanted me to stay and offered
$20 per month more if I would agree to him replying to Bookers that
I was no longer interested. I told him to give an honest reference, and
when Bookers replied then I would decide. Barnard then spoke with the
forest manager, Mr. Howe and Mr. H.W. Gray, the general manager in
Georgetown, and they decided to appoint me to the executive staff of
CDC in April 1954.

In 1957, after about two years under direct control by CDC, I went
for my first three months' vacation. On my return Barnard told me that
he had suggested to head office management that I should be transferred
to the remote Ikuribisci camp to work and live. Well, that was never
in the initial arrangement and I would also be required to do the field
manager's job along with forest accountant and get the least amount of
pay. Around 1956 while Bruce Farrar had been working at Wineperu,
his father, Cecil Frederick Farrar, visited and as his firm was the auditors
of B.G. Timbers Ltd., C.F. Farrar took the opportunity of reviewing

the cost-accounting system with me. After this, Bruce told me that his father was very impressed with my ability and should I ever decide to leave Wineperu, he would offer me employment. Now that I was being requested to leave Wineperu under dubious circumstances, I wrote to Bruce Farrar and he apparently showed the letter to his father. The next thing I knew, I was invited to an interview with Fitzpatrick, Graham and Company, a prestigious accounting firm, the only firm of chartered accountants in British Guiana since 1905, for which Mr. Cecil F. Farrar was a senior partner.

I went for the interview on Christmas Eve of 1957 and Farrar introduced me to the other two partners and then sent a letter by messenger to my home in Georgetown that same day confirming that they would take me on immediately or they would wait for the three-months notice required under my employment contract. In fact the letter arrived at my residence by messenger even before I myself returned home. Fitzpatrick, Graham did the auditing for all the major businesses in the country. I joined the company in April 1958 as a senior audit clerk, and within a year I was made an audit manager. From 1 January 1959, Farrar decided that I would take over some of Russell Rickford's audits so that Rickford could pay more attention to the Bookers' Industrial Holdings Group.

I took over audits of BG & Trinidad Mutual Life and Fire Insurance Companies as well as the Demerara Mutual Life Assurance Society. That was when I got to put into practice purchasing and selling of investments, cum div and ex div, and I at last saw where I was going wrong when I was taking postal tuition some 10 years earlier.

The auditing procedures were improved when Farrar in 1960 introduced an internal control and accounting questionnaire, which allowed us to do examinations on test-check bases. One day, Farrar asked me to get out the Demerara Mutual Life file, and go back about five years previously to see where he had written down some concerns about the control over printed premiums receivable. Demerara Mutual had branches in Trinidad and Barbados, and agencies in Grenada, St. Vincent, Dominica, Monserrat, and Antigua. While applying the accounting control questionnaire I noticed that the entries in the cashbooks at the head office were merely transcribed entries of bank deposit slips reported by personnel at the branches or agencies. There was no accounting control over the cash receipts and the premiums received – no actual receipts were being submitted to the head office to show that all payments on the mortgages and loans had been made, and this practice had been going on for years. When the examination was finished, we wrote a report that was about 5 to 7 pages long, pointing out the grave weaknesses in accounting and control. This was about August 1960.

Sometime around September or October somebody in Barbados sent an anonymous letter to the Demerara Mutual Life head office raising some concerns about the handling of mortgages and premiums, etc. and that letter was tossed into the garbage. Now the actuary for Demerara Mutual Life Assurance Society was a white man named E.N. Pelham, in England. Farrar had on more than one occasion expressed to Pelham his misgivings over the accounting control of these printed premiums receivable, but nothing was done by the Society to correct these shortcomings. As it turned out, a copy of the letter from this anonymous person was sent to Pelham, and right away he forwarded it to Farrar, who sent a coded message to the partner in Barbados, requesting that a surprise cash count be carried out immediately. The investigators found that the originals of the receipts for payments on thousands of insurance premiums, mortgages and loans on policy were issued but these very payments were not reported to head office and consequently the policy records in Georgetown showed the payments to be still outstanding. The duplicates of the receipts were found in the Barbados office, stashed away in drawers and boxes, but the monies received were never deposited in the bank. What was happening was that two women bookkeepers were receiving the payments and they had devised a scheme to rip off the company.

A retired secretary/accountant of Demerara Mutual, Hugh Cannon, was called back to do a special investigation. He and Ruth Fowler were sent to Barbados and they checked every policy holder to verify that the original receipt was in his or her possession but for which the premiums were never deposited. When totaled up, it was a hundred and sixty odd thousand dollars. They learnt that these two women were pocketing the renewals of premiums for their own use. The insurance would not lapse, but the premiums for these policies were noted as not paid, in arrears, or being late. When the payment due date came up again – annually, semi-annually, quarterly or monthly – these ladies would take the renewal premium and apply it to cover the amount due for the previous period, while they themselves contributed the interest penalty accrued on the overdue payment. This practice of letting premiums lapse for a while was not uncommon because there were people who couldn't afford to pay the full amount at one time. In the case of life insurance policies there was often a residual cash value, so the late payments were not vigorously pursued. But the women were committing fraud, enriching themselves and hiding the crime. In the English auditing system this is called teeming and lading – delaying the submission of deposits and altering the payment slips relating to subsequent deposits – in essence, this is like digging a hole to fill a hole. This situation arose because Fitzpatrick, Graham could examine the records only at the Society's head office in Georgetown and was not authorized to check the records at the branches and agencies. When Cannon came back, he shook my hand, and he said, "Mr. Pierre, a very good job you have done. Thank you."

I could tell you many more stories like this, with the same sort of nonsense. Anyway, the three senior partners at Fitzpatrick Graham retired. Farrar left first, followed by Milliken and then Ridler. Ridler left in 1966, the year of Guyana's independence. There were other fellows from England who came in as partners, but in my estimation, they were not of the same caliber as the original three. Shortly before 1970 when I was doing an audit for the Demerara Oxygen Company Limited, (Docol), I chatted with William Lieu, the assistant manager/accountant there. I told him I was getting fed up with the management at Fitzpatrick, Graham, and if Docol had a vacancy I would consider working for them. Some time went by, then suddenly out of the blue Stan Wilson, the manager of Docol, phoned me. I went for an interview with him and he offered me this newly-created post – chief accountant – starting April 1970.

Docol, a privately-owned company founded by an American and a Scotsman from Trinidad, wanted to increase the price of the various gases that they were manufacturing. They had to go to the Ministry of

Trade and Industry to get permission to raise prices, but they couldn't produce the relevant costing data to get approval. The rate of exchange was varying and the Guyana dollar dropping. Docol could only calculate the price for calcium carbide, used to make acetylene, and for caustic soda, used for oxygen manufacture, and so on – the raw materials. But as far as costs of manufacture and other expenses were concerned, no figures were available. In fact, the management of finances was done by calling Barclay's Bank on Monday morning to find out how much was in the account. Wilson was going on feedback from his secretaries and learnt that the staff was getting fed up and wanted to join a union. Well I don't believe in that kind of management; you can't run a company on favoritism and nepotism – that's when you are looking for problems. So I accepted the job and the first thing that hit me was seeing the mess they were in. There were four clerks doing records of their cylinders, and another four doing the store records, all six months or more in arrears.

Docol had some 2½ million dollars worth in cylinders but sometimes they had to shut the plant down because they didn't have any cylinders available, even with these four chaps – two in the day and two at night, 24 hours a day – working on records. The records were kept on an NCR machine, and, being six months in arrears, this information was virtually useless to the company and to the customers as well. In addition to that the inventory consisted of about 10,000 items in about six different locations and they couldn't tell the inventory, and what was where. Right away, just like at CDC, I set up different operating accounts, one for the oxygen/acetylene, one for carbon dioxide. But the big headache was to split the assets, because all they had was one lump sum figure for plant and machinery, so I had to split these as best as possible. Secondly, I got the cylinder records put on computer. Then I reduced the clerical staff from four to two, making one an internal auditor who had to go to each branch to take inventory twice per year to satisfy our auditors – this is called a perpetual inventory system.

It was through this re-organization of accounts management that we noticed that the branch where Arnold Chee-A-Tow was the manager was losing an abnormal amount of items, including regulators for oxygen and acetylene welding. These things were about $500 a piece.

Nobody could figure out what was going on and, poor Arnold, he was brought to head office with DeCaries taking over. But the losses persisted. Now there were only three people working at that branch – DeCaries and two others – and one of them felt that it was the janitor, the cleaning woman, who was stealing these things. So a requisition was sent to restock this Georgetown branch with regulators from the main store at Eccles and they began to watch the movements of the janitor and the regulators. It was noticed that the regulators displayed in the showcase were untouched and the items were disappearing only from the unopened boxes kept in the back store. So one day, immediately after the janitor left the storeroom, one of the managers went in to check the boxes, and indeed a regulator was missing. When she had gone past the gate, they summoned her back and had her empty the bucket. There, covered by the dirty wash-water, was the regulator. This woman was stealing these things and selling them for $15 each to a Chinese fellow who ran a general store. She was fired, and, mind you, everybody in the company used to get 15-months pay each year, because they all would get an extra month's pay as a bonus every four months, but apparently this was still not good enough for her.

A similar situation was uncovered at Mackenzie. There were these big crawler draglines with 15-, 20-cubic yard buckets that came in for repairs. While the crawler was in motion, the driver had to have the bucket up in the air so that he could see ahead. So when the repairs were done, the bucket would be raised as it passed through the security gate. There were two security guards who would scrutinize the cabin area, but they didn't think about having the bucket lowered for inspection. It was these very buckets that were hauling away generators, coils of wire, 400-amp cables, equipment, and all manner of things, right over the noses of the security guards.

Control and accounting for the gas cylinders was also a big headache. So I introduced a deposit method. A cost deposit of $110 was set for each cylinder and then the rental fee would be waived. Within the first nine months the cylinders started to appear and we also collected $110,000 in cylinder rental – all this was money previously going down the drain and we had been considering that another building the size of the entire plant might be needed for storing more cylinders. Before this time various small repair shops used to get the cylinders when the employees of our major customers sold them on the side. The repair shops then discarded the empty cylinders, sometimes by the side of the road. Also, we might be supplying the Transport & Harbours Department with oxygen and acetylene gas to be sent to the penal settlement at Mazaruni where they were used for ship repairs, and when they were used up T&HD never thought of sending them back to us. But with the deposit system, it made economic sense for users to return the cylinders. Sometimes customers would bring in cylinders but the unique numbers engraved on them showed that we needed to give the credit to a different purchaser. We didn't bother to ask how the party returning those cylinders had managed to acquire them. Our major customers appreciated that our system of control was indeed fool-proof.

While I was at Docol I went to my first seminar in Bermuda on cylinder and inventory control for members of the National Welding Supplies Association, primarily Americans. I took along a sample of our monthly printout for inventory and cylinder control with one or two examples of estates and individual customers. Don Wyatt was the president of the Association, and he gave the address, describing recent developments in the industry. He stated that the greatest amount of assets, money tied up, that a gas business had was in cylinders. He explained that goodwill and trust might work for a small company to keep track of the cylinders and inventory, but once you grew to a certain size, you had to have either a manual or a mechanized system of control for this inventory otherwise you would be depending on SWAG. He asked the audience if anybody knew what SWAG meant, but nobody could answer. Mind you, in attendance were big boys from Liquid Carbonic, Airco, Dupont, Miller Engineering – giants in the industry. Wyatt then explained that SWAG stands for Scientific Wild Ass Guessing. There was considerable laughter at this remark. Later, I showed Frank Wiltshire, Jr., secretary of the Association, how we controlled the inventory and cylinders. I was the only person from the West Indies and South America, and he was so surprised that I, coming from a Third World country, was using a very effective accounting system. I showed how we were able to determine exactly where all our cylinders were, as well as having the ability to calculate the average time of use for the cylinders purchased by certain customers. You know, one of the officials at that conference wanted to offer me a job on the spot. I told him I was already working for an American, Paul Hugo Scharwienka, who had inherited the business from his parents, the founders of Docol.

I enjoyed working at Docol. I would never have thought of leaving Guyana, because I considered that I had the best job so far in my life. I had my expenses paid whenever they sent me abroad, and enjoyed a very good benefits package. Then in about 1970-1971 the government pushed harder to carry out the nationalization program. This affected us directly as well as indirectly through our customers. But the thing that really made me consider leaving was when the government indicated that it would be introducing compulsory service in the military – a proposal that included children from the age of eight going to special youth camps in remote areas. So, in 1973, when my elder boy was five years of age, my wife and I decided to apply to emigrate to Canada. The application was sent to the Canadian Immigration Office in Port-of-Spain, Trinidad, where the visas were issued. Before you know it, I received a reply saying that they didn't think that I could establish myself successfully in Canada – I wasn't even given a chance for an interview. I realized that with only a few years of elementary school education (and being 45 years of age) that it would be difficult to get approval, and so I was resigned to my fate.

At this time, there were a number of people from China, or Macau, in Guyana who were about to go to Canada for a visit. My wife, Norma, ran our travel agency and was arranging visas for them. As a service, she would also accompany them to the Canadian High Commissioner's office in the Bank of Guyana building, since the Chinese could not speak English well. The Canadian representative, Mr. Butler, had a brief chat with Norma, asking her about the state of the country and whether she was thinking of emigrating, to which Norma replied that we were turned down, for not being capable of establishing ourselves in Canada. She then asked if he was willing to have an interview with me, and Mr. Butler agreed.

Going to the interview, I took along a letter of recommendation from Stan Wilson, the general manager of Docal, as well as a strong testimonial from Fitzpatrick, Graham. Butler inquired whether I could get a letter to vouch for my practical ability and I asked him if he knew Mr. Farrar, the senior partner of Fitzpatrick, Graham, explaining that I could go right away and get a letter from Farrar. He suggested that I do so. Farrar immediately dictated a letter and sent it off directly to the Canadian visa office in Trinidad. The letter stated that although I may lack any formal qualification, I have been self-educated to a very high standard and that during the twelve years of service my work was in no way inferior to other qualified members of the staff. Furthermore, as a member of the Canadian Institute of Chartered Accountants he would pay regular visits to Canada, and was of the opinion that I would have absolutely no difficulty in establishing myself successfully in Canada within a very short time. Moreover, he considered that I would have a great deal to contribute to any community that I may wish to reside. Within two weeks of that letter arriving, I was requested to attend an interview. At that interview, not five minutes had passed when the Canadian official said, "We were a bit hasty in our first decision with you."

On 18 May 1974, we arrived in Vancouver, where Farrar's nephew, a partner of a chartered accounting firm, was resident and it was he who arranged a job for me, knowing my ability as an accountant. He even let us stay in his home in North Vancouver until we bought our own home. I joined his firm of chartered accounts at the New Westminster branch, and the first assignment they gave me to do on my own was the accounts at Shoppers Drug Mart stores. Usually, CA students would be sent to do this job – nobody else wanted to do it, because the caliber of bookkeeping was so primitive. You had to virtually write up the financial statements that the stores wanted, and make journal entries because the bookkeepers didn't know how to pass a journal entry. Well I couldn't give a damn, since it was part of my work. Eventually I ended up doing the accounts for 19 branches, because the vice-president of finance was so pleased with my work, which, he said was much better than what they were getting from our head office in Vancouver. I worked for that accounting firm for six years.

Alan Herriera, a fellow employee at Fitzpatrick, Graham, formerly from the Port-of-Spain branch, was working for Butler Tire and he asked me if I was interested in taking over because he wanted to go back to

Trinidad. He did the bookkeeping for Butler and managed to stabilize the company's financial position, but he was not as experienced as I was. When I joined Butler Tire I found that the situation was something like the early days at Docol – they were operating on SWAG. They were virtually bankrupt, because the assets weren't in existence and the stock was grossly overvalued. Butler had a plant to retread tires. These retreads were owned by Butler and were used by Doman Industries. There was a 30% markup on these tires, which was charged to the Butler branches, even if the retreads were still in storage at the branches. I told the auditor that where I came from, I was taught that a company cannot make a profit within itself. So the stock figure was incorrect. I forget how much it was but maybe a hundred thousand dollars. They were paying income tax on income that didn't exist.

Butler Tire operated with a $300,000 revolving loan from the Bank of Montreal. But the conditions were that Butler could not buy assets that, cumulatively, would be more that five thousand dollars per annum, without their permission. Butler couldn't pay themselves any dividends, and they couldn't withdraw any money from the loans, or pay themselves interest on those loans. In addition to these restrictions Butler had to supply quarterly accounts for the bank to inspect, and from time to time the bank manager, or other representative, would pay a visit to see how things were going. Do you know, within a year, I turned that $300,000 loan completely around, and then it was the bank that owed us $450,000?

I'll tell you how I did that. Butler Tire was an independent distributor for several tire manufacturers – Michelin, Goodyear, Goodrich, Firestone, Bridgestone. There are two seasonal sets of tires, summer and winter, and we had to stock up with enough before each season started. Sometimes we would have to order some two million dollars worth of tires and would pay for them over a few months. The tire manufacturers offered a 2% purchase discount on tires bought in a month if we paid for the tires before the end of the following month, say between the 25th to the 28th. In some cases Butler was also being used to supply the tire manufacturers' own central billing customers. The purchasers were billed directly by the tire manufacturers and Butler was given a commission for such sales. Up to this point, we were taking the 2% credit on the net accounts payable to these manufacturers, and this net amount included deductions for the commissions as well as expenses incurred on behalf of the manufacturers for promotional and other extraneous items. However, in practice, Butler was buying the tires outright from the manufacturers, and storing them until the customers required them. Furthermore the tire companies didn't permit us to return them. After I looked at the invoices I noticed that we were entitled to 2% on our purchases of those tires and I told the accounts payable clerk to take the 2% discount on the gross purchases. When one of the manufacturers objected, we referred the matter to our legal advisor and he agreed with our interpretation. So, where originally we were getting only $8,000 a year for the purchase discounts, this rose to $96,000 per year.

Another matter that I changed was the way we were dealing with Doman. This was a big lumber company that was using our tires, paying us just for the mileage used on the tires. Now some of these tires were on 8-wheel or 16-wheel trailers for which there was no method to record the mileage. In addition, the trailers were sometimes contracted out to other companies, and that use was also not recorded because the amount of mileage that Doman reported was for only their own trucks. The cheapest tire was a bias-ply tire that would cost $250, but Doman wanted Michelin steel-belted radials that were $1,400 each. With the large number of trucks and trailers and two sets of tires (for summer and winter), even at the $250 value this meant that more than a million dollars of Butler's tires – Butler's assets – were being tied up by Doman. This was no small matter. If there were a work stoppage at Doman, then Butler would get nothing for all these assets. So I drew up an agreement that would pay Butler a basic sum of $40,000 per month or else the mileage, whichever the greater. Eventually, the two parties agreed to a basic monthly payment of $20,000 or mileage. Would you know, shortly after the agreement was signed in 1981, there was a strike in the forestry industry, lasting for about six months, so Butler received $120,000 that they would not have gotten before.

After I was at Butler for four years, the youngest son in the Butler family brought in his wife to run the business and they fired me. I took them to court and was awarded some $28,000 for wrongful dismissal. Within a year of my leaving, the business went bankrupt and the bank seized the assets and sold them off. It was the father of this bankrupted son who had founded the Butler Tire business in 1922, and it grew until there were several prospering branches. However, before he died in the 1960s, I heard that the founder had told one of the branch managers that if that son ever took over the business, he would wreck it.

You know, what I have seen in the way things are run in this country, there's a lot of skullduggery at all levels – in business and in local, provincial and federal affairs – and people and government are being short-changed all over the

Joe Pierre at the office of Butler Tire, Burnaby, B.C. (1982). *Joe Pierre.*

place. Well, as I was taught when I used to be auditing for Fitzpatrick, Graham, you never volunteer information, especially to auditors and lawyers. If they don't ask, you don't volunteer information, don't open your mouth.

Multi-Cultural Education

Cheryl Stinson, Née Yhap

It was my 17th birthday in the summer of 1969 when we arrived in Vancouver, coming across Canada by train from Toronto. That was also the year that my father, Lawrence Yhap, turned 50. Back in Guyana he had been a civil servant all his life and rose to become a District Commissioner (DC) who was in charge of administrative affairs for a specific region on behalf of the government. He then was appointed to the Ministry of Home Affairs and was a key figure in planning the visit of Her Majesty Queen Elizabeth II in February 1966 as well as the celebrations for Guyana's independence on 26 May a few months later. After independence some changes were introduced in the civil service, one of them being the lowering of the compulsory retirement age from 60 to 55, with the option to leave at age 50. Dad felt that the political situation in the years just before and after independence was no longer very attractive and that it would be best to leave before he became too old to adapt to a new country. My parents also had my own education in mind and wanted to get me settled in higher education as early as possible.

My education in Guyana during my formative years was considerably interrupted because of Dad's appointments as DC to different parts of the country. My Mum Esther would recall that she hardly had time to get the drapes hung when Dad would receive notice that he would be dispatched to another region. For me, the moving was not much of a problem . . . I would quickly pack up my toys, games and books, jump in the car and off we would go. However, my schooling suffered because I might be placed in a class where I was a little ahead in the subject from my previous school and so I became bored. Otherwise I might be placed in a more advanced class for which I didn't have the grounding to catch up easily. I don't know if this decision was made by my parents or the teachers, or both, to decide that it would be fine to have me be challenged but sometimes it was quite a struggle for me to keep up. In addition I always entered not knowing a single soul and because I was the DC's daughter some kids were very hesitant to be more than classmates. They felt that they had to keep their distance. My parents would choose my friends from among their own circle of associates, perhaps the regional doctor, engineer, church or charity worker, who had children. But some of those kids, quite frankly, I didn't like. Perhaps they were 5 or 6 years older than me and really weren't interested in a playmate that much younger. In fact I often had nicer friends at school whose company I enjoyed but they didn't want to come over to play, finding the thought of playing at the DC's house rather intimidating. I of course mixed with children of different racial backgrounds, particularly those of African and Indian origin, who made up the majority of Guyana's population.

This disrupted type of education continued until I was in my teens. In the home environment the situation was rather more stable since Dad, as DC, had the services of a full staff – housekeeper, cook, driver, gardener and a washer woman who also did the ironing because Dad had to be impeccably dressed in a starched white shirt while Mum did a lot of charity work and would wear billowing cancan-type dresses. As for myself, I needed to be sent off to school in a clean, ironed uniform. My responsibility at home was to take care of the pets. We had ducks, chickens and lots of dogs. I even raised a newborn rat after it was found abandoned when the maid was cleaning behind the stove. She wanted to toss it into the river but I decided to rescue it. I named him Mickey. It progressed from sucking on a milk-soaked piece of cotton wool to a really fat rat, having been pampered with whatever food I was eating as well as thick cream skimmed from the scalding of fresh cow's milk. It was kept in a bird cage on a table but eventually gnawed its way to freedom one night. My pet-caring routine started at 6:00 a.m. when I would head downstairs, put on my little gumboots and go outside to clean the chicken coops, gather eggs, provide food and water, and then feed the dogs. After that I headed upstairs, took a shower, dressed for school and by that time breakfast would be ready.

When Dad worked for the Ministry of Home Affairs in Georgetown I was admitted to St. Rose's Ursuline Convent, my parents' first choice, where I sat for the Common Entrance Examination in preparation for getting a higher education. That opportunity came when I was accepted to Vancouver City College to study sciences. I was keen on becoming a veterinarian but that was an impossible goal because of our family's financial circumstances. Dad didn't have stable employment while Mum did some odd jobs and then worked at Eaton's, a large department store. Dad tried all sorts of avenues to find a job, without success. One day he found out that Canadian Pacific Airlines (CP Air) was hiring and so he jumped on the bus and headed to the CP offices. A very nice gentleman interviewed him but felt that Dad was much too over-qualified for the posted job and would not remain with CP. Dad replied that if he were offered a job he promised he would not leave simply because he became bored. This is how Dad started out in the mailroom at CP, doing very basic work while learning the system. He eventually retired as the Manager of Rotables, responsible for the inventory of parts required for the repair and maintenance of the whole fleet of planes worldwide. Each part had to be catalogued regarding its origin, history of use, location, subsequent repair, distribution and disposal. In the days before computerization it required a lot of paperwork and disciplined organization.

For my part, a change in career course was necessary and I learnt secretarial sciences at Vancouver City College, which included typing, Pitman shorthand and using the Dictaphone. Mum did shorthand when she was secretary at the Chinese Embassy in Georgetown when she was young. So she fished out all her books and I had a deluge of material to study. After graduating I did a couple small jobs before being employed to work for Dr. Bert Allsopp, a fisheries expert from Guyana, who was with the International Development Research Centre (IDRC) with the local office at the University of British Columbia. In addition to doing regular secretarial work, I would make arrangements for various international visitors, who spoke varying degrees of English, making sure that they were properly hosted and their itineraries in order. Bert would frequently be travelling and I often had to run the office by myself. On some of those occasions I needed to call the IDRC head office in Ottawa and one of my main connections there was Paul Stinson. He was a program officer looking after various agricultural, food and nutritional sciences projects. After a few years Paul flew to Vancouver on a short business trip and that was the first time that I could put a face to his voice. On a subsequent occasion the supporting personnel from the outlying offices were invited to Ottawa. The prevailing impression was that Ottawa was a rather staid place where political talk was the order of the day. Staff members at IDRC's head office were therefore instructed to make sure that the girls from out West weren't unduly exposed to political banter. I had an enjoyable time and got to know Paul better, after which we maintained regular correspondence.

For a long while Paul had been eager to travel rather than be tied to a desk job and had submitted a request for an overseas posting, preferably in Asia. Suddenly, in 1980, it came through – he would be assigned to Singapore. He informed me that he could be away for up to five years, with limited opportunities to get back to Canada. I told him that I was happy with my job in Vancouver and had never given a thought of leaving. I also knew that I wouldn't go to Singapore unless we were married. So in June of that year we were married and within a week we flew to Bali for a week's honeymoon before hurrying off to Singapore to start his job. Paul had visited Singapore earlier and had scouted around for suitable accommodations. He had prepared a list of potential apartments and when we arrived it didn't take me long to make a decision.

I was quite at home in Singapore, simply because it's multi-cultural, everybody spoke English and the weather is like Guyana's, beautiful for me. We lived in an apartment building that had 80% locals. The aromas of curries, stir fry cooking and more came wafting through my balcony. There were four apartments on our floor, next to us at one time was a British guy with an Indian wife; she cooked some wonderful curries. On the opposite side in the other two apartments were local Chinese and maybe a Malaysian family. From below and above us came the sounds of Chinese music and during Chinese New Year I could hear the shuffling of mah-jongg tiles, and ladies laughing and chattering. They soon realised that I did not speak Malay nor Chinese, but they spoke English and would say hello, hello. We never really had deep conversations or visited each others' apartments but if I ran into a problem I knew that I could certainly go knock on their doors. But I never had any trouble, and nobody ever questioned why an expatriate was living there.

Singapore was impeccably clean. Everything worked, the infra-structure was so reliable. I don't think I ever saw a traffic light that didn't work. But they tend to go a little bit overboard with some of their little by-laws. Some of their rules can frustrate the heck out of you but at the end of the day you just have to chuckle and say well there could be worse laws than this. My passport bore a stamp stating

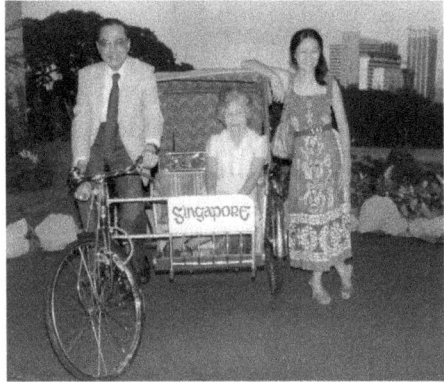

My parents visited us in Singapore in 1983. *Cheryl Stinson.*

that I was not permitted to get employment. Paul had the required work permit and the authorities made it clear that I did not. I had hoped that I would be able to work unofficially at the Canadian Embassy. But I soon found out that I was ranked rather low on the totem pole because they had to employ a certain amount of local staff and then they had their own Canadian staff that had transferred over there. Next on the list were the wives of the Canadian diplomats, if they wanted work. And then came people like me . . . and I never managed to get my foot in the door. One wife of an IDRC employee was a model in Canada. She was a tall, very striking girl with blonde hair and in Singapore there was a shortage of tall, striking blondes. The managers of clothing companies thought she looked very nice wearing their outfits and when they wanted to set up a fashion show she very often got the call to stroll along the catwalk. I think she was paid for it and I don't know how she managed it. Maybe she had a good agent. I know she did some charity work too. But most of the other wives did not work.

We spent four years in Singapore, until 1984. I was happy there and my husband was happy too in his job, he so enjoyed the travelling. Actually I always say that I lived there for four years and Paul lived there for maybe a year and a little bit more – he travelled over 200 days of the year. And he learnt very quickly that I was the type of wife that he could leave behind and I wouldn't be staring at the walls and pining away. I think that had to do partly with the fact that I was an only child. I was accustomed to doing things alone, I wasn't bored with my own company. I know that some of the wives did not like their husbands being away so much. When the wives got together they really voiced concern, almost distress, that their husbands were gone for three weeks, or not even a full two weeks, and would be going off again for two more weeks after coming home for only a couple days. As long as I had something to do, I was happy. I didn't have any help in the house and I took classes at the Art Academy. I wanted to enrol as a full time student but they were full and the fellow I talked to said there is no way that we can give you a spot. However, if you want to come as a drop-in come with your easel and your pencil and set yourself up in a corner. The instructors will know that you are a drop-in and they'll give you as much attention as anybody else. I complied and joined other students in the class going for degrees, serious art students doing art history. I only attended classes in charcoal drawings since I liked the idea of having just a piece of paper and a stick of charcoal with which to create something. I also started doing batik and I studied under a fellow who was very well known in Singapore. He had done many of the government contracts for visiting dignitaries such as the queen and heads of state. The government would commission a batik from him to be presented to the important guest. I really learnt a lot and that was a whole new style of art. I also did a fair bit of volunteering for the SPCA and all these things kept me busy.

Paul wanted to do an MBA and opted for a one-year course at the International Institute for Management Development (commonly known as IMEDE) in Lausanne, the French section of Switzerland. Paul was on a student visa and mine was as a wife of a student. Each year every graduating class would present a gift to the school and all kinds of gifts had been presented over the years making it harder and harder each year for the next class to figure out something different. It also had to be something that they could afford, because everybody would be chipping in for this gift. At the time IMEDE was tossing around elaborate plans for a new building. There would be an underground university while retaining part of the existing staid building. The student body decided to present IMEDE with something to remember what it looked like so they approached me to do a complete drawing of the whole IMEDE facility, with all the trees and the lawns and everything intact – not a photograph, but a drawing. I had to start working on that fairly early and I was sure glad that they let me know what their intentions were because I put a lot of hours into that project; while Paul spent months at his desk, I spent months at the easel. The students had the original of my large charcoal drawing framed and then presented it to the Institute. The students also had a plate made which they used to create the formal invitations for the graduation gala. Just before graduation one of the professors contacted me and asked if he could have permission to use it as his Christmas card to send out to his colleagues and business associates. For me that was confirmation that the drawing was a success.

I took the opportunity to study French, which kept me busy. A year went by very quickly, just like that. We lived in a little place called Lutry, just outside Lausanne, on a hill with grapes growing on the slopes. Our apartment was the size of a postage stamp and looked over Lac Léman which presented an incredibly beautiful scene: just across the lake you could see France where, at night, the twinkling lights of the towns stood out in the darkness. We watched as the grapevines sprouted and turned green and later saw the pickers with special baskets on their backs harvesting the grapes. We had a Volkswagen Golf, with standard shift as is common in Europe, and in the evenings I would drive down to pick Paul up at IMEDE. He usually took the train to get there in the mornings. One night the snow started to come down and wouldn't stop. By the time we decided to get moving and drove to the foot of the hill leading to our place, we knew that there was no way that the car was going to make it. So we parked it and began walking up that hill, but I was not looking forward to that climb. On the way up we paused now and then to look around. It was one of the most beautiful nights I have experienced in my life. It was like a Christmas scene created by Charles Dickens. Even though it was bitterly cold, I can't remember being cold. I just recall the lights from the windows and the lamps, the glistening slope of the hill, the snow-laden trees and the clearness of the night even though snow continued to fall heavily. I half expected to see little kids come running out wearing old fashioned clothes – girls wearing little bonnets and boys with caps and knee-high boots, truly like a living Christmas card.

After our stint in Lausanne we went to Basel, the German section, and Paul started working with Ciba-Geigy. We had a beautiful apartment in a place called Pratteln with an Italian caretaker. We got along well. Most people didn't speak English but I used my recently-acquired French to communicate. I started studying German to keep busy but found it hard. The local food wasn't as nice as in Lausanne, in my opinion. We had a nice neighbour downstairs, a bachelor who was Swiss German and on occasion we invited him to dinner. He enjoyed my curry – Guyanese style, I might add. The ingredients were easy to find, particularly from shops owned by Asians who brought in just about everything under the sun. We stayed in Basel for two years where Paul's job had him sitting behind a desk, mainly. He was beginning to get bored and longed for a travelling job like what he had in Singapore. But before that could be granted he had to prove himself in the field, so Ciba-Geigy sent him back to Canada.

We lived in Mississauga, on the outskirts of Toronto, while Paul was doing product promotion which required him to go knocking at the doctors' offices, waiting to be called in, and explaining the new drugs that Ciba-Geigy was producing. After about a year he was promoted to Product Manager and put in charge of reps who were now doing the door-knocking. He was again back in an office job and we both figured that there had to be more to this, having taken the time to acquire an MBA degree. Then he was informed that he had proven himself and would be posted to Zimbabwe, which was considered to be a hardship posting.

In late 1986 Paul took up his position as General Regional Manager for southern Africa, covering a little bit of South Africa, Zimbabwe, Malawi, Mozambique. We were provided with a house in Chisipiti in the eastern section of Harare, a large place with lots of yard space. The house was owned by a white Zimbabwean landlord, managed by a white house agent and was previously occupied by a white Zimbabwean family. I inspected the house and found a few things that needed tuning up and repairing. I then said, I want to see the servants' quarters. "What?" was the response. I repeated, "I want to see the servants' quarters!" This surprised them but they led me in. I was really shocked at what I saw. They had tried to sweep it but the place required a good scrubbing, and it needed to be painted. It wasn't derelict, but it was neglected terribly.

I had the place scrubbed, repainted, and swept out nicely. I had the bathroom completely scrubbed, but the fact remained that only cold water was available. So that meant that for the greater part of the year the staff were not bathing properly. Yes, it can get quite cold in Harare. I said this is not going to work. I called a German fellow who ran a plumbing company and told him I wanted hot water in the servants' quarters. He said, There is no way we can run a pipe from your house out to them, and the landlord, I can tell you right now, he's not going to let you do that. He continued, I do have a solution – a Steamy and all I do is cut the pipe above the shower head and install it there. I noticed that shower head was right over the toilet and the theory was that as the occupant showered the toilet would get cleaned. I don't know how the plumber obtained his supplies, maybe brought in from South Africa or on the black market, but they were quality parts. The kettle-like device containing a heating element was eventually installed. It was connected to an electric switch, and on turning it on a stream of comfortably warm water would be produced. The plumber cautioned that the element would eventually burn out depending on how often it was used but it could be replaced.

At the time we had a gardener named Norman and his little boy was in town. Norman sent his son to have a shower and for the first time in his life that boy was bathing with warm water. Norman had to literally drag the boy out of that shower, because he just stood under there until Norman finally said, You can't burn out the element on the first day, Madam would not stand for that. Later I discovered that the nannies, after their shift, were showering before they went home. If they didn't get a chance because they were going to miss their bus they would come early in the morning and take a shower. And then I discovered the guards were showering before they went home. It took a lot of new elements to keep the Steamy going!

The landlord wouldn't pay for the water heater although it was a permanent installation and the contract said that any improvements that remained in the house would be reimbursed. But what that referred to was improvements to the house, not the servants' quarters. He said, "We don't treat our servants like that." The attitude of the landlord was quite representative of many white Zimbabweans. Our neighbour had a houseboy, Noah, with about four or five kids living in a small place. One day there was a lot of wailing from next door and Noah's employer came over and asked for understanding, explaining that one of Noah's sons had died and the wailing would traditionally go on for about three days. Our landlord happened to visit during that mourning period and he heard the wailing to which I said that their little child had passed away. He said, They'll replace it in no time! That was his total and complete comment. He was a nice gentleman who would sit and talk intelligently with me, but this is us and that's them. We once attended a small dinner of five people at the home of a French-American expatriate family when the dining table conversation got around to the problem of getting their washing machine back in working order as parts usually had to be obtained from South Africa. The lone Zimbabwean, a white woman who was impeccably dressed and well educated, must have found it irritating listening to these expatriates lamenting the problems of an appliance which she apparently did not have. Finally she piped-up, "We don't have that problem. At our house the washer is black!"

I employed several servants in Zimbabwe. I had a house girl named Irene although I used to do my own cooking. When my twin boys were born in 1991 I hired a nanny and she eventually asked for help because after my twins started to walk they discovered that when the nanny was chasing them it was strategic for each to run off in a different direction. She would just stand there and shout in exasperation, "Madam! Madam!!" I got her a young assistant and things were more orderly then. The gardener Norman loved to cook, and especially to bake. He would not hesitate to drop his rake or hoe, quickly wash up and run into my kitchen. In those few minutes Norman would have changed from his gardening overalls into stiff white attire. I didn't

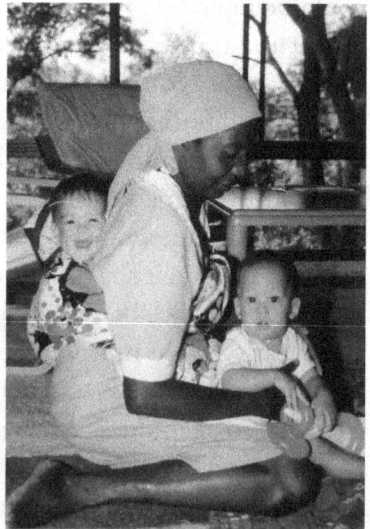

Our nanny joined us for a vacation in South Africa in January 1992. It was her first trip outside Zimbabwe. *Cheryl Stinson.*

require that but the family before us demanded that he be dressed like a proper cook and so he just assumed the same would be the case with us. I said, Norman if you're just coming in to help me in the kitchen perhaps you can just take off your overalls if they are very dusty and make sure your hands are clean, but I don't expect you to change into whites; only if we are entertaining, then it would be nice if you are in white. He said, Madam I have so many of these white things, if I don't wear them, what am I going to do with them?

I did a lot of charity work in Zimbabwe, particularly for the Epilepsy Support Foundation. I got connected to them because one of the drugs that Ciba-Geigy was introducing was for epilepsy. They would have these fund-raising events and one of the things that was very popular was cakes baked with outside ingredients – better quality flour brought in from South Africa, vanilla essence, almond flavouring and things like that, items that were hard to get locally. Every time we took home leave I would return to Zimbabwe with packages of almonds, walnuts, good quality baking powder, etc. Or if we went down to South Africa I would buy there and bring them back. So my cakes would rise a little higher or be somewhat lighter. I would call Norman in and he would help with the cleaning, beating the eggs, mixing the batter and decorating. I would bake 4 or 5 cakes and donate them to the foundation's bake sales or their Christmas sales. Sometimes they would sell for $50. Sounds like a lot but it was Zim dollars. I would always bake some extra for the house and staff which we would all share.

Handling a snake at a wildlife refuge.
Cheryl Stinson.

The staff included guards who would patrol the grounds within our walled compound. I had one guard on day shift and one for nights. Things were beginning to get a little rough in Zimbabwe and on the news or in the newspapers there were reports of people getting roughed up in their homes. I felt it appropriate that we should ask for an armed guard even if it was going to cost more. We spoke to the supervisor of the guard company. He said, No madam, the only guards who can carry guns are those of President Mugabe, and the banks . . . our guys can only carry sticks. I then requested two guards, because Paul was then doing a lot of travelling and I was now by myself with the babies. But they didn't even have a stick, so on a trip to South Africa I bought about four sjamboks. They're long whips that the South African police use for people control and riots and can be lethal. The sjambok has a handle that tapers off to a long whip made from a kind of a rubber. It doesn't snap or crack like a whip but delivers a solid whack that is guaranteed to produce a resulting scream. I armed my fellows with the sjamboks and they loved them. They used to walk around swishing them in practice. Some of them hit themselves by mistake because they were long and curled back snapping them on their ankles or wherever. You'd hear them yelling and then laughing since they felt silly. Norman, our gardener, said he preferred to wield an axe handle in a confrontation, and I got one from the hardware store . . . without the blade. The guards would come down the street at a certain hour to take up duty for the afternoon or evening shift, and each guard would peel off to go to his assigned address. Each wore a green uniform with a red neck kerchief. Some of them had helmets. When I asked whereabouts they met in town I was told that they came from the local town office at Chisipiti. I said, That's funny I'm always in Chisipiti, I don't remember seeing an office there. He explained, Yes Madam you know the big tree, that's our office, we meet under there; if it rains we just huddle closer under the tree.

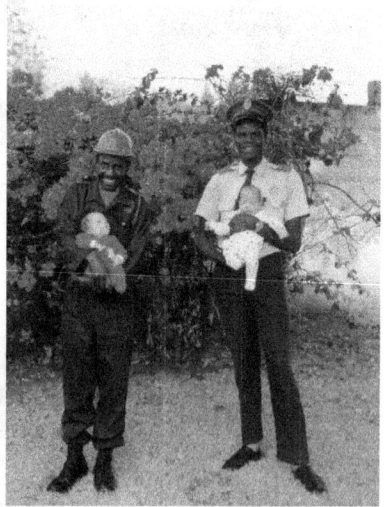

Elisha and David, trusted guards, with the twins in our walled compound. *Cheryl Stinson..*

I had regular guards whom I liked and trusted but they didn't always come because they might be on holiday or sick. So I always wanted to know who was on duty and I would at least call them to say good evening and ask their names and gently admonish them to not let me catch them sleeping. Usually Norman would have acquainted himself with the guard in advance, and would come and say to me, "Madam you have a new guard tonight," or "Madam it's the usual Elisha," and I would make a cup of hot coffee or cocoa with sweet biscuits every night particularly during winter.

In the yard there was a most wonderful avocado tree, higher than the house. One morning Norman came running and exclaimed, Madam the avocadoes are gone. Apparently either the guard was in on it or he was up near the front gate sleeping or talking with someone while a thief was helping himself liberally to the low-hanging fruits. I got out a sheet and called the guard to hold it. I told Norman to climb the tree and get all the avocadoes that are almost ripe and toss them down to the sheet. They were huge avocadoes, each about 4 to 5 inches across. I asked for some cloth bags to be brought from the house and I told Norman to fill 10 bags with the avocadoes, some ripe and others almost ripe. He must have thought I was going to sell them or give them away to friends but I had been counting mentally: first there's the home, then Irene the house girl, my two nannies, Norman, the two regular guards. Besides these, I reckoned on Noah, the neighbour's houseboy who was really nice to us, our landlord and the house agent. I told Norman, Make sure they are all even, with some green ones mixed with some ripe ones, tie them up and just line them up outside the kitchen right there. When the time came for the guards to switch I called the one who was going off duty and said, OK you can take one. They all were really surprised because they were not accustomed to a family sharing things with servants. Each of the staff was asked to take a bag. At that time they were beginning to feel the pinch of food shortages and some of the guards told me they would eat one or two, have the wife sell some and send the green ones to other family members upcountry. Once the guards realised that they were going to partake in the bounty, they guarded that tree better since Norman told me that from his quarters he could hear footsteps in the night and know it was the guard from the sound of his boot as well as his cough.

I had no qualms sharing stuff with my staff, especially if the items were in excess, still usable or would go to waste. Elisha, our guard, was quite a good runner; he was hoping to represent Zimbabwe. He ran with shoes, but I don't know how they stayed on and he couldn't afford a pair of new ones. Actually his feet were a little smaller than Paul's so as soon as Paul's running shoes got a little too worn for him I used to take them, scrub them, replace the laces and give them to Elisha. The excited runner would push cloth into the toe area so they didn't flop around and cause blisters at the back. Then he would pull the laces tightly and off he would go running. He would sometimes run to come on duty and now that he was hot and sweaty he'd use the Steamy shower quickly.

In Zimbabwe the staple food was milimeal, made of ground corn. It was rather like flour and used to make sadza which is a very stiff porridge that is solid enough to be rolled by hand. The locals would cook that with every meal. The milimeal came in massive 50-pound bags which the average Zimbabwean could not afford to buy. Not only was inflation reducing their buying power but also a 50-pound bag was too much for the average family. I would go to the local supermarket, small by North American standards, and ask the manager very quietly whether any milimeal was available. He might say that a shipment just came in and some would be put onto the shelves. I let him know that I didn't just want some, I wanted a bag. The bag would be loaded in my car at the back of the store and I would hurry directly home to have Norman divide it up for distribution to all staff including the guards. I couldn't sell the milimeal to my servants nor could I give some to the household staff and sell some to the guards . . . to me that was unconscionable and would not have brought harmony to the home turf. Sometimes I would arrive at the supermarket and know that milimeal had arrived because of the *long* line-up outside the store; women with children on their backs, men without work trying to get some food. I always felt that my staff was genuinely grateful and cheerful about my efforts to acquire essentials for them.

When I became pregnant everybody in Canada expected me to return there for the birth. This was especially so after they heard that I was having twins and they tried to persuade me not to leave it too late, it's a long trip. My doctor was a nice white Zimbabwean man who indicated that my pregnancy was going fine and it was really my choice.

Ultrasound examinations were performed at a private clinic run by a black Zimbabwean doctor who kept an eye on me every two weeks. His name is Steven and I named one of my sons after him because he was really so very nice. The birth was uneventful and the babies were healthy so I don't have any regrets with my decision to stay in Zimbabwe.

In all my travels I found the Zimbabweans, both black and white, were among the nicest people. The children I found particularly charming. They have a distinctive manner of expressing gratitude and greeting when they meet you – they would clap, just a gentle clap. They rarely wave or shake hands, just clap, even the littlest children. It's so sweet.

In 1993 Paul again worked for IDRC trying to improve the production and utilization of bamboo in India. We were posted to New Delhi where we had a nice house. The American Embassy women's group maintained a directory of employees, like a hand-me-down list with recommendations, but I quickly found out that great recommendations didn't necessarily mean great employees. I had a lot of unpleasant experiences dealing with hired staff and the caste system was definitely something that I needed to think hard about to overcome the consequences. One of my house rules was that every member of the staff had to wash and dry his hands before coming into the house from the bathroom. The bathroom was attached to the house but with an outside entrance. One day the cook had gone to use the bathroom and in no time at all he was back in the kitchen. I said, Did you wash your hands? He responded that he would wash them here, in the kitchen. I emphasized the importance of cleaning up *before* entering the kitchen. He still continued to come into the house a few times with unwashed hands. I tried to determine why he was doing so and it was like pulling teeth. Tara, the houseboy, had no issue complying with my house rule, especially since he was cleaning the house, playing with the twins, handling the kids' toys, learning English by reading the children's books, and so forth. Eventually I got them to fess up: I had put a bar of soap in the servants' bathroom as well as a towel, which I would change regularly. Tara belonged to a lower caste and the cook looked down on him. Because Tara used the bar of soap, the cook did not want to touch it. So he preferred to have unwashed hands in contrast to this lower caste man with clean hands, but he still considered himself superior. I couldn't put two bars of soap . . . there wasn't enough space anyway . . . so I got a pump system and I said, Use your elbow and the soap will come out. That was accepted, and I provided them with paper towels as well.

Later on we had a fellow, Russell, who was very skinny, with somewhat long, grey hair, and who called me memsaab. He wasn't sure himself how old he was because records were not kept when he was born. From his recollection of British and Indian historical events and his age at the time he averaged that he was probably 90 years old. Paul and I calculated that he was *at least* 90. It shocked me that such an old person still wanted to find work but he could cook the most delicious dishes. He had learnt from the British in the days when there was no air conditioning. When summer came in New Delhi it would be HOT, and the British women would pack up their families and go up to the cooler highlands, taking their hired staff with them. The men, attended by a skeleton staff, would stay and work in the city up to a point. Russell was accustomed to packing up the kitchen, taking so many months' supplies, going up with memsaab and her family and pampering her in the cooler regions. He was at home in the kitchen and I trusted him, because anytime he wanted something he would ask me, and that included for even a small, inconsequential container. But he had one annoying habit. As soon as I walked in the kitchen he would drop whatever he was holding and jump to attention, stamping his right foot next to his left one and standing upright with stiff backbone and even stiffer upper lip. The Queen's guards might have been impressed but it startled the daylights out of me. I pleaded with him, Don't do that, you make me jump, you actually scare me. It took me a really long time before I broke him of the habit. However he would still stiffen up, turn around and acknowledge my presence but the stamping was gone, to my great relief. But that was the way the British trained him, and I don't think he ever got accustomed to my presence in my own kitchen.

Russell got sick a few times, especially when the weather turned cold and his aging lungs could not cope. I had room for only one servant and I gave it to Russell although his family lived maybe 10 to 15 minutes from us. They refused to take in the old man in case he died and then would become a great expense for them. So since he had a job he should live at memsaab's place and it then would be her problem. I provided him with a heater, but he still got sick and I had to take him to hospital. On a couple occasions I sent the driver to notify his family that Russell was in hospital and that they had to take food for him because the hospital didn't provide food. I instructed the driver to drop in every day and quietly find out from the hospital staff if the family was bringing food. He learnt that they would take food only on some days. I told the driver that on the day he realizes that he not being fed to go to a hawker's stand, buy him something warm and I would repay him. We then brought Russell home as soon as possible, because if the driver were to take him to his family, they would refuse to even open the door. It was not unusual for the hospital doctors to discharge a patient before they felt it best, especially if the patient was being difficult and didn't want to stay. So they would write a prescription and let him go. I made sure that Tara the houseboy would check on him and buy food at the hawker's stand if necessary. Fortunately Tara was willing to do that and Russell didn't mind. Finally after many months Russell just got too weak and weary. He was in no condition to work at all. So we took him to his family and I don't know what became to him. I'm sure that in his productive years he would have earned a decent salary from the Brits and able to maintain his family well, but when he became old and sick he was considered a burden to them.

Russell was the best worker I had. There were some who lasted only one day. Within that time it was clear to me that they were unsuitable and would be dismissed with a day's pay. Some drank on the job, or were extremely rude, or stole. I had a driver who complained to Paul that I had promised to give him a bottle of Scotch along with his salary. If he thought that I would give a bottle of Scotch on Friday for him to drink all weekend and then have him come in on Monday morning to drive my children to school, he should think again. I had another driver who was very good but I had been warned that out of the blue he might not turn up for work. His name was John and he spoke perfect English. After a few months of flawless employment, he suddenly didn't appear. Apparently, after he earned a certain amount of money, he would quit working and when the money ran out he would put his name on the list, present his resume and have some other unsuspecting soul hire him. I asked him if there was something that made him unhappy working for me. He responded, No, no, no, I don't feel like working.

Another driver, who regrettably did not last long, worked for a considerable time as the personal driver for Indira Gandhi's daughter-in-law. He was always on time, impeccably dressed and flawlessly polite with enough English for us to get along. However, he had the perplexing and annoying habit of always driving on the centre line, the dividing line between us and the on-coming traffic. He would only swerve back into the correct lane when on-coming traffic honked or obviously was not going to give way, like a truck. No matter how I tried to demonstrate to him, with the aid of the children's play town, that he must stay on the correct side of the road – no, he would meander back to straddling the centre line. Then I figured it out. As driver for an official car which was always accompanied by police out-riders, he would simply drive down the centre of the road as the out-riders cleared the way ahead. And this, unfortunately, was a habit he just couldn't break no matter how much I pointed out that I was not connected to the Gandhi family nor did we have out-riders.

I once had a cook who was drunk, completely sloshed. I told him that he was fired and retorted that I couldn't fire him. He considered that it was the man of the house who was in charge even though I was the one who hired him and he had never seen Paul before starting on the job. I summoned the guard and told him I would count to three and if the cook was still there the guard should physically throw him out. The cook refused to budge. He snickered and felt that the guard was "one of us." The burly guard promptly put him out on the street.

Apparently my Chinese features confused the hired staff which sometimes led to a quick turnover. They seemed to like to work in Asian households. A Japanese woman, for example, perhaps would not know much English, did not talk a lot or would be hesitant about speaking up. The employees were on home territory and would proceed to rule the roost, giving instructions on how things should be done, when they would leave work and so forth. But I spoke English and was not afraid to show my temper if needed. Some of the younger ones that I hired were just a nightmare. They had the opportunity to earn a decent salary, work in clean surroundings and they all wanted to work with expatriate families. The inside joke among the expatriates was that if the servants worked for an Indian family the memsaab would be beautifully and expensively attired with a silk sari, draped with gold jewelry, and charm her guests in elegant fashion. Then she'd step into the kitchen, slap the maid and kick the cook for any perceived glitch and step back out to again charm her guests. They said that was very common, simply because she belonged to a higher caste. So that's why it puzzled me when some of them had the opportunity to work for an employer who would not treat them like that, yet they misbehaved to the point of having to be dismissed.

I went to one home that was outfitted with an elevator. It was maybe three or four stories high and I rode in the elevator and ended up in the basement where the husband and the many sons had their offices. The husband's office was a fantastic room, and just behind his beautiful desk were two Ming vases that were probably as tall as myself. There also were ornate hand-carved wooden pieces, ivory tusks, and jade. It was an unbelievable display of wealth. All the servants were dressed in white, with seemingly staff for each floor. The family were merchants and it made me wonder how many millions of rupees were coming in to maintain a home like this, as well as driving Mercedes cars and educating their children abroad. That's where I really saw the extremes of wealth and poverty, superimposed on the caste system.

I once took my 3-year-old sons to have their hair cut at a New Delhi five-star hotel where the all-male clients were also having facial saunas, pedicures, manicures etc. To stay out of the way while the barbers worked on the boys I squeezed myself nearby next to a little cubicle where I could also see what was going on inside. I soon realized the used towels that were being used for the clients' facials etc were being dropped through an opening in the cubicle that had a basket on the other side. I then observed a barber shop employee, in this five-star hotel and in the privacy of the cubicle, dutifully retrieve towel after towel, neatly re-fold them and take them back into the barber shop for use on the next customer.

In August 1994 the plague broke out and it was getting out of hand. People were burning clothes and appeals were broadcast asking the masses to avoid traveling. Tara was due to have his leave, about 10 days, and he and his wife were going up country on the typically overloaded train as usual. I told Paul that Tara may be healthy now, but no way did

I want him to go up country by that mode of transportation and then come back to our house. It was too much of a risk particularly for our two kids. So we approached Tara and asked if he would wait until the scare was over. He responded, No, I have a wedding, I have this and that to do. I told Tara that if he were to wait we would pay for him and his wife to travel first class. He went for that, and he stayed. I think he delayed his trip by about two months and by October the health scare and panic passed after causing more than 600 casualties. The plague proliferated from the lack of cleanliness. Hygienic practices left much to be desired. Often when I went shopping in New Delhi I saw a kid run out from a store, drop his pants, relieve himself on the sidewalk and go back inside. No one blinked. Piles of such droppings could be seen everywhere. You had to be very careful where you stepped.

The indifferent attitude towards sanitation really gave us great concern. When we went up to Agra to see the Taj Mahal it was like driving through a cesspit. It was a long drive taking a few hours and a dangerous one too with lots of transport trucks barreling along on narrow roads, some with no lights and hardly any brakes. Even though we thought of taking a break in the journey we didn't stop to use any of the "sanitary" facilities. After we got to Agra we found that it wasn't any cleaner. A similar experience occurred in going up to Jaipur.

Nevertheless, despite these sanitation challenges and often arduous road trips with two accommodating, patient toddlers in tow, we always looked forward to visiting the various cities where historical monuments were to be viewed and with the aid of a knowledgeable guide we would soak up the intriguing histories of eras gone. Believing that travel is an invaluable education there was no way that we were going to forfeit the opportunity to see as much as we could of India and sample the

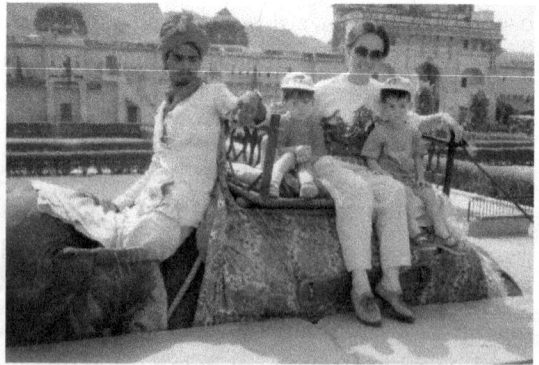

Taking an elephant ride in Jaipur. *Cheryl Stinson.*

different curries and delicacies from the local region or state. Several visits were made to the Taj Mahal, one of which was in the dark when we each were provided with a torch by the guide. The twins, clutching their torches, were given special attention by the guide who took great delight in showing them the wonderment and beauty of the various colored marble and inlaid stones by shining their torches from behind. The visit obviously made a lasting impression on the boys because from then on they always referred to the "Torch Mahal." There was no denying that on leaving the big cities en route to our latest sight-seeing destination the natural beauty of the countryside was at times breathtaking and I often regretted that we did not stop more often to snap more photos, and when we did we very often failed to capture what we actually saw. However, we do have albums to remember those trips and now years later, when for the twins things are almost impossible to recall from such a young age, we can pull out the albums and pour over the pages.

We had to be very careful in the restaurants we chose and inevitably went to places like the Hilton Hotel where we expected that the food would be fresh and properly prepared. We had more stomach problems in that country than we ever had before, no matter how hard we tried. We installed an ultraviolet water filtration system for the kitchen, based on the recommendations of other expatriates. There was nothing more disconcerting than to host a party and have guests telephone the next day to report intestinal troubles. Every year when we returned to Canada on home leave I would have everyone undergo a complete medical examination. One year Steven was discovered to have a parasite. It was so rare that the lab specialists had to look up reference materials to identify it and the doctor couldn't even pronounce the long Latin name. She didn't know how to treat it but had a godfather who was a parasitic specialist at UBC. On learning that Steven was three years old, he cautioned that medications would harm the child. However, the parasite was one that flourished in unclean conditions and if the food and water Steven was ingesting was clean and he kept his hands nicely scrubbed, the parasite would not survive. Towards the end of our two-month homeleave a stool test was taken and Steven returned to India with a clean bill of health.

After two years working for IDRC, Paul accepted a job with

Boehringer Mannheim, another Swiss pharmaceutical company, and we moved to a farmhouse outside New Delhi. It was one of the most beautiful homes I've ever lived in. We were surrounded by other farmhouses and many of them were retreats for wealthy Indian families. The grounds were huge and surrounded by an 8-foot concrete wall topped with shards of glass. There were two buildings on the premises that provided accommodations for seven employees, four of them being gardeners, or malis, because of the vast area of lawns. I did have some trouble getting reliable hired help, including guards who slept on the job, but eventually I gathered a group that I was happy with.

When Diwali, the Festival of Lights, was coming up, I planned a surprise for them. I went to the bank and made a big withdrawal. Indian money in general is tattered, almost falling apart to the touch. I told the bank manager that I would like to have new notes because most of them would be as gifts. I didn't specify that it was for my servants or else he might ask why I was giving so much money in the first place and would have promptly said the bank was out of new notes. He counted out some spanking new notes and I bought several red envelopes for the money and tied them with gold thread. I told the servants that I would allow everybody to work until noon on the day before Diwali, and then they could take off to enjoy the festivities. I needed the guards to remain but I wanted to know how many other staff preferred to stay behind. They quickly replied, No, no madam we're not going to go, we'll be around. I said, OK, just have fun, but don't get drunk, and don't fall into the swimming pool. Late that night, just before the boys were to go to sleep there was a knock on the door which was very unusual. Bopaul, the houseboy, who also looked after the pool, said, Madam can you come please? I stepped out and found the whole of the back grounds was lit up. We had a long driveway with a lovely roundabout and a beautiful fountain. There must have been two or three hundred candles stretching to the gate, beautiful lights going on and on. The boys were still in their pyjamas when I pulled them out take a look.

The next day the servants put marks on the children's foreheads, wishing them well. I called the servants and I said, I'd like to wish you all Happy Diwali. I had also prepared a hamper for each of them. It had a blanket, cooking oil, jam, peanut butter, sugar and matches and a few other essentials. I took a flat basket with the envelopes and approached Vishnu, the eldest gardener, and invited him to take one. They assumed that I would have given my houseboy more than I would have given them as outside malis but once I held out the basket it was obvious that the envelopes would all have the same amount. The old fellow was very humbled that I went to him first and gave him the honor. He should have stopped working a long time ago but he needed to support his family. Vishnu bowed slightly and was hesitant. I said, Take one Vishnu. He didn't speak any English and Bopaul said something to him. Vishnu gingerly took an envelope and bowed gratefully. I was so glad I had prepared my surprise gifts for them knowing that the night before they had prepared all those beautiful candles as their own special surprise for the boys and me. They obviously spent a significant amount of time collecting fat to serve as fuel, preparing little candle holders, almost like pop bottle caps, and making the wicks out of string. It was really a touching gesture and an illuminating display of their appreciation.

During all our time in India the boys attended the American Embassy school which enrolled pre-schoolers from age 3 and regular students up to grade 12. There was a nice mix of children including Germans, Swiss and Italians as well as a few Indians kids from wealthy families . . . a mini United Nations. They were instructed by Indian teachers who were obviously educated in the U.S. or England. They came from upper class Indian families and had teaching degrees. The boys left the house in the morning at 9 o'clock and I'd pick them up at 2 or 3. I would prepare their little lunch bags and off they'd go. The little children learnt reading, writing, computing (featuring cartoon characters) and had outdoor activities including swimming, tours to museums and watching the older kids playing soccer. There was a fantastic library that looked like a library in a modern North American high school. As the twins approached their fifth birthday I began to consider their ongoing education and opted to return to Canada where they could go into kindergarten that took 5-year-old children and continue on to high school. I felt that my decision to stabilize their education was the right course for them when they were accepted at Cornell University in Ithaca, New York.

From Calypso to Samba

Rosaliene Bacchus, née Fung

Leaving Guyana

My life spiralled out of control as I watched my husband descend the stairs into an abyss. It was a Wednesday morning, March 4, 1987. "If you don' wanna go, I goin' without you," Jerry said, without looking back. Fear took control. My stomach churned, my head swirled, my vision blurred. My husband was on his way to the Brazilian Consulate in Georgetown. We were moving to Brazil. The well-being of our sons, one and three years old, was at stake. Fear disturbed my sleep with thoughts of them losing their hair and eyesight, and suffering from paralysis and dementia, as a result of thallium poisoning.

Two months had passed since I left my secretarial job at a bank in Georgetown to assist my husband with his home-based pastry and catering business. It had flourished since its small beginning three years ago. Jerry had learnt to make pastry with his three elderly aunts — headed by Auntie Rosie Ho-Yow — who ran a well-established catering business. "Me alone can't sell to the whole of Georgetown," said Aunt Rosie, the day he asked to learn the business. He was a fast learner and I became his apprentice. We made Chinese cakes, star cakes, pine tarts, cheese rolls, meat patties, Swiss rolls and, at Christmas time, black cake. Now, two women helped him with the pastry-making and a guy took care of purchases and deliveries.

During the years following Guyana's independence in May 1966, we had adapted to black-outs, storing water in buckets, and food shortages. We had lived through the racial disturbances; riots; workers' strikes; the Jim Jones and his People's Temple scandal in November 1978; the assassination of Jesuit priest, Father Bernard Darke, in July 1979; and the assassination of Walter Rodney, leader of the Working People's Alliance, in June 1980.

Members of our families, relatives, school friends, and work colleagues left our shores for the United Kingdom, Canada, the United States, and other distant lands. By the end of 1981, my father, Phillip Edward Fung, and I were the remnants of our family in Guyana. For many Guyanese, survival depended upon money and foodstuffs received from abroad. For others, hope lay in a better future reunited with their loved ones overseas. For me, it was a time of loss and isolation.

During the period 1982 to 1986, the ban on the importation of wheat and other basic food items, in the name of self-reliance, created a new profession: the Guyanese "trader." These entrepreneurs traveled to Brazil, Suriname, the Caribbean Islands, and the USA to purchase food and other items for resale in Georgetown and other major cities. They faced constant harassment from customs and border officials who either seized their goods or demanded bribes. The police raided bakeries and trampled confiscated bread made with wheat flour. They arrested and jailed a few individuals. This did not deter clandestine trading, mainly across the Corentyne River border with Suriname. The local rice flour substitute could not make fine pastry; obtaining wheat flour for our pastry business became difficult and risky. Government repression of the parallel market proved difficult since it filled a vital need for our people. In the late 1980s, the government eventually approved the construction of stalls in a section of downtown Georgetown, off Water Street, for traders to market their goods.

To worsen our plight, thallium poison entered our food chain and threatened our lives. In July 1986, the Roman Catholic press disclosed the government's use of thallium to kill rats on the sugar plantations. Some high official had ignored the fact that, since 1973, the World Health Organization had prohibited the use of thallium as a rodenticide because of its extremely high toxicity. The health authorities advised all users of cow's milk to test for thallium poisoning. Tests done by the Government Analyst Department on myself, husband and sons revealed a high level of thallium in our blood. (The Analyst Department later discovered that their testing equipment was defective.) They advised us to take potassium and referred us to the Georgetown Hospital for treatment. By then, pandemonium had broken out in Georgetown. We waited in long lines at the hospital among irate and frightened citizens.

The doctors treated us with Prussian Blue which stained our mouths a deep purple color. My heart ached at the sight of the purple stains on the mouths and white vests of my one- and three-year-old sons.

I wrestled with Fear that night of March 4, 1987. I chose to leap into the unknown like a woman hurdling herself from a burning building into the black night.

Jerry booked our flight for March 26th. He wanted to get out fast. Saying goodbye to relatives and friends severed our bond with our past, our world. What do you say to friends who have been part of your history? The exodus from Guyana — following our country's independence — separated families, destroyed friendships, and robbed our young nation of its talent. When it is your turn to leave, you can say nothing to relieve the pain of your departure, of your own abandonment. I was leaving the country of my birth, the country that I loved, the country that had moulded me. I spoke English; I had grown up with cricket, the steel band and calypso.

Journey to Fortaleza, Ceará, Northeast Brazil

At 5:00 a.m. on Thursday, March 26, 1987, Georgetown slept as we set out for Timehri Airport. Fear sat beside me as we waited at the airport for our Guyana Airways flight to Boa Vista, capital of the State of Roraima in northern Brazil. Guyana was small-fry next to Brazil, the world's fifth largest country. To cut costs, Jerry had planned a week-long, four-leg trek. Fear can be persistent; he drowns you in self-doubt. Will you make it safely to your destination? It's a four-thousand-mile journey from Boa Vista to Fortaleza, in a strange country. You don't speak the language. Do you have enough money to start a new life? Will you find someplace decent and secure to raise your kids? Will they get a good education? Will you find work? Will you learn to speak Portuguese? Will you . . .? Sometimes, it's hard to get Fear to shut up.

Boa Vista, just 70 miles distant from Guyana's southern border town of Lethem, stretched out below us like a spider's web within the Amazon Forest. You're descending into a trap, said Fear. But Brazil's smallest and most remote state capital impressed me with its good roads, public telephones, well-stocked supermarkets, and large shopping center with all that one needed. The people we met were friendly and helpful.

I drifted on the notes of their musical language. The scantily-dressed population in this dusty and steamy city gave it an informal, holiday atmosphere. On our first night in Brazil, we slept to the hum of an electric fan in a tiny hotel room.

On the next morning, we left Boa Vista at 7:00 a.m. en route to Manaus, capital of the State of Amazonas, by bus. The 20-hour bus trip, covering over 470 miles, required two bus drivers — dressed in uniform and tie in spite of the heat. The passengers comprised mostly of Guyanese traders, Brazilians, and our family. To minimize expenses, we bought two tickets and held the boys in our laps.

At the city limit, the paved road became a red dirt road that meandered through a wide corridor in the Amazon Forest. I revelled at the immense walls of dense trees. The drivers maintained a steady fast pace even when crossing wooden bridges without railings. As the bus sped across, the air current swished under the bridge. Thrilling and frightening! The bus traversed two rivers by pontoon. At a rest-stop clearing on the route, we stopped for lunch. All went well until our drivers advised us of a broken bridge ahead. I have no idea how they got the news. Repairs were underway. It was now late afternoon. Just five hours more to Manaus. The drivers took us back to the rest-stop where we had lunch. Later that night, with little available accommodation, the majority of us slept on wooden benches and chairs under a blanketed sky. The symphony of insects and blood-thirsty mosquitoes kept me awake for most of the night.

In the afternoon on the following day, our bus started out again. It arrived at the broken bridge by early evening. "We're going to have a passenger exchange with buses coming from Manaus," said one of our drivers. Three buses from Boa Vista awaited two buses from Manaus. Our Guyanese companions became vociferous. All passengers retrieved their luggage. We had to cross a makeshift bridge: a plank about two feet wide, over fifty feet long, and about ten feet above the river bed. While I stayed with the boys, Jerry made two trips with our suitcases. Two Brazilian men carried our sons across. I was the last to cross. Fear attacks you in unexpected ways and places: walking across a plank. Unarmed, you face Fear with a furtive look. When you escape his grip, you triumph.

While we waited next to our luggage by the roadside, the clamour of six o'clock bees intensified the overall confusion. As shadows melted into night, my uneasiness mounted. Fireflies danced in the black jungle. The headlights of the first bus approaching from Manaus pierced the darkness. Chaos erupted as who should board the bus. The drivers awarded me first place as the only woman with children. As my sons and I waited in the bus, Fear prodded me with thoughts of being separated from my husband. When the drivers allowed him and some other passengers to board the bus, Fear took a backseat.

We slept on the bus as it moved on to Manaus. Early in the morning, we awoke when the bus stopped owing to an empty tank. We got off to stretch our legs and climbed up the hillside to a small red-clay-brick cottage. Jerry chatted in Portuguese with a woman who offered us tiny cups of strong black coffee. I later discovered that this hospitality to strangers is a characteristic of the Brazilian people. We arrived in Manaus on Sunday morning, March 29th, at 8:00 a.m. — a journey that lasted 49 hours.

We stayed three days in Manaus with Jerry's Guyanese friend. The bed rest was a luxury. Manaus, located in the heart of the Amazon Forest on the bank of the River Negro, is a large and densely populated city of over one million (at that time). The stores downtown boggled our eyes with goods that were prohibited or unavailable in our hometown, Georgetown. Their integrated bus system impressed us. The Amazon Theatre, built in 1896 with materials and by artists brought in from Europe, exuded the grandeur of Brazil's past. An evening at a street fair of local handicraft products delighted our senses. What a creative and talented people! Enthralled, we watched two young men dance *capoeira* — martial arts movements in slow-motion — to the string music and chants by members of the group.

Capoeira performers. *Ronald Cesar.*

When we left Manaus, we headed north eastwards — towards the Equator — by air to

Belem. Jerry had contemplated taking the ferry boat along the Amazon River to Belem: a five-day voyage during which passengers slept in hammocks. I thought it too rough for our sons. In contrast, the interior of Brazil's Varig airline jumbo jet seemed more like a theatre. Everything was bigger in Brazil.

Belem, the capital of the State of Pará, lies on the River Pará — part of the Amazon river system — about 60 miles inland from the Atlantic Ocean. In Belem, we embarked on the fourth and final phase of our journey by bus, a 30-hour trip covering almost 1000 miles with stops for lunch, afternoon snack and dinner. Passing through Belem, our bus jostled with other buses, cars and pedestrians on the congested roadways. Giant trees lined the wide main streets. Churches with squares stood out amidst other buildings. Travelling in a south-easterly direction, our bus traversed the northeastern States of Maranhão and Piauí. The vegetation changed from dense forest to scattered trees and shrubs in open expanses of land. We passed through several small towns and areas of isolated dwelling units.

On Thursday, April 2, 1987, we arrived in Fortaleza, around eight in the morning. Lots of sand lined the sides of the street where we spent our first eleven days. Our long and exhausting journey across the north and northeast of Brazil had come to an end.

Fortaleza: Our New Home

Fortaleza — the Portuguese word for 'fort' or 'fortress' — was named after Fortress Schoonenborch built by the Dutch in 1649. When the Portuguese expelled the Dutch in 1654, they renamed it *Fortaleza de Nossa Senhora de Assunção* (Fortress of Our Lady of the Assumption). Fortaleza became the capital of the northeastern State of Ceará on April 13, 1726, long before the conception of British Guiana.

Ceará is smaller in area than Guyana but, in 1991, had a population of 6.4 million. Almost 2 million lived in Fortaleza alone — far more than the 764,000 estimated inhabitants of Guyana in 1990. Sixty percent of Ceará's interior region is semi-arid — known as the *sertão* — covered with shrubs and cacti. Low levels of rainfall in this region prohibited the development of sugar plantations. Due to long cycles of drought in this region, with light showers whenever it does rain, Ceará is a land of eternal sunshine. Coupled with a 356-mile-long coastline of sandy beaches, the State became a mecca for tourists. Each beach has a beauty and characteristics of its own, a refuge from the relentless heat — ranging from 79°F to 82°F in Fortaleza.

In *Centro* (downtown) museums, churches, fortresses, theatres and other buildings of Portuguese architecture from the 18th and 19th centuries stand side by side with modern office buildings, commercial centres and hotels. Statues and monuments are reminders of great personalities and events of Fortaleza's colourful past. Older *praças* (squares), framed by large trees and benches offering shade and rest, differ from modern concrete *praças* with water fountains.

The littered streets of downtown *Centro* tarnish the beauty of its architecture. The constant flow of people on the sidewalks slows down movement in *Centro*. Office buildings and hotels rise up ten stories or more overhead, trapping noise in their tunnels. Cars, bumper to bumper, crawl through the narrow streets. Buses pass non-stop on the main streets feeding the downtown district.

Luxurious five-star hotels and apartment buildings line Fortaleza's beach front. Upper-class residential areas compete for the ocean view and cool sea air. Tall apartment buildings of various designs and colours dominate the skyline. Throughout the city, one- to two-storied homes are interspersed with apartment buildings. Brick red convex-shaped ceramic tiles cap concrete houses. *Favelas* (slums) exist side by side: in abandoned lots, along the railway line, on sandy hilltops and slopes, and along the banks of rivers that overflow with every heavy rainfall.

Beach front area of Forteleza. *Bete Maciel.*

Billboards and signs in another language attracted my attention. My vocabulary included the Portuguese equivalent for good morning, good afternoon, good night, thank you, please, excuse me, and sorry.

As I watched and listened to the children at play, I soon learned the Portuguese for: come here, give me, move out the way, stop it, wait for me, and let's go.

With the help of my husband's friend in Fortaleza, we rented an apartment in a condominium complex located in the outskirts of the city.

Settling In

Our new home was hidden away in an extensive area of drab concrete housing units with concrete stairways — familiar to us only on the movie screen. The four blocks, each four storeys high, weaved in and out, forming a concrete labyrinth that disoriented unsuspecting newcomers. Canopies of cashew nut and mango trees provided shade and fruit. In our small two-bedroom apartment, the walls and low ceiling closed in on me.

Two weeks after our arrival in Fortaleza, my four-year-old said, "Mummy, I wanna go home." His two-year-old brother, thumb in mouth, held onto his shirt.

"This is our home now, darling," I said. "We're not going back to Guyana."

Their adventure was over: Time to settle in. It would take some time for them to accept this as their home.

The administrative building housed the office of the *síndico* (elected manager), a *mercadinho* (small green grocery), and a kindergarten school with seats for twenty kids. Along the back road, a small dry goods shop and another green grocer provided other options.

The roads that circled the condominium were unpaved. Years later, during municipal elections, the district mayor had these roads asphalted. Internal roads made of sand and stone hindered speeding. The sandy play areas delighted my sons but neighbours warned us that the sand was unhygienic. They cautioned us not to sit on the hot outdoor concrete seats. "You'll get sick," they said.

We learnt that the crystal-clear tap water was unsafe for consumption. As recommended, we boiled and filtered water for drinking and cooking. The popular red earthenware filter became a fixture in our kitchen.

"Don't throw toilet paper in the bowl," said my husband's Guyanese friend. "It'll block the sewerage. Put it in a garbage bag." It was difficult to get accustomed to what was, for us, an unsanitary practice. Even more difficult was to witness impoverished children and adults forage in the garbage disposal area. Every morning when I went out with the garbage, I would see this corpulent male and female couple seated on the ground, opening and sorting the contents of garbage bags spread out around them. It was repulsive and heartbreaking.

As the only English-speaking residents, we became an attraction for the children. Whenever I took my sons outside to play, they encircled and gaped at us. They frightened my kids; I felt like a monkey in a zoo. What a relief when I discovered an area at the back of one of the buildings where my sons could play without spectators!

Growing up in a small city, I had rarely used the bus. Our school, downtown, and recreational areas were all within walking or riding distance. In Fortaleza, it was suicidal to use a bicycle. Without a car, the bus was the best means of moving about in this large city. Never before had we seen so many buses. Getting the right buses to our destination became important knowledge for survival. Travelling in the city buses immersed us in the struggle of Brazil's working class. To get to work on time, people crammed into buses. The invasion of my physical space disconcerted me. Getting off an overcrowded bus meant pushing your way between bodies jammed in the aisle.

Some men take advantage of the close proximity in public buses and trains to rub themselves against women. Years later, I tried to escape such abuse but the beast accompanied my every move towards the exit. His ejaculate caught me on my right ankle as I prepared to get off the bus. The anger and repulsion I felt that day fuelled my determination to overcome and succeed.

While conversing, Brazilians stand or sit very close and touch each other a lot. Whenever friends and family meet, they hug and kiss. While men perform a half embrace and tap each other on the back of the shoulder, women kiss both sides of the cheek without touching the skin. Male and female friends also greet each other in this way. Their *calor humano* (human warmth) and passionate use of language for expression contrived together to contaminate me to the core.

Obtaining Permanent Resident Status

Before our 90-day visitor visas expired, we contacted a Brazilian international lawyer for assistance in applying for permanent residence. When he could not help us, Fear became my constant companion. In my dreams, Fear conjured up visions of burly policemen with holstered guns slung low on their hips — a common sight in the streets downtown — dragging us from our home. At every knock on our door, Fear grabbed my hand: "Don't open! They've found you." When Jerry did not return home at his usual time, Fear taunted that the Federal Police had arrested him.

While I asked God to show us the way, we started a home-based pastry business and soon had three regular canteen clients. Our sons began studying Portuguese at the kindergarten school in the condominium compound. The Lord answered my pleas for help in an unexpected way. On October 3, 1988, Brazil's President José Sarney signed a decree-law permitting all illegal residents who had entered Brazil before July 1, 1987 to regularize their residential status. We learnt about this through an article titled (translated), *"Foreigners who entered illegally in the country can stay,"* published in *O Globo* newspapers in Rio de Janeiro. We obtained a copy of this article from one of many Brazilians who helped us over the sixteen years we lived in Brazil. Fear warned that the announcement was a trap set by the government authorities to uncover the estimated 500,000 illegal residents in the country. "Go to the Federal Police Department, present your passports and apply for the provisional registry," said our international lawyer. "It is the best way." Fear remained alert like a sentry.

We were well-received by the Federal Police officials and were always treated with respect. They issued us temporary visas valid for a period of two years. Armed with this document, we applied for and obtained work permits. We could enrol our children in primary school and obtain public medical care. When our temporary visas expired, the Federal Police Department renewed it for another two years and initiated our application for permanent residence.

The application process was a complex one. It required a series of medical examinations; submission of the results to the Ministry of Health; photographs and fingerprints by the Federal Police Department;

written and signed declarations from my husband, me and my boss; and payment of the stipulated fee for each of our four applications.

When my sons and I received our Identity Cards for Foreigners with Permanent Status in 1993, my husband was no longer in Brazil. Disenchanted with the difficulty of making a decent living in Brazil, he had returned to Guyana in March 1991.

Earning a Living in Brazil

My sons were six and eight years old when their father unexpectedly left Brazil. To raise them alone in a male-dominated culture forced me to extend the limits of my capabilities and endurance. Sole responsibility for their well-being and safety threatened to inundate me. Yet, I had struggled too much over those first four years — finding a new profession, learning Portuguese, adjusting to Brazilian life — to abandon the journey and begin again in Guyana. Fear called me crazy and foolish for taking on the task. In the years ahead, friends called me courageous, a heroine, and a warrior. I learnt to take one day at a time.

Earning a living wage to provide for myself and sons was my greatest challenge during a period of high inflation and periods of recession. Workers could not stretch low wages to meet the monthly rise in the cost of living. Bursts of hyperinflation in 1989 (1,863%) and 1994 (2,489%) boggled the mind. With no experience in handling such a volatile economic situation, I had to learn survival skills from the people around me.

During the 16 years that we lived in Brazil, we coped with six economic plans and five currency changes: cruzado, novo cruzado, cruzeiro, cruzeiro real, and real. In 1990, we juggled three different currencies in circulation. Each plan merely served to temporarily slow inflation. Businesses, large and small, sunk in the turbulent economic waves. Job insecurity bobbed on the surface.

When my husband left Brazil in 1991, I was working as an import-export assistant at an international trade consultancy firm. For the first time, I formed part of a small family-owned firm. With them, I obtained my foundation in import and export operations. Alone with two sons, I had to move on but the friendship forged with that family grew over the years. Their support, acceptance within their family circle,

By 1992 I was able to provide for myself and my sons in Brazil. *Rosaliene Bacchus.*

and many kindnesses buoyed me throughout the years.

The gradual reduction in import tariffs under the Collor Plan (1990) opened new job opportunities with companies operating in international commerce. I obtained a position as import-export analyst, then later promoted to the manager's position, with a fresh melon producer, exporter, and importer. Two conquests during this period improved our lives: the acquisition of a cheque account and credit card. I could buy on credit and take advantage of the common practice among major retailers of fixed-monthly payments with post-dated cheques.

Constant price increases made it meaningless to save to buy costly items, such as a refrigerator or colour television. When you raised the amount, the price had already galloped ahead. High interest rates included in the fixed-monthly payments sometimes doubled the final cost of the desired item. For workers earning the minimum wage or salaries fixed to the minimum wage (my case), this was the only option.

With mounting inflation and prolonged drought in Ceará, the melon exporter faced bankruptcy. Salinity increased in its shrinking reservoirs. Uncertainty and insecurity plagued our head office team. Fear returned to stalk me. I had strange dreams. When I let go of the European melon market and joined the team of an importer-wholesaler-retailer firm, I set out on a new path uphill.

Working in the wholesale and retail businesses brought new challenges, excitement, and achievements. As the company grew, I grew as an international trade professional. But the smouldering volcanic Brazilian economy rumbled as I climbed uphill. The Real Plan in mid-1994, equalizing the real with the US dollar, did not tame the dragon. In January 1999, the cost of imports erupted with the devaluation of the real against the US dollar. With molten-laden foreign payments, the company reduced its imports and initiated downsizing. Tensions rose within the company. Throughout the year, I said goodbye to people with whom I had shared many happy moments. Choked with the fumes and ashes of rising exchange rates, the company ceased its import operations by the end of that year. My position as import manager became obsolete.

Achievements that paved a better life for me and my sons were threatened. With my increased income, we had moved to a ten-floor apartment building in an upper middle-class neighbourhood — a ten-minute walk distance from the Beira Mar promenade and seaside.

When my turn came to leave the company, I had to plod up another rocky slope. My next work contract demanded the most both as a professional and a breadwinner. The finished cow-leather producer and exporter was another first in many aspects: a joint-venture enterprise, a factory environment, and highly technological and complex operations. I gained the opportunity to learn and grow with competent executives who allowed me to develop my full potential in the global market.

The factory was located in another coastal city, over forty two miles away. The company provided transport by bus to and from the factory for all professionals resident in Fortaleza and its environs. As I awoke before cock-crow to be ready for pick-up at 5:20 a.m., I caught up on lost sleep on the one-and-a-half-hour bus ride to the factory. The administrative staff began work at 7:00 a.m. Breakfast and lunch were served in the dining hall to all staff members. As export sales manager, I did not always take the 5:00 p.m. bus back to Fortaleza. The company provided alternative transport for those of us who worked late. With the long days and working weekends, I depended on my adolescent sons to assist with the household chores. They were a great support. Their shopping and cooking skills came in handy when our apartment became the venue for weekend overnight matches, following the release of the first Halo Xbox video-game. Our living room and balcony bulged with young people. What a joy!

Family and Social Life

Frequent get-togethers of family and friends were a normal part of life in Fortaleza. People take time out to enjoy the good that life offers. Perhaps, this is their way of turning life's lemon into lemonade — an expression I often heard. Low-income families take care of each other by pooling their financial resources. Family units are strong and supportive of its members.

Enjoying a snack in downtown Fortaleza. *Rosaliene Bacchus.*

Beach front promenade in Fortaleza where I often walked with my sons. *Bete Maciel.*

In Fortaleza, children are an important part of family life. Family-owned businesses plan social events for their staff with families in mind. My sons have many happy memories of birthday and Christmas parties shared with bosses and friends from my workplace. Weekends are time for a day at the beach or at a *sítio* (country house). Rare trips to famous beaches — like Jericoacoara, Canoa Quebrada, and Beach Park — added adventure to our lives.

Praia do Futuro, a popular beach in Fortaleza. *Bete Maciel.*

Revelers at the Carnaval de Aracati.
Domikado.

Various cultural activities throughout the year enriched our lives. Before Lent, there is the *Carnaval* in Rio. Every state plays carnival in its unique way. In Ceará, the population left Fortaleza on Thursday evening. Most of them headed for the beaches and did not return until the night before Ash Wednesday. Five days straight spent on non-stop drinking, dancing, and revelry to music provided by singers and bands on *trios elétricos* – large trucks equipped with modern sound systems and a platform on top for the artists. Carnival in Aracati was the most popular. Those without money found their way to the beaches with just the clothes on their backs and slept wherever they fell in exhaustion.

With a conservative and strict upbringing, I was never able to be part of such festivities. We remained in the city where all forms of commerce, including the cinemas, closed for business. For me, it was a well-needed break from the pressures of work. It was a bad time for my sons as most of their friends left the city. For those of us who remained in Fortaleza, there was the Maracatu parade. Participants, with face and hands painted black, dressed in costumes reminiscent of the Portuguese and French monarchy. Moving through major streets in downtown Fortaleza, they danced to the rhythm of African drums.

One aspect of Brazil's carnival fascinated me: the Samba. It differed from the Caribbean rhythm that coursed through my veins. I never mastered the samba like a native but I was imbued with its rhythm and movement.

The folkloric *Festas Juninas* during the month of June contrasted with Carnival. June commemorates the feasts of Saint Anthony (June 13), Saint John (June 24) and Saint Peter (June 29). The Brazilian people are very religious. Many of them had little shrines in their homes, dedicated to Mary or their favourite saint. Unmarried women invoke

Saint Anthony for husbands. Saint John is the merrymaker and protects married couples and the sick. Saint Peter is the protector of widows and fishermen.

The June Festivals are celebrated with the bonfire and the *quadrilha* (square dance) to the sound of the accordion, triangle and *zabumba* (leather drum). Young women dress like early Portuguese farm workers: colourful skirts and straw hats with two long hair-braids. Their male partners paint on moustaches, dress in patched overalls with straw hats. I watched with pride as my sons performed in their school festivals. Together with our neighbours, we enjoyed another *Festa Junina* organized by our condominium management team.

My sons and their school friend dressed up for Festa Sao Joao.
Rosaliene Bacchus.

Then there is Brazil's passion for football (American soccer). Just as we Guyanese learn and play cricket from a young age, Brazilian children learn to kick a ball as soon as they are able to walk. In the beginning, my sons had no interest in football and did not play well. Over time, I observed with satisfaction as they had fun playing football with the other boys in the condominium playground. It was a rite-of-passage for them. Our passion for football was born with the 1994 FIFA World Cup. Since then, we have rooted for the Brazilian team in all its World Cup matches.

During the World Cup, the air would be charged with a contagious energy that swept us along with its current. Yellow and green buntings — the colours of the Brazilian flag — livened the streets like a town fair. Brazilian flags fluttered from passing cars. All business and other activities came to a halt during the matches of the Brazilian team. Buses stopped on their route at the nearest restaurant or bar with a television where the driver, conductor and passengers could watch the game.

While my sons stayed with their friends, I watched most games with work colleagues. We jumped up, screamed, hugged each other, and set off fire crackers with every goal. We suffered whenever our team missed a goal, obtained a penalty or a player was hurt. To win the World Cup is a matter of great national pride for the Brazilian people. During the 2002 World Cup, management at the leather factory where I worked set up a giant screen and a satellite dish. In this way, the entire tannery and administrative staff could view the game from the factory floor. Such moments were precious and bonded us with the people of our adopted homeland.

The Brazilian television network that brought us the FIFA World Cup is an integral part of Brazilian working class life. It provides not only entertainment for all ages but its newscasts and programmes also help form public opinion. I was pleased with the numerous programmes available for children. But the level of female nudity on many shows, reflected in the Brazilian way of dress, shocked me. In time, what my conservative mind had judged as vulgar became a natural part of our everyday life in this hot and dusty tropical coastal city.

The Brazilian *novela* (soap opera) is of great importance in daily life. In the evenings, there are three *novelas* from Monday to Saturday at six, seven and eight o'clock. The *novela at eight* on Rede Globo, featuring the country's top actors and actresses, is the most popular. Main characters of polemic *novelas* are often a topic for discussion among neighbours and work colleagues.

I got hooked on *novelas* after following episodes as a language-learning exercise. I gradually understood more as my vocabulary increased. I also gained an appreciation for the high quality of Brazil's film productions and acting performances. When each *novela* ended, I even missed my favourite characters.

Living With Poverty and Violence

Novelas served as an escape from the poverty and violence that were part of our everyday life. The middle and upper classes hide behind high walls topped with electrified wires. Gate-keepers control movement at entrances to apartment buildings.

Yet, you cannot escape from the poverty and the violence in Fortaleza. Pockets of *favelas* are located within and on the fringes of high-value residential areas. The homeless, of all ages, roam the streets in downtown Fortaleza and target women and the elderly. Open-air restaurants along the beach promenade attract beggars. At some street corners and traffic lights, bandits rob motorists of their watches, wallets or handbags.

There existed a general sense of insecurity. Men were being shot and killed while standing outside their homes or waiting for a bus. Children were kidnapped while playing in front of their homes, in parks, and shopping centres. Women were seized while withdrawing money from ATMs and taken to machines around town to deplete their bank accounts before being released. Wealthy businessmen or members of their family were kidnapped and held for ransom.

My sons and I could not allow the violence to imprison us. As we went about our daily activities, we trained ourselves to be alert to our surroundings, when walking on the streets, and using the city buses.

Like a true Brazilian, I got together with friends after work on Fridays for a happy hour to eat barbecue chicken hearts with a cold drink. At weekends, whenever possible, we enjoyed the sunshine and waves at the beach. We savoured the fried fish, cooked crabs broken with a wooden stick, and boiled salted unshelled shrimp. Men and women quenched their thirst with cold beer. Children played in the sand, raced the waves as they rushed inland along the shore, and built sand castles. Peddlers walked the beach barefoot, offering sunglasses, suntan lotion, lotion to bleach body hair, straw hats, and jewellery made from natural materials. Others pushed small two-wheeled thermal carts filled with *picoles* (popsicles) of various flavours. The sound of their bell attracted the children like flies to a drop of syrup on a table top. Under the sun's gaze, even parents enjoyed this icy treat. The sculptured, bronzed young women wearing the *fio-dental* (thongs) paraded along the seaside. The anxieties of the past week were washed out with the tide. Who could ask for more?

Guyanese with a Brazilian Heart

Lying on the beach in Fortaleza, I discovered the calming effect of the ocean's rise and fall. I had had to face situations that I had never anticipated that night on March 4, 1987 when I fought with Fear.

Together, my sons and I faced and overcame each obstacle, each hurt, each loss.

When you raise young children in a foreign culture without the support of an extended family, your voice is just dust in the wind. There was no Guyanese or Caribbean community in Fortaleza. I had to conquer Fear. I had to go with the current or remain stranded on the bank. Yet flowing with the stream did not mean drowning my values, principles, and world vision — fruits of my upbringing in Guyana.

Some traditions are lost and replaced with those of the new homeland. Others are ingrained. I learnt to cook a few Brazilian dishes; I added them to our Guyanese cuisine. At Christmas, friends and neighbours looked forward to receiving a piece of our Guyana black cake.

As immigrants, we have to make profound changes to adapt, survive, and succeed in our new environment. Part of me is still Guyanese, but I was inoculated with the Brazilian *jeito de ser* (way of being). Their celebration of life captured my heart; their suffering imprisoned my soul. Today, I am a Guyanese with a *coração brasileiro*. My heart continues to beat in tune with its rhythm; my soul continues to rejoice and cry out with its people.

Scenes from a Life in Music

Ray Luck

Ray Luck was appointed Member of the Order of Service of Guyana on being conferred the Cacique's Crown of Honour in 1992. Born November 18, 1942, of the fourth generation of the Luck family in Guyana, he is the son of Albert (Cowie) and Claris (Nannie) Luck. As a concert pianist, teacher, adjudicator, and lecturer, Ray has toured on five continents. His CDs – 'Souvenirs of Venice and Naples' and 'Dukas-Schmitt' – appear on the websites www.claudiorecords.com and www.rayluck.com

"Life is not what one lived, but what one remembers and how one remembers it in order to recount it."
                    Gabriel Garcia Marquez in 'Living to Tell the Tale.'

* * * * * * * *

Beginnings

A few years ago, as I visited a friend's home in Port of Spain to relax before a concert performance, I found her elderly mother giving a piano lesson on the veranda to a young student while others awaited their turn. This scene struck a familiar chord since it reminded me of my lessons with my first music teacher, Millicent Joseph. From the age of six, two afternoons every week were devoted to piano lessons with theory and aural training on Saturday mornings. Thus my sister, Beverley, and I progressed every year through the graded exams set by the Associated Board of the Royal Schools of Music in London. From the age of 10 or so, juggling primary school and music lessons was difficult. I stayed after normal school hours for the 'extra' lessons that prepared us for the 11+ government scholarship exam. On music lesson days, I would then pedal a mini-bicycle from Smith Church Primary School in Hadfield Street to Mrs. Joseph's in Queenstown, followed by an equally long journey of endless pedaling to our home in Kingston. There seemed little to enjoy in this period of my life. What made it burdensome was that even though I understood that learning was serious business, children were nevertheless subjected to a regimen of fear and intimidation imposed by teachers. Their mantra seemed to be "You will learn by hook or by crook!" These early experiences no doubt left an indelible mark and influenced my own approach to teaching. As a teacher, I would be compelled to find more positive ways of communication.

Teenage Years

Thankfully, high school years at Queens College were less stressful since learning was no longer associated with coercion. For me, the smorgasbord of new school subjects opened vistas, and though we were kept on our toes scholastically - at general assembly, each name in the school was read out periodically according to academic placement in class - we were left very much to learn at our own pace. As I matured, I quickly recognized the link between effort and personal fulfillment.

At age 14, a major change occurred in my music study when through happenstance I became a student of Ruby MacGregor (sister of Mrs. Joseph). Mrs. MacGregor, recognized with the MBE for her contributions to music, was the most respected music teacher in all of British Guiana. Her musical accomplishments in New Amsterdam were legendary. To my good fortune, she moved to Georgetown in 1957, when with Mrs. Joseph's blessing I transferred to her. Ruby MacGregor's most remarkable traits as a teacher were her vivid personality and ability to inspire (I recall her relating her impressions of a recital by the pianist-composer, Ernst von Dohnányi whom she had heard at the Edinburgh Festival, and as she relived this experience it was as if I myself were hearing the pianist in the concert hall). Largely self-taught, she brought a lively curiosity and practical approach to her teaching, and as ABRSM representative in New Amsterdam, she told me that she often sought answers to musical questions from the visiting examiners when the exams were through. She shared her library of music textbooks and LP recordings, and we spent many hours together discussing various artists' performances. At this stage, my study of music theory included counterpoint and fugal writing, subjects that I would encounter later in the B.Mus. curriculum. Four years of lessons with Mrs. MacGregor seemed to whiz by in which we accomplished much – a Distinction in the final Grade 8 exam and a number of diplomas, the LRSM, as well as Licentiate and Fellowship diplomas from Trinity College of Music, London.

The British Guiana Music Festival, founded by Lynette Dolphin and Eleanor Kerry in 1952, set musical standards and provided performing opportunities for musicians of every ilk and all ages. I participated in the first festival (in the Under 10 Piano Solo class) and grew up sharing a range of musical experiences with many others. From an early age these festivals taught us to respect and acknowledge the talents and successes of our peers while getting used to performing on stage.

In London and Paris

The decision to make music a lifetime career was easy for me but caused concern in others. At 16, I was recommended for the Caribbean's ABRSM scholarship but declined this in order to complete high school. At 18, I juggled career paths but music eventually trumped the other options of a UWI scholarship to study mathematics and a place at Cambridge to study medicine. Most likely I had gained my parents' support through my obvious commitment and musical accomplishments to date. With no other artist figure in the family, they had no clue where such a career choice might lead, but fortunately, they believed that with one life to live, one should be happy in one's choice. Serious music study is at heart a vocation, and my parents' unequivocal trust in my judgment equipped me with a lifelong confidence. During the months of career-juggling, Mrs. MacGregor had remained silent and when told of my decision to study music, commented, "A cork will float no matter how much you try to sink it."

London was a culture shock as one would expect, but before long I was ensconced at a British Council hostel in Knightsbridge along with a few hundred Commonwealth students adjusting to life in Britain. At the Royal College of Music I enrolled in London University's B.Mus. course, while studying piano first with Antony Hopkins, and then Cyril Smith, one of the most sought-after professors. One private piano lesson each week provided little music interaction with other students – except for weekly College concerts – and in general, the scheduled music lectures were very dull. Little did I know that at the end of my second year (1963) this would change after receiving a bursary to attend the Dartington Summer School. Located on a beautiful Devonshire estate, the Summer School featured eminent European teachers, composers, and performers. Its informality, high-energy buzz of students and artists, excellent master classes, and concerts created an exciting and stimulating environment. I performed in Yvonne Lefébure's master class and was charmed by her vivacity and personal warmth, and above all, I was in awe of her mastery and command as an artist-teacher. She spoke only French and though I missed subtleties (O-level French seemed in the distant past), the stamp of musical truth in her teaching was unmistakable. Moreover, the camaraderie among her students from Paris and their respect for her made a great impression on me. At the end of my stay at Dartington, Mme. Lefébure invited me to audition for a scholarship at the Paris Conservatoire. That autumn (how well I remember the colorful foliage in the gardens at Versailles!) I went twice to Paris for the two-stage *concours d'admission* – playing a Chopin Nocturne and Beethoven's 'Appassionata' Sonata in the first round, and Weber's 3rd Sonata, the *morceau imposé* memorized in three weeks, for the final test.

Yvonne Lefébure had played for Debussy, Ravel, and Fauré; her professors included Dukas, and as the protégée prodigy of the eminent French pianist, Alfred Cortot, she had gained the Premier Prize at the Conservatoire at age 11 playing the 'Appassionata' Sonata. Work at the Conservatoire was rigorous – besides general music classes, each student in the piano class of 12 performed in twice weekly master classes. It was a revelation to hear such a large range of repertoire performed and taught at this level. Incidentally, this would serve as excellent training in pedagogy! The intensity in class continued into the end-of-year exam. Each year those passing the first stage of this exam were assigned a specially commissioned composition to be performed from memory for a second jury. Winning the Premier Prix at the end of my first year was noteworthy but also bitter-sweet since I could no longer remain in the class. However, this award entitled me to enter the Conservatoire's Chamber Music class which I did and gained another Premier Prix at the following year's concours.

The year after Paris was spent completing the B.Mus degree, while studying with the British pianist, Denis Matthews (specialist on the music of Mozart, Haydn, and Beethoven) on an award from the Countess of Munster Musical Trust. In 1966, I returned to Paris on a French Government scholarship and prepared for international competitions. For better

Ray Luck performing at a concert.
www.rayluck.com

or worse, music contests provide training for performing in the most exacting conditions – and in 1967, I emerged second prizewinner in the Geneva International Music Competition. This success was the springboard for a debut recital at the Queen Elizabeth Hall in London in December 1969 resulting in the positive headline review, *'Fine Beethoven by Guyanese Pianist'*, in London's Daily Telegraph.

To North America

In considering my future at this stage, I thought that it would be ideal to find an artist-in-residence position at a university or college that demanded both performing and teaching skills. In the 1970s such jobs were typical at North American universities while fewer than a handful existed in Britain. But how could one aspire to such a position? On a concert tour in Canada in 1973, friends in Calgary had spoken highly of György Sebok, a Hungarian professor at Indiana University, and when I reached Toronto, I decided to tour three schools in the US – Juilliard, Peabody, and IU at Bloomington – to inquire about music doctorate programs. Indiana University, the largest with 3000 music students, was the most welcoming and affordable, and so in January 1975, I left London and arrived in the middle of winter to commence graduate study. It was a revolutionary change in education systems (e.g. the basic term 'credit-hour' had to be explained), but there were definite advantages – the semester system allowed entrance in the middle of the school year, teaching assistantships were available, and the easy informal access to professors was a most pleasant surprise. Prof. Sebok's studio consisted largely of international students (mainly from Asia and Europe), the result of his constant travel abroad. At IU, he had designed the Performer's Certificate, an advanced course for international music students, and on my arrival he encouraged me to enroll in this program. I told him that I already had diplomas in excess and was interested only in the doctorate degree in order to achieve a long-term goal. I knew that the highest 'paper' qualification would be the only guarantee to satisfy a future employer. My firmness must have unnerved him, and he ended the discussion, "Well, do the doctorate if you wish." I discovered later that he meant this literally since I was left to plan and work through the degree requirements entirely unaided, though he appeared at crucial moments to lend moral support. As a teacher he was the right person for me at the time. With very few words, he offered rare insights into one's performance that would be revelatory later in the privacy of the practice studio. A quasi-metaphysical mind-set went hand in hand with his holistic view of piano-playing – mental, physical, and musical – that led to a constant awareness of the relationship between effort and efficiency. I completed the degree in three years, and afterwards remained so fascinated by this philosopher-musician that I attended his summer music workshops in the alpine village of Ernen in the Valais region of Switzerland.

Two years as visiting lecturer at the University of Maryland at College Park intervened before I was appointed associate professor of music at Randolph-Macon Woman's College in Lynchburg, Virginia. From my arrival in 1980, this small liberal arts college of 750 students welcomed me into its community and offered a plethora of professional opportunities. Indeed, shortly after my arrival, the College sponsored me in a debut solo recital at Alice Tully Hall in New York's Lincoln Center. Other highlights were an arts trip to Java & Bali, a tour of China, and time off for two Fulbright teaching fellowships to the Caribbean (1994) and Greece (2001). The exceptional qualities of life that I found on this campus – acceptance on one's merit regardless of background, nurturing of students and faculty, an honor code that, for example, made proctoring of exams unnecessary – made this sojourn a happy time. In addition, the College provided funds for personal professional projects, and awarded me an endowed chair in music. After 22 years I felt the urge to return to a warmer climate, and in 2002, moved to a neighborhood in Saint Petersburg, Florida, that reminded me of the ones that I knew in Georgetown.

The Caribbean

Ever since my first Caribbean concert tour (sponsored by the Guyana Government in 1969) that began in Guyana and Suriname and wound its way northwards from Trinidad to the Bahamas, I have maintained musical contacts in the region. In 1998, I taught one term at the St. Lucia School of Music where I now return each July to conduct an international piano workshop. These connections are important to me, and the people whom I have met and the serendipitous happenings on these visits have been memorable.

From that first tour, I learned it was a priority to check the piano and the tuner's expertise at each stop-over. In Dominica, the young tuner revealed that his name was Handel. Surprised, I asked him, "You mean, Handel, like the composer?" He said this was so and informed me that his siblings were also named after composers – a brother, Purcell, and sisters, Palestrina and Paganini! I was intrigued and curious to meet his parents. Handel arranged a visit, and as I stepped out of the taxi, a shingle outside the house stated, 'John Christian, Teacher of Commerce and Music'. At the top of the staircase, Mr. Christian rose to greet me from his desk and after shaking hands, he thumped the wall behind him a few times with an open palm, repeating, "THESE ARE THE GREATS!" The wall was decorated with picture postcards of famous composers. The large room that I had entered was furnished with a number of musical instruments and typewriters. Somehow this

Ray Luck tutoring a student in Dominica. *www.rayluck.com*

all seemed vaguely familiar, and then I recalled my childhood home. As long as I could remember, my father had supplemented high school teaching with afternoon classes in typewriting, shorthand, and book-keeping. The gallery of our home at that time was converted into a classroom with typewriters, and of course, there was a piano in the living room on which my sister and I practiced. What a cacophony it must have all made – the clack of typewriters and Czerny! After my concert, Mr. Christian came backstage proclaiming, "One hundred percent! One hundred percent!!" He obviously was giving me his seal of approval.

Again, on the theme of pianos and piano tuners. In 1994, when I arrived in Montserrat for a concert, I found a tourist-type American dressed in beachwear and flip-flops tuning the piano, and it soon became obvious that this young man knew precious little about tuning. By necessity the tuning eventually evolved into a cooperative venture between him and me. As he hit the piano keys and wielded the tuning lever, I grunted 'higher' or 'lower' to indicate the adjustment. In this way we made progress. Finally on reaching the highest notes, I was left speechless when my host blurted out, "But why are you worrying with those? You don't play up there, do you?!" A year later, it was a shock and most unsettling to see photos of Plymouth, deserted and obliterated in Soufrière's ash.

In fall 2000, I had come across a news report that a British expedition had delivered a grand piano to a village in the Amazonian rainforest. Intrigued by this, I thought it would be a great adventure to locate and play this instrument. I showed the newspaper clipping to Michael Gilkes, visiting professor at R-MWC, and we both became enthusiastic about planning a trip. Michael obtained permission from the Government, and set about to organize a 10-day expedition to Masakanyari, the only Wai-Wai settlement in Guyana, where the grand piano was located. In March 2002, our party assembled in Georgetown: videographer, two sound technicians, piano technician – Remington Ally from Toronto and an American anthropologist completing her field-study of the Wai-Wai. The first day we flew to the Rockview Resort at Annai in the south Rupununi, then the next morning, our small plane took us further south to Gunn's Strip, located an hour's walk from the Wai-Wai village near the Guyana-Brazil border. Remington spent two days overhauling the innards of the piano, much to the fascination of the children who took delight in seeing themselves framed in the digital camera. The instrument that emerged had a warm beautiful sound and perfect playing action. The benab which housed the piano was lit by flambeaux for the concert in the evening. The villagers, young and old, first sang hymns in Wai-Wai accompanied by two young guitarists, and following a brief introduction to the music, I played a program of Bach ('Jesu, Joy of Man's Desiring'), Villa-Lobos ('Jungle Festival'), and Hugh Sam's

Wearing the native head dress at a visit to an Amerindian village. *www.rayluck.com*

arrangements of Guyanese songs, 'Small Days'/ 'Rick, Chick, Chick'. At the end of the evening, each member of the audience – children and adults alike – approached and shook my hand in quiet acknowledgment of mutual gratitude. It was a thrill to 'discover' this new audience in my native Guyana.

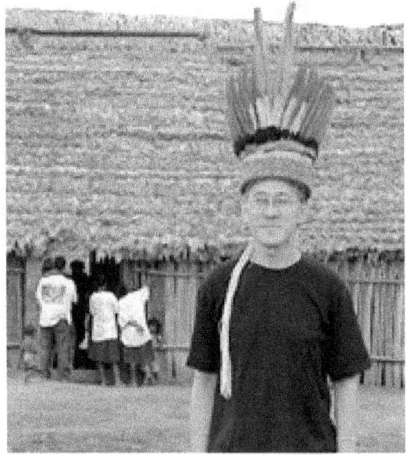

China

I had found that the inability to speak Chinese presented an enormous cultural barrier when meeting Chinese nationals in the West. It was as if they were unable to grasp the enormity of the diaspora and unaware that previous generations had settled in far-flung places. Thus prior to my first visit to China in 2000, I spent 16 weeks learning Mandarin to explain at a basic level, for instance, that I was 'Overseas' Chinese. Without fail, this effort elicited broad smiles instead of the previous blank looks of incomprehension. My interpreter then proceeded to elaborate on my origins and to explain why this ethnic Chinese person was without-language. Three years later I returned to Shanghai and when I went to perform a piano recital at the Kai Ming Theater in Suzhou, I became aware of the strong desire of many Chinese to speak English. At the concert, an emcee introduced each item on the program in Mandarin and at the end of the program, some of the audience came on stage to greet me. There was one memorable moment when a boy, about eight years old dressed immaculately in a military-style uniform, edged his way forward, shook my hand and asked in a British accent, "How do I become a musician?" This concert

Ray Luck at the Kai Ming Theatre, Suzhou.
www.rayluck.com.

in Suzhou had followed three weeks of adjudicating piano classes at the Hong Kong Schools Music Festival. There I had listened to 3000 young pianists and wrote a comment sheet for each performer. These young musicians were keen to excel, and like the young boy in Suzhou, they were intent to get to the root of things. A teacher needs to get to the root of things in passing on the legacy of what one has learned and experienced. Also an eager and receptive student may appear at any place and at any time. Together student and teacher will embark on the wonderful journey of discovery and that gives music meaning and emotion.

Around the World

Vivian Lee

When I look back on the past, I never would have thought that so much of my travels around the world came about from a football. But, in many ways, the soccer ball, itself looking much like a miniature world, gave me a kick-start for many of my activities and course in life. Starting from when I was a teenager attending St. Stanislaus College in Georgetown, I was active in football and was noticed by the manager of the Artillery Team, one of the top teams in the country. I joined the Gunners, as that team was called, but this required that I be "enlisted" in the military, although in practical terms this was more like "being on the list" of the Auxiliary. But this "tour of duty" took me to Trinidad for training and drills. My football skills as a striker caused me to be selected to represent Guyana in international matches. But then I myself was struck on the cheek

St. Stanislaus College was started by Jesuits in 1866 as a grammar school for boys. *Isabelle Lee.*

in a collision during a game resulting in a bone fracture. I took a vacation in Barbados to recuperate and it was during my stay there that I thought hard about whether I wanted to continue being a civil servant. I resigned my job and opted to go to the United States to learn

Vivian Lee, who became a First Lieutenant in the Auxilary, is shown with his parents. *Viv Lee.*

the business of laundering and dry cleaning so that I could help in the laundry that my father had established in Georgetown.

It was while I was in New York and New Jersey that I got interested in a course in broadcasting. Upon my return to Georgetown I was warmly greeted as a returning hero, because I was known in Guyana as a football star of sorts, having on one occasion scored the game-deciding goal against Surinam. This acclaim helped me when I set up my Ace Advertisers business. Then it was through my success in advertising that I was asked to be the president of the British Guiana Table Tennis Association. Through an opportune fund-raising dance, we were able to collect sufficient money for me to take the table tennis team to Jamaica.

The success of Ace Advertisers allowed me to go for visits to Barbados and Trinidad, especially during the Carnival revelries in Port-of-Spain. During all this time, my interest in football never wavered and even after my participation as a player ended, I was still on the football field as a referee. When the World Cup for football was scheduled for Mexico in 1970, I wanted to go, especially since I realized that I had not taken a long vacation in some 3 to 4 years. I arranged for my son, Ronald, to run Ace Advertisers, while I would be away for about three months. Eric Rohee told me that he also wanted to go. I wrote to the agency in Mexico and I found out about the tickets and the necessary travel arrangements. Then I told Eric that things were under control, and gave him the prices for the various tickets. Then Eric asked me about hotel accommodations. I said, I'm not worried about a hotel, we must be able to get a place. But he said, you know everything must be sold out at this time already. I said, "Man, I going, even if it turns out that I must find a girlfriend or somebody to put me up somewhere."

Football referee Viv Lee at GFC grounds, Georgetown. *Viv Lee.*

Brazil was my favorite team and I bought two sets of tickets in my name to see all the matches that Brazil would be playing. I got tickets for Mexico City to see the opening ceremony and the opening match, as well as the final, and the rest of the tickets were for the Group 3 matches in Guadalajara, featuring Brazil and England. Then Eric told me he would not go, and wouldn't require the tickets. I said, don't worry I'm going to sell it when I get there. Typical of me, I was willing to take the chance but he decided not to go without reserved accommodations. I guess our fates were not the same. When I went there and got off the plane, I told the taxi driver, "Hotel, Hotel." Well I couldn't speak Spanish but they knew the word "Hotel" and he opened his mouth agape giving the impression: where the hell you expect me to find a hotel at this time. So we drove to one hotel – no vacancy. We went to another – nothing doing. We tried yet another – no luck. Eventually, I think maybe at the fourth or fifth try, there was a room available – and the name of the place was Oxford Hotel. It was a little squeaky place, a walk-up with no elevator. On the third floor the guy ask me if I wanted it. It was a room, and it wasn't too expensive. I said yes. What the heck did I care that it was a walk-up, I wasn't going to be living there permanently and after I set out in the morning, I would be gone for the whole day. But I was so glad to get that hotel I tell you I would have slept in a dump. So I thought about how things turned out – Eric, man, you should have come. I had a wonderful time. I saw all the matches that I wanted and sold the remaining extra tickets right there. There was a girl from the travel agency sitting there selling tickets and she bought back my ticket right away with a full refund.

After the World Cup I decided I would tour the USA. I bought a two-week Greyhound bus pass and crisscrossed the country. Wherever I met with folks from Guyana I would do an interview and send back the tape for broadcast on the radio. Then I visited Canada, but not the western region. After that, I went over to England, and there I bought a car, a Morris with relining front seats, which made it convenient for me to sleep in the car. I had gone before to England, but I'd never been to France. My grandmother (my mother's mother) was French so I wanted to go and see what France was all about. I crossed the English Channel and my first port of destination was Holland. I then headed north to Denmark and Sweden and I came back and went to Milan in Italy. During all this traveling I would pick up hitch-hikers and in this way I met with people from Holland, Mexico, Japan and other countries. Back in Guyana, Ace Advertisers used to do advertisements for Fiat motorcars and so I went to visit the car assembly plant in Milan. I spent an afternoon there, and asked a girl at the factory about any points of interest in this area. She recommended Mont Blanc[1] and gave me directions.

The most direct route was the Mont Blanc Tunnel that connected Italy and France, and just at the entrance to this tunnel I picked up a couple of French girls who were hitch-hiking to France. Somehow, going through that tunnel, it seemed like the story of my life – a long period of darkness and then glorious sunshine when we reached the other side. It was a beautiful sight and we took some pictures. The date was 5 September 1970. One of the girls was quite friendly and curious about the place from where I came and so we exchanged addresses. After touring in France, I continued on to Spain and Portugal, before going back to London. I then had the car shipped to Guyana while I took a plane back home.

I began corresponding with the hitch-hiking girl – her name is Isabelle – and we made an arrangement to meet in London for Old Year's Night celebrations. At this time my marriage had already broken up and my children were grown and taking care of themselves independently. Well, London is a busy place and by the time I caught a train to get to Heathrow Airport I was late by about half an hour. She was not a happy lass, commenting, The first time you make a date and you show up late. But anyhow we were happy to be together in London and spent Old Year's Night at a lovely dance there. Unfortunately, she had brought only light clothing and we had a hard time getting a taxi to go home. We waited for half an hour, running from one side of the street to the other, trying to flag down a taxi. Anyhow, I proposed and she accepted so my return to Guyana I wrote her mother telling her that I would like to marry her daughter. We got married on 29 May 1971 in Cluses, Haute Savoie, her hometown in the French Alps.

On the way back to Guyana we stopped in Barbados, and had an

---

1   Located in the Alps, Mont Blanc is the highest mountain in western Europe.

Viv and his bride Isabelle at their
civil marriage ceremony in Clues.
Viv Lee.

Celebrating Isabelle's 21st birthday
at Ace Advertisers in Georgetown.
Viv Lee.

enjoyable time. Actually, she was rather courageous. Her father had died
the year before and she had four brothers and three sisters and she was
the only one to leave France. It was upsetting for her mother and strange
for her too. But her eldest sister came down with her for the trip, and
she enjoyed the whole thing. It was a very different life for Isabelle but
she soon began to love it. My advertising business was one of the largest
and our position in Guyana was very good. We lived a comfortable life,
and had a cook and a maid to take care of the children with whom we
were blessed. But this "good life" for us lasted only until 1979, when we
decided to leave Guyana.

The events resulting from Guyana's independence in May 1966 were
the main causes for us leaving Guyana. Personally, I was happy to see
independence arrive. I recall sitting in the park there as they lowered the
British flag. I told my daughter Jennifer (from my first marriage) that I
felt proud that "this is our own country now." As Guyanese were saying,
We're now responsible for our own destiny. Like them, I was hoping

Viv and Isabelle's home in Georgetown
from 1972 to 1979. *Isabelle Lee.*

that we would have leaders and good fortune to push us ahead to become a strong nation on our own. But it wasn't to be.

Shortly after independence some things appeared as if they were on the right track. But then local conditions got worse and it looked like the leaders were not very practical in what they were aiming to do and how they were going to achieve it. In the late 1960s the government introduced restrictions on imports. At first I thought it was a good thing not to depend so much on the outside. The idea of growing your own food sounded good to me – it would make us more and more independent. But the restrictions on the importation of household goods caused my clients to suffer in sales. What did we have to advertise now? Nothing more – our shelves are bare. The little bit that we got would be sold in no time. So less and less advertising requests came, but I would still have stayed on in Guyana because I used to tell everybody, This is my country, the one that I love, right? I am staying. But teachers were affected, schools were affected, and I felt that the education standard was sinking. I had two young kids, Tony, and Delicia, and I wondered what lay in the future. I had to think of their education and future prospects.

At this time, my wife was enrolled at the University of Guyana. Then Prime Minister Forbes Burnham wanted all the people who wanted to graduate from the university to serve a period of time with the Guyana Defense Force. Isabelle would need to go to the interior of the country for training and active service. I could have gone to see the officer in charge of the postings for GDF, because I knew him well. However, I decided against that as it would have been unfair because all others had to do service. Isabelle was expecting our third child so I said, let's forget your B.A. degree and this military duty obligation. She didn't complete her schooling and we made plans to leave the country. I sold out the business and gave away my stuff. I guess I was never meant to be rich. I quit and we made arrangements to go to France.

It was virtually impossible for people to take their financial assets out of the country, unless they resorted to bribery or the black market. Well, the thought of being caught was the thing that really scared me. Imagine Vivian Lee, who was a well-known personality, trying to get his own money out of Guyana. I decided to leave my money in Guyana and concluded that whatever God has in store for me, He would take care of us. So we left with not much more than the clothes in our suitcases. All that they allowed us to take was my old motorcar, with permission to ship it abroad, and a couple hundred dollars in foreign exchange. So all my money was left in Guyana to use whenever I can visit my beloved country and give a helping hand.

We left for France and we started life all over from scratch. Here I was in a foreign land at the age of 60, and the trouble was that, having worked for myself, I had no pension or retirement plan to provide an income. Even so, when we left Guyana we had no qualms about taking this big step and being alarmed about how we would live. Fortunately, Isabelle's mother had a room for us and while it was a place to make a start, we had the three young children, and we didn't want to stay too long with the old lady.

Cluses is a beautiful little town in the French Alps, some 40 kilometres southeast of Geneva. Jobs for my wife were difficult to find locally and she eventually got one at Digital Corporation in Geneva. I started to teach English. We used to go around the town putting up little stickers to advertise my English lessons as we didn't have money to advertise in the newspaper. My very first student was a young man and I taught him in my mother-in-law's kitchen. Isabelle went to apply for a job at a company called Alcatel, a big company

Viv Lee adjusting to French cuisine and lifestyle (1982). *Viv Lee.*

in the technological business. The manager explained that they didn't have anything right then and he asked about her husband – what was he doing? So she said that he taught English. From that I got a job teaching English at Alcatel – to their executives, mostly. We made arrangements to hold lessons at varying times, depending on the schedules of the students. Since I was living only five minutes away from the company, I used to ride a bicycle or I could walk. It was very convenient.

Isabelle's job at Digital in Geneva was fantastic. By working in Switzerland and living in France, we had the best of both worlds because the Swiss franc was stronger than the French franc. So we did quite well and saved our money. Soon we had enough money to think of buying a house. Cluses was really too small a town to get a good job, and so we moved over to Annecy, where we rented a beautiful little apartment, not far from a lovely lake with the mountains around it. Isabelle would leave for Geneva in the morning at 7:00 o'clock and would stay till 5:00 or 6:00 p.m. I had to take care of the children. The children could walk to school from where we were living and I would be at home preparing their "lunch" and so on. Alcatel also had a branch office about 10 kilometres away. I didn't have a motorcar and had to ride my bicycle there. The area was hilly and on some hills I had to get off and push the bike because the road was too steep. I arranged my classes with the executives to fit my time. During their 7- to 8-hour day they could always fit me in because I just wanted between 12 and 1:30 p.m. to be reserved for the kids, and also to be home by 3:30 when they came back from school. So that arrangement worked well. Many of the lessons were one-on-one with the student and then I started to get more students. I taught everything – pronunciation, grammar, the lot. The executives were more or less learning to speak and how to express certain things in English. Sometimes they would have correspondence to show me and wanted to have something corrected.

I didn't have too much trouble adapting to France, with the benefit of having a French wife. When we were traveling together I had no problem. I started to speak a little French, picking it up here and there, but the majority of the conversation was with her. We joined the church, attended meetings and things like that. Through my teaching we made a lot of friends, some of whom still stay in touch to this day.

Originally, before we left Guyana we planned that we would not live in France for more than five or six years. The idea was that we had three children, whom we wanted to learn to speak French (like their French mother). So we arranged to stay in France to give them a good grounding in the French language. But with English being the major language in the world, I wanted them to eventually have English as their mother tongue, with the benefit of knowing two languages. So in 1984, our 5th year, we started to consider what to do next. In 1985 we made an application to immigrate to Canada. You know, when I think of all the people who get entry into Canada on pretexts, it makes me wonder. There we were, with money and fluency in both English and French, but we had to go down to Marseille two or three times to see the Canadian immigration officer and the man kept asking why we wanted to leave lovely France. We couldn't understand why he wanted to discourage us.

At that time, my eldest daughter Jennifer was living in Toronto. She had come up to go to secretarial school and then she got a job and was allowed to stay permanently. So cited her as a relative in Canada. We had brought three children to France, born to Isabelle, and the eldest, Tony, was 12 years old when we started to apply to go to Canada. Although being born in Guyana, he was schooled in France and his French was better than his English. So. In order to give him a head start, we sent him to Maryland, USA, where my eldest boy, Ronald, was living. He was able to attend public school there, but at first, he had a hard time because the local children used to laugh and call him "French boy." However, he was quick to learn and soon caught up. Interestingly enough, a daughter Mary was born to us a month before we received our immigration papers to Canada. Although born in France, she was the only one who didn't learn French. She later learnt the language by attending French immersion school in Canada.

Leaving France was financially better than leaving Guyana. At least, we had some money that we had saved in investments. Digital, where Isabelle was working, had branch operations in Ontario and Quebec but she didn't like the thought of going the colder areas of Canada. She had read so much about the Vancouver's mild weather, and had become so accustomed to the nice warm climate of Guyana that we opted for Vancouver although we had no job, no friends, no family, no "nothing" there. We landed in Vancouver on 8 December 1985 on a foggy day, and we did not expect anything more than a very bleak Christmas. Everybody was celebrating Christmas and here we were with four kids living in a hotel. We stayed there for two days and we found a bed and breakfast place in Vancouver. The owner invited us for Christmas dinner. We began our search for a house to buy, because we wanted to get settled as soon as possible. We enlisted the services of a real estate agent and told him that we had two kids who would be attending primary school. He showed us a house in Richmond next to Tomsett School and we bought it. We felt that this was great, we wouldn't have to worry about sending them to school, and our older boy's high school was not far away. The house was not far from the Vancouver International Airport, some 7 to 8 kilometres away, where my wife was able to find a job. I have always felt that God guides our lives, and things worked out relatively smoothly for us in settling in.

We wanted to buy a TV set and I was speaking to a guy in the store about various models and he said, "You know what: you sound like a Guyanese." I said yes, and I told him my name and he told me his surname – Fernandes. I asked him, "What is your father's name?" He replied, Marcellinos, but he shortened it to Mark. I told him that Marcellinos Fernandes went to school with me in Guyana at St. Stanislaus College. I didn't know how many people from Guyana were in the Vancouver area, but after locating some, a few of us got together and, in 1986, I founded the Guyanese Canadian Association of British Columbia in my kitchen.

I managed to get a job as a salesperson for children's university scholarship insurance, which, for a monthly premium, provided a larger sum of money for tuition fees when the child grew up and qualified for university. I did that for about three to four years. After that I decided to go back to school. I enrolled at the University of British Columbia and spent four years there doing my BA in English Language. I graduated in 1994.

I didn't make use my university qualifications, per se, and then got this idea for the board game about world travel. I felt that it had to be educational as well as entertaining. From 1995 we started to do research for the game – geographical names, historical events, social studies, travel terminology, and more – and we decided to call the game "Flying High – Around the World in 80 Plays" with the objective to get from the starting point to the end of the journey, 80 playing squares away, while accumulating travel dollars based on answering questions correctly, with the possibilities of encountering weather or flight delays, travel promotions and the like. The educational features came from questions, e.g. about geography, or cultural customs, that would have to be answered to determine awards and the next square that you could go. The game was launched in 1996, and was given a three-star award from the Canadian Toy Testing Company – the highest possible rating. We decided to include a feedback form in the game and through this we received several helpful suggestions, resulting in us designing a Junior Edition for those aged 6 to 9, as well as a Challenge Edition for the "pros."

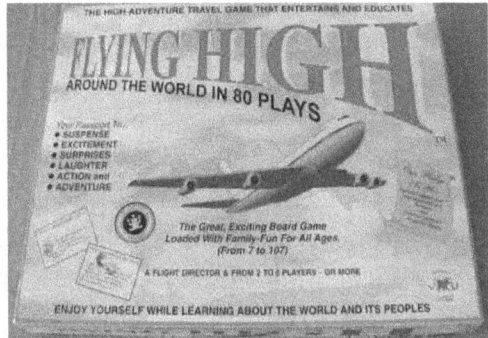

The game was very much a family enterprise. My wife and I were the main designers, while the children were the testers, critics, advertisers and promoters. But the biggest hurdle has been in marketing. All in all, sales were fair but we needed to have significant capital to really push the product, to go up against the big companies that spend millions upon millions of dollars in promotion and advertising. We approached some large stores, such as The Bay, and in 1998, they were willing to put the product on their shelves, but, to me, it is questionable whether this represented a good breakthrough. Essentially we were just given some shelf space and we ourselves had to maintain the records and the stock of games. Also, because we are an unknown manufacturer, the game would frequently be shifted to a less accessible shelf, in favor of other famous board games. Furthermore, if the games were gone from the shelves but were not checked through the cash register, we had to take the loss ourselves for these stolen games. When The Bay bought out Zellers stores, we were given the option of consignment sales at

Zellers. In this case they would take a limited amount of stock but take responsibility for the sales. For this they wanted a 40% cut, which was just barely acceptable to us. Then, if they offered a big discount sale on the games to clear the stock and sold them for $15 or $10 each, the return we would get couldn't even clear our costs. So we have been doing sales the hard way – by ourselves – going to malls, schools, exhibitions, etc.

We also went to schools to show the game and were greeted with various attitudes. Some school principals said that it was up to the School Board to decide and wouldn't even look at what we had, while others had some flexibility in their decision-making and said they would let the children have a try. In some cases we got permission to hold a half-hour demonstration during the school lunch break. We also have some small independent stores, one of which is owned by a Guyanese fellow in Ontario called Creative Learning, and he has sold many games for us. A lot of sales have come through referrals, from people who have heard from others about the game, and in this way the word is getting around, and not only in North America but also in other countries, such as Australia. If the product does take off like we would hope, we ourselves would be flying high – and around the world.

In 2004 I turned my creative talent to publishing an anthology "Super Seniors – Beyond 65 and Fully Alive." Thirteen writers from across Canada contributed 21 of the real-life stories and I wrote seven, of what we hope are INSPIRATIONAL examples of senior women and men living healthy, active lives in body, mind and spirit. Copies of this definitive work of some social significance are obtainable from Viv Lee through www.superseniors.net.

Having enjoyed my 85th birthday on 27 August 2004, I am looking forward to a few more years of activity so that I may qualify for a place in the next anthology.

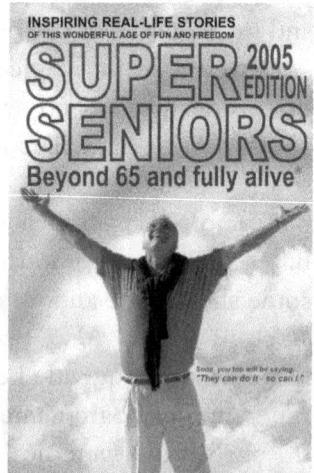

At the Antipodes

Colin Ying

British Guiana

Mr. Brown, my Geography teacher at Queen's College in 1958 when I was in Third Form, drew the class's attention to the countries of the world beyond the boundaries of British Guiana, and explained, "If you were to take a needle and run it through the earth, it would emerge in the Antipodes." And so he referred to the island continent of Australia on the other side of the globe. I thought, "What an absolutely remote place; I would never go there." Of course at my age, Georgetown was the centre of the known world, and my only recollection of travel outside British Guiana at the time was to Barbados on a holiday with my parents, brother and sister. Later, during my secondary school days at Queen's College, my parents took us in tow to visit other West Indian islands – Grenada and Trinidad.

Nineteen years after my geography lesson when I had first heard of the Antipodes, I set foot in Sydney, Australia. My inquisitive wanderings as a university student, and later as a university lecturer, brought me here by a circuitous route. I left BG to pursue tertiary liberal arts studies in Canada in 1965 for four years, went to England for four years to study law from 1969 (after a brief return that year to Guyana, as it had become, when I worked in the Ministry of External Affairs), took up a three-year university lecturing appointment in Singapore at the University of Singapore in 1973, and then came to Australia in 1977 after I accepted another lecturing appointment at a new law school in Sydney. I have lived in Sydney since then, reversing my impetuous childhood dismissal of the Antipodes as a place to visit, much less settle in. However, to say that my settling here was planned over time is hardly true. Curiosity and life take one to unexpected places, and mine has been a journey that started without an ultimate destination in mind, where the transit stops shared a somewhat common history and link with Guyana. They were all at one time colonized by the English and became a part of the British Empire, so English was widely spoken and understood, facilitating communication for me.

In reflecting in 2004 on what I might write in this chapter, I thought back to my life in BG (as it then was) up to the age of 18, when I started on my overseas travels. These memories, naturally less than immediate or clear now, were not of exceptional or newsworthy events, but of common place events and experiences, largely inconsequential in the grand scheme of things, but bringing back a sense of place and a feeling of nostalgia. So I recalled the warm to hot humid tropical weather, mitigated by the northeast trade winds, a carefree existence full of childhood games, later dominated in my teenage years by academic study at Queen's College and church life at the D'Urban Street First Baptist Church, started by American missionaries. I could see in my mind's eye on the streets of Georgetown phalanxes of bicycles, the favoured mode of transport by many of us; ash from the seasonal burning of sugar cane crops prior to harvesting; soot in my eyes from a steam locomotive as I travelled on trains on the East Coast and the West Coast and leaned out of the window to feel the rushing air, before diesel locomotives took over; the buzz of Stabroek Market; the soaring timber structure of St. George's Cathedral; the muddy waters of the estuaries of the giant Essequibo, the smaller Berbice and the still smaller Demerara Rivers; people in the vast majority who were black- or brown-skinned (persons of "colour," as one might say today, although a Nigerian friend from my university days in London would delight in telling me that black was not a colour, but an absence of colour), so that those of Chinese ancestry like myself stood out. In the land of six peoples, as BG was called, the Chinese that I knew accepted their status as a minority group, largely adopted the local customs and way of life, and happily endeavoured to blend in with the mainstream culture.

My earliest recollections of life outside my known universe of BG were the Caribbean islands of Barbados, Grenada and Trinidad. In each, while the language was common, the accents were charmingly different from what to my ears was the flat BG accent; the beaches were beautiful and inviting; the sea was a fascinating deep blue; and the roads were hilly. My first foray outside the tropics was in 1964 when my parents took us to England and Scotland to visit my elder brother, who was then a student at Aberdeen University. On that trip, I flew in a jet for the first time, a Boeing 707, high above the clouds, higher than I had ever been in a propeller-driven aeroplane, where the soft pervasive golden hues of the setting sun fascinated me. My first venture to a country in the temperate zone and in the First World further opened my eyes and experiences. I felt a sense of history, the coolness of the weather, the orderliness of life, and relative seemingly affluence everywhere I looked.

The West: Canada and England

That set the stage for my enthusiastic embrace of studies and life on my own in 1965, after I completed secondary school studies at Queen's College, and went to Canada to study Arts at the University of Manitoba. In Canada, and especially in Manitoba, the winters are extreme and the farthest from the tropics that one could have imagined. I found Canada a vast, marvellous but freezing country. The popular French Canadian folk singer, Gilles Vigneault, captured its essence for me in the opening lines of his famous song, and no one has summed it up better:

> Mon pays, ce n'est pas un pays, c'est l'hiver.
>
> Mon jardin, ce n'est pas un jardin, c'est la plaine.
>
> Mon chemin, ce n'est pas un chemin, c'est la neige
>
> (My country is not a country, but winter.
>
> My garden is not a garden, but the plains.
>
> My path is not a path, but snow)

My time in Canada, for all its distance geographically and culturally from Asia, imparted in me a growing consciousness, only subliminally felt in BG, where it carried no great significance as far as I was concerned, that I was ethnically Chinese. This was due to the fact that I became aware that almost invariably all whom I met during my student days in Canada so regarded me, even if I was not born in, and at the time had never been to, China or Asia, nor (perhaps because of my lack of exposure to Asian-born Chinese previously) felt an identification with persons from that part of the world. The most distinctive feature of being Chinese is, of course, the ability to speak Mandarin or a Chinese dialect, and my inability to do so in the context where Canadians expected me to be able to do so caused me considerable angst. So much so that I eventually remarked to my mother's aunt and her son (my second cousin) whom I first met in Canada, "I think it would be best to introduce myself always as Guyanese, and never say that I am Chinese." Their vehement reply was, "You will always be Chinese." It was a message that the passage of time and encounters with others reinforced. Although my mother's aunt had been born in BG, she left to see and live in China, as did most of her siblings, long before I was born. In time she married a doctor from Swatow, Peter Pan, had two sons and moved with her family to North Borneo (now Sabah, part of east Malaysia) when the Communists took power in China, before migrating to Canada after her husband passed away.

In 1966, the year after I arrived in Canada for university studies, BG became a sovereign country in its own right, Guyana was born, and three year later in 1969 I moved to London for another four years to take up law studies at King's College and sit the Bar exams.

The East: Singapore

In London, I met and formed close friendships with several Malaysians and Singaporeans, who encouraged me to visit Southeast Asia. I had been vaguely aware that my mother had an uncle who, like my grand aunt whom I had met in Canada, returned to China many years ago, before I was born, and who had moved to Singapore when the Communists took control of China in 1949. 1970 was the era of cheap air charter flights, so driven by curiosity to see that part of the world where Chinese and golden-skinned people predominated, I hopped on board a charter flight to the Orient for the first time, taking myself back to the tropics in visiting Malaysia and Singapore. These two neighbouring countries, in a real sense the antipodes from Guyana too, were once united in a federation, which was dissolved in 1965.

The smells that greeted me in those two countries in 1970 (fragrant durian, mangoes, road side cooking aromas coming from the incredible variety of spices), the tropical heat and humidity, the mouth watering cuisine and the energetic bustle of places where Chinese were highly visible and in large numbers, were memorable, as were the sights, the history and the observable way of life of the people there. I met my mother's uncle and family for the first time. My aunt and four of their six children were born in China, with the last two born in Singapore. As both Malaysia and Singapore were once British colonies, like Guyana, the shared colonial heritage made communication easy. After that first taste of Southeast Asia in 1970, I returned to Singapore in 1973 to work at the University of Singapore, after I had completed my studies in London. The friendships so easily made and cemented when I was a student there, and the very pleasant memories of my visit to Singapore in 1970 lured me back.

My Singapore experience lasted a bit over three years on this occasion. During that time, I met and married a Singaporean, Ong Chwee Hua, a *peranakan*, or Chinese whose ancestors had settled in the areas around the Straits of Malacca. Such Chinese adopted and fused with Chinese traditions and cuisine the language, mode of dress and cuisine of predominantly the local Malays of the region. There are clearly parallels between the *peranakan* of the Straits of Malacca and the Chinese of Guyana, who over generations had largely assimilated the Guyanese culture and way of life.

I enjoyed living and working in Singapore for the duration of my three plus years. The discipline, dynamism and single-mindedness of Singaporeans, harnessed under the guided democracy of Lee Kuan Yew, had to be admired. And yet Singapore in 1977 could be a restrictive place, physically only 640 square kilometres in area, more a city than a state, subject to tight political and social controls. As a Guyanese, I remained a foreigner, and, as with all foreigners, needed Singapore government approval before I could marry Chwee Hua, a Singapore citizen, in Singapore. So it was that when my employment contract with the University of Singapore expired in 1977, I looked further afield in the region, and, after the Foundation Dean of a new law school in Sydney invited me to apply for a lecturing position there, became aware of the island continent of Australia, eight hours flight from Singapore, the antipodes that I had never dreamed I would ever see.

The Antipodes

Thus in 1977 I arrived in Sydney, Australia, another relic of the British empire, but geographically much closer than Guyana to Singapore, a fact that greatly relieved my parents-in-law. Going to Australia seemed a logical step for me to take at the time. After all, it was an acquaintance from the Australian High Commission in Singapore that had supplied Australian champagne for our wedding in 1975.

Australia is a big and varied country, a continent in its own right. I am happy with my decision to come here, at first for only three years, and then eventually to settle permanently in Sydney once I chose to apply for Australian citizenship in 1987. The people are on the whole friendly, easy-going, unpretentious and un-class-conscious. The climate in Sydney and along the entire southeast coast of the continent (where most Australians live) is mild, pleasant and agreeable, conducive to an outdoors lifestyle. If Canada is a land of snow and winter, Australia for me is a land of sun and summer, much closer to the tropics than to the arctic (or the Antarctic). I like that warmth and brightness. The image I associate with Australia is that of the sun shining in a cloudless deep blue sky. And Australian beaches are magnificent, with sparkling blue or turquoise water, rivalling the best of the Caribbean beaches, although swimming in some areas can be hazardous because of deadly or toxic marine life (some uniquely Australian), such as the saltwater crocodile, the blue ringed octopus, the box jellyfish and the irukandji jellyfish.

In fact, the Australian land mass is so large that its regions cover a range of landscapes and climates. Those that like snow and wintry weather can go to the Snowy Mountains in the Australian Alps, as well as the mountain ranges in the Victorian Alps, or settle in Tasmania. Far north Queensland, the top end of the Northern Territory and northern Western Australia are tropical or sub-tropical. The red centre of the continent is desert and gorges, blisteringly hot in the summer months, tolerably warm in the winter months. Along the southeast coast, the climate is temperate and Mediterranean, although the good-natured barb habitually flung at Melburnians is that Melbourne is capable of producing temperatures across all four seasons in a single day.

Some aspects of Australia remind me of Guyana. For instance:

- Before federation in 1901, Australia consisted of six separate British colonies, and Guyana too was formerly a British colony.
- The population in both countries is low, particularly in comparison with their neighbours (Venezuela and Brazil for Guyana, Indonesia for Australia), and the vast majority live on the coast, with few inhabitants in the interior, which in Australia is desert while in Guyana it is jungle.
- There are just over 20 million people in Australia, occupying 7,692,024 square kilometres (or 2.6 persons per square kilometre), while Guyana has about 706,000 people over 214,970 square kilometres (or 3.3 persons per square kilometre).
- Both countries are commodity producers and exporters.
- Cricket has always been the national game of both countries. Australians love the touring West Indian teams, especially since the notable series that included the first tied Test in Brisbane in 1961.
- When I was growing up, Guyana was known as the land of six races, a melting pot. Although Australia was at one time intent on religiously retaining and reinforcing its Anglo-Celtic identity by adopting a White Australia policy, officially abandoned in 1973, it is now truly and irrevocably multicultural.

Indeed, with the abandonment of the White Australia policy, Asian immigration has increased. Particularly in the larger cities, the Asian presence is highly visible, as is Asian cuisine, which Australians have taken to enthusiastically. There has been a positive change in public attitudes to Asian immigration since the 1970s, and diversity is actively promoted officially. By way of contrast, in the mid to late 1800s, with the discovery of gold in New South Wales, Victoria and the Northern Territory, when large numbers of Chinese entered those colonies to work the gold diggings, after white prospectors had apparently exhausted them, they were subject to racial vilification and violent attacks, not dissimilar to the treatment meted out to the Chinese gold prospectors in California during its gold rush days.

That is not to say that the Australia of today is free of racial prejudice or is perfect. Racist groups exist, but are a tiny minority, even if vocal. Australia's treatment of asylum seekers, particularly children, has been justly condemned by human rights groups, and the country has yet to reach an accommodation with the indigenous peoples whose occupation of the continent predated the Anglo-Celtic invasion in 1788. As with many indigenous peoples around the world, Australian aboriginals have much to be dissatisfied with. Despite an occupation of this great southern continent for over 50,000 years, colonial and Australian governments never recognized claims by aboriginal tribal groups to the land until 1988, the accepted view until then being that the continent was *terra nullius*, or land belonging to no one, before the English convicts arrived in 1788 to settle here. Even after 1988, aboriginal customary rights and title to land could be overridden by private title conferred by the Crown, and any claim to land by them was restricted to land remaining in public ownership. Marginalized culturally and economically, Australian aboriginals are plagued by alcohol, drugs and the malaise that afflicts a people caught in a world from which they feel alienated. And yet one must marvel at the comparative lack of a stridently militant aboriginal attitude that might seek to reclaim the land of their ancestors who had lived on this continent for so many thousands of years before 1788.

Nevertheless, there are many individual Australians generous of heart and full of good will. They make the difference. While finding paradise on earth is impossible, life here is as good as it gets, as my childhood in Guyana once seemed too to me. Guyana and Australia were never at the centre of world power or seismic events, and still are not, but each must cultivate her own garden, as Voltaire's Candide concluded. Happiness is within reach in either place.

When The World Came Crashing Down

Barbara Sohan

Barbara Sohan is a descendant of 19th century immigrants from China, with ancestral connections to the Chung Tiam-fook, Ho-A-Hing, Ho-Ten-Pow and Chin-A-Fat families. She was born in 1942 in Georgetown, where she grew up and attended St. Sidwell's Anglican School, Demerara High, and Carnegie Home Economics School.

* * * * * * * *

My mother lived in Blankenburg, West Coast Demerara, with two brothers, Wilfred and Arthur, and a sister, Evelyn. My mother's name is Clarice Ten-Pow, the daughter of Alexander "Loy" and Alice Ten-Pow. Clarice had three children for Harold Tiam-Fook, who lived in Brickdam, Georgetown, but he never acknowledged my brother Ronald or myself. When Ronald and I were seven and six years old, Harold took all three of us children from my mother. Later that same year my mother went to our school and got us back. The only way she could do so was when Harold was not around. She came to the school and asked us all if we wanted to go with her. My brother and I said yes and my sister Joan, the eldest, said no. Joan stayed with her father until times got very hard for her and she tried to come home several times, and my mother took her in on all those occasions. We were then living in Lodge Village, Georgetown, and my mother met this gentleman, Albert Hing, who married her and with whom she had four children. Albert Hing supported us and brought us up, while my biological father never lifted a finger for us. There was no running water in the house (we had to fetch water from the well), no stove, no refrigerator. We built a fireside made out of mud with two holes in the top where pots could be placed. There was a hole in the front where kindling and cow dung could be inserted to get the fire going. As little children, we had to cut the wood to make the fire, scrub the stairs every day, wash clothes by hand, and iron clothes with an old-fashioned, solid metal iron. On holidays we would go back to my grandmother to spend some time with her and help her with her shop. In those days we would wrap the flour and sugar in one-pound packages and prepare small packets of salt or butter to be given away with any purchases of flour or bread. We helped her to fetch water. There was no electric lighting and she used a vaporized kerosene lamp (called a gas lamp) and oil-burning lamps with adjustable wicks; we showered in the kitchen with buckets of water, and the toilet was an outhouse. It was quite an experience.

After we grew up my grandmother would come to town to order goods for the grocery. I would have to meet her at 7 a.m., before I went to school. She would bring us little goodies and give me a small piece. I would also have to go to the market to shop so we would have food for that day since we had no refrigerator. All this had to be done before I went to school. I also was a member of the YWCA for many years where I learned to do a lot of handwork like knitting, crochet, and embroidery, as well as dancing and cooking. I would go to evening classes to learn shorthand and typewriting.

In 1964, Clive Sohan and I got married in Georgetown and we had a daughter, Astrid, two years later. We lived on Fourth Street in Alberttown, and had a neighbor who had immigrated to the United States and he would come back many times a year to Guyana. He was a chauffeur working for Barclay's Bank on Wall Street, in New York. Clive was very encouraged by what he was told so he decided that he wanted to go to the States. I had worked at the bus company as a cashier and then I stayed home after Astrid was born, while Clive worked at Bookers hardware department as a payroll clerk. Can you imagine – we lived on his salary, which was either $25 or $32 a week. In Guyana things were getting bad. People were stealing and there was rioting, with Blacks and Indians fighting among themselves, and at times the situation got really terrible, with stores being burned and looted. We didn't want to stay in such an environment. Clive did not have the necessary qualifications but I had a dressmaker's certificate, issued by the government, and this kind of trade certification was very helpful in getting a visa to the U.S. Clive took my papers to make an application at the U.S. embassy, not knowing that one of our family friends was working there. She approached him one day and asked him what he was doing there. He told her he wanted to go to the States and she helped us with the necessary procedures from there on. In a matter of months we were in the States, but we left Astrid with my mother because she was just one and a half years old at the time.

We arrived with 1,200 Guyana dollars, which was equal to US$500, and our two suitcases. We came into New

Barbara and Clive Sohan about to board the plane to the U.S. *Barbara Sohan*

York in the heart of winter – in December of 1969 – with a coat that I had made and another one given to Clive by a friend. It had snowed before we landed and then the rain fell so it became slushy and I had to walk in the slush with my shoes because I had no boots. We did not know many people at the time – one was Clive's brother-in-law who had come up the year before to study and he was living in a bachelor apartment, which is just one room with a roll away bed. That meant that we had to stay in a hotel at $60 per week. We had no idea about what we needed to do in winter, and the room was very cold because we did not know that we had to turn on the heat, so we froze that first night. On many nights I cried so much. I missed my home, my daughter, and here we were living in the cold. In those days you did not get your Green Card when you landed, and the Immigration Office would mail it to your home but we had no permanent address because we were staying at a hotel. So we never got our Green Cards when we should have, and this meant that getting a meaningful job was a little tricky. In any event, jobs were very easy to come by although the pay was very low but we were willing to take anything.

After one week of searching, Clive got a job in a factory packing belts and they also hired me to cut the belts. The man said he liked us so we were both able to work at the same factory. Clive would get off earlier than I did, and the nights became dark so early. We were not used to all of this, and in addition we had to buy breakfast, lunch and dinner every day from restaurants and diners. We would eat breakfast at a diner and have lunch at work, delivered from places where we could order as a group, and for dinner we would stop off at a restaurant and eat out. Clive made $100 and I made $98 a week. The subway fare was 15 cents and you were able to get a bus transfer for the same money. Three weeks went by when one of Clive's relatives called him and invited us to Brooklyn. We were living at a hotel in Manhattan, on 72nd Street, so we went to visit her in Brooklyn. She heard our story and found us an apartment a week later. Accommodations were very easy to come by in those days so we moved to Brooklyn into a one-bedroom apartment that had millions of roaches and hardly any heat. We had no furniture although the young lady before us left her bed and we bought her dinette set. We slept on her bed until our own bed that we had purchased was delivered. We also bought a TV set and that's all that we acquired at the time. We lived there for three months and when we left the landlady never gave us back our security deposit. I was so hurt – no one had ever robbed us before. I then had to go to the Immigration Office to reapply for our Green Cards, which, fortunately, did not take very long to come. As soon as we got them we left the factory. Clive managed to get a job at Citibank as a reconciliation clerk. The test was so easy he actually helped another person who was applying for a job – he showed the guy the answers. I was employed at Remington Electric Shaver as a payroll clerk. I worked there for a year and then got a job at Chase Manhattan Bank, first as a teller, then as a teller supervisor. I later transferred to a desk job as a reconciliation clerk and became the supervisor for that department.

After nine months in the States I went to Guyana to see Astrid. During those nine months I would send money and clothes for her, and my mother would write, but she would not tell me things that Astrid would go through, e.g. my poor baby would cry every night and could not sleep. My father had to walk her every night because she missed me at a year and a half – that was very young age to leave her. Clive never went back to Guyana. When I applied for Astrid to join us I had put down my parents' names as well as those of my brothers and sisters. We knew it was just a matter of time before they would arrive. After a year and a half they came, when Astrid was three years old, and by then we had moved to a two-bedroom apartment. The landlady, who was a Guyanese, was very strict and we had signed a lease for two years. We could not have friends staying over for any period of time. At one time we had a friend from Guyana visiting us and the landlady turned off the hot water while we were at work, trying to save a few bucks. This was very upsetting. I went down to her apartment and told her off.

Almost at the end of those two years my parents, brothers and sisters came with Astrid. We saved every penny we had earned and bought a place so we stayed for only about two weeks to a month at the old apartment. There were eight of us altogether and it was rough. Our money was not enough and I had to support my family. When you first arrive in the U.S. everything would be new, so you can imagine our grocery bill! By then we were like strangers to Astrid so we had to start all over again to develop our bonds. We bought a two-family house and rented out the upstairs. My parents lived in the basement and we lived on the main floor. My father got a job at a factory distributing German chinaware made by Villory & Boch, and, of course, all of us have dinner sets from that company. My mother stayed at home and helped to take care of Astrid while my brothers and sisters went to school. A couple of years later Clive's parents came up to stay permanently, so we all crowded together and lived as one happy family. Astrid started school when she turned five years old – she went to PS181, a public school. She was too young to start off in Catholic school, but after a year we sent her to Holy Cross School for the rest of the seven years we lived in that house. We did think about having other children, and actually we wanted to have three, but after we got here life was so difficult there was no way I would want to bring a child in this world to endure the hardship and suffering.

I left Chase Manhattan Bank after working there for almost nine years. Astrid was spending too many hours by herself and she was ten so I stayed home with her for a few years and then I started to pursue a job in New Jersey, closer to home. School was across the street and she came home for lunch. She used to play softball after classes. She then started high school and would write short articles for the school bulletin. She also helped with the schoolbook and would go ice-skating on weekends. Astrid did tap dancing after school and learned to play the accordion. When Astrid was a teenager, my friend and I would take her to the disco at the Copacabana on Sundays and she had a lot of nice friends that she still has until now. Whenever we would go to dinner or to shows we would take Astrid because I wanted her to grow up knowing everything and not being afraid of going on the subway. By that time we were beginning to pay back taxes so Clive learned to drive and then I also learned. We bought a car, for which we could get some tax deductions, and it was a lot of fun with Clive showing me how to drive – you cannot imagine the experiences I had going down the main streets of Brooklyn. Astrid was growing and I did not want her to grow up in Brooklyn so we bought a house in the suburbs – in New Jersey. It was a four-bedroom house which we still own after over 25 years. I gave my parents the house I owned in Brooklyn because I did not want to be bothered to go back to Brooklyn to collect rent and we showed them how they could make it work. They were afraid they could not manage it so we showed them the way. My parents still live there right now and do not want to move. They are so old it would take a stick of dynamite to move them out. Clive's mother died from a massive heart attack after a couple of years in Brooklyn, and Clive's father lived with us until he joined Clive's sister in Canada where he died about ten years ago from diabetes, cancer and other health-related problems.

When we moved to New Jersey and was painting our house, Clive received a phone call from a friend regarding a job, which had been offered to her. She could not do it so she called Clive to tell him she had recommended him for this job at Société Générale; it was a job he could not refuse – right up his alley with all the trimmings. They doubled or tripled his earnings, took care of our mortgage and all those other perks, and he remained at that firm for as long as we have lived in this house. During all that time he used to commute to New York everyday, driving sometimes one hour or else one and a half hours. I, on the other hand, worked for different companies. After a few years I went back to work for

The Sohan home in New Jersey. *Barbara Sohan.*

Revlon in New Jersey, left there and went to work for Hercules Chemical Company, where I was a payroll clerk, and then joined MCOSS as a payroll person. I used to arrange the pay for all nurses, aides and office staff and after that I got another job at Holmdel Township Board of Education working for two doctors of education. I was the bookkeeper as well as the payroll person paying the superintendent, the business officers and all the teachers. This is where I was when I retired after working for 14 years.

Astrid graduated from high school and right away I thought she should go to England to get the experience of traveling abroad so I bought her a ticket to London and Paris. She went with two other friends and spent two weeks staying at my sister who lives in London, and also at Clive's cousin, who had a son their age, so she had a great time on that trip. Whenever we went on vacation we would take her with us; we took her to Vancouver and also went to Calgary to visit with my friend. When Astrid came back from England she wanted to work so she got a job as secretary for about a year then she got another job at International Flavor and Fragrances where her boss recognized her potential. He told her she was pretty much wasting her time being a secretary, so he got her a job in the computer department. She took off with it and they could not contain her. She left after some time and took a job at Johnson & Johnson for IBM where she worked on the E-mail desk during the day, and in the evenings she would work for a friend doing interviews on the computer for a great deal of money. Then she started complaining that everyone was making more money than she was so I said, if that's the way you feel, do something about it. So she went out and took this job at Marsh and McLennan, currently known as Marsh. She worked there for three and a half years and was doing very well, so much so that within that time she ended up being Assistant Vice-President of Global Technology Services. She worked very hard, had a great boss and loved every moment of her job. She had great friends and was loved by all at her workplace. She excelled on that job. Astrid could not sit still in college, she made four or five attempts and finally gave up. I guess in looking back she did not choose the right courses, she learned all about the computer on her own through self-study and practical experience. She took a couple of courses with company sponsorship and she was smart – she had a lot of common sense and could grasp anything on the first try. Astrid was very involved with compiling the family tree, and she would go to family reunions with her laptop computer in order to fill in all the missing pieces. She loved to do research. I cannot begin to tell you all the many qualities she had – she was feisty.

Clive and Barbara's only daughter Astrid. *Barbara Sohan.*

Astrid worked at Marsh on the 95th floor of the World Trade Center in New York. She and her 12 buddies, as she would call them, were there on Tuesday, September 11, 2001. I was at work and I called her at about 8.15 a.m., like I used to do every morning. We talked. I said, hi Astrid how are you, and she said, oh Ma, I have a project to finish by 8.30 . . . got to go. About half an hour after that I heard a buzz in the office and the girls were saying there was a plane crash but did not know where it was, as we did not have a TV in the office. However the accounts mushroomed within about five minutes as calls kept coming in. Everyone knew that Astrid worked at the World Trade Center, so I called her . . . but I could not get through. I called my girlfriend at her home to get her to find out from the TV what was going on, then I tried to call Clive but all the phone lines to New York City were down. I began to receive a number of phone calls. Astrid was able to use one of her colleague's BlackBerry beepers and was E-mailing messages to her co-worker (Jennifer) who was supposed to be at work but was not there that day. Jennifer called Mark, Astrid's boyfriend, and then he called me. In the first message I received it said that she was OK and was trying to get out. The next one described that fire and smoke were coming. The last message I received was, "Could you tell my Mom and Dad I love them very much." At that moment I had the gut feeling that it was all over. My boss sent me home and by the time I got there, the second tower was falling. From the time I got that last message I could not stop crying. Within that time I received phone calls from all over Canada, London and from all my friends – that's why I did not leave work earlier. My sister, Kim, came over we stayed glued to the TV hoping we would see Astrid running around somewhere. In the meantime, Clive decided not to come home, fearing that he would miss a phone call from her telling him to come and get her, even though I felt I would never see her again, based on her last phone message. Nevertheless, we still clung to a faint hope . . . love is not a word we would throw around freely so when she said it, it was a cue from her. Eventually Clive came home and we started to make phone calls to the hospitals. No hope. On Wednesday, we stayed at home glued to the TV, hoping that we would see her. No hope.

On Thursday, Clive was planning to go to the Armory, which was set up for everyone to go and see a master list, compiled from the hospitals, of all the dead and treated victims. However, I could not entrust it all to him so at 4 a.m. I decided I would go with him. I called my sisters, brothers and friends. We all got together and met up at the Armory – nine of us – and we split up, each one taking a different hospital. The girls from my office came over and made posters with Astrid's picture and phone number. It was now 6 a.m., at which time I called our photographer to get a copy of one of the pictures we had taken as a family on August 11, 2001, exactly one month before the incident. We were supposed to have taken them a year ago and I said to Astrid that we have to do this now. We had also arranged to have our vows renewed for our 35th wedding anniversary, and Astrid was going to walk down the aisle with us. After that we were going to have a party – on September 22, 2001. Astrid was helping to plan all these things and was excited about the plans. So we sat for hours at the Armory and finally saw the list – but no Astrid. By this time we had learned that her whole department had been wiped out so whenever we went looking we would look for the others also, because if we saw them we would see her through them. But it was to no avail. At the Armory we filed a missing person's report, and a DNA report. We were treated very well – there were chaplains, priests, Red Cross, police, AT&T. You were able to make all kinds of phone calls free of charge. Food was provided and there was no want for anything. When we left, the TV stations were out at the street corners so we were able to connect with a lot of networks. We were on Channels 2, 5, and 7, as well as London, Canadian and quite a few other TV stations. We also appeared on a TV program, the Iyanla Vanzant Show, which was trying to help the victims to get on with their lives.

It was now Saturday and nothing had been found, so my hope was slowly dying. We then went to Marsh and they had a debriefing of the events that took place as best as they knew and they tried to answers questions regarding their employees. Then they took us back to the Armory, but by then the crowd had become a lot smaller, so Mayor Guliani set up Pier 94 as a one-stop facility where applications could be made for various funds. There were people to help you to do everything, and again you did not have to worry about lunch or dinner – everything was there for you. When I came home in the afternoon my neighbors would come over with hot food . . . every day a different one. Some of the teachers would come by and leave soup and different things at my door. My neighbors held a candlelight vigil outside my house and my

Mom had a candlelight mass arranged in Brooklyn for Astrid, by which time I had to start thinking of a memorial. It was held on October 6, 2001, and all the girls at the office participated in helping to arrange the program and different things so that I did not have much to do. It was wonderful – 600 people attended and the church was packed. All my family from Canada came and all offered lots of support. I then started to go to counseling for one year.

In November of 2001 I hired an aviation attorney in Manhattan who has experience with a lot of cases, including the Lockerbie disaster,[1] so I have every confidence he will handle my case very well. We went to Pier 94 and filed for a death certificate. An attorney was there to help us and we filed for all the other available claims, but every time things seemed to be settling down, something else would come up. I received a letter saying that Astrid's driver's license was found, so Clive went to retrieve it. Would you believe . . . it was intact, which said to me that she wanted to be found. I can only imagine that she must have ditched her pocketbook and kept her license on her person.

We were settling down again when two policemen came to my door. It was April 6th . . . a Tuesday. I will never forget that day for the rest of my life – they said that they had found my daughter. Well, all hell broke loose; it was worse than when I knew she was not coming home. It now became a reality that I had to accept my daughter the way she had become, which was the most difficult thing to do. I never cried so much before. They wanted to take me to the hospital and I would not let them, so they went and brought the priest over and then my counselor. It was about 5.30 to 6.00 p.m. and by the time they left it was about 11 p.m. By then I had calmed down and went to bed with swollen eyes. It was a good thing that Clive was home, off sick that day, and a friend of mine was over visiting, so I was not alone. I had to gather my thoughts and do things all over again to hold another memorial and a burial – it took place on the April 10, 2002. When we had first gone to the funeral parlor, there were papers to be signed asking if we wanted to be notified if any more body parts were found. I had taken a chance and said no, and that all worked out for the best, because they found her body intact

---

1   On 21 December 1988, Pan Am Flight 103 was brought down by a bomb over the Scottish town of Lockerbie, killing 270 people.

– her left hand was broken as well as one of her feet, and she was identified by her dental records. We have cremated her body, and kept the ashes, and we cannot decide what to do with her remains right now.

I spoke to the coroner's office to find out what had been found and they told me, everything. Then I spoke to the detective who was working on her case to find out where she was found. She was on the south side but she had been working in the northeast section. What had happened was that she came down the stairs closest to her but the plane had crashed there. The place was a blazing inferno so she went looking for an exit on the other side but got knocked out by the fumes. I thought they would never find her, when you saw the intensity of what had happened. Her hair was singed down to one inch, and that was because she was lying there for several months.

Things have started to settle down, but we still have to go to court and relive the situation all over again. We have since sued Osama bin Laden and all those people who were helping him financially – both on the international and the domestic fronts. I went before the judge in October 2003 so we are waiting to see what will become of it.

I remember Astrid as an intelligent go-getter, with lots of confidence. She went after what she desired. She loved her father so much – just a couple weeks previously, I was out and she said to him, let's go to lunch. That was something she loved to do every once in a while, as well as taking him to a show, just the two of them alone. She and I would go shopping together, and she was just beginning to enjoy our timeshare,[2] which we let her use, and in this way she went to Jamaica and Antigua. Astrid also did quite a bit of traveling on her own. Clive and I have enjoyed traveling to various places in the past 14 years, using our three time-shares. In 2000, we went on a tour to Beijing, Hangzhou, Xi'an, and Shanghai about 4 years ago, and in the following year we went to Bali, Singapore, Thailand, and Hong Kong, so we are enjoying the fruits of our labor. Clive will retire at the end of 2006, by which time he would be half a year past 62, and before then we will have a 60th birthday party

---

2   A property, usually in a resort location, that is purchased and available for use for an agreed number of weeks per year. The contractual agreement allows the owner to spend an equivalent time period at another timeshare location anywhere in the world.

for him. We will be looking to buy a little house in a warm place for winter when the time and right place appears.

If I had to do it all over again I would do the same thing I did before. Although Astrid did not understand in the beginning, she got to appreciate where we were coming from and she loved her parents. I do not have any regrets; we did not have any loose ends – we were the kind that would speak our minds at the time. If she had something to say she would do so, and if I had something to say, I would. We had some good times together, the most important thing is that she knew we loved her and we knew she loved us, even without receiving her last message. The only regret I have is that I did not have the opportunity to say goodbye for the last time, and to tell her how much I love her.

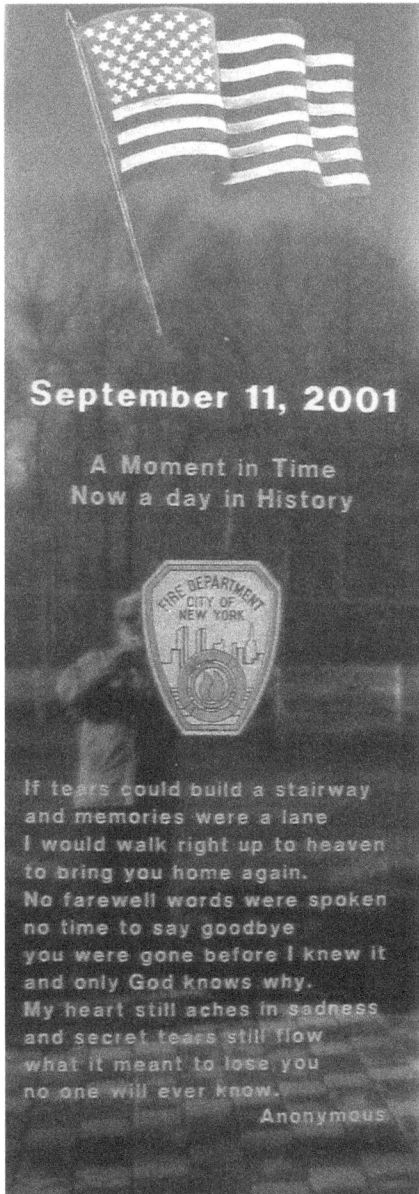

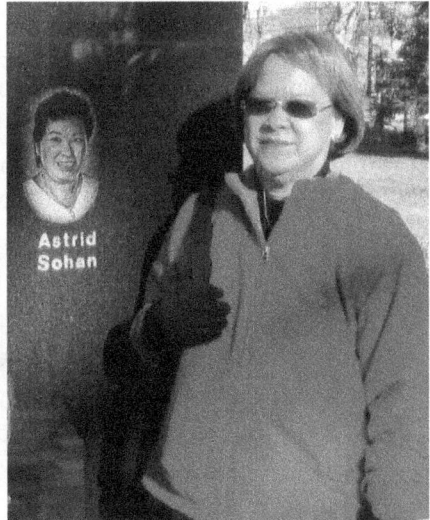

September 11, 2001

A Moment in Time
Now a day in History

FIRE DEPARTMENT
CITY OF
NEW YORK

If tears could build a stairway
and memories were a lane
I would walk right up to heaven
to bring you home again.
No farewell words were spoken
no time to say goodbye
you were gone before I knew it
and only God knows why.
My heart still aches in sadness
and secret tears still flow
what it meant to lose you
no one will ever know.
                Anonymous

Astrid
Sohan

Barbara visits the memorial for Astrid and the plaque with the commemorative poem. *Barbara Sohan.*

Blown Away

Paula Stehling, née Sue-A-Quan

I was born in Georgetown in 1951 and grew up there. My parents owned Sue-A-Quan's Ice Cream Parlor and I attended St. Rose's High School, which was located not far away. After graduating I joined Royal Bank of Canada, but was with the bank only a few months when my immigration papers to Canada came through in November 1969. Two of my sisters were settled in Toronto and one of them, Fay, a graduate in mathematics from London, England had sponsored me, the youngest of four children in the family. Unfortunately my father died suddenly shortly after his 61st birthday and this happened during the same week that my visa arrived. The visa was valid for only a few months and the plan had been for me to go alone to Canada and my parents would follow at a later date. With the changed situation my mother and I departed for Canada in March 1970, she on a visitor's visa.

Shortly after landing in Toronto I looked through the newspapers and saw ads for positions at an insurance company and at Canadian Imperial Bank of Commerce (CIBC). I applied to both and they both responded with offers but I took the bank job because the pay was two dollars a week more. I started as a teller and then moved my way up, staying with them for ten years. In February 1975 I got married to Jim Stehling, a Canadian fellow, and three years later we had a baby girl. I took two years off on maternity leave and then went back to banking, this time with Canada Trust. I worked there for 16 years.

By the late 1990s Jim and I were getting tired of Toronto's cold winter weather and we considered going to Florida. Jim had an uncle who was an aide to the president in the U.S. and he told us to apply through the American embassy. We did but they never responded and it was not until much later, just before Jim's uncle died, that we found out that he didn't think we were serious or else he would have sponsored us. If not for

Jim Stehling looks over the summer scene with revellers enjoying the backyard pool at his Toronto home (July 1987). *Trev Sue-A-Quan*

his misunderstanding we would have been living in Florida by now.

In late 1995, when winter was beginning to chill us once again, Jim saw an ad in the *Toronto Star* requiring an experienced carpet installer for a project in the Cayman Islands. Floor installation – carpets and tiles – was Jim's area of expertise and he asked me where the Cayman Islands were. I took out a map and found a little dot in the middle of the Caribbean region and showed it to him. "Is it warm there?" he asked, and I said, Yeah. After taking a moment to think over the possibilities Jim decided to phone the number posted in the ad. The man who answered was in London, Ontario and he told Jim that once he returned to the Cayman Islands he would send a ticket for Jim to join him there.

In December Jim found himself in a hotel in George Town, the capital of Grand Cayman Island and discovered that the 'employer' did not know anything about carpet installation and the intention was to see how much Jim knew about laying a new carpet and overseeing the workers. The job was at the spacious restaurant on the second floor of the airport terminal. The work had to be done at night after the customers had left and the restaurant was closed. Jim went there for a couple nights to look at the ongoing work. He didn't get paid but he considered that the week's accommodation was an acceptable arrangement. Jim did indeed find that the climate was warm and except for being taken for a sightseeing drive he did not go around out on his own because he had never before ventured outside of Canada by himself. Besides, it was kind of scary with the traffic in the British dependency traveling on the left side of the road.

In February 1996 we decided to take a week's trip to the Caymans on our own initiative to explore possibilities in more detail. Jim and I handed out resumes and we were delighted when a couple companies expressed interest in employing Jim (although not the one that had brought him over initially) and one of them was ready to start the paperwork for medical examinations, work permit application, etc. One of the banks was also willing to consider employing me. In the Cayman Islands the regulations specified that only when one person had a 'strong' enough application would a permit be granted for a dependent to accompany the applicant. So the bank had to apply for a permit on my own merit and it turned out that my permit was contingent on Jim also getting employment. We decided to leave our daughter in Toronto to complete her schooling while in the care of my sister Fay and my mother. Our work permits were valid for one and two years but they were renewable. Over the years my status in the bank rose through promotions and my permit became the stronger one so that technically I could put Jim on it as a dependent. The system, controlled by the Immigration Department, was such that neither a carpet installer nor a mid-level bank employee was considered to be earning a sufficiently high salary to support a dependent – only a professional bank trust officer could qualify.

The working arrangements with Jim's employer were not ideal and he found himself being shuffled off to minor jobs or being over-ridden in making decisions that affected the quality of the work. After six months Jim lost the job. However, the nature of floor installation in Toronto had caused him to also become skilled in general house construction and this ability caught the attention of a large property management company. He was hired to take charge of all manner of building maintenance and construction, including repairs.

Jim enjoyed his work, the warm weather and the crystal clear ocean surrounding the island. He adjusted well to driving on the left side of the road, and noted with interest that the cars owned by the residents carried yellow license plates while rental cars were fitted with white plates, apparently to let everyone know that the drivers of rented cars may be performing unexpected maneuvers. Then one day he was driving along normally and was hit head-on by a car driving on the wrong side of the road – it was a car with a white license plate. Jim suffered some fractures and bruises but was able to resume work after a week, although in a bandaged state.

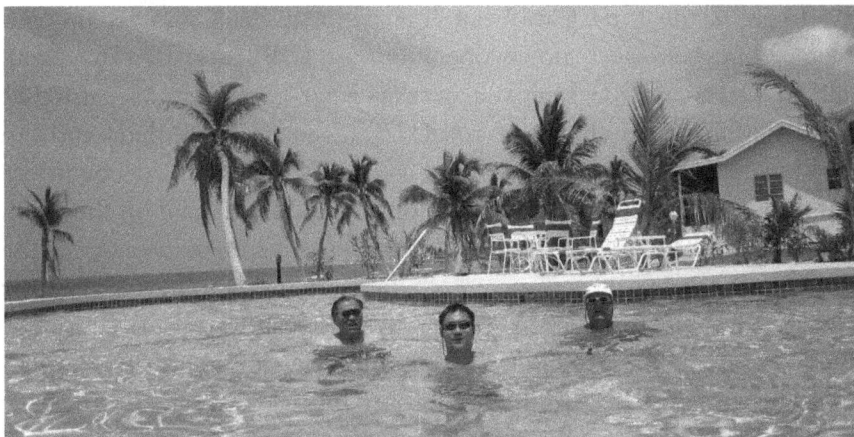

Outdoor swimming is a year-round pleasure in the Cayman Islands. The condominium owners and their guests can choose between the luxurious pool or, a few steps further on, the Caribbean Sea. *Trev Sue-A-Quan.*

About a year later Jim was at a work site where a display booth was being set up to promote a real estate development project. He went to plug in a power tool and was blown away – thrown back across the room from a severe electrical shock. Apparently a worker had earlier incorrectly installed the electrical outlet. Fortunately the building was where Jim's doctor had his office and he was taken upstairs by stretcher and hooked up with monitoring devices to check the state of his heart and vital signs. I received a call when I was at the bank and I rushed over and stayed with him for some two hours until things appeared stable. But his condition had to be monitored for about two more weeks.

Because of these setbacks, Jim lost quite a bit of weight, some 50 pounds, and he decided to do bicycling to keep himself in shape. He would go riding after 4:00 o'clock in the morning when the weather was cool and there was not too much traffic on the roads. One fateful day he went out at 4:30 and was struck by a hit-and-run driver, who left him lying on the road. Somebody came along, picked him up and called the ambulance. The collision resulted in a concussion to his head and ever since then he has had trouble with equilibrium, maintaining his balance. He recovered otherwise but one day he was working on a ladder and toppled over, breaking his forearm. With these incidents coming one after another there was a period of about six months when he was not actively working.

In 2002 the First Caribbean International Bank was set up as a merger between the regional operations of CIBC and Barclay's Bank and in October 2003 I moved over to First Caribbean as Customer Service Manager in charge of retail. I enjoyed my work there and Jim and I were now nicely settled on the island. We bought a two-bedroom condominium in Spotts, a few miles outside George Town on the south side of the island. Our home was literally a stone's throw away from the ocean. We reveled in the warmth of the sun and could go for regular swims in either the ocean or the nearby pool that was available for use by the residents of the condominium complex. Coming from Guyana I easily became accustomed to the laid-back lifestyle and lack of efficiency in doing some things, which seemed to be a trait in many less-developed countries. I liked to make friends and discovered several other people of Guyanese origin through their accent. I also became friends with many Canadians in a place where many such ex-patriates worked and congregated. One day I was driving along the road and offered someone a ride. Patricia Parker turned out to be a fellow bank administrator from Canada and we struck up a close friendship.

Jim was active in the church, being a drummer in a band that played religious songs in modern style for the First Baptist Church of Grand Cayman. He also developed another interest, which I shared. Back in Canada he had kept some budgies and after we moved here somebody gave him a Cayman parrot, named Charlie. The bird was not in good condition because he had suffered a wound of some sort but we took care of him and he prospered with us. Word got around about Charlie's well-being and one day we got a call from a person at the National Trust, an organization that has the goal of preserving Caymanian historical places and wildlife, particularly birds. A Cayman parrot had been found on the road in very bad shape. One of the wings was badly cut and she was close to dying. The National Trust gave us the bird and we lovingly nursed Cindy back to health. We really enjoyed having the birds and after this we acquired cockatiels, a lovebird and some doves. Once we were given a dove that was a pet to its previous owner and it really took a liking to Jim. It would follow Jim around the house walking behind him like an obedient puppy. The vet knew that we were capable of taking care of birds and she would let us know when a wounded bird was found or abandoned. Invariably Jim would go and pick up the bird hoping that a nice home would later be found for it. But sometimes the bird became another one in our growing family. By the summer of 2004 we had 13 birds in our collection.

In early September of 2004 the news came that a tropical storm was forming in the Caribbean. As it grew in strength it was named Hurricane Ivan. We watched on the television as Ivan devastated Grenada on the 7th of September. The forecast showed that it was heading for Jamaica and Cuba, with the Cayman Islands also potentially in its path. Although hurricanes are a regular occurrence on the Caymans there had not been a severe one for more than 50 years. However, the forecasters indicated that this one could grow into a really big storm. Accordingly, the government issued advisories for people to leave the island or take refuge in designated locations. Guidelines were also published in the papers describing the materials and supplies that should be stocked and kept handy. It was not a mandatory evacuation, in which case huge transport planes might have been brought in to take everybody off the island, but those who lived near the ocean were advised to leave their homes and go to a secure shelter. The Canadian embassy was also in contact with us indicating that two planes were being made available and asking if we needed assistance in leaving the island. But Jim and I made the decision that we were not going to leave the birds to go blowing in the wind, and since the shelters did not take pets it meant that we would have to ride out the storm at home.

On Thursday, 9th September people were getting anxious and several of the bank employees did not show up for work. The bank managers decided to close the bank at 1:00 p.m. and by 1:30 we began to make preparations to weather the storm . . . papers and documents were stored away, computers disconnected and covered up, valuable materials moved to the vault. I knew that by the time I got off work there would be long lines at the shops and a shortage of some goods so earlier in the day I had called Jim and urged him go to the supermarket to stock up with supplies. He got two large bottles of water, packets of dry food, batteries, etc., as well as sheets of plywood to board up the house.

The next day we finished boarding up the windows of the house with help from one of his workers and a neighbor. The bank was closed for the day to allow the employees to make their necessary preparations. We watched the TV and listened to the hourly reports on the radio about Ivan's progress, and the news was not good. Leaving Jamaica in a wake of devastation Ivan was picking up strength and becoming a Category 5 hurricane, the strongest degree, and it was heading on a westerly course – straight for the Caymans.

On Saturday, 11th September the bank's CEO called us after he saw how bad the hurricane had hit Jamaica. Knowing that we were close to the ocean he advised us to go to the bank. He himself had left his suite in the Hyatt Regency hotel and gone to Patricia's home, which was located further inland. We told him that without the birds we were not leaving. Five minutes later he telephoned again and said that things were getting worse and that Patricia and her husband, Larry, along with himself were going to move to the bank. We again declined his urgent request to evacuate and hung up the phone. By now it had begun to rain and all day the birds were in a state of agitation, screaming their heads off and flying back and forth. An hour later the CEO called and said that a decision was made that the people seeking refuge at the bank would be put on the second floor and that we could come with the birds and be on the first floor. I said in that case I would come. But the problem now was how to take all our birds. The CEO said he would come over and he and Larry arrived in their cars to help us carry the many large cages to the bank because they were more than could hold in Jim's pickup truck and my car. We completed the move when it was getting dark, with rain pouring down and wind beginning to pick up.

The first floor of the bank, where my office was located, now became our home base. Because of the birds we were the only ones on that level because it was considered better to have the people placed at a higher elevation. Then we noticed that while we had grabbed our suitcases with valuables we had forgotten to bring our own emergency supplies of food and water in the rush to get out. However, we did have an ample supply of birdseed, perhaps enough to last two months. Fortunately Patricia and other colleagues were kind enough to share their foodstuff with us. We were informed that electricity would be cut at 8:00 p.m. when it was expected that the storm would become even more severe and from then on we were in the dark, literally, and unaware of what was happening

Trev and Xiaoli Sue-A-Quan join Paula Stehling (right) in front of the First Caribbean International Bank where the bank's employees took refuge when Hurricane Ivan struck the island in September 2004. *Trev Sue-A-Quan.*

outside. The radio signals stopped, phone lines went dead and cellular phones were unable to transmit. We didn't bring any bedding or pillows and we made the best we could by lying down directly on a small area of carpet in the cash room just outside the vault. During the night the storm hit with great force and a window on the third floor was blown away. The water came pelting in and dripped down to the second floor and then to the first floor. Our carpet bed became damp but we had nowhere else to sleep. Jim had come down with a bout of pneumonia before Hurricane Ivan arrived and we had also forgotten to bring his medications and his condition was getting worse having to sleep on the cold wet floor.

Hurricane Ivan was absolutely terrible. The winds howled and every so often we would hear a crash, bang, thud as a galvanized sheet from a neighboring roof and other airborne objects came crashing into the side of the bank. The storm seemed to stall over the island and kept battering us throughout the whole of Sunday. It rained non-stop all day and through the gloom we could see trees keeling over, cars rocking and debris flying through the air. Water started to accumulate on the first floor and there were no signs that it would go down so the CEO allowed us to move the birds into a vault on the second floor. Then the water supply went off and we were unable to flush the toilets. The washrooms soon turned into stinking cesspools. With the lights out people had to use flashlights to see their way to the toilets and some people were not as careful as others in trying to keep the place in a sanitary condition. Perhaps they could not see what they were doing . . . or, then again, maybe they could.

Hurricane Ivan terrorized us until Monday and it was not until the afternoon that the winds died down sufficiently to allow people to venture out. We needed to go home to get Jim's medicine and some food, as well as some bedding. The water had drained off from several places while other locations were still inundated. But the roads were strewn with mud, sand, rocks, trees, parts of houses, personal belongings, furniture and even fish. Many cars and boats were completely destroyed and buildings demolished or washed away. We got within a few hundred yards of our home and came upon a huge obstacle completely blocking the way. It was a large section of our neighboring complex that was sitting squarely across the road. Mariners Cove Apartments was a 62-unit building and the force of the surging water had torn the place in two with one portion ending up on the road while an even larger part was washed into the ocean. Hopes for our own home sunk when we saw the kind of

A large part of Mariners Cove ended up on the road. *Courtesy of Terri Merren, author of "Hurricane Ivan Survival Stories," The Mill Press, Jamaica, 2005.*

Some seaside concrete buildings remained standing but sustained water damage to the interior while coconut trees were bent and uprooted by the hurricane. *Philip Nadeau.*

destruction the hurricane had brought to this huge complex as well as noting the numerous uprooted trees and smashed cars we passed on the way. We parked the pickup truck and walked around the severed building, going through pools of mud and grime as we negotiated our way past the various objects strewn here and there.

When we reached our home it looked fairly intact from the outside but after we went inside all we could see was destruction. The roof of the building had been torn off and water had come through the upstairs condominium into ours leaving ankle-deep pools of water in some places. Our own ceiling had been wrecked with portions hanging down precariously. Furniture had been pushed around and debris and broken glass were scattered everywhere. The walls were thoroughly soaked and falling apart, with drenched and ruined artwork sagging down. The porch where some of our birds were kept had collapsed and everything was washed out. It came as a surprise to us that after only a couple days of being away our appliances – microwave, stove, washer and dryer – were already rusting, most likely from the salty seawater whipped up by the ferocious winds plus the humidity and heat. We tried to collect things that we needed or could salvage and filled two suitcases of supplies. We got Jim's medicine but as soon as the cabinet door was closed the whole cupboard unit came crashing down. As we headed back to the pickup truck we noticed that a bulldozer had been able to clear a narrow path on the roadway such that single file traffic could get through. The police were there directing traffic but they stopped us from walking through the cleared section, allowing only motorized traffic to pass. We tried to get a ride from some passing cars but no one would stop to take two mud-covered strangers into their vehicle. By now it was getting late in the afternoon

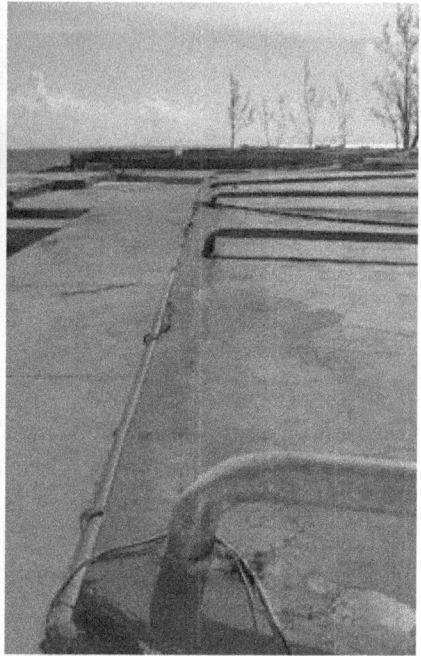

The bare foundation was the only thing remaining of the Mariners Cove apartment complex. The bent posts were once vertical and held up a perimeter fence.

Mariners Cove ended up as a huge pile of shattered possessions and memories.

Photos courtesy of Philip Nadeau, a resident of Grand Cayman Island.

The island was devastated with many collapsed buildings and debris strewn everywhere. Maintenance crews worked hard to get the roads open.

The force of Hurricane Ivan caused this car to end up in a pool of water with a dumpster on top while the boat was severed and blown on to dry land.

Photos courtesy of Philip Nadeau, a resident of Grand Cayman Island.

and there was a 6 p.m. to 6 a.m. curfew in place and we had to get back to the bank in a hurry. When the policeman saw our plight he stopped a vehicle and commanded the driver to take us. We only needed to get past the remains of Mariners Cove, some one hundred yards or so, to get to our pickup truck.

After returning to the bank that Monday evening we evaluated our situation and our options. For certain we could not go home and earlier in the day I was part of the management team discussing when it was feasible to re-open the bank. The decision was made that the bank would be open for business on Thursday. It was really a stressful time for me, having to deal with business matters, trying to figure out how best to get the operations going again, having an ailing husband as well as a flock of birds . . . at least they were keeping quiet about the situation, most likely because they were in unfamiliar surroundings. It was decided that we should move up to the third floor, which had been vacated by staff of CIBC who had moved to Barclay's Bank House a few months earlier. The place was now a construction zone with open ceilings, wires hanging down and dust everywhere. With no water or cleaning products and we tried our best to clear away as much dust as we could. Patricia had been able to go home and she retrieved an air mattress for us, which was a real luxury. Then, later in the week, Jim managed to get a bed and some pillows and that was heaven. With the storm now abated the generator at the bank could be turned on and a pump was installed so that water could be drawn from the cistern below the building. Water was collected in pails to finally flush the toilets. Fortunately we did not have any sewer backup in our building or else that would have resulted in a real mess.

While Jim went about fulfilling his employer's assignments he tried to obtain the necessary building materials to get our home back in habitable condition. Of course there was great demand for these products but because many of the suppliers were on good working terms with him Jim was able to get hold of much of the required materials. With electricity on the island still out of service it was hard going to work efficiently and we knew that we would have to stay at the bank for a while longer. It turned out to be six weeks. The bank had a toaster, coffee maker and fridge and I had my own electric kettle and frying pan so we were able to make breakfast and simple meals. The supermarkets were open although there was not a big selection of goods in the early days following the storm. There was a lady who opened a food service downstairs and we often relied on her for dinner. A shower was then installed for our use. It was set up on the stairway, which was made of tiles, and consisted of a hose that piped water from the cistern up to the first floor, going through a window that had to be broken to let the hose pass through. Jim and I had to pretend that this was like camping out, even though camping was not one of our favorite activities. We placed the bed inside the vault but slept with the door open. When we left I had to shut the vault and spin the combination lock because in those desperate times some people were stealing other people's things as well as money from the bank. It was sad.

The air quality after the hurricane was bad, with a lot of particulate matter in the air and the trees barren of leaves that would otherwise trap the dust. Charlie, our parrot, got very sick. He started wheezing, stopped eating and had diarrhea. I had to take him to the vet, and we nearly lost him. I had to hand-feed him for a while but he recovered. The other birds were OK. A pair of cockatiels even gave birth – laying and hatching an egg but unfortunately the chick died. But the pair mated again and had two more young ones that survived. Actually, having the birds turned out to be a blessing in one way – they saved our vehicles from being wrecked. Back at our condominium compound there were cars that had the roof torn off, completely wrecked or significantly damaged from being flooded with water. With our cars at the bank's parking lot they suffered relatively minor damage. One windshield was badly scratched from things crashing into it, the brakes had to be reworked having been soaked with water and a few new dents had appeared. We also needed to replace some tires having run over various nails, spikes, glass bottles and similar sharp objects. We did have insurance coverage but when the time for renewal came, which was two months later, in November, our premiums went up from $400 to $1,200. So we essentially ended up paying the price.

At the end of October the bank decided that we could no longer stay there and we were told to leave. One of my friends, Ann Record, kindly took us in. She had a huge 4000 sq. ft. home and an electric generator and she offered us her daughter's room with an adjoining washroom while the daughter moved to sleep with her parents. The birds were placed in the garage. It was sheer luxury compared to the recent experience at the bank. Ann also had a person who came to clean and cook and after the stress at work it was wonderful being able to come back and have dinner and a refreshing shower without having to worry about household chores. Jim would go out from 7:00 a.m. to 7:00 p.m. struggling to get our house repaired as well as meeting the heavy demand for his skills from his employer and others. He was also struggling to overcome his pneumonia and for a while he had to stop and try to regain his health. During all this time we were using our own savings to buy the materials and pay for the reconstruction work. Meetings were held with the insurance company every Saturday and we asked them for an advance. We were granted $30,000 and that helped but still did not cover the outlay of some $90,000 that we needed to get the house in good condition. Admittedly, we did some upgrading of the appliances, porch and laundry room but the costs were still greater than the $50,000 amount that the insurance company eventually paid us. Even so we considered ourselves fortunate compared to those who had no insurance at all. Electric power was restored on the island in early December and we were able to move back home in mid-December.

A year after Hurricane Ivan had devastated the Cayman Islands Jim and I watched as the news came through on the TV that Hurricane Katrina was gathering in strength and heading for New Orleans. We heard that some concerns were being expressed about the dikes and that some locations would be reinforced but we felt that the authorities were badly underestimating the effects of the storm surge and the power of the wind and waves. The people should have been given orders for mandatory evacuation and arrangements made accordingly. When thousands of people were directed to take refuge in the Superdome I told Jim that I didn't think that was a wise idea. Having gone through a situation at the bank that was much smaller in scale with some 36 people and a few sets of washrooms I expected that the facilities at the Superdome would quickly become overwhelmed and the stench overwhelming.

Even though we had spent money to fix up our home nicely we did not know how long it would remain our home. This was because our status as residents of Cayman Islands is currently under review. There was an election in the spring of 2005 resulting in a change of government and a new bill was passed which limited the period of residence to seven years, after which every non-Caymanian person would have to leave, for at least two years. We were made to understand that the intention was to place restrictions mainly on those from Jamaica, the country with which the Cayman Islands were very closely associated until 1992. Unfortunately, the new law has also affected many of the people on which the island depends to make its economy function properly. The regulation specified that a person who has been here for more than eight years could apply for permanent residency at any time between the 8th and 10th years. We had already been living here for 9 years and so we made our application in July 2005. Now we have to wait. The tricky part is that the decision by the Immigration Department is not necessarily based on whether the person's skills are needed but perhaps on a quota of some sort. In an attempt to strengthen our case I declined an offer in May 2006 to transfer to a different bank assignment and decided to accept a position at another financial institution that would be even higher in grade than what I had already reached. But we have to prepare ourselves mentally and physically for the possibility that we might be served a two-month notice to leave the island and have accumulated various pieces of luggage and crates. We have survived Hurricane Ivan but we still do not know if it would be through bureaucratic procedures that we might be blown away.

Banking and Batabano

Cecil Chan-A-Sue and Camille (Chan) Short

In 1503 Christopher Columbus happened upon the Cayman Islands when he was blown off course on his way from Panama to Hispaniola. The number of turtles sighted at Cayman Brac and Little Cayman was so great that he called the islands Las Tortugas (The Turtles). The larger Grand Cayman Island was discovered later and the group of islands became a source of turtle meat for the pirates and buccaneers that roamed the Caribbean. The islands were renamed Cayman from the word caiman, a local name for the crocodiles that were also found there. In 1655 the Cayman Islands came under British control and jointly administered as a dependency of Jamaica. The close association with Jamaica lasted until 1992 when Jamaica opted to become an independent country. Cayman decided to remain under British rule.

With little in the way of natural resources the Cayman Islands have developed a flourishing tourist industry while venturing into the world of finance after a law was introduced in 1966 to make Cayman a center for banking and financial services. The airport was formerly a small airstrip built in 1953 but has now become a busy entry point for international flights bringing millions of tourists who come to play in the sunshine and swim in the clear Caribbean Sea. They of course help to promote the financial well-being of the country, although the banks have been doing fine on their own accord as a off-shore location for financial services. Four centuries after Columbus two Chinese Guyanese set course for the Cayman Islands, and each has helped to contribute to the islands' development, while making Grand Cayman Island their new home.

* * * * * * * *

Cecil Chan-A-Sue was born and grew up in Guyana. After completing his high school studies he was employed at the Georgetown branch of the Royal Bank of Canada. He belonged to the generation that saw the transition from written records to digital processing – from pen and ink to data entry machines. In those days there would be an individual computer at each branch to maintain the records for the various aspects of banking needs as well as the accounts of individual customers. This required a considerable amount of keyboard typing to input the data into the large NCR machines. The computerization operations were successfully completed by Cecil and in 1982 he was asked by Royal Bank to go to the Cayman Islands to assist with the automation of the bank's records there.

Arriving in George Town Cecil went diligently to work. It was a major adjustment getting used to the new environment although he was too busy to be concerned, sometimes working seven days of the week trying to get everything set up properly. He found the island to be rather quiet and reserved, and there was no television station. This, on the other hand caused people to interact more with one another and so he got to know his neighbors and socialized with them. Over the years Cecil rose in rank and authority and has now accumulated many years of loyal service to the Royal Bank.

The concept of having Cayman Island become a financial and banking center was approved by the island's authorities who offered tax advantages to individuals or corporations that were not available in other locations. In addition to being a tax haven the Cayman Islands offer privacy of accounts, with confidentiality maintained by the banks; financial transactions are not reported to the home country of the individual person or corporate entity. As a result, the Cayman Islands have, within a few decades, become the leading center for offshore banking and a conduit for money flowing from one country to another with financial transactions exceeding a trillion dollars per year. There are no taxes levied on individuals, corporations or property – the country's revenues are generated from duties on all imported goods, real estate transfers, fees and licenses.

With the advent of the internet and desktop computers, the data processing operations for banking became an extensive network that spanned the globe. Cecil was involved in this transformation of the computer systems for the bank. Computers have facilitated the documentation and execution of banking transactions. They have also allowed the banks the ability to monitor the movement of funds to ensure that the transfers are for legitimate purposes. The stories of people walking in with suitcases of cash trying to hide ill-gotten gains in the Cayman Islands are the stuff of Hollywood, Cecil explains. He admits that in the early days a few clients of that category were able to do so but such a practice would not be permitted today. Safeguards and procedural checks have been introduced to prevent the Caymans from being a location where money can be laundered. There are no numbered accounts and those wanting to do business with the banks must have accounts set up in their own names or as registered companies. In addition, the Cayman Islands government is a signatory to cooperative agreements with some countries regarding the exchange of information under certain circumstances as well as a participant in various international agreements regarding money obtained from illegal operations. Anti-money-laundering laws have been introduced with provisions such as "dual criminality" whereby indictable offences in other countries are considered to also be crimes perpetrated in the Cayman Islands. These regulations make the Caymans a very difficult place for hiding "dirty money" and they give assurances to the financial community that appropriate safeguards are in place to make the Cayman Islands the best place to conduct legitimate monetary transactions.

Cecil is well settled in the Cayman Islands and enjoys the clean atmosphere, not only in the business sense but also because of the ocean and living environment. The community is small and there is relatively little crime. Although there is not a wide selection of cultural activities as compared with, for example, North America, there is no place in the world that one can have everything in life. The peace and high standard of living in the Caymans are just fine in the trade off. Cecil also gives back to the community as a volunteer with Meals on Wheels. His boss was once the president of the Rotary Club and the organization was looking for volunteers to deliver meals to needy folks. At lunchtime on Fridays he would take the meal packages to the people on his assigned route. On the Friday of the weekend when Hurricane Ivan hit in September 2004 businesses, including the Meals on Wheels kitchen, were closed and food deliveries did not resume until some two months later, in part because of the damage sustained by the food preparation facilities and in part because some volunteers had lost their vehicles. Some of the people served by Meals on Wheels had families to go to, some left the island, and others indicated that the meal service was no longer needed. When deliveries resumed the number of people on Cecil's route had dropped to about seven, and it takes him about half an hour to complete.

The Rotary Club is the main organization offering Meals on Wheels and raises money for the program through fund-raising drives, while also getting some support from the government. Over time the people receiving the meals have developed a friendship with Cecil and he became one to whom they could pour out their difficulties. For Cecil, their problems helped to put his own life in perspective.

* * * * * * * *

After working for Barclay's Bank in Georgetown for three years Camille Chan decided that is was time to leave Guyana. The political climate and economic prospects were not encouraging. Her elder sister had gone to Canada to study and there she married a civil engineer. When Camille's brother-in-law noticed an ad in the paper for an engineer to work on the expansion of the highway system in the Cayman Islands he applied and was offered the position. With family members now settled in the Cayman Islands Camille joined them there. After arriving in George Town she applied to Barclay's Bank and to Bank of Nova Scotia (Scotiabank). Barclay's offered her $200 a month plus consideration for her three years' service in Guyana towards her benefits while Scotia's offer was $225. Camille was reluctant to give up the three years of credit but in those days twenty-five dollars was a significant amount and so she chose to work for Scotia and stayed with that bank for nine years. She then joined Butterfield Bank in a managerial position. Camille married and raised a family in the Cayman Islands, her husband being a Guyanese who had come to the island country when he was nine years old.

Camille found that the Cayman Islands, while being a wonderful place to live and work, had a reputation of being rather conservative in outlook. This can be attributed in part to being an island nation as well as having a strong church-going tradition. The goings-on in the world can easily be ignored since the benefits of being an offshore tax haven have been realized primarily through paper or computer-based transactions rather than having to deal with clients in person and being drawn into their affairs. With the financial world needing the support of other related enterprises, such as insurance, legal offices, financial management, investment planning and the like a number of companies have emerged to offer these services efficiently using a relatively small community of

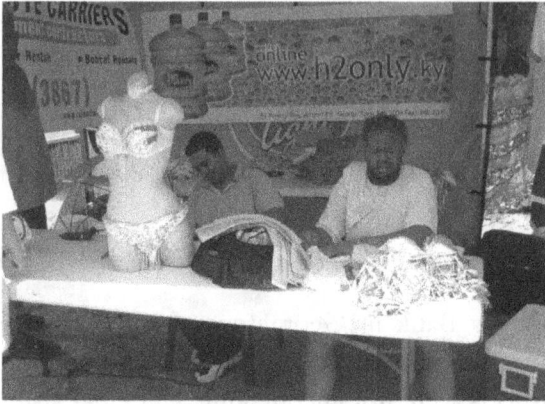

Batabano participants making costumes. For a fee the public can join a band and get to wear these colorful carnival outfits. *Trev Sue-A-Quan.*

professional people, most of whom are expatriates from the U.K., U.S., and Canada. While Grand Cayman does offer a warm climate year-round and lovely beaches with crystal clear water, a routine of a swim after work tends to become monotonous. There is a limited choice of social, cultural and entertainment facilities and activities. Many expatriates choose to go "off-island" on a fairly regular basis to get a change of scenery and enjoy perhaps a Broadway show, mountains, rivers, international sports competitions, winter activities or "big city life." Camille found a way to express her joy and enthusiasm on the social scene by supporting Batabano, an annual event in April with music, dance and street parades.

Batabano (bah-tah-bah-NOO) was the brainchild of Dave Martins, a Guyanese who had formed a singing group the *Tradewinds* that became popular in the 1960s. Dave and his band chose to settle in the Cayman

An elaborate costume being prepared for the parade. *Trev Sue-A-Quan.*

As is typical in Trinidad's carnival, huge colorful costumes are created that need to be supported by large frames with wheels. *Trev Sue-A-Quan.*

Music plays a huge part in promoting the mood and liveliness of the Batabano celebrations. In 2006 Byron Lee and the Dragonaires, a popular Jamaican band known throughout the Caribbean, was a major attraction. *Trev Sue-A-Quan.*

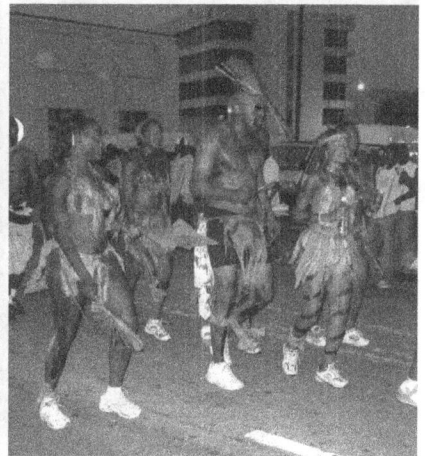

Participants in the 2006 Batabano parade. *Trev Sue-A-Quan.*

Islands in 1981. Dave had been doing the occasional fund-raiser for the island's Rotary Club. On one occasion, after being requested to do one more event, he suggested to David Peynado, his friend and Rotary member, that a serious annual fund-raiser be starting along the lines of a Trinidad-type carnival. Peynado hesitated for about five seconds, and then said, "Let's do it." Martins organized the event and started planning it with Peynado. Presentations were made at a couple of Rotary meetings to explain the idea. Many of the club's administrators were from outside the Caribbean region and didn't have a clue about carnival.

Frankly, several of them were very skeptical.

The initial reaction to the first Batabano was fantastic with a lot of the more uninhibited people in the country (Caymanians as well as expats) joining in. Camille (Chan) Wight, Consuelo Ebanks, Graham Thompson, Reba Dilbert, and Raglan Roper, were some of the early devotees who provided their skills and enthusiasm. Huge crowds turned out, and there were lots of costumes. The event raised a lot of money. In the second year, Bernard Ramsay, who had carnival experience (or playing mas') was brought over from Guyana to run workshops on wire-bending, costume production, use of materials, etc. There was one feature had to be changed following the inaugural Batabano: the mudders were out. In the early years of Trinidad's carnival, following World War II, some of the poor people who could not afford fancy clothes smeared mud and clay on their bodies to create a decorative effect, and perhaps a disguise if so needed. The authorities and banking officials in George Town were not amused when some of the mud ended up on their streets and buildings. Getting down and dirty did not quite fit the image that the orderly financial community wanted to project. Dave Martins ran Batabano for three years, on behalf of Rotary, with big support from David Peyando, as well as from other Rotarians like James Ebanks and Donnie Smith, Eddie Balderamos, Rick Burgos, etc. The popularity of the *Tradewinds* probably helped stir initial interest in the idea, but the crowd really responded to the product.

From the beginning, however, Dave Martins pointed out to Rotary that this activity was not part of Caymanian culture, and that they would have to put some money into developing the event mainly through finding a method to propel it forward, beginning with the school children. Dave wrote a long paper to this effect, spelling it out for them, but Rotary didn't follow through. Also, on its own accord, Batabano showed signs of wanting to go more into "show business" rather than merely parading in costumes, and Dave exhorted Rotary to encourage this (it was the local pulse) but they didn't pursue that either. Early on, as well, the brevity of the costumes and the suggestive gyrations of the participants who cavorted along the streets raised some hackles among other things. This aspect was never treated properly, and eventually Rotary pulled out of running Batabano full bore. They succumbed to the negative feedback they were getting, and handed over the operations to a private group. To this day the critics continue to hold the opinion that revelation should be obtained from the bible rather than from the exposure of significant amounts of flesh resulting from the wearing of skimpy costumes. In reality more skin could be observed on the island's famous Seven Mile Beach on any day of the year and the spectators of the carnival are generally more in admiration of the colorful costumes rather than the attributes of persons wearing them. Nevertheless, Batabano has grown over the years and has been gaining more favorable attention from schoolchildren, government officials, corporate sponsors and tourists. While being a contributing part of the island's financial success Camille also continues to be in the forefront of the Batabano activities, organizing, publicizing and promoting events as well as leading her group of revelers as the carnival band weaves through the streets of George Town.

Camille (right) and her companion leading their band of revelers through the streets of George Town. *Trev Sue-A-Quan.*

Astronauts in China

Andy Lee, née Lam

In October 2003, China launched an astronaut in a short orbital flight of the Earth. This accomplishment was promoted as a highlight in China's recent development in the fields of science and technology. Just over a century before, China was the 'sick man of Asia,' a backward nation struggling to gain respect in the world while burdened by the imperial dynastic system that had dominated for thousands of years. But even before the entry into space, the term 'astronaut" was already being applied to several Chinese. These were the ones who had made great financial leaps forward from the capitalist-style economy that was introduced in the 1980s under the guise of 'Socialism with Chinese characteristics.' Several of the successful Chinese entrepreneurial men were able to enjoy a lavish lifestyle, with houses, cars, material goods, fine clothing and privilege. They then took flight to various developed nations, where they purchased impressive mansions and placed their children, and quite often, their wives, to establish a foothold for the future in a strange but more secure society. The businessmen would return to China to supervise their prospering enterprises so as to maintain the flow of profits that would enhance the affluent standard of living to which they had quickly become accustomed. The frequent flights to and fro between China and their families earned them the name 'astronauts.' These are Chinese-style commuters in the modern era.

Admittedly, the astronaut families represent a small percentage of China's people, but because the population base is so huge the astronauts are appearing in the (tens of) thousands. Their impact at home and abroad is significant, extending beyond the economic sphere into cultural and social habits. Meanwhile, the majority of China's peoples are peasants and laborers, with the more successful ones sampling modernization through gadgets – fancy cars, cell phones, CD players, karaoke and the Internet. At the same time the poor remain relatively poor, unable to reach the heights that the astronauts attain. A glimpse into the lives of these different strata of society in modern China was gained by Andy Lee, who went to Beijing in September 2002 to teach English. During her vacation time Andy traveled across China with her recently-made friends as guides. As a fifth-generation Chinese in Guyana with her residence in London, England, she describes in a down-to-earth style the perspectives of someone with Chinese ancestry and appearance, together with a Guyanese upbringing and openness, and the ways and sentiments of a person from the developed world.

* * * * * * *

Mouse was never a student of mine. She tagged along with Zhang Yang one Thursday because ZY asked me to teach him English. Mouse and Zhang Yang were an item until SARS. Mouse is a very intelligent girl, but lazy. She spoke very little English when I first met her way back in September. Within a few months she became my best success story without either of us trying. The problem with Mouse, she moseys along at a slow peaceful pace and she has a doleful countenance, which makes me want to slap her to wake her up. But she is quite comfortable being dragged through the backwoods. Moon and Mouse are the only two people in China I would consider taking on a journey through China . . . they don't answer back.

ZY really needs to be mentioned, because he typifies so many beginning learners of English. Zhang Kai Sheng or Zhang Yang to his family and friends is an unknown entity. I met him Wednesday morning in the corridor whilst waiting for the bell to go. He asked if I could teach him English and be his friend. At least that's what I heard. I said, yea fine come round at 6 p.m. on Thursday. At 6 p.m. on Wednesday, this apparition appeared, flask 'n all. I told him as politely as I could – tomorrow at 6:00, OK? Morning or afternoon? For Heaven's sake, who on Earth is going to teach English at 6:00 in the morning – get a life, man. When he came over he attempted to explain his plan. "I speaka Eengrish bad. My teacha is Chinese and he teacha me Eengrish languagge (with full emphasis on the ge). I teacha uu Chinese." So I start by making him try to say 'speak' without the 'a.' Next, I was in the middle of getting rid of the 'ge' in language when he suddenly started prattling away and writing. He actually was trying to teach me Chinese. James was in the background doing emails and I could see his whole body shaking with laughter. That's not all: "I wan be yo frena. Uu beautiful. Uu call me Zhang Yang, uu my frena. I studentt, uu teacher, I call uu teacher? I wan talk wi uu. Uu meeta me tomorrow at 6 oclacka on futaballa feel."

Zhang Yang and Mouse still come for lessons on Thursdays. I'm trying. When he comes across a word he just cannot pronounce I say, "tell me what it means?" with the hope that maybe we could forget that word and use another. When he duly reads the meaning I cannot help from collapsing with laughter. Omigosh, I feel bad sometimes, but his pronunciation is the absolute pits. Hey, I should tape it!

27 Jan 2003

Mouse and ZY had queued up for 6 hours on the Friday night for tickets and managed to get us the slow train sitting in varying degrees of upright on hard seats. That is, 14 hours on hard seats stopping at every bloody station on the way. Train travel in China is as complex as it gets. Firstly, we cannot book more than 4 days in advance. Then we cannot book return seats! And we have to go to the station in the place of our embarkation to buy tickets. Hence, there is absolutely no way you can plan to be in any place at anytime specially in the Spring Festival holiday when the whole of China's population has somewhere to go.

Mouse is typical Chinese. She whispers to me at dinner "We haven't got a bathroom. You bathe everyday, don't you? I'm sorry." This is what we now know as a 'need to know as you need to know when we think you absolutely need to know.' Poor poor Yo.[1] Poor us! Mouse is a happy jolly girl. Yo loved her to bits because Mouse tended to her every need. We eventually arrived at Siping just after midday and had a long taxi ride to Mouse's village. "Mouse, how much farther to your home?" "Nearly there." Mouse's English is relative. We were nearer to her home than to Beijing is what she meant.

We had boarded the train around midnight so we didn't see much from BJ to nearly Shenyang. Shenyang is a new major city just north of BJ. That means, industry. We bucked and rolled along the NE flat lands of China for hours through small farming villages, towns and cities of all sizes and colours and at various stages of modernity and dilapidation. I was happy to see the old factories standing forlorn and desolate, brand new bright buildings pointing skyward and believe it or not, brightly painted! The weather changed rapidly from snow in BJ to

---

1   Yolande Chin, a dear friend from Trinidad joined Andy on this adventure to China's countryside.

frosty, to sunny, cloudy, smog - just about every phenomena. Every inch of land is under cultivation and ploughed and seeded by hand. It's a poor poor county. Tall sheaves of dried corn stacks piled outside each house. This is fuel for the winter. In the distance on the left the mountains of Mongolia. A bleak desolate land. Oh, and barely a sliver of snow in the furrows of the fields.

On to Mouse's home. It's a village of about 600 people. Red brick one storied houses built about 12 years ago by the Gov and prematurely aged by the weather and the harsh dusty plains as is its inhabitants leathered to the colour of the earth. It is a fair sized home with 2 bedrooms, kitchen and hallway. The main bedroom is also the living room, that was our home for 3 days and 3 nights. The 'kang' was about a third of the room. It is best described as a heated concrete platform covered by a sheet of lino. We ate, slept, held audiences on this platform. At eating time a round short legged table was placed in the middle. At night padded quilts and blankets were laid out for us to sleep on and in between. It was deliciously warm and comfortable. We were told that the daytime temp was about - 11 and night - Lord knows but as you lay there you could feel the heavy cold air boring

Andy Lee (right) enjoying a meal on top of the multi-purpose kang, with Mouse and her mother in attendance. *Andy Lee.*

into your skull. At night too, No. 1s were done in the slop bucket in the middle of the hallway. Everyone was aroused when this was being done as nothing is secret. There were 2 slop buckets, one for the kitchen waste which fed the chickens in the yard and the other one . . . Yo never saw where that went. God it was cold. The outhouse in the back of the house was the sluice affair. I naturally corked up until Harbin. On our second day we went to the market on a donkey bus. Market days are held on the 3rd, 13th and 23rd of each month. It was packed with

Andy sits in the front row seat of the donkey bus, with Yolande Chin peering over her right shoulder, while going to market in rural China. *Andy Lee.*

shoppers getting ready for the Spring Festival. Villages are not remote or at any great distance from one another but in weather as cold as this they seemed many many miles distant. Our bus fetched neighbours shopping whilst they legged it home themselves. A friendly inquisitive day. Most of our stay was spent demonstrating the computer. Curious inquisitive beings awed by having their photos taken and displayed instantly on the screen. Magic lantern. Perplexing and confusing because they all have TVs and DVDs.

The markets were filled with a variety of goods with the approach of the Spring Festival (Chinese New Year). *Andy Lee.*

29 June 2003. Jingo Po Hu (Jing Po Lake)

Heilongjiang, read: Hei (black) long (dragon) jiang (river). Ha er bin is the capital city of Heilongjiang. I'm up here for a week to fix my papers for next year and to check out the facilities and things. At least that was what

I had intended to do. Others seem to have big plans for me on THEIR minds. It would be asinine to traverse this vast country alone, so I invited or, in fact, jumped at the chance of having a 'local' guide and interpreter – in the form of Moon. Moon was a student of mine who showed, in his class, the best chance of comprehension . We'd been roaming Beijing together for several months and although we got lost or misplaced due to his complete absence of directional sense, we always found where we'd set out to find . . . eventually. We also found many places, which we didn't want to find, and this unique quality was what I felt would make the journey worthwhile. And it did.

This all begun one day in May . . . during the SARS crisis, when we teachers of English were virtual prisoners, quarantined in our residences in an effort to stop the spread of the disease. It must have been after the 6th. I used to go over to the campus for a part of the day, everyday – just to keep sane, you understand. Moon, Cheng, Alex and I would play ping-pong everyday or sometimes just sit. Not much chatting on my part because they speak Chinese and I don't. One day Moon and I were chatting about our 'dreams.' He said he dreamt he would travel China. Oh boy, did I jump at that! Here I am straining at the leash to have a chance to drive China. That, and along the Silk Road . . . but that particular stretch will have to wait for a little bit longer.

Next day.

"Moon, I've been thinking…" I began.

"Yea?"

"Would you go with me?"

"Where?"

"Traveling China."

"When?"

"This summer."

"How long?"

"Dunno. However long it takes."

"Where?"

"Everywhere. Maybe nowhere and all. Just driving."

"Driving?"

"Yea. In a car…."

Chance. That's what I think it was – chance. Everything seems to be happenchance. I happenchanced to be born. YEEEEEEEes!.

~ ~ ~ ~ ~ ~ ~ ~

Sometime around hungry the road sign said Baidaihe so we made a slight detour to lunch there.

"How do you do this?" Moon queried.

"Like this," I demonstrated, calling on ample Guyanese expertise in dealing with whole boiled crabs.

"$@#%," he exclaimed, with obvious shell-shock.

"You want this . . . the back?" I invited.

"YOU have it."

Say no more. One slurp and it's gone. There! I taught Moon how to deal with crab. After lunch we paid our way onto the beach for a stroll. Chinese don't swim for fun. The sport is growing slowly and it's not on the PE agenda in schools. Chinese won't go sunbathing because to have darkened skin denotes peasant stock. Besides, the umbrella industry would collapse if there weren't a need to take shade from the sun.

The public beach has a levy of 20 yuan a head. You will find that everywhere you visit has to be paid for. There were a few swimmers or knee-deep waders in the sea. Most of the men dressed in dark coloured trousers and long-sleeved shirts, shoes and socks in hand. The women stayed out of the water under umbrellas with their stocking socks firmly strangulating their ankles. A few brave souls did get splashed. This was Moon's first sight of the ocean and probably such a vast expanse of water. He did not take his trainers off to dip his toes in the water. No different from many other Chinese. Where I come from, we used to splash in any puddle we could find. On a hot day we'd cool off in the duck pond!

~ ~ ~ ~ ~ ~ ~ ~

Somewhere near Shenyang, Moon phoned his aunt's friend, Adam, who has a factory there and maybe he will 'putusupforthenight.' If we don't like the accommodations then we could find a hotel. OK. Hit town at about 6.30 p.m. just before dark. Phoned for directions and was told to ask for such 'n such road where we would see a factory with a blue roof. **Cannot miss it.** (Australian for: you will surely miss it.) Asked at the tollgate. Asked the old man. Asked the yobs. Asked a nice couple. Asked a taxi driver who wanted to charge 50 yuan. Asked at another tollgate. Must have asked the whole of Shenyang by 9.30 p.m.! It's not easy to follow "go straight, head north, then east, west" etc. in the dark, and when there are train bridges, road bridges, tollgate bridges, its only fair that they should be more specific than *'everybody knows the bridge.'* To put it simply, we should have turned right at the old man. Found the road as I mentioned above and tried to find the blue roof. Specifics are nice, I always say. It was the factory that was blue and because it had a flat roof, that feature was not visible from ground level.

Just make a note here that the giving and taking of directions in China is, at the best of times, a complex affair. . . . as complex as Bubba (in *Forrest Gump*) giving Anne of Green Gables directions to the Boston Tea Party. It's really rather silly asking local folk directions because they haven't necessarily gone to where you are going except by bus and they never needed to find it themselves. A whole generation missed school some years ago and reading is not their forte so tuck the map away and read the body language.

The cultural divide between the East and the West is very pronounced in that Chinese, for more than one reason, are incapable of issuing specific instructions. A simple compass direction, i.e. north, south, east or west (sometimes with the slight variations of east-north, east-south, west-north or west-south), is regarded as adequate.[2] Daytime, or in the dead of darkness, is immaterial. Why? They have an inbuilt compass. Their homes, cities, towns and villages are built on a north/south (or an east/west) axis. (Except for Tianjin, which from the late 19th century was under European occupation and influence and resulted in streets laid out on a diagonal axis, confusing everyone including the locals.) Dialect, accent and body language all combine to make a mess of comprehension. Mandarin was prescribed to unify this vast nation. But did you know that people in Shanghai have their own language which is completely different to the language spoken in Beijing, which is different to anything else in the rest of the country, which ignores the rest of the country and communicates in whatever mmm's and ahh's

---

2   In Chinese, east and west precede north and south in using combined directions, the reverse of the custom in the West.

they remember? And I haven't yet mentioned Fujian Province, which has an unknown quantity of dialects, plus Guangdong with its international language and food, which we had all believed defined the 'real' Chinese language and culture!

Adam was born in Southern China and when he was a little nipper, he and his parents immigrated to Australia and lived there for 30 years. He is the manager of a water pump factory in Shenyang. Last winter, owing to a very cold winter and heavy pollution, he shut down the place for six weeks and went to visit his family still living down under. Adam has soaked up Aussie culture and accent – very laid back and hospitable. Whether this was due to the Aussie or Chinese culture, it turned out to be fortunate, as there didn't seem to be much action in the factory anyway. Since it was long after dark his cook rustled up two bowls of noodles each topped with a fried egg and garnished with green onions and precious dried shrimps, which he kept stored in a glass jar. I think he was a mite bit surprised that we hadn't stopped for a bite to eat before visiting the factory because it must have seemed impossible to him for anyone to get lost for two and a half hours in Shenyang (or any other city in China, for that matter!).

Above the factory floor is the workers' dormitory. Each room had a single bed and the worldly goods of somebody else. The squat toilets were downstairs and the cold water came on at about 5 a.m. The water supply is controlled by the neighbor, who thinks the pump needs a rest from 8 p.m. to 5 a.m. I couldn't have a shower because there wasn't one. Adam was such a kind and lovely person I hadn't the heart to turn down his hospitality. But then, at that time of night, he probably didn't think of "conveniences." Must have been way past everyone's bedtime for we didn't see a single other soul, but heard movement – the banging doors echoing through the whole building, and my door specifically, because if I'd shut it properly I couldn't get in without disturbing Adam who by this time went over across the courtyard to his quarters which was part of the office. After dinner, Moon went to the toilet. When he came back I needed to 'go,' and he said, "Don't." Men rarely think cleaning a priority in their routines.

Early next morning, Adam and I chatted a while about China and to some extent his disillusionment with business and education in general.

It's really a Catch 22 because small businesses like Adam's, which manufactures circulation pumps for central heating systems, haven't got much chance without the wherewithal to export nor to make much headway in the home market which cannot sustain such a specialized tool. We could have mulled over both subjects for years as there was so much Adam could say.

Waited in a side street near Kentucky Fried Chicken imaging that I was seeing a bit of China that nobody else sees because KFC doesn't open for another half hour and blow if I'm going to leave my car parked after what's-her-name said that they break in and steal things . . . Spent some time staring at the porno carved in stone on the building opposite. KFC that morning was absolutely delicious. I'll never say a bad word about KFC again especially how now I wager a KFC, as in "Wanna bet a KFC . . ." whenever there is a bet to be made. I'm two KFCs down.

~ ~ ~ ~ ~ ~ ~ ~

26 June

The trickle down economic miracle hasn't made it up to Heilongjiang. Roads to the volcanoes are atrocious. The problem is that they have no sound rock base under the thin skin of asphalt. Trucks thunder over the roads puncturing the surface and this makes for chicken pox pattern potholes and/or rivulet-ribbing. It's not the big expanse of potholes that we feared, it was the small deep ones barely visible to the naked eye. Banging over them is a fearful feat; dodging them is the sport. Every vehicle swerves, ducks and dives to avoid these menaces. Not to be outdone, the edges where the bridges meet the road are optimum in the tire-bursting competition.

I always felt guilty whenever I uttered "oops." At the really bad bumps my passengers would bounce their way to the roof. Moon swears I was driving too fast purposely. This was our first real experience of China's road mending scheme. What happens, the Road Menders would choose the worst group of potholes, mark the area from the middle of the road to the edge for about 40 feet. Then they would cordon off the area with flagged ropes, and plant a couple more flags. And then proceed to dig down to about four inches. After that, I don't know what they do because we've never been around at the close of play. This is done simultaneously along the whole road, be it one inch or 1000 kliks. A journey that should be one hour easily becomes six. "Oops" could also mean, "Heavens above, why don't they have proper road mending warnings? In Canada, they have students tramping a few hundred metres down the road waving flags, being thorough nuisances to the general public." Luckily, we saw only one truck sinking into a bridge on this road. Later, down South, it was horrendous.

~ ~ ~ ~ ~ ~ ~ ~

1-2 July

Back in Ha er bin that afternoon we went to the porcelain market. Thousands of porcelain pottery and figurines were displayed on rickety stands in the open air. Cheap, cheap and cheap, and it was bargainable again. Wow!

After Moon negotiated for my things that I figured I would buy for Mrs. Sun, I wandered back thinking that the vendors hadn't smartened up to the fact that I was Yingguoren[3] and therefore 'rich.' Wrong. Boy, they can spot a foreigner a mile away. Anyway, sportingly, the 'egg' man accepted my 50 yuan and when I got to the 'vase' man I had less than the 120 yuan asking price. I re-bargained:

"Duo shao?" (How much?)

"120"

"70"

"Bushi, 110"

"Bushi, 75"

"Bushi, 110"

Obviously we had reached a stand-off here.

"Ok," I surrendered, and with the biggest smile and a wink of the eye, I emptied my silk purse onto the table.

"65," I pointed out.

"Dui, dui." (That's right.)

Thumbs up and the biggest smiles and winks all 'round . . .

WOW!!!! Jeepers! Best bit of bargaining I've ever every achieved. Lord, was I pleased with myself. Packed my egg and my vase in the

---

3 A person from England.

van and stood waiting with Duan until they took our spoils back to the apartment. It was a good day.

That night we dined with Duan, who'd brought my papers. Lee, who is also from Sunderland (the university that had arranged for me to teach in China), phoned and I invited him to meet us at the restaurant. Lee and I talked nine to the dozen about the whys and wherefores of our experiences in China so far. I'm sorry but this evening was the first time I used my brain in conversation since Moon and I were alone on the Jingshan Expressway. Any foreigner in a foreign country will have had the experience of being deaf and dumb and completely ignored. I had to bite the bit for the few days in Ha er bin because I had to do business. I've had to tolerate this many a time.

~ ~ ~ ~ ~ ~ ~ ~

Back on the 201 to Shenyang. This time we won't visit Adam. For one, Moon doesn't understand his English. For two, experience is experience and I need a proper hotel.

"If we find that big road with the TV station, we'll find a good hotel," Moon glowed. "Go up there."

"That's the ring road."

"You sure?"

"Ask."

Somewhere on a big road: "That's a hotel. No, not that one . . . that one."

Moon went in to check out the hotel. It's cheap – 100 yuan. That OK? OK. And you can park here without paying and breakfast is free in the morning. AND it's got air conditioning. Hey, what the heck? It's got everything a girl could want. Shortly after, on the third floor . . .

"The air conditioner doesn't work," I advised the attendant.

"Open the window."

"There's no towel."

"You have two towels."

"Where?"

"There."

"What? These pieces of rags? I use this stuff for mopping the floor."

~ ~ ~ ~ ~ ~ ~ ~

The next big town with smoking stacks and a network of train tracks playing noughts 'n crosses over the road was Anshan.

"What's this place?"

"Anshan Iron & Steel."

"What do they make?"

"Dunno." (Dunno, is the generic term for *'I don't know the word in English so don't ask me.'*)

"It's a rich place," I declared.

"How you know?"

"Nice houses, big cars AND SUVs."

~ ~ ~ ~ ~ ~ ~ ~

Dalian is one of the prettiest seaside resorts. It has the sense to hide its huge factories in valleys and the beaches are worth going in for a dip. There is a hotel complex on one of the beaches with a beautiful golf course and a little man plucking weeds out of the absolutely pristine lawns. This time, too, we toured the dock areas. Understand, a lot of our 'touring' comes because we're lost. We were looking for a gas station. Dalian has miles and miles of 'flyovers' for motor transport and we could see tops of gas stations but it takes guesstimates and guts to reach them. U-turns on fast highways are pretty dangerous but absolutely necessary. Lunch at an upscale restaurant (an ex-cinema) was a self-service affair. Not expensive by our standards – 59 yuan a head. Nothing significant except the abalone, which we could not afford – 600 yuan for one.

This was one place where a Westerner would feel quite at home. Was there anything Chinese? No, not really. Along with Qindao, Dalian is very Western and prosperous. Of the two cities, I would choose Dalian.

4 July. Car ferry to Yantai

As with most things in China, tickets are only valid on the day they are bought. The paperwork involved in purchasing a ticket for the car ferry was beyond me. Passport, birth certificate, driver's licence, visa, and they might have missed asking us for our medical records. There wasn't much space for vehicular traffic. Not by our standards. Most of the vehicles were trucks. Foot passengers came in two buses. There were three classes of sleeping – bunks, seats, and floor. I wasn't offered the cheapest tickets. The journey was about six hours and I slept soundly all the way over. Just as well that it was a night crossing because the bars and restaurants were shut or non-existent . . . a pretty Spartan affair. There is a fee of 20 yuan to go on the upper deck. There is something strange about Chinese and water. They are not great swimmers. On board the ferry and, as I recall, the Yangtse Chinese tourist boat, passengers are not allowed to roam the decks unless accompanied by the crew. We got locked up tight and the only thing to do was to sleep.

~ ~ ~ ~ ~ ~ ~ ~

Looking for the gateway to Taishan is like looking for a needle in a haystack. The mountain is there, in full view. Not really magnificent in the realms of mountains and as we were going round and round it, I began to evaluate the futility of trying to find the way up to the top. Sign posting is such that we at one time headed away from the mountain although we could see we were pointed away from it, believing that maybe there was a shortcut . . . or even a proper way. Nevertheless, as we were slowly skirting round the foothill, the local craftsmen and women displayed their wares on rickety trestles – bits of pottery, teapots, carvings, rocks, broken furniture, just about anything that could passably resemble something worth looking at. Methinks, myself, that a few busloads of white tourists once passed through and for the hell of it, bought up some old stuff which has now led to all the rubbish being flogged as antiques. However, we stopped at a group of these hawkers to look at the 'local' specialties. Polished rocks, supposedly from the holy mountain – that's IT! These can be bought anywhere in China and there must be a factory somewhere painting the black veins to make picturesque trees and flowers and scenery to make the purchase that much more special.

The hotel at the cable car station has seen better days. Maintenance, maintenance. Cleanliness. Plumbing. I was introduced to my room, which was self-contained with shower and toilet bowl and with the warning: if you want to do big business, use the toilet in the yard. I'm getting too old for this nonsense because next morning, the hotel was totally secured and the toilet for the big business was on the outside!

Cicadas and donkey meat for dinner. Over priced for we could have caught our dinner on the way up the mountain road. In ancient times and in more recent times, Chinese are known to keep cicadas in ceramic cages – there are specialty collectors who gather these rare and pseudo-rare cute containers. They tell me that they appreciate the sound of cicadas. I hear it all the time – tinnitus. Drives me bonkers sometimes.

~ ~ ~ ~ ~ ~ ~ ~

The bods in Tiananmen are rebuilding and reinventing China. They are building megaliths of modern monstrosities alongside old style pavilions and pagodas. Hangzhou is a prime example of rebuilding Ming and Qing style buildings lost to wars and the Cultural Revolution. Around West Lake (Xi Hu) the parks and gardens are replanted with mature trees and shrubs. From my first visit two years ago, Hangzhou has and is going under a massive transformation. What was once the promenade lined with Western-style hotels is being superseded by something which is in the process of being built at the expense of a piece of the lake. My first impression was, 'They've moved Hangzhou.' Hanzhou is a massive working city. A tourist sees only tiny part of life in the urban complex. To be fair, it's the same with most touristy cities around the world, though in most Chinese cities the demarcation line between the tourist, commercial and suburban areas are well defined and unless one explores, never the twain shall meet.

~ ~ ~ ~ ~ ~ ~ ~

Jingdezhen[4] is the dirtiest city so far – noisy, grimy, hot and steamy. People are all over the place. So many people sitting round doing nothing. Shop keepers cannot be bothered to attend to customers. Cheap luminous plastic goods spew out on to the pavements. Old wooden houses. This area is also a pine and bamboo forest. Dirty water with rice grains get thrown out on the street. Open sewers, terrible roads. Traffic absolutely horrendous. Not many private cars. Lots of little jitneys, pedestrians, motorbikes. The pottery market is not worth the trip. Ornamental jars by the thousands. This is one city where the council is putting money in

---

4   Considered the leading city for production of ceramics in China.

their pockets. To think that this place puts out porcelain in vast quantities, surely they could do something better for themselves?

Turned right on the main road on a no right turn and got stopped by police. He took me over to see the road sign and I said "Oh." Then he gave a lecture and said I lost points and I said I didn't understand so he said did I see the sign and I said no it should be bigger. He smiled and let me off. He wanted to know how I got my driver's licence. Mouse told him that the Beijing police speak English. I'm assuming that he thought I'd paid for my licence but maybe he hadn't noticed that just about every other driver in China had their licence printed in the Kodak print shop.

~ ~ ~ ~ ~ ~ ~ ~

21 July

Had another close shave with the police. On the Zhengzhou/Wuhan expressway, I got clocked driving at 132 km/hr and was nearly booked when we went through the tollgate. The kind policeman let me off since I was a foreigner, elderly, and a woman who doesn't speak Chinese and is driving around China. Pays to be all these things.

One of the benefits of SARS was to expose the unsanitary conditions of the nation. On CCTV9, a TV station that broadcasts the world over, the Chinese government seems to send messages that China is changing its ways and the people are becoming 'clean.' CCTV9 actually is not seen by many Chinese in China and presumably do not realize that they have dirty habits. There is no change in anybody's eating habits, i.e. communal bowls and dishes. The villages are as unsanitary as ever. The ponds that are dry and filled with rubbish in the summer are full of rubbish and standing water in the wet season. Why have this pond of sometimes putrid water? To drain the village and prepare in case of flood. Can't you use the water? No need, enough rain. Drain the ponds because all they breed are germs and mosquitoes. Where will we put the water?

I decided to give up because of the heat and headed home to Beijing on the 21st from Xiangtan. Since we were passing thru Zhumadian, it was only polite to drop in to say 'hello' to Mama, Moon's mother. Mama talked about the days of starvation. She cannot remember the awful drought of 1959 when it hadn't rain for three years – she was just two years old. Her parents were starving so they left their village and moved into town to work for wealthier families in order to earn whatever little money they could to buy food. In those days there was no food on the farms and people ate grass and trees and tree bark or indeed anything that moved or lived. In the first year they ate the green grass, the next they ate the roots and shoots and in the third year there was nothing. As we drove through the mountains and hills, the trees are obviously not primary forest but the whole area is completely green and vegetation abundant and luxuriant. It is hard to remember that starvation did happen in such a seemingly fertile land. But it did.

This summer, as in every summer, there is flooding, drought, earthquakes, hurricanes. Somehow I missed them all. Moon trembled as we drove through southern Anhui Province because his mother told him there was flooding. And indeed, some of the fields did seem to be under water and he did point out a house under water but there are many fields flooded for planting rice. There are duck and fish ponds all over the place. He just got a bit nervous. Anyway, he soon went back to Beijing and Mouse came to take his place.

~ ~ ~ ~ ~ ~ ~ ~

If only I could speak the lingo. . . . There are many advantages being able to say "ting bu dong" (I don't understand). You get to do exactly what you want because after returning the rebukes with crass English to demonstrate that you cannot understand the restrictions they want to impose upon you. Many a times I adopt my English Matron self and bluntly refuse to understand "mei you" (don't have it) or "bu shi," (is not) or whatever. Now that I understand a little bit more, the counter-measures are more aggressive and at machine-gun speed. For example, yesterday I went to buy myself a Subway at my local Subway. It was the first time I went on my bike because other times I drove the two corners. Well, it's in a 3-star hotel complex and there is a guard directing traffic on the forecourt. Bikes are not allowed on the hallowed parking lot. Why, for Heaven's sakes? In a country where only a tiny elite can afford a motorcar, why deny the poor majority the right to ride over the forecourt to Subway or even Wang Jing Gao Oo? I just told him where he could park HIS bike and went in to get my Subway. Poor boy. Sometimes I really do feel sorry for people like him but he will get away allowing that little incident because I'm a foreigner.

I often wonder how they can tell I'm a foreigner. I feel complimented and comfortable when I'm ignored as 'oneofthem.' My clothes, shoes, umbrella and trappings where all bought or made in China. I might sometimes display a foreign trait but on the whole, I think I'm 'invisible.' OK, I still wobble a bit on my bike. But I do ride up the wrong side, ignore anything aback of me and pop out in front of oncoming traffic. Just like everybody else. I do say 'oops' from time to time and smile nervously. Oh, that might be the thing. Nobody smiles. Well . . . very few. Normally, they stare and stare and stare. Normally, I feel like bashing their faces in. . . . Oh never mind, that's on a really bad day.

~ ~ ~ ~ ~ ~ ~ ~

Our first drive to Beidahe was on a near empty expressway, suffering from the repercussions of SARS. A few big black cars, popular amongst the glitterati and a throwback from the days when being in such a vehicle meant you were 'somebody.' The first ones made locally in Changchun were the RED FLAGS. These days, Volkswagons, Audis, Toyotas, and any other car manufacturer who came earlier have been making their version of the Red Flag. They all look the same to me! Their days are numbered though because private motor vehicles are being sprayed in various colors. The 'in' color at the time of writing is silver-white. Uncountable trucks in either blue or army green and all listing at a near 45-degree angle grind along at 10 km/hr often three abreast. These juggernauts are a menace. More often than not, motorists are forced to zip through and around them. Luckily they move so slowly and steadily that if judged precisely, you can squeeze through the gaps. . . . But the real danger is the overloading of the trucks. They are heavy and quite a few shed their loads. On one occasion a private bus drove near enough and shaved its top off on the overhanging 3-wheel tuck-tucks that stuck out over two lanes. Jingshan Expressway – this is the main artery road to the North. It's a new expressway and in fairly good condition right up to Shenyang. Tollgates in Hebei and Liaoning Provinces occur at about every 50 kliks. All expressways, in good or bad or disastrous condition, are littered with tollgates and this is a heavy cost when driving through China. The speed limit is between 110-120 kliks but if there is no radar then there is no limit. Speed throughout China is in directly proportional to the number and speed of the trucking traffic . . . with local variations, of course.

Our second trip to Beidahe was on a Saturday, long after SARS. Jingshan Expressway was packed to the hilt with weekenders and day-trippers. There were convoys of family cars parked along any 'safe' place waiting for other friends to arrive. Other convoys were driving at full speed with warning lights flashing between a tightly packed motorway. Why? Because they were a 'group.' At other times drivers would stop to relieve themselves. The sheer madness of these new car owners is unfathomable. Last year 48,000 people died in road accidents. Rubber-necking is a must and once one stops to witness the cause of the hold-up and to take photos of the gruesome ones, one drives away with utmost satisfaction. A hold-up is not exactly a hold-up. It's more of a speed-up. As soon as traffic starts to slow down that's when the aggression comes to the fore. Nobody likes to be beaten and drivers risk life and limb swaying and serving between lines of vehicles. If the truth be known, best way to drive through China is to get down off the highways and travel the byways. Driving in China varies, like the dishes, cultural variations from city to city, highway to back roads. Beijing is a civilized, modern city with bland food, fairly polite slow drivers. Also, orderly pedestrians and barely a bike or scooter. It is normal for faster drivers to zip around with ease.

Chinese expressways are a pleasure to traverse. Every single klik is 'finished' in heavy-duty crash barriers on both sides and in the middle. Topiary, shrubs, flowers and the gardeners and sweepers necessary to keep the passing pleasant and heart-stopping at the same time. Every gardener plants a little red flag to warn passing motorists of their presence. Time and time again, however, at 160 km/hr it is impossible to pick these out. Sometimes it comes as a complete surprise to see a tiny face peering out from between the shrubs. Their bikes and 3-wheelers parked casually in the emergency lane block one's quick passage past the heaving trucks. Must be the longest garden in the world where it is a pleasure to weed the beds . . . where one can wander at leisure, dreaming of being in one of the speeding bullets that zip by at a hair's breath. Though I think to them it's only a job. Expressways are one of the cleanest places in China being swept daily from end to end and some. The panorama is not dissimilar to any other in America, England or Canada.

Traveling by private car is a phenomenon in China. I don't know how they learn to drive but judging from the driving test I had to take to get my Chinese licence, any idiot can get a licence. Foreign drivers only have to know where the ignition key goes and they'd pass the test. For the locals, it is rather simple because there is a testing park with proper corners, road markings, speedway bends and a few pedestrians (?). I believe it must be simple because there was moss and grit on the areas we didn't use. Foreigners are tested on Friday mornings only. Four would-be drivers and the police examiner in the one car. Each driver is given a number and when your turn comes up, you exchange places with the driver. The most important thing you have to do is put on your seat belt. People have been known to fail for forgetting that little detail!

~ ~ ~ ~ ~ ~ ~ ~ ~

17 January 2004. Suiping, Henan Province

This cold morning, wrapped up in an eiderdown duvet and slowly toasting on an electric blanket, I begin to revise and reflect on my impressions thus far. On the 29 August 2003, I first came to Beijing to teach at Beijing Institute of Machinery, located at Qinghe, just beyond the 5th ring road on the outskirts of the vast city. Myself, three Americans, one other English and a Japanese were contracted to teach English in whatever form to 'university' students. We had all come to China for various reasons; I to find my roots, James (the half-and-half Chinese) fresh from Trinity College was doing his gap year; Eric a professional teacher who wants to teach in China as did Kyoko, Japanese teacher who came to study Chinese; Bob, fresh from university in America and could not find employment; Jeffrey, first generation Chinese born in the U.S., also fresh from university and considered aimless by his parents so he came to China to appease them. Incidentally, Jeffrey stayed for only three months as the teaching was 'too much' and he missed the comforts of the USA.

Comforts and soft living of the West? How so? Beijing, one of the largest cities in the world, capital of a vast country that is progressing and developing so fast that has the financial wizards on Wall Street in a spin? The whole world watches while the city is growing upwards and outwards. The buildings in the city center sprung up like toadstools in the field. Glass and steel needles puncture the sky, or the smog that blankets the city. Kilometers of raised roads circle and dip through the city creating more space for the two million vehicles that seem to be constantly together crawling and belching fumes that create the modern-day atmospheric sludge that is the bane of our cities today. It is with some pride that Beijingers would tell you that the car fumes are creating the unhealthy air.

Yesterday I was taken to visit a 'poor' family. It was an exercise in endurance. Not so much that the family was poor for the spending power is relative. What I mean is that maybe they had little by way of material possessions and sustenance. What they had was common to almost all the people in their village and in this area. No heating in their homes, no furniture as we know it. A few short wooden chairs that were probably handed down over the generations because they are all proud that there were no nails to keep them together. One bedroom which housed the whole family whenever they were all together. A rickety old table that served as the kitchen, dinning and total utility table, i.e. covered in flour where they made dough for mantou[5] and dumplings. A dresser piled high with almost all the family possessions. The slab of pork hung from the rafters. Pictures of Mao and famous fabulous women, school certificates, calendars, and family photos hung on the walls. All were faded and dingy with dust and wet rot. The floor made of red bricks caked in clay and covered with the droppings of the family, seed cases, sweetie papers and dirt and dust. The mud and grit formed a dyke around the room. Under the dresser was packed with God knows what and all covered in dust and clay. Naked light bulbs (2) hung in the doorway to the storeroom and one to the bedroom. The walls were packed clay patted on to red bricks. The roof was tiled and padded inside with straw.

The blackened kitchen shed leant on the wall. It was about 3 ft x 3 ft, dark, a brick stove that held one iron wok (which probably never moved since it was first installed) and an iron pot. Straw and twigs were fed in

---

5 Steamed bread, shaped like a hemisphere, and a staple in the diet of northern China.

to it through a hole in the short side. There was a set of rickety shelves to store dishes and other kitchen utensils. Straw, ash, mud and half inch clay was the floor. Washing was done with a bucket of water brought over from the neighbor's well.

In the courtyard in the far corner was a shed, which served as the toilet. The other far corner was a straw covered chicken coop for one laying hen that provided the family with eggs. The dog also had its own straw covered area and was seemingly permanently tied under it. Between the kitchen and the toilet was an unused pigpen and a duck pond filled with the family garbage. The yard itself was bare earth and at the time of my visit, sludgy clay.

The adults were dressed in clothes seen in magazines of the 50s and 60s. Women dressed with colorful scarves and colored coats; the men in jackets and big coats. Some of them were in army jackets and coats. The children all wore identical tracksuits provided by their schools. The girls wore silver earrings in their pierced ears and jeweled hair-bands.

~ ~ ~ ~ ~ ~ ~ ~

The greatest disadvantage is living in a country that uses a language unknown to me. I can say that it is good that my sons do phone from time to time and there are other foreign teachers with whom I can speak fluently. Sometimes I feel as though my brain has atrophied because it's not only because simple communication is sadly lacking, it's that the 'cultural' difference plays a great part in being able to converse. Commonality is rare in a country that has been locked up for so long. Not only has the nation been estranged from our world but also each village, each town, city, province, is as different as it is diverse. Meaning: Beijingers are considered sophisticated and advanced. Peasant farmers and their families are most certainly at the very lowest level of worldly intelligence. I walk the very thin line of arrogance and conceit. Forgive me, for I think I am the ignoramus, lacking sufficient information about China and the Chinese.

~ ~ ~ ~ ~ ~ ~ ~

Teaching in China

In every school there is bound to be the wild bunch and I've got them. It's the Freshers coming to study English because they're going to Ireland after three years here and, boy, they are about to let the whole world know. Had them first time on Thursday and I immediately wrote home to say I'd be on the next plane out of Beijing. It was with some trepidation that I poked my head around the door that morning. The room was quiet and about quarter full. As is my wont, I chatted with some of the girls – I have to sorta cast a web because you never know who can understand a simple question like "How many in this class?" The room filled up slowly and no worries until the 'wide boys'[6] arrived . . . one minute to the hour. Banged their way right to the back, banged and clattered the desks, chairs and bags and sat down with not so much of a backward or forward glance in my direction. You know the scenario. Soon as they got settled I pointed, "you, you, you . . . OUTA HERE. When you come back in sit in the front row." They meekly got their things together went out and stood around in the corridor. I waited a couple of minutes and beckoned them in. Headed right for the back again like any decent wide boy and I said uh, uh. I pointed to the front and they did as told. Lesson One – take no bullshit. The two who came in a bit later tried the same game and they were stopped in their tracks. You might say "well done" but to tell you the truth, I just did what came naturally. Didn't think of cause or consequence like is my usual thing… and it worked. The boys actually were the best speakers in class and because they sat in front I was able to glean a lot more than if they had they sat in the back. It was a stroke of luck.

James, Bob and I have that same class and we had planned to share out what we would do with them. James had them on Thursday afternoon. James nearly committed suicide after. He spoke Mandarin to them as well. They gave him hell. The monitor, Chris, (every class has one) advised him that maybe he didn't control the class. Boy, did I feel good after THAT! I'm still in with a chance.

Time in class today was spent getting to know each other. Getting to know what they need to know. Some may wonder why the exodus from such an up-and-coming country. Why would the sudden 'freedom' result in irresponsibility and arrogance. There is a belief here that anything outside of study, work, and scratching for a living is taboo. I

6   In-tune or with-it boys.

get the strangest feeling that these people just don't know what's going to happen to them when they leave university. No it's not like the West where the economy, environment etc. limit choices. Here, it's because they really have no idea what to do with what they are learning. "English is a tool." "I want to work in a foreign company or a company dealing with foreigners." "Translator." "I want to be a CEO." What's a CEO? What sort of trade? What sort of business? They haven't a clue. Some of them will probably end up working in the big hotels, if they are lucky, because they can speak English. There is just not enough scope or resources to cope with natural progression or enthusiasm. I've a growing frustration with the negativity in the air. Yes, I know they have limited resources. I know these students have to be careful with their money. I know they worked hard to be here. But where is the joie de vivre so typical of our university students?

Every day is a new beginning and a new revelation. It is I who needs to be taught. It is I who has to come to grips with Chinese and Chinese culture. I've been reaching out of my Western ideas and ideals and most of all my Western cultural background. Yea, there is a deep divide. The difference between me and the other teachers is simple, they are here to teach and they, except Bob, seem fine with their classes because they have come to accept the cultural divide. I am romancing with China and its people and I've got to come down to earth and smell the roses. Being a teacher, and especially for me who thought this would be a breeze, is a huge responsibility. It is indescribable.

~ ~ ~ ~ ~ ~ ~ ~

Yesterday James and I went walking (tiptoeing) through the local district. It's certainly not modern Beijing. It's a maze of narrow streets with dirty shops, food vendors, smelly alleyways, staring eyes, chickens, suspect puddles – the real China. I really don't have to cook cause I could get all sorts of cooked meats and vegetables . . . and very cheap. James is half Chinese and turns up his nose at this sort of thing but he loves being the center of attention. I can walk where I want and nobody would give me a second glance. Eric says I have Hakka blood because my high cheekbones are typical of Northern Chinese and the Hakka people migrated from the north. Eric is an anthropologist as well.

I'm learning Chinese. Not because I really, really want to. Seems everybody wants me to learn the language. I'm being given books . . . perhaps they think it's a shame that a Chinese can't speak the language! Of course it much easier learning it here than in London. I'm still at a lost how to pronounce 'tse.' They speak with their teeth clamped shut and the tongue pasted onto the bottom teeth.

Eric does the ordering for us at the restaurants and when he doesn't come James tries. Mostly we just point at the dishes the other people are eating. The following are translations from the noodle shop where we lunch: Fire mountain under snow, mixed three in pieces, elbow flower in soy, man and wife lung slices, beaten cucumbers, fragrant flower birth rice, and sand pot spare ribs. We really do miss out on oodles of the good stuff because the food on the other tables always seem to look much better than ours. Oh, must say though, we tend to take note of the numbers on the right hand side. When we first arrived we could have afforded just about anything because its all very cheap. Now that we've had our pay packs, a meal above 8 yuan is pretty expensive. We've now stopped buying drinks in restaurants and instead of an average of 12-15 yuan each we're down to eight. James and I always have to have kebabs with our noodles. The Americans are quite easy with meatless food.

At times I regret taking on this work because I know I will get so involved that at the end of it I won't want to leave. Kings and Queens we are not. It's more like the Red Cross, the Life Guards throwing out lifelines and pulling in more than we can carry. I don't know about making money out of this. I don't know how to refuse pleas for help and at the same time I don't want to overstretch myself or get too bogged down. Maybe as time goes on I will get harden to it all.

~ ~ ~ ~ ~ ~ ~ ~

I'd asked Eric Ecko (Gao Ying Chao) from B0201 a week ago if his father, a doctor, would monitor my blood pressure. "No problem." Next day he confirmed his father's agreement and we set the date for yesterday. Day after that he said his father would have a car pick me up at nine outside the college gate. Day after that he tells me, "No food." Eric is monosyllabic and spaces his words at 24 hours intervals. Yesterday the car and his father's assistant duly arrived at the school gate. She (Zhang

....) is a new breed of Beijinger. She owns and drives her own car, traveled Europe, has a big apartment, husband who has a partnership selling food to white-collar workers and was very friendly and outgoing. I shut my eyes and we could have been in London, Toronto or anywhere else but Qinghe.

On the way to the hospital, she tells me it's an army hospital. All the staff there are army personnel. Drove into the car park and found no free spaces so she parked right across two others. I was introduced to Gao De Hong, a very nice 49-year-old man. He is head of the Laboratory section of the hospital. For the next two hours Zhang and Dr. Gao took me through all the testing departments. After the hospital round, they took me to a posh restaurant nearby. You get to know the level as soon as you drive into the car park. Four boys suited out in bellboy uniforms and white gloves ran up to the car and yanked open the doors. A bevy of six cheongsam beauties sing a chorus of "welcome" as you enter the restaurant where you are met in the lobby by about four tour guides who navigate through widely spaced tables all beautifully covered in pink and green damask cloths and dotted with proper wine glasses, un-chipped crockery and chopsticks on stands. I knew then that I was in the wrong place. Coming from the boonies of Qinghe with the battery pack and rubber hose wrapped round my torso, it was most certainly not an in place for me. I remarked – this must be a high-class restaurant! No, it's about middle class. Through out the whole meal I announced mentally, "Forgive me China, I was wrong, you are indeed modern and with-it, and in fact, better than anything in the West." We ate off Western dinner plates, cut the goose foot and huge mushroom with steak knives and forks, ate the rice with a teaspoon, drank tea out of the wine glasses, picked demurely at the peanuts and baby bamboo shoots with chopsticks, tumbled curried chicken sealed in little foil packets onto our plates, poked and prodded the steam fish, which as you know comes as the finale and by which time I could eat not another morsel. So, I have all the leftovers neatly boxed in my refrigerator to be eaten when I can find time to fit it in between the hot pots, kebabs, duck and lamb shanks (from over the road) and all the other stuff from Nos. 1-6 Buddhists eateries, the Christmas place, the fairy lights . . . It's our way of identifying our various dining spots.

~ ~ ~ ~ ~ ~ ~ ~

Ok, let me explain further. We are up against a no-win situation here. We are supposed to be teaching them modern everyday English. But whenever I say "Don't use that word," like tobefrank, moreandmore, and so on they tell me, teacher that's what we have to use to pass the English exam! I've seen some of the exam papers and they are right. It's antiquated Chinese English. I had a hard time explaining not to use 'play with myself.'

This weekend we went to Tiantan – Temple of Heaven. Lots and lots of walking. Ten yuan for the park and 20 yuan for the complex. You guessed it – we just walked around the park. Then to Hepingmen – the antiques market. Oh what can I say? There are all these ancient buildings with dragons and gargoyles and pretty maids all in a row. It's all been built specially for tourists! Every time I think, hey, how cute, they tell me, "Oh, that's new." No Chinese go shopping in the antiques market. No Chinese buy Beijing glass or paper-thin porcelain. They're buying Benzes, Audis, and BMWs. They are eating mountains of food at expensive restaurants. Food is wasted like you never could imagine. Oh man, our meal here in Qinghe comes up to about 45-60 yuan for six and we are stuffed at the end of 4-6 dishes. In Beijing you'd be hard pressed and embarrassed if you should spend under 60 yuan for two. Yesterday, at a new-style Korean barbeque fast food eatery, my partner and I shared one plate of meat and veggies. The family at the next table had two plates of meat each and pyramids of food piled round. We spent 58 yuan and shudder to calculate just how much THEY spent.

Mrs. Zhang told me a few things about the hard times. I remember most of it but thinking they are so far away from prying eyes and have land to grow their own crops I was surprised and dismayed when she said they grew wheat, rice and corn in those hard times but were allowed to eat only the corn. The boys grew up on corn. The Zhangs regard themselves as very lucky because they have three boys. Yes, this is not Beijing or Shanghai. Traditions passed down through the ages are still practiced here. Third son will marry in two years time when the family is able to buy him a 10,000 yuan bride. He's invited me to the wedding. I must remember to leave that day whenever it be to celebrate his marriage. The people in that village and thousands, maybe millions of villages like that, are born live and die without ever going into a city or further than perhaps a 5-mile radius of their homes. Unbelievable.

~ ~ ~ ~ ~ ~ ~ ~

At the beginning of my new career, I asked my students 'What will you do in the future?' Everyone prioritized the health and welfare of their parents. What if you won a lot of money? I'll buy my parents a house and give them money for the rest of their lives. We in the West rarely think like this. We rarely have to think this. In China they have to want to because it is so, so true – the hardships life has given them. Oh, I apologize, deeply apologize, to all my students to whom I said, "But your parents must have made some provision for their old age!" Oh China.

~ ~ ~ ~ ~ ~ ~ ~

In February 2004, I receive a letter from Sunderland University informing me that my appointment for next year will be in Guangdong Province. I don't know exactly where in Guangdong – it's a 45-minute bus ride from Guangzhou at a private institution. I have asked that my teaching be lumped together so that I could have at least three consecutive days off. The dean is the mother of a friend of mine and she is rather anxious that I teach – the only foreign teacher!!!! Also she wants me to do a few lectures to at least 100 or so students, bringing them closer to our 'culture' etc. I will try to stay down that way for at least two years before moving on again.

This has been an amazing turn of events for me, since I will be in the very region from where my ancestors (and many of the 19th century immigrants to Guyana) originated. It was my interest in knowing more about my roots that made me apply to teach in China in the first place. Now I will have a better chance to learn about my history and 'culture.' It still seems like a dream.

ABOUT THE AUTHOR

Trevelyan A. Sue-A-Quan was born in November 1943 in Georgetown, Guyana. He is the great-grandson of an indentured labourer who left China in 1873. Many of the second-generation descendants of these Chinese field workers became shopkeepers, including the author's grandfather.

Trev Sue-A-Quan's generation was the one that typified the transition from shopkeeping to professions based on higher education. Trev attended Queen's College in Georgetown and attained B.Sc. and Ph.D. degrees in Chemical Engineering at the University of Birmingham, England. He immigrated to Canada in 1969 but then pursued a career opportunity with a major oil company in Chicago where he conducted research in petroleum processing and fossil fuel utilization. Eight years later Trev headed to Beijing, China, becoming Senior Research Engineer at the Coal Science Research Center. He spent five years there and in 1984 returned to Canada with his wife and son. They now make their home in Vancouver, Canada.

Trev's interest in the Chinese in Guyana came from a curiosity about the circumstances that caused his great-grandfather to leave his native land. That history was told in his book *Cane Reapers: Chinese Indentured Immigrants in Guyana*, completed in 1999. A sequel *Cane Ripples: The Chinese in Guyana* describing the lives of the Chinese who settled in Guyana was published in 2003. Many of the subsequent generations of Chinese-Guyanese migrated to other countries and their experiences are related in this book, *Cane Rovers: Stories of the Chinese-Guyanese Diaspora*.

Visit the **Chinese in Guyana: Their Roots** website at
www.rootsweb.com/~guycigtr

E-mail: Canereapers@Lycos.com

www.ingramcontent.com/pod-product-compliance
Lightning Source LLC
Chambersburg PA
CBHW070550270326
41926CB00013B/2263

* 9 780097 335572 7 *